THE STRATEGY BRI

The Strategy Bridge: Theory for Practice is an original contribution to the general theory of strategy. While heavily indebted to Carl von Clausewitz, Sun-tzu, and the very few other classic authors, this book presents the theory, rather than merely comments on the theory as developed by others. The author explains that the purpose of strategy is to connect purposefully politics and policy with the instruments they must use. The primary focus of attention is on military strategy, but this focus is well nested in discussion of grand strategy, for which military strategy is only one strand.

The book presents the general theory of strategy comprehensively and explains the utility of it for the particular strategies that strategists need to develop in order to meet their historically unique challenges. The book argues that strategy's general theory provides essential education for practicing strategists at all times and in all circumstances. As general theory, *The Strategy Bridge* is as relevant to understanding strategic behaviour in the Peloponnesian War as it is for the conflicts of the Twenty-First century.

The book proceeds from exposition of general strategic theory to address three basic issue areas that are not at all well explained, let alone understood with a view to advancing better practice, in the extant literature. Specifically, the book tackles the problems that harass and imperil strategic performance; it probes deeply into the hugely underexamined subject of just what it is that the strategist produces—strategic effect; and it 'joins up the dots' from theory through practice to consequences by means of a close examination of command performance.

The author takes a holistic view of strategy, and is rigorously attentive to the significance of the contexts within which and for which strategies are developed and applied. The book regards the strategist as a hero, charged with the feasible, but awesomely difficult, task of converting the threat and use of force (for military strategy) into desired political consequences. He seeks some control over the rival or enemy via strategic effect, the instrumental produce of his instrumental labours. In order to maximise his prospects for success, the practicing strategist requires all the educational assistance that strategic theory can provide.

The Strategy Bridge: Theory for Practice

COLIN S. GRAY

OXFORD

UNIVERSITY PRESS

OXFORD

UNIVERSITY PRESS

Great Clarendon Street, Oxford, OX2 6DP,
United Kingdom

Oxford University Press is a department of the University of Oxford.
It furthers the University's objective of excellence in research, scholarship,
and education by publishing worldwide. Oxford is a registered trade mark of
Oxford University Press in the UK and in certain other countries

First published 2010
First published in paperback 2016

Published in the United States of America by Oxford University Press
198 Madison Avenue, New York, NY 10016, United States of America

British Library Cataloguing in Publication Data
Data available

Library of Congress Cataloging in Publication Data
Data available

ISBN 978–0–19–957966–2 (Hbk.)
ISBN 978–0–19–877912–4 (Pbk.)

To the love of my life, Valerie.

Foreword

You hold in your hands the first original and serious work on strategy of the 21st century—perhaps the first such book in decades. Written by someone who has thought widely about this topic, read deeply in its history, and contributed to its practice, it belongs on the bookshelf of students and practitioners alike.

The truth is, many academics and decision-makers think that no such thing exists. I once heard an eminent historian assert that Clausewitz was wrong (i.e., that war is not, and cannot be, a continuation of policy by other means), and that strategy, in the sense of the use of force for political ends, was meaningless. He was working on a history of World War I at the time, and it seemed not to have occurred to him that a similar view among European soldiers and politicians might have had something to do with the dismal course of that conflict.

It is easier to grasp strategy in theory than to put it into practice, and not least because strategic decisions only rarely present themselves as such. To be sure, in some cases they appear as first order choices about a course of action. More often they appear as incremental choices which may undo seemingly unshakeable principles. Thus, President Roosevelt and his advisers had decided on the principle "Germany First" in 1941, as they contemplated war against the Axis. But in practice hard choices about a counteroffensive in the Solomon Islands, or a landing in North Africa in 1942 rather than France in 1943 substantially modified a simple concept.

Strategy takes different forms in different political and technological periods. Many in the English-speaking world have attempted to wish away the problems strategy addresses—the Islamist terror and insurgency campaigns spearheaded by, but not confined to Al Qaeda; the prospects of a proliferated world, beginning with violently inclined states like North Korea and Iran; the rise of a China that is feeling its strength and willing to assert and display it.

In some ways the Cold War reduced the study of strategy to a dangerously abstract set of precepts about the construction of unused and possibly unusable arsenals of nuclear weapons, or to counterinsurgency directed against nationalist guerrillas. The challenges that lie ahead are far more complicated, varied, and dare one say it, interesting. And this book is a very good place to begin thinking about them.

Dr. Eliot A. Cohen
Robert E. Osgood Professor of Strategic Studies
Johns Hopkins SAIS
Washington, DC

Preface

Scholars need to be ambitious, occasionally. Once a decade, I have sought to write a fairly bold book that was more challenging to research and write than is the norm. As a defence professional, albeit these days one with some teaching duties, it is all too easy to take one's conceptual capital more or less as it happens to be, and simply plug it into the security problems of today. However, from time to time, with decade long intervals, I have attempted to give something myself to the canon of strategic lore with which we all must operate. *Strategy Bridge* is the third of my ventures over the frontier (the first two were *War, Peace and Victory* in 1990, and *Modern Strategy* in 1999). This time, I have gone for broke and have attempted to present the general theory of strategy, with the addition of as little supplementary material as possible, lest the central plot be obscured. No doubt I shall be moved at some time in the future to write *Strategy Bridge II: The Missing Chapters*.

Unavoidably, all that I can do here in the main theory chapters is to rearrange the deckchairs on our strategic conceptual flagship. By this admission I mean simply that there is nothing new to be discovered about the general theory of strategy. It is all there in the classics, as well as in historical practice, of course. But the theory does need to be rearranged for our times, just as the classics have to be reread for some fresh interpretation, as our historical context demands. *Strategy Bridge* is designed and written primarily to be strategic theory, not commentary on the strategic theory we have inherited from the past. My attitude towards the 'classical' strategic theorists, Carl von Clausewitz especially, is one of deepest respect and profound gratitude, but not of worship, critical or otherwise. As the references in this text attest abundantly, my debt to the great Prussian is priceless. However, the general theory as exposed and developed here deploys Clausewitzian concepts and arguments only as they fit this exercise. It has been my good fortune to debate Clausewitzian theory with a number of most competent colleagues over the years, a running contest that is apt to lead us astray. I am concerned lest we focus unduly upon the interesting question 'what did Clausewitz mean?' at the expense of the rather more important question, 'was he right?'

Strategy Bridge is both as short and as long as it needs to be. Strategy is a complex subject, with many facets that have to be identified and explained if one is not to mislead the reader. Beyond the core theory chapters (Chapters 1 and 2), and the contextual chapter on politics and war (Chapter 3), I have limited the text to just four vital foci. These are problems (Chapter 4), product–strategic effect (Chapter 5), command performance (Chapter 6), and the endeavour to control (Chapter 7). Each of these latter chapters addresses a subject that I have found underexplored and poorly explained in the literature of strategic studies. Chapters 4–7 emphatically do not comprise deckchair reorganization.

If some readers should find my prose to be tough sledding for bedtime perusal, it may nonetheless serve well enough as homeopathic medication for insomnia. While I have sought to write accessibly, I can well believe that my final efforts, even with expert editorial assistance, have not always soared to felicitous heights. Poetry, this is not. In case anyone is wondering, although the content of this book has taken many years to mature, no part of this text has been published separately.

It is customary, as well as necessary and just, to cite the help one has received in the push to produce a book. *Strategy Bridge* is obviously a career capstone effort—for good or ill—after more than four decades of theorizing, advising, and teaching, resident at different times in three countries. It follows that since I enjoy a wonderful accumulation of friends, colleagues (past and present), and valuable networked contacts, my acknowledgement paragraphs easily could expand seriously out of hand.

I wish to recognize appreciatively the critically important financial support that I have received from the Earhart Foundation of Ann Arbor, Michigan. I am grateful to the Foundation, its excellent President, Ingrid Gregg, and its Board of Trustees, both for their long-time support for my research students, as well as for this book, specifically. Also, I am deeply in debt to my friend, colleague, and Head of School at the University of Reading, Dr. Philip Giddings, who has always encouraged and usually has tolerated the behaviour of a not invariably cooperative book-obsessed professor.

Eliot A. Cohen truly is a 'maker of modern strategy'. For many years, I have benefited from his writings on many aspects of strategy; both his commentaries on the defence issues of the here and now, and his deeper studies of enduring matters. Knowing how busy he is, I can only offer my profound thanks for his taking the time and making the effort to contribute the Foreword to *Strategy Bridge*. Eliot is a strategist who is always worth reading, as his high reputation attests.

My intellectual debts are much too numerous, and even opaque, for me to attempt to list industriously. Given that I belong to a community of fairly intensely communicating contemporary scholars and practitioners, that my subject has been performed in practice forever, everywhere, and that it has always attracted theorization in some form or other, it is difficult to avoid innocently unintentional plagiarism. Heavy footnoting, a dense thicket of references, a massive bibliography, should all help protect one against the dreaded charge, but still the danger is existential to the modern scholar. When one has been reading and talking about strategy and all its works for forty-five years, it is not always unambiguously obvious just what was the provenance of a favoured idea or notable fact. All that I can do here is to apologize to those who may feel slighted by my silence as to their direct and indirect contribution to this text. I have tried to reference fairly and fully, but alas perfection is only a goal to be sought, not a realistic aspiration. What I can do with high confidence is name a few of the scholars whose work has influenced me significantly here, perhaps particularly when I have not agreed with it in some respect. I am appreciative of the contribution to my understanding of strategy made by Antulio J. Echevarria II,

Williamson Murray, Frank G. Hoffman, Jeremy Black, Hew Strachan, Lawrence Freedman, Edward N. Luttwak, Stephen Cimbala, and Theo Farrell. These very few comprise only the shortest of what could be a long list indeed. And, need I say, the first name on my list of mentors has to be Carl von Clausewitz, followed not too distantly by Sun Tzu and Thucydides. Among the modern writers on strategy I have named, there is no doubt that Antulio Echevarria has had the greatest influence on me, even when we have disagreed. His study of Clausewitz is the finest work on strategy that I have read in many a year.

Next, I appreciate the confidence shown in me and this project by my editor at Oxford University Press, Dominic Byatt. There is no adequate substitute for an editor who believes in a book. In order to bring an unruly manuscript to some good end, I have required the expert services of my ever patient manuscript preparation person—typist does not begin to express the grim reality of the mission—Mrs Barbara Watts.

There is no verbal formula that can express adequately my debt to my family. The best that I can offer is a simple 'thank you' to Valerie and Tonia for encouragement, toleration, and support, far above and beyond...

Colin S. Gray

Wokingham
July 2009

Contents

List of Figures

List of Tables

List of Abbreviations

AWPD-1	Air War Plans Division 1
BEF	British Expeditionary Force
COIN	Counter-Insurgency
EBO	Effects-Based Operations
EMS	Electromagnetic Spectrum
GPS	Global Positioning System
GWOT	Global War on Terror
JFC	Joint Forces Command
KOYLI	King's Own Yorkshire Light Infantry
MAD	Mutual Assured Destruction
PLA	People's Liberation Army
RAF	Royal Air Force
SAC	Strategic Air Command
SDS	Strategy Deficiency Syndrome
SHAPE	Supreme Headquarters Allied Powers Europe
USAAF	United States Army Air Forces
USN	United States Navy

Theory should cast a steady light on all phenomena so that we can more easily recognize and eliminate the weeds that always spring from ignorance; it should show how one thing is related to another, and keep the unimportant separate.

Carl von Clausewitz,
On War (1832–4; 1976)

The value of strategic concepts is to be found in their ability to provide some way through the tangle of international relations. Rather than being propelled into recklessness by a surge of popular feeling or stunned into immobility by contradictory advice, policy-makers need concepts to enable them to appreciate the likely dynamics of the situations in which they find themselves and evaluate alternative courses of action.

Lawrence Freedman,
Deterrence (2004)

Without a theory the facts are silent.

F. A. Hayek,
Quoted in John Keegan,
A History of Warfare (1993)

And although it is a spirited thing to deal with material of which one has not made a profession, nonetheless I do not believe it is an error to occupy with words a rank that many have, with greater presumption, occupied with deeds. For the errors I make as I write can be corrected without harm to anyone, but those that are made by them as they act cannot be known except with the ruin of empires.

Niccolo Machiavelli,
Art of War (1521; 2003)

Great commanders can lead their countries to calamitous defeats.

John Lee,
The Warlords: Hindenburg and Ludendorff (2005)

Strength is power; happiness is the objective [of using power]. [Power and success are interrelated]. Power is of three kinds; so is the success resulting from its use. Intellectual strength provides the power of [good] counsel; a prosperous treasury and a strong army provide physical power and valour is the basis for [morale and] energetic action. The success resulting from each one is, correspondingly, intellectual, physical and [psychological].

Kautilya,
The Arthashastra (fourth century BCE)

When the Goodman mends his armour,
  And trims his helmet's plume;
When the goodwife's shuttle merrily
  Goes flashing through the loom;
With weeping and with laughter
  Still is the story told
How well Horatius kept the bridge
  In the brave days of old.

Thomas Babington, Lord Macaulay
Horatius Keeps the Bridge (1842)

Introduction: Surviving Clausewitz

Carl von Clausewitz is not dead. The ideas of the greatest of all theorists of war live on in the unfinished masterpiece, *On War*, a book written and partially revised between 1816 and 1830 and first published in three volumes between 1832 and 1834.[1] Those who have proclaimed the death of the Prussian's theory have yet to present a convincing case, though it has not been for want of trying. But there is a significant problem with *On War*. It has become unduly dominant an influence over the minds of strategic theorists. Courtesy in no small part to the high praise it was accorded by Europe's most celebrated contemporary soldier, Field Marshal Helmuth Graf von Moltke (the elder), *On War* has enjoyed unchallenged pole position among general treatises on war and strategy since the early 1870s. The theorist, his theory, and the book that contains it have become nothing short of super-iconic. So influential is Clausewitz today that there is a sense in which all strategists, certainly including this author, are Clausewitzians. His ideas are an integral and inalienable part of our strategic education and discourse, whether or not they are accurately interpreted and appropriately deployed, and whether or not we agree with him.[2] We cannot escape the intellectual reach and grasp of *On War*. Its careful study reveals beyond room for a reasonable doubt that Clausewitz fully merits the highest of high esteem in which he is held near universally as a strategic theorist. The trouble is that a truly hegemonic theorist, theory, and corpus of writing can hardly help but stunt, even prevent, the growth of other theories. The challenge to strategic theorists today is to know how to use Clausewitz's approach, ideas, and turns of phrase—while being careful of the translation from the original German, as well as the Prussian context of the early nineteenth century—without being so captured by them that original, let alone critical and even sceptical, thought is discouraged. A massive tree casts a giant shadow. Strategic theorists can forget that their primary duty is to be clear as to what they mean; it is not to try to be faithful to the Clausewitzian canon. The latter is important with respect to understanding what the Prussian most probably intended us to understand. But the former is more important. Clausewitz has had his say, at great length. He, at least, was entirely unambiguous as to his role: it was defined as a duty to educate, not to train. Clausewitz donated us a priceless work of theory for our education, not a manual of doctrine for our obedient instruction. We must not allow strategic thought to be reduced to textual analysis of a sacred book.

Strategy Bridge is deeply Clausewitzian in that the author has been educated by the master and holds him in profound respect. No attempt is made in these pages to effect a clear separation from the ideas for which *On War* is justly renowned; such a foolish endeavour would certainly fail, and deservedly so. However, *Strategy Bridge*, by the author's most determined intent, is not a book about Clausewitz's theories of war and strategy. Rather is the chief purpose to make some original contribution to the understanding of strategy. Clausewitz looms, as he must and should, as a powerful contributor to the theory outlined and developed here, but that is the totality of the role he is allowed. It is plausible to suggest that some people who might have been strategic theorists of the first rank, in practice limited their achievements to a lower order of merit because they could not, or would not, break free from Clausewitzian discipleship. *Strategy Bridge* seeks to help break the grip of Clausewitzian theory upon strategic thinkers and executors, to the degree to which that grip has become unhealthy. While it is important to appreciate the Prussian's thought in the cultural context of his time, debate over 'what Clausewitz really meant' can slide into a barren scholasticism. Theorists of an inventive kind would employ their talent to better effect were they to ask, 'what do *I* think about this problem?'. All too often it seems as if strategists today are fearful of venturing into a dangerous world without the fearsome firepower of Clausewitz in the closest of close support.

None of the above should be read as criticism of *On War*. His assistance, even guidance, should be sought and employed for all it is worth. But also what is needed today is a willingness on the part of strategic theorists to be independent of mind, indeed original if this is possible and useful. Since there are no new ideas in strategy, it is more than a little challenging to strive to be original, of course. When the title of this Introduction specifies 'Surviving Clausewitz', it indicates the problems that occur when deep respect slips into uncritical acceptance. It is not easy to give a master work its due, all the while remaining one's own person as a strategic theorist. By way of acknowledging some personal guilt, I cannot deny authorship of an essay with the following message: 'If Thucydides, Sun Tzu, and Clausewitz Did Not Say It, It Probably Is Not Worth Saying.'[3] This was a deliberate overstatement for the purpose of making the point that the trinity of great authors just named is worthy of the highest regard. Most of what is presented in the twenty-first century as bold new strategic theory, innovative doctrine, and practice, that is a radical change from preceding behaviour, is readily locatable in the three classics and in the ever contestable historical record. In the 2000s, Americans rediscovered best practice for counter-insurgency (COIN) and realized that they were committed to 'hybrid warfare' fed by enemies posing 'hybrid threats'.[4] Meanwhile, Britons celebrated their latest big idea, a 'comprehensive approach' to irregular conflict.[5] By the late 1960s, the US government, the Army in particular, knew how to succeed at COIN, but the domestic

American political context had ceased to be permissive of the protracted effort involved.[6] Its foes in South-east Asia in the 1960s and 1970s had posed nothing if not hybrid threats in complex conflicts. As for the 'comprehensive approach', this excellent idea has long been known by another name, grand strategy. One thing of which we can be certain is that the big novel idea of today will have a long historical provenance.

Steven Metz was only half-correct when he wrote in 1994 that 'it is time to hold a wake so that strategists can pay their respects to Clausewitz and then move on, leaving him to rest among the historians'. Alas, he fell considerably short of half-correct when he proceeded to claim that

> Despite the efforts of brilliant minds to adapt and update his theory, Clausewitz does not adequately account for much of the real or threatened armed violence of the late 20th century, whether revolutionary insurgency, nuclear deterrence, or counternarcotic trafficking.[7]

It is necessary for strategists to do much more than simply 'pay their respects' to the Prussian; they need to understand and absorb his theory with as much historical empathy as possible. Although in the opinion of this strategist, Clausewitz's theory is valid for all periods and all forms of warfare, as well as for conflict behaviour short of actual warfare, his must not be regarded as the last word on the subjects of war and strategy. Just as Clausewitz left his large and untidy manuscript in need of revision, so we must treat strategic theory as a living field. The theory rests upon fundamental propositions and explanations, but in addition it is always in want of historical and functional contextualization. As Chapter 1 explains, in common with war, strategy has an enduring nature but an ever shape-shifting character. Clausewitz should not be left 'to the historians', as Metz suggests, but rather has to be augmented and when necessary challenged as the most vital contribution to strategic thought available.

It is somewhat humbling to realize that there is only one strategic enlightenment. In his wonderful comparative study, *Masters of War*, Michael I. Handel discovered, or believed he had, profound similarities among strategic thinkers considered comparatively across time and cultures. Handel is basically correct, though he exaggerates transcultural commonalities. He assays the proposition that there are two 'radically different Eastern and Western approaches to the art of war', and finds it unpersuasive. He rejects the culturalist theory of 'opposing paradigms'.[8] In his words again: 'I concluded that the basic logic of strategy, like that of political behaviour, is universal. To say otherwise would be akin to asserting that Russia, China, Japan, and the United States each follow distinct theories of physics or chemistry.' This is either right or, at the least, is highly plausible. However, for a large caveat, Handel overstates the good argument that strategic thought provides universal, rather than culture-specific, truth. *Strategy Bridge* strives to find and develop a general theory of strategy explicable in terms that should be universally and eternally valid. But, in addition, it identifies a general theory adaptably applicable to the many specific forms that strategy can and must assume if it is to meet the particular needs of time, place, character of enemy, and forms of warfare.

Some historians are uncomfortable with the claim that the theory of strategy is eternally and universally authoritative. The valid point is registered that strategy in its modern meaning was a word that did not appear in the literature until the 1770s. In 1771 and again in 1777, French author Lt. Colonel Paul Gideon Joly de Maizeroy referred to strategy in terms compatible with common understanding today, as also did Jacques-Antoine Hippolyte Comte de Guibert in 1779. Until the late eighteenth century, theorists and practitioners would seem to have succeeded in using every verbal formula to refer to what Maizeroy and we understand by strategy, except the word itself. Edward N. Luttwak notes that '[a]s with many scientific terms, the word "strategy" (French *stratégie*, [sometimes *dialectique:* CSG], Italian *strategia*) is a Greek word that no ancient Greek ever used'.[9] The Greek words *strategos* and *strategia*, respectively, referred to a general and to generalship, narrowly understood. The truth of the matter is that security communities around the world have always done strategy as we understand it today, but they have called it such only for the past 200 years. Because our distant predecessors did not employ the word strategy, it does not follow that they failed to grasp the meaning of the concept in terms that we would find familiar, and still less does it mean that prior to the 1770s no one did strategy. To illustrate my claim: probably the finest example of what today we must call grand strategic reasoning was expressed by King Archidamus of Sparta in 432 BCE, with reference to his polity's prospects for success in the possible war with Athens that was then under public consideration. If the Greeks (and Byzantines, also Greeks, albeit Romanized ones) did not think strategically—functionally in our modern usage—Thucydides could not have written, or transcribed perhaps, Archidamus's brilliant speech, and Byzantine Emperor Leo VI could not have written his non-trivially strategic *Taktica* in ca. AD 904.[10]

In his brilliant and much celebrated long essay on Tolstoy, Sir Isaiah Berlin employs the Greek fable of the hedgehog and the fox. The poet Archilochus wrote: 'The fox knows many things, but the hedgehog knows one big thing.'[11] Berlin argues convincingly that Tolstoy wished to be a hedgehog, armed with a universal unifying theory of history. Alas, in practice he was a genius of a fox, perceptive about the details of the diversity of people and events. This metaphor is helpful in understanding my endeavour in *Strategy Bridge*. Like Tolstoy, in motive if not in skill, I strive to identify a universal theory of strategy, while accommodating theoretically the historical richness of actual strategies, which is to say of plans in action with their consequences. Whether or not I have succeeded well enough is a judgement I must leave to the reader.

There is a need for strategic thought to move on with, not from, Clausewitz. Strategy is so difficult a subject to understand, let alone to practice successfully, that *On War* is essential as the outstanding intellectual guide. The challenge, to repeat, is to know how to use Clausewitz prudently. This means employing his ideas and his method of analysis with a care to historical context. Also, there are some areas that have to be explored, explained, and fitted into a strategy whole, indeed a gestalt as Handel suggests usefully, that Clausewitz either neglected altogether, left dangling incompletely treated, or simply—to risk a charge of apostasy—misunderstood.[12] None of these remarks on the advisability of reining in an unduly respectful view of Clausewitz impacts on my belief that if one has to follow a strategic intellectual giant, the great Prussian stands as the only candidate for guru. Fortunately, though, there is no self-evident necessity to freeze the boundary of strategic theory according to a world view from the 1810s and 1820s.

It is nearly a decade since I published *Modern Strategy*.[13] It contained a great deal of strategic theory, but it was not designed or written with theory exposition as its principal mission. Although inevitably there is much common ground between that book and *Strategy Bridge*, their chief purposes are quite distinctive. *Modern Strategy* sought to plough the entire field of modern strategic behaviour, and had a great deal to say about strategy in general and Clausewitz and other strategists in particular. However, it did not aspire to develop a general strategic theory of its own. Some vital elements for such emerged in the text, but that was mainly as a by-product of other concerns. Overall, *Modern Strategy* told a story characterized by timelessness and a unity of strategy's many dimensions. Ten years on, *Strategy Bridge* is not content merely to talk theoretically, as well as practically, about strategy. Instead, it specifies and tests a theory of strategy. I am not fully convinced that the indefinite article is most appropriate, except to signify an all too sincere authorial modesty. The true position of this theorist holds that there is only a single general theory of strategy, as Handel claims. *Strategy Bridge* is an effort to assemble the diverse major pieces of the strategy puzzle and turn them into a coherent unity, a theory worthy of the ascription. With thanks to Archilochus and Berlin, *Strategy Bridge* invites assessment as the effort of a would-be strategic hedgehog.

The public need for a coherent and contemporary general theory of strategy is evident both from the literature extant and, even more, from the daily evidence of real-world strategic malpractice. General theories of strategy of high quality, classics if one will, are in conspicuously short supply. In fact, the voluminous literature on so-called strategic studies contains an abundance of scribbling on nearly every conceivable topic save for general strategic theory. An important reason why Clausewitz is so prominent an intellectual influence, both when he is well understood and when he is not, is because *On War* has no genuine competition. Other reasons include the quality of Clausewitz's theorizing, of course. As I have suggested elsewhere, only half in jest, Clausewitz may have performed too well as a theorist.[14] Perhaps his rather ragged and incomplete, but brilliant, theory of war left insufficient intellectual room for succeeding generations of theorists to make their mark. This speculative claim is implausible as stated, yet it does point to a problem raised already. It can be difficult to find intellectual breathing space on a stage that must always accommodate the Prussian as a virtually living presence. Whatever the reasons, there are very few general theories of strategy that warrant the iconic status, 'classic'.

In the highest category of classic status, there are only three entries: Clausewitz's *On War* (1832–4), far advanced in first place; Sun Tzu's *The Art of War* (ca. 490 BCE), which is perceptive while being terse to a fault; and Thucydides' *The Peloponnesian War* (ca. 400 BCE), which interweaves historical narrative with strategic insight.[15]

As was explained above, our modern definition of strategy cannot be dated earlier than the 1770s, and was by no means fully developed, let alone authoritative, through Clausewitz's lifetime. It is testimony both to the persistence through time of generically identical or very similar challenges, and to the enduring merit in these authors' analyses that we can locate their writings within a modern paradigm of strategy that makes sense to us today. It is understandable why historians may find the view taken here of these historical classics to be anachronistic, a challenge that this author attempts to meet in Appendix C. However, such would be a mistake, because the core subject matter that today we identify as strategic existed as a function and had to be exercised in all past periods. That was so no matter how the challenges of the time were explained and ordered by the ideas then current in the words of the languages then extant. For illustration, Alexander's Macedonian army was dependent upon logistics, even though this term is modern, (the science of supply and movement) being attributed to Baron Antoine Henri de Jomini.[16] Should some doubt remain over the validity of our backfitting modern strategic ideas in assessing, say, ancient Greek thought and behaviour, readers might care to note the following judgement by two Greek strategic theorists of today. In their potent study of *Thucydides on Strategy*, Athanassios G. Platias and Constantinos Koliopoulos advise as follows:

> We conclude by presenting a number of strategic concepts as they appear in Thucydides' text. Naturally, Thucydides did not use contemporary strategic jargon. Nevertheless, one cannot help but be impressed by the remarkable clarity and dexterity with which he uses a multitude of supposedly modern concepts.[17]

In addition to the three masterpieces by Clausewitz, Sun Tzu, and Thucydides, works by five other authors merit mention and qualify for a second category of esteem. Specifically: Niccolo Machiavelli's *The Art of* War (1521), and *The Prince* (1532), just clear the bar for classic status, primarily for reason of their insight into the nexus between an army and the society it serves; Jomini's *Art of War* (1838), a book which has had great influence up to the present day, for good and ill; Basil H. Liddell Hart's *Strategy: The Indirect Approach* (1967, 4th edn.), which offers much valuable strategic education, in addition to a contestable general theory of its own; J. C. Wylie's *Military Strategy: A General Theory of Power Control* (1967, 1989), the best book of somewhat, but only somewhat, original general strategic theory published in the twentieth century;[18] and Luttwak's *Strategy: The Logic of War and Peace* (1987, 2001), which develops a general theory around the useful insight that a paradoxical logic is uniquely characteristic of strategy at every level of conflict. In third and fourth categories of merit, I place, respectively, the twentieth-century American strategic thinkers, Bernard

Brodie and Thomas C. Schelling.[19] These authors yielded understanding of strategy in the nuclear age that has application beyond their historical context: in short, they have contributed to strategy's general theory. Of course, there are many more books, articles, essays, reports, and briefings that have value. But for those in search of an education in the fundamentals of strategy, the books just cited comprise the canon. Some readers may judge timeless quality and intellectual grasp rather more restrictively than I, and prefer to claim simply that understanding gleaned from the study of Clausewitz, Sun Tzu, and Thucydides, can suffice for a sound education in strategy.

My principal intellectual debts have just been acknowledged. From time to time, I may misread or inadvertently misuse Clausewitz, Sun Tzu, and Thucydides, but theirs is the reasoning that provides the arches which support *Strategy Bridge*. Why the bridge metaphor? Because no other idea so well conveys the core function of strategy. This idea of the strategy bridge, in common with possible alternative metaphors, is open to challenge by pedants. For example, a material bridge is a passive construction to be used simply for traffic that is usually, though not invariably, two way. The strategy bridge, however, is not passive, at least it should not be. The strategists who hold the bridge are tasked with the generally inordinately complex and difficult mission of translating political purpose, or policy, into feasible military, and other, plans. Theirs is the task of turning one currency—military (or economic, or diplomatic, and so forth) power—into quite another (desired political consequences). This near alchemical process necessarily involves the manipulation of two distinct currencies, military effect and political effect, via the potency of strategic effect. Overwhelming virtues of the bridge metaphor include its merit as a simple image that is universally accessible and comprehended, and the singularity of its ubiquitous, transcultural, function. A bridge, even a metaphorical one, has to connect two distinctive entities or phenomena that otherwise would be divided. In the proverbial nutshell, this is exactly the function of strategy. If one subscribes to the value in the bridge metaphor, it ought to be impossible to fail to understand why strategy matters profoundly.

Chapters 1 and 2 present, explain, and defend the theory of strategy. The theory offers a master narrative, a dominant compound concept. *Strategy Bridge* argues that strategy seeks control over an enemy's political behaviour, and that the threat or use of military force will be more or less prominent among the instruments of power that strategists orchestrate in their bridging function between means and ends. The key terms are control, force, bridge, and effect. To emphasize political control as the ultimate purpose of strategy is to ensure that one does not lose the plot in the course of theorizing or, even more likely, of strategy execution. Although the practice of strategy strictly does not require the threat or use of military force, such action will always be plausibly possible. If this condition is not met, one is not dealing with strategy as it is understood in this book. The concept of the strategy bridge is extraordinarily significant because it draws attention to the vital distinction between means and ends. Strategic effect refers to the consequences of behaviour upon an enemy. The effect can be material, psychological, or both. Control is sought via restricting an enemy's ability to resist and also, perhaps, his will to do so. Obviously, the two should be closely connected, at least in the minds of rational policymakers.

I acknowledge readily that identification of control over the enemy as the overriding purpose of strategy is entirely unoriginal. Clausewitz advises that 'to impose our will on the enemy is its [war's] object', and Wylie insists that 'the aim of war is some measure of control over the enemy'.[20] Their messages are the same. One threatens, or fights, in order to influence the political, strategic, and military decisions that can trigger, or which order, inimical action. *Strategy Bridge* heavily endorses this idea as comprising the core of the purpose of strategy.

Some people may wonder why the theory of strategy is alleged to be so important, since strategy inherently is a practical business.[21] Why do abstract ideas and ahistorical propositions matter? The reason is that theory moves the course of history. Human behaviour is driven by theory. Theory provides the consequentialist beliefs that enable us to make decisions rationally, if not always reasonably. Theory tries to tell us that *if* so and so is done, *then* such and such should be the consequence. Theory, the realm of linked ideas, yields meaning to our world. By and large, we judge behaviour according to our beliefs about its most probable consequences. The conduct of statecraft, let alone of war itself, rests inalienably upon theory. The beliefs, cultures more broadly, of rivals and actual belligerents, rest overwhelmingly upon theoretical tenets which may be largely speculative. Chapter 1 delves at some length into the nature, functions, and character of theory. For the purposes of this Introduction, however, it is necessary only for me to register the claim that the theory of strategy has a most intimate connection with strategic practice and malpractice. Strategic behaviour, especially that of a directly military character, comprises strategic ideas in action. Strategic ideas as theory move world history via strategies as plans in execution.

Strategy Bridge is designed to identify, explore, explain, analyse, and assess. Fundamentally, in Part I, 'Theory', it develops and analyses the general theory of strategy, with many debts to the classics (Chapters 1–2). Perhaps I should claim simply that this book presents the theory of strategy in a new way, since I cannot claim to have discovered anything of significance that was unknown to the court strategists of ancient China. Chapter 3 contextualizes the theory of strategy with respect to politics and war. Part II, 'Practice', comprising Chapters 4–6, applies the dicta of the general theory to specific major areas wherein their relevance and value is explored and explained. These chapters discuss: the many difficulties that harass and can frustrate the strategist, especially the inconvenient presence of a self-willed enemy (Chapter 4); the concept, material and psychological realities of strategic effect, which is to say strategy's output (Chapter 5); and command performance with strategy by strategists (Chapter 6). The Conclusion brings all elements of the grand narrative together by explaining how the theory of strategy aids practice by bringing order out of the chaos of under-governed strategic intellectual space in its pursuit of control.

Much confusion can be prevented by identifying two levels of analysis for strategy. I approach strategy: (1) as general theory; (2) as specific operational plans, which is to say as strategies. In this manner, the analysis is able to cope with both truly general and general but specific (i.e. partial, as for, say, air power, or special operations) theories of strategy, while avoiding needless complexity. The general theory must educate the people whose duty it is to draw up specific historical plans of action. Recognition of this distinction is true to reality and precludes any cause for unease over reference both to strategy and strategies. For illustration: in 1943–4 Supreme Headquarters Allied Powers Europe (SHAPE): comprised people and processes that were the product of education in general strategic theory, as well as of experience as interpreted by culture; developed specific joint and combined operational plans for the invasion of German-held Western Europe; and oversaw the detailed specific operational plans developed by and for geography-limited kinds of military forces. Hedgehogs and foxes should be allies.

Accepting some risk of overcomplicating matters, I can specify a subordinate category of theories that have more in common with strategy's general theory than they do with specific historical strategies as plans. This somewhat interme-diate level of theory comprises general theories specific to particular geographics or functions. For example, there is general theory for air power and sea power, and indeed for special operations. These specific general theories, to hazard an apparent oxymoron, comprise a transmission belt of ideas between general strategy and strategies as plans unique to time and place. All references in this book to strategies, plural, apply to actual strategies chosen to cope with real, or believed to be real, historical strategic problems and opportunities.

The value of strategic theory can depend not only on the willingness of practical people to learn, but also on the merit, or otherwise, in the theory to which they are exposed. It is essential that the theorist of strategy never forgets that he or she writes primarily not for the edification and possibly the amusement of other theorists. Instead, strategic theory should intend to achieve the better education of executive strategists, their political masters, and their military agents. It is in this spirit and for this purpose that the discussion must open with a broad-fronted offensive intended to secure the commanding heights of a useful general theory of strategy, one that must educate those who draft and execute the specific strategies of historical experience.

NOTES

1. Carl von Clausewitz, *On War*, tr. Michael Howard and Peter Paret (1832–4; Princeton, NJ: Princeton University Press, 1976).
2. Recent scholarship on Clausewitz, the man and his writings, includes: Beatrice Heuser, *Reading Clausewitz* (London: Pimlico, 2002); Hugh Smith, *On Clausewitz: A Study of Military and Political Ideas* (Basingstoke: Palgrave Macmillan, 2005); Andreas Herberg-Rothe, *Clausewitz's Puzzle: The Political Theory of War* (Oxford: Oxford University Press, 2007); Antulio J. Echevarria II, *Clausewitz and Contemporary War* (Oxford: Oxford University Press, 2007); Hew Strachan, *Clausewitz's On War: A Biography* (New York: Atlantic Monthly Press, 2007); Hew Strachan and Andreas Herberg-Rothe, eds., *Clausewitz in the*

Twenty-First Century (Oxford: Oxford University Press, 2007); and Jon Tetsuro Sumida, *Decoding Clausewitz: A New Approach to On War* (Lawrence, KS: University Press of Kansas, 2008). The leading intellectual biography remains Peter Paret, *Clausewitz and the State* (New York: Oxford University Press, 1976). Clausewitz and his magnum opus certainly are not suffering from any recent neglect. Michael Howard, *Clausewitz: A Very Short Introduction* (Oxford: Oxford University Press, 2008), is a small gem.

3. Colin S. Gray, *Fighting Talk: Forty Maxims on War, Peace, and Strategy* (Westport, CT: Praeger Security International, 2007), 58–61.

4. US Army and Marine Corps, *Counterinsurgency Field Manual: U.S. Army Field Manual No. 3–24, and Marine Corps Warfighting Publication No. 3–33.5* (Chicago, IL: University of Chicago Press, 2007); Frank G. Hoffman, *Conflict in the 21st Century: The Rise of Hybrid Wars* (Arlington, VA: Potomac Institute for Policy Studies, December 2007); and David Kilcullen, *The Accidental Guerrilla: Fighting Small Wars in the Midst of a Big One* (London: C. Hurst, 2009).

5. (UK) Cabinet Office, *The National Security Strategy of the United Kingdom: Security in an Interdependent World*, Cm. 7291 (Norwich: Stationery Office, 2008).

6. See Andrew Wiest, ed., *Rolling Thunder in a Gentle Land: The Vietnam War Revisited* (Oxford: Osprey Publishing, 2006), is a fine collection of well balanced essays.

7. Steven Metz, 'A Wake for Clausewitz: Towards a Philosophy of 21st-Century Warfare', *Parameters*, 24 (winter 1994–95), 126, 128.

8. Michael I. Handel, *Masters of War: Classical Strategic Thought*, 3rd edn. (London: Frank Cass, 2001), xvii.

9. Edward N. Luttwak, *Strategy: The Logic of War and Peace*, rev. edn. (Cambridge, MA: Harvard University Press, 2001), 267. For a useful brief discussion of Maizeroy and his discovery, though not celebration, of strategy, see the helpful discussion in Azar Gat, *The Origins of Military Thought: From the Enlightenment to Clausewitz* (Oxford: Clarendon Press, 1989), 37–43.

10. Thucydides, *The Landmark Thucydides: A Comprehensive Guide to The Peloponnesian War*, ed. Robert B. Strassler, rev. tr. Richard Crawley (ca. 400 BCE; New York: Free Press, 1996), 45–7. I am grateful to Hew Strachan for insisting that I recognize the lack of historical provenance to the modern meaning of the English word strategy. I must persist, however, in arguing that we humans have always needed to think and behave strategically as the concept is understood today. I am under-impressed by the fact that prior to the 1770s our European languages did not deploy the word for strategy in the meaning we assign to it now. For a somewhat different point of view, see Hew Strachan, 'The Lost Meaning of Strategy', *Survival*, 47 (autumn 2005), esp. 35. Williamson Murray and Mark Grimsley, 'Introduction: On Strategy', in Murray, Macgregor Knox, and Alvin Bernstein, eds., *The Making of Strategy: Rulers, States, and War* (Cambridge: Cambridge University Press, 1994), 1–23. See the excellent entry on strategy by J. P. Charnay in Andre Corvisier, ed., *A Dictionary of Military History*, ed. John Childs, tr. Chris Turner (Oxford: Blackwell Reference, 1994), 768–74. Charnay credits Lt. Colonel Paul Gideon Joly de Maizeroy (1719–89) with the first recognizably modern use of the word strategy, though he was not averse to substituting *dialectique* for it. Intellectually, the breakthrough year for a tolerably clear recognition of the vital distinction between tactics and strategy in our modern understanding of the word, was 1771, with Maizeroy's translation of Byzantine Emperor Leo VI's (The Wise's) 886–912, *Taktika*. Leo writes of *strategike* (Greek). For his own writing on the subject, see Maizeroy, *Théorie de la guerre, Où l'on expose la constitution et formation de l'Infanterie et de la Cavalerie, leurs manoeuvres élémentaires, avec l'application des principes à la grande Tactique,*

Suivie de demonstration Sur la Stratégique (Lausanne: 1777), lxxxv–vi, 299. Maizeroy titles the third part of this book, 'De la Stratégique ou Dialectique Relativement aux Opérations de la Guerre'. I am much indebted to Beatrice Heuser of Reading University for drawing my attention to Maizeroy's translation of Leo. R. R. Palmer appears to credit Jacques-Antoine Comte de Guibert with first introduction of the modern sense of strategy, as *la Stratégique*, in his *Défense du systéme de guerre moderne* (Paris: 1779). However, Maizeroy would seem to have scored before him. See Palmer, 'Frederick the Great, Guibert, Bülow: From Dynastic to National War', in Peter Paret, ed., *Makers of Modern Strategy: From Machiavelli to the Nuclear Age* (Princeton, NJ: Princeton University Press, 1986), 107 n27. See Appendix C, Conceptual '*Hueys*' at Thermopylae? The Challenge of Strategic Anachronism.

11. Isaiah Berlin, *The Hedgehog and the Fox: An Essay on Tolstoy's View of History* (New York: Mentor Books, 1957), 7.
12. Handel, *Masters of War*, 345–51.
13. Colin S. Gray, *Modern Strategy* (Oxford: Oxford University Press, 1999).
14. Ibid. ch. 3.
15. Sun Tzu, *The Art of War*, tr. Ralph D. Sawyer (ca. 490 BCE; Boulder, CO: Westview Press, 1994); Thucydides, *Landmark Thucydides*.
16. See D. W. Engels, *Alexander the Great and the Logistics of the Macedonian Army* (Berkeley, CA: University of California Press, 1980); and Baron Antoine Henri de Jomini, *The Art of War* (1838; London: Greenhill Books, 1992), ch. vi. A successful demonstration of the value of apparent theoretical anachronism in the study of strategy is David J. Lonsdale, *Alexander the Great: Lessons in Strategy* (Abingdon: Routledge 2007).
17. Athanassios G. Platias and Constantinos Koliopoulos, *Thucydides on Strategy: Athenian and Spartan Grand Strategies in the Peloponnesian War and Their Relevance Today* (Athens: Eurasia Publications, 2006), 257. Essentially the same point is made by the American historian, Antulio J. Echevarria II, when he writes: 'While the decisionmaking that Tartar bands used to formulate policy might appear less sophisticated than those of modern states (which is debatable), they proved no less effective in developing strategies and direction for military force in pursuit of political goals. These objectives emerged as a product of resources available to the Tartars, their geographical position as a composite of Turkish and Mongol nations located in Central Asia, their nomadic culture and traditions, and the influence of Islam.' 'Dynamic Inter-Dimensionality: A Revolution in Military Theory', *Joint Force Quarterly*, 15 (spring 1997), 31.
18. Niccolo Machiavelli, *Art of War*, tr. Christopher Lynch (1521; Chicago: University of Chicago Press, 2003); id., *Discourses on Livy*, tr. Julia Conaway Bondarella and Peter Bondarella (1531; Oxford: Oxford University Press, 2003); id., *The Prince*, tr. Peter Bondarella and Mark Musa (1532; Oxford: Oxford University Press, 1998); Jomini, *The Art of War* (1838; London: Greenhill Books, 1992); Basil H. Liddell Hart, *Strategy: The Indirect Approach* (1941; London: Faber and Faber, 1967); Luttwak, *Strategy*; and J. C. Wylie, *Military Strategy: A General Theory of Power Control* (1967; Annapolis, MD: Naval Institute Press, 1989).
19. Bernard Brodie, ed., *The Absolute Weapon: Atomic Power and World Order* (New York: Harcourt, Brace, 1946); id., *Strategy in the Missile Age* (Princeton, NJ: Princeton University Press, 1959); id., *War and Politics* (New York: Macmillan, 1973); Thomas C. Schelling, *The Strategy of Conflict* (Cambridge MA: Harvard University Press, 1960); id., *Arms and Influence* (New Haven, CT: Yale University Press, 1966).
20. Clausewitz, 75; Wylie, *Military Strategy*, 66 (emphasis in the original).
21. Bernard Brodie, *War and Politics* (New York: Macmillan, 1973), 452.

Part I

Theory

1

The Theory of Strategy, I:
Enduring Nature, Changing Character

QUESTIONS AND DEFINITIONS

There is but a single theory of strategy; its function is to educate those whose profession it is to hold open a bridge between politics and action. Those people are strategists. Theory has to expose the general nature of strategy as well as explain the elements that shape and drive specific historical strategies. It is in the nature of strategy for its historical, specific, character to be ever changing. The former is as constant as the latter is not. The theory must explain both. Examination of strategy's hydra-headed character gravitates towards the twin compound behaviours of strategy-making and strategy execution. Chapters 1 and 2 provide the conceptual tools with which any and every aspect of specific historical strategies—the general theory of strategy expressed and revealed in particular contexts—can be considered. At least that should be so, provided the general theory is crafted well enough. Because specific strategies in history reflect application of the tenets, the dicta, of general theory, it is essential that the subject be approached, treated, and practised holistically. Strategy and strategies, theory and practice, must be seen as one. Theory should be able to help educate the realm of practice by assisting people to think strategically. The general theory of strategy may be compared to a skeleton key that can empower strategists conceptually, by means of opening every door to every character and kind of strategic challenge. The general theory key cannot itself solve problems, but it should enhance greatly the ability of its users to perform effectively.

The general theory has to answer four fundamental questions.

1. What is strategy?
2. How is strategy made, and by whom?
3. How is strategy executed?
4. What does strategy do?—consequences.

The general theory must explain strategy as an eternal idea, function, set of challenges, and behaviour. How these persisting aspects are made manifest in actual strategies, which is to say in specific plans, is the realm of strategy's multi-headed, inherently transient character. Chapters 1 and 2 provide a common framework of general theory for the understanding of both strategy's single

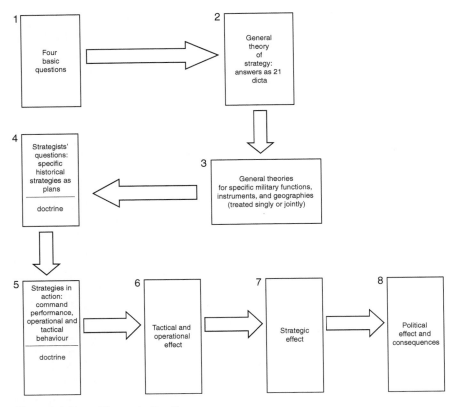

Figure 1.1 From Theory to Practice

nature and its many characters. Figure 1.1 lays out the barest of bare bones in the skeleton of strategic theory and practice.

Strategy must be approached both as general theory for the education of practice and as historical plans and strategies chosen and executed by strategists on the authority of politics. It follows that theory should be helpful to identify not only the questions that theorists must answer, but also the ones that responsible strategists need always to keep in the forefront of their minds. These are the strategists' questions, proper recognition of some of which I owe to the wisdom of an outstanding historian and strategic theorist, Philip A. Crowl.[1]

1. What is it about? What are the political stakes and how much do they matter to us?
2. So what? What will be the strategic effect of the sundry characters of behaviour that we choose to conduct?
3. Is the strategy selected tailored well enough to meet our political objectives?

4. What are the probable limits of our (military) power as a basket of complementary agencies to influence and endeavour to control the enemy's will?
5. How could the enemy strive to thwart us?
6. What are our alternative courses of action (and inaction)? What are their prospective costs and benefits?
7. How robust is our home front?
8. Does the strategy we prefer today draw prudently and honestly upon the strategic education that history provides?
9. What have we overlooked?

Although I have edited and added to Crowl's 'Short Catechism', I do not believe that our combined and amended list presented here contains any element to which he would have objected. Questions are our best friends for the invention and refinement of strong useful theory, and they are the lethal enemies of poor theory.

Before we can proceed to identify the content of the theory of strategy, it is essential that the key concepts should be defined with as close to crystal clarity as possible. If we neglect to define terms carefully the result must be confusion. The author himself may be confused, while even if he was not confused at the outset, terminological ambiguity is certainly going to weaken his argument and mislead readers. Clausewitz never wrote more accurately than when he claimed that

> The primary purpose of any theory is to clarify concepts and ideas that have become, as it were, confused and entangled. Not until terms and concepts have been defined can one hope to make any progress in examining the question clearly and simply and expect the reader to share one's views.[2]

The coining of definitions is a task fraught with peril. Alas, nowhere is this claim verified more easily than with respect to the concept of strategy. As this and later chapters explain, strategy is an idea, a function, a behaviour that almost begs to be abused as a consequence of misapprehension. Since ideas drive actions, intellectual confusion must promote confused activity. The needed definition of strategy has to be 'right enough', which is to say it does not have to meet any and every objection, but it must highlight the core of its subject and it must not mislead. Without casting aspersions upon alternative definitions preferred by other authors, this theorist advances here the most vital definitions authoritative for argument in this book.

Over the course of many years I have favoured a number of different definitions of the concepts treated immediately below. Quite often I discovered that even the criticisms of my conceptual usage that had some merit, tended to come with biases of their own that threatened the core integrity of the argument. Most commonly, the charge of undue exclusivity (e.g. too narrow a military focus) carried the viruses of undue inclusivity and consequent loss of focus. In short, it is all too easy to lose the plot as result of a praiseworthy effort to draft the perfect definition. People, even scholars, are apt to forget that definitions are intellectual inventions; they cannot be true or false. Here are the concepts and their meanings most central to the integrity of the arguments developed here about the functions of the strategy bridge.

1. *Vision*: A concept of the desired condition that serves to inspire, and provide moral and political authority for, policy preferences and choices.

2. *Policy*: The political objectives that provide the purposes of particular historical strategies.

3. *Strategy* (content neutral): The direction and use made of means by chosen ways in order to achieve desired ends.

4. *Grand strategy*: The direction and use made of any or all among the total assets of a security community in support of its policy goals as decided by politics. The theory and practice of grand strategy is the theory and practice of statecraft itself. In the words of John Lewis Gaddis, it is 'the calculated relationship of means to large ends'.[3]

5. *Military strategy*: The direction and use made of force and the threat of force for the purposes of policy as decided by politics. Military strategy exists as generic general theory (as in Clausewitz, and here in Chapters 1 and 2), as well as in historical strategies. The latter have to be approached both as uniquely distinctive plans and in terms of their consequences (strategic effect, ultimately). Definitions that identify strategy and strategies only as plans should be rejected because they fail to grip the essence of strategy, which is its instrumental nature. Strategy has to be expressed in strategies as plans, but most significantly it is about the intended consequences of the operational and tactical behaviour advanced by those plans.

6. *Operations*: Combinations of purposefully linked military engagements, generally though not necessarily on a large scale. Operations are strategy as action; they appear as plans (strategies), as combat, and as consequences (effect).

7. *Tactics*: Actual military behaviour, most especially, though not only, directly in combat (fighting).

8. *Military doctrine*: Guidance, mandatory or discretionary, on what is believed officially to be contemporary best military practice.

9. *Strategic effect*: The cumulative and sequential impact of strategic performance upon the course of events.

10. *Strategic history*: The influence of the threat and use of force upon the grand narrative of general history. It is necessary to be vigilant lest 'strategic' is equated too narrowly with the military narrative. However, overenthusiastic contextualization of military matters in a sophisticated search for the whole grand strategic story carries the serious risk of understating the relative historical importance of organized violence for political ends.

Because there can be only one general theory, the imperial definite article in the title of this chapter is appropriate. Strategy per se, the function, cannot differ among cultures and historical contexts. The general theory applies to China and Russia as much as to the United States and Britain. But when one talks about, say, Russian strategy in Afghanistan in the 1980s, or American strategy in Iraq in the 2000s, one must notice the many differences that derive from the distinctive contexts for these two cases of applied strategy. Strategic theory is authoritative at just two levels of domain: the strictly general, and the general but specific or partial (e.g. to cyber power or counter-insurgency) to geography or particular function. This split provides a clarity resting upon empirical realities that is essential for the avoidance of needless confusion. The general theory of strategy covers both grand and military strategy. Of necessity, it is abstract and sweeping. Contrary to appearances, however, the focus of this book is very much on practical matters, because such is the nature of strategy. Security communities have specific strategies, they 'do' strategy. In every real-world historical case, the character of the chosen strategies should be obedient to the meaning and major implications of strategy's general nature, and general, but specifically partial natures, if those strategies are to prosper in the live-fire or pike-thrust test of strategic history. For example, although the general theory is beyond cultural influence, particular strategies preferred by historical belligerents most certainly are not.

Given the recent 'cultural turn' in Western strategic analysis, it is especially important to understand and sustain in practice a clear distinction between strategy in general and strategies as specific operational plans.[4] For application, the general theory of strategy needs filling out in detail with respect to each unique historical moment. Strategies change with their contexts, but, whether they be jointly land and air, or narrowly naval or space, in application they cannot evade the reach and grasp of strategy's general theory. The most general theory provides inspiration and more for the design of general theories specific to limited tools of strategy (armies, navies, special operations forces, and so forth). So that there should be no ambiguity about the theoretical framework employed in this book, Table 1.1 sets out the relevant elemental architecture.

There is always a danger that the theorist will proceed one or two steps too far, and as a result will pass the culminating point of victory for clarity and utility. I accept the peril, but lest my faith is misjudged it is probably prudent to adopt the Nelsonian approach and identify the strategic theoretical equivalents of the great admiral's advice that no captain could go far wrong if he placed his ship alongside one of the enemy's. These are the rules of engagement for productive encounter with strategic theoretical matters:

1. Maintain clear distinctions among policy, strategy, and tactics: these three magical words translate as purpose, ways, and means. The three are interdependent, but there should be no confusion as to the descending ranking of relative significance, from policy, through strategy, to tactics. Poor tactics can be rescued by superior strategy, while poor strategy sometimes can be saved by excellence in policy. Tactical superiority is likely to prove disastrous when

Table 1.1 Strategy: The Function and Levels

1. *Strategy* (function, content neutral): the relations among ends, ways, and means; inescapable, pervasive, ubiquitous, universal, eternal. Understood strictly as a function, strategy must ply its trade of ends, ways, and means at every level of war and warfare. These levels usually are identified in the Trinitarian framework of strategy, operations, and tactics. Functionally appreciated, strategy is done operationally and tactically, though there is merit in privileging the elementary binary of strategy and tactics.
2. *General theory of strategy* (grand and military): validity independent of all historical contextual detail.
3. *Specific (partial) general theories of strategy*: for particular military (et al.) instruments and functions (e.g. for space power, cyber power, sea power, special operations); valid for all times, places, and circumstances.
4. *Grand strategies*: historically specific choices, every one unique.
5. *Military strategies* (overall): historically specific choices, every one unique.
6. *Military strategies specific to one or more military instruments or functions*: for example, historically specific 'joint' or air, or special operations campaign plans (*strategies*), developed and executed coherently as a part of overall military strategy.

strategy is weak or policy is ill judged: soldiers would be doing the wrong things well, and for the wrong reasons.

2. One has a strategy, which is done by tactics.

3. Strategy and tactics, though functionally distinctive, are both about the answers to why, how, and what questions.

4. Strategy and tactics meet in the ubiquitous command function at every level of behaviour. Strategy and tactics are locked together by the command function.

5. Neither strategy nor tactics has integrity one without the other. Strategy bereft of tactics literally cannot be done, while tactics innocent of strategy has to be nonsensically aimless.

6. Clausewitz was content to theorize about warfare with reference to the elementary binary of strategy and tactics. The invention, or discovery, of an operational level interposed between strategy and tactics, though officially orthodox in the Western world today, is not unproblematic.[5] The general theory of strategy does not need to recognize an operational level to warfare, the merit in such recognition is distinctly contestable and appears weaker or stronger from one historical strategic context to another. It is prudent to maintain that any construct that can impede cooperation between tactics and strategy should be regarded with a sceptical eye. The concepts of an operation and of operational art by its commanders are not at all dubious, but the postulate of an operational level to warfare is challengeable. What matters is that tactics should serve strategy, and vice versa. On balance, it is the judgement of this theorist that the problem lies not so much with the idea of an operational level of war intervening between strategic and tactical levels, but rather with poor performance by strategists who fail to impress their strategic designs sufficiently upon their operational and tactical level commanders.

Of recent decades, an operational level of war has been endorsed officially by many countries' military establishments, but there are under-recognized reasons why we should be careful in our enthusiasm for the idea. In principle, it should be valuable to work with the concept of a campaign that requires a strategy, which is to say a plan or plans, for the direction of tactical behaviour. But, in practice, to postulate an operational level of warfare intervening between strategy and tactics is to accept risks that are easy to overlook. Specifically, to the military professional, military operations and so-called operational art may substitute inappropriately for overall military strategy. The military person is ever likely to feel most comfortable in the allegedly politics-free zone of military operations. The peril lurking as a consequence of the tactical-operational nexus is matched by the danger in the strategy–operations connections. The strategist is all too likely to short-change his grip on tactical matters because he believes, mistakenly, that he need only grasp the operational. So, far from preserving a vital enabling bridge between strategy and tactics, the theory and practice of an operational level of war, on occasion at least, may function as a barrier rather than a two-way transmission belt. This is only a caveat, not a heretical claim eccentric to thoroughly modern military minds. It is, however, useful in its warning not to impede performance on the necessary strategy–tactics connection. If politician-strategists and soldier-strategists are content simply to sponsor strategy that is left to be executed by operational artistry using tactical behaviour at an operational level of war, the necessary strategic artistry is likely to be missing from effective guidance of the action. When military campaigns are conducted by military virtuosity for unduly military reasons, the tactical–strategic nexus is apt to be thin indeed.

Chapters 1 and 2 provide the theoretical architecture necessary for the comprehension of all strategic behaviour. Although the argument has to be largely abstract and bloodless, it is written with the practical needs of pragmatic people in mind. In almost all respects the theory of strategy exposed in these chapters lends itself readily to translation for real-world specific applicability. By way of illustration, the theory claims as a general truth that strategy is more difficult to devise and execute than are operations and tactics. It is no great step to change strategy to 'specific strategies' for one to leave the rarefied world of the theorist and enter the realm of practice. Bernard Brodie has written that:

> Strategic thinking, or theory if one prefers is nothing if not pragmatic. Strategy is a 'how to do it' study, a guide to accomplishing something and doing it efficiently. As in many other branches of politics, the question that matters in strategy is: Will the idea work? More important, will it be likely to work under the special circumstances under which it will next be tested?[6]

This is highly plausible, albeit with a reservation on Brodie's specification of efficiency as a requirement of strategy.[7] There should be no need to defend theory from assault by both hostile or merely sceptical strategic practitioners, planners, and 'shooters'. But, unfortunately, the need is all too pressing. Indeed, ignorance of the value of theory for practice is so widespread that it has to be dispersed and badly trounced before one can proceed usefully into the body of the argument. Therefore, as a necessary overture to presentation of the main body of the theory of strategy, the next section explains what theorists can bring to strategic performance.

THE MEANING AND VALUE OF THEORY

Theory and practice meet on the strategy bridge. In an important sense strategic planning can only be a theoretical exercise. When officials make a plan for action they are expressing a belief and hope that the behaviour specified will produce the desired results. This 'if . . . then . . .' consequentialist reasoning is theory in action. Nearly everything that impinges upon issues of war and peace comes down to applied theory. There is no escape from the toils of strategic theory, not even for the most apparently pragmatic of people. Clausewitz was largely correct when he wrote:

> Incidentally, we repeat again that here, as in all the practical arts, the function of theory is to educate the practical man, to train his judgment, rather than to assist him directly in the performance of his duties.[8]

Strategic theory as understood by Clausewitz is not overly helpful in particular cases, but then it cannot be designed to be so. The general theory can only educate, not train for all-case victory. In order to win, our strategist needs to outperform their strategist in the practical realization of the dicta of general theory.

What is theory? Strategists and their critics are wont to deploy the term recklessly, either deliberately evading, or simply ignoring the fact that it is eminently contestable. Social scientists typically mean by theory a set of propositions, even a single imperial one, the truth of which can be tested. In the words of Robert Boyle from 1664, scientific method is 'investigation by hypothesis subjected to rigorous experimental cross examination'.[9] In this way our bank of strategic knowledge can grow fatter and healthier. Notwithstanding the respect for the scientific method just indicated, it so happens that testable propositions are hard to draft for the field of strategic studies. In the 1960s, it was commonplace to refer to the Vietnam War metaphorically as a laboratory for escalation. In truth the War could be nothing of the kind. For the scientific veracity of a theory to be established, every test of the idea for the behaviour in question must yield the same outcome. World history, with all its complexities and uncertainties of cause and effect, cannot possibly be used to test hypotheses or propositions in a rigorous manner, following the basic experimental method of the harder sciences. Experiments need to be controlled. The idea is close to absurd with reference to strategy in execution, since warfare is violence applied with few rules for control. Indeed, the terms of engagement, the rules in a particular conflict, will be integral to the stakes in the struggle. The necessary role of an enemy eviscerates the foolish notion of war as a controllable experiment. That said, it does not follow that the social scientist, perhaps the social scientific historian, must abandon all ambition to locate a reasonable enough approximation to strategic truth. This author confesses to adhering to a distinctly old-fashioned positivism. I believe that we can and should try to understand the nature and shifting character of strategy, and that the product of strategic enquiry as strategic theory in which we can repose confidence is attainable.

There should be no tension between theory and practice. Given that strategic theory must serve the world of action, and that that world is shaped and even driven by ideas, the only challenges, as here, are to discover both the eternal secrets of the subject and to learn how to apply them in practice. These tasks are difficult, but far from insuperable. The first necessity is for the utmost clarity over definitions and levels of analysis and application.

In answer to the question, 'what is theory?'—many answers have equal authority. The *Oxford English Reference Dictionary* insists that theory can refer to: a supposition that purportedly explains something, a speculative view, an abstract thought, testable propositions, and an exposition of the principles that govern phenomena in a science.[10] Recall that Brodie was content to equate strategic theory simply with strategic thinking per se. We do not endorse such a permissive attitude to the meaning of strategic theory, but neither are we enamoured of approaches that seek the scientific certainty of the physical sciences, principally through quantification. Instead, we identify a set of statements, not quite maxims, that is both descriptive and, in a sense, is normative also, as well as silently prescriptive by implication. The theory outlined below and in Chapter 2 explains the nature of strategic behaviour; is abstract; has been discovered in historical practice, so it has been tested by experience; and overall constitutes the principles that rule all strategic activity. On the basis of these diverse claims, what follows in this chapter and in Chapter 2 truly is strategic theory.

What does theory do? To quote the Prussian again, 'Theory exists so that one need not start afresh each time sorting out the material and plowing through it, but will find it ready to hand and in good order. It is meant to educate the mind of the future commander, or more accurately to guide him in his self-education, not to accompany him to the battlefield.'[11] No one has offered a better explanation of the function of general strategic theory. Racing forward to the present day, Harry R. Yarger of the US Army War College suggests helpfully that:

> A theory of strategy provides essential terminology and definitions, explanations of the underlying assumptions and premises, substantive propositions translated into testable hypotheses, and methods that can be used to test the hypotheses and modify the theory as appropriate.[12]

The only difficulty with Yarger's approach to strategic theory is that it appears to encourage, even demand, an impossibility. How can we test strategic hypotheses when, as noted already, properly controlled experiments conducted in the quest for scientific truth cannot be conducted? The best that can be done is to found strategic theory upon what can be learnt from strategic history. But, since historical evidence is always incomplete, and the course of strategic history is ever contested by historians as they reconstruct the past to suit their ideas and interests, any theory that can rest only upon our reading and rereading of the past is unlikely to be thoroughly reliable. I assert that the general theory of strategy identified and explained here is true. The basis for such a seemingly extravagant claim is the belief that there is a real unique past to be explored and understood. The theory of strategy has not been deduced from first principles by a process of rational thought, but rather discovered from a process of historical investigation, flawed though the process and its product must be. General strategic theory should be thought of as lying immanent in the strategic history of our past, much as Michelangelo saw a complete statue as reposing immanently in a block of marble. This is why one needs to approach general strategic theory with the definite rather than the indefinite article. In the eyes of many post-modern theorists, people determinedly relativist and constructivist in approach, the view taken here of strategic theory must seem close to absurd. So be it. If you believe that there are no general truths discoverable about strategy, and war and peace, then *Strategy Bridge* is not the book for you. Let there be no misunderstanding on this point: I insist that there is an objective scale of soundness for the spectrum of potential offerings that one may call strategic theory. Truth in the theory of strategy is not a matter for subjective individual, even national, preference; all efforts at theory are not created and do not merit respect as equals. A bold but foolish theorist may insist, for example, that strategy should not be constrained significantly by logistical problems, or that as a general rule the enemy's preferences can safely be ignored. As a would-be educator of practical strategists, such a theorist would encourage the design and conduct of flawed strategies by commanders sufficiently ill-advised as to take his ignorant theoretical nostrums seriously.

GENERAL THEORY

Any attempt to design a new general theory of strategy could only be eccentric and misleading. Everything necessary for a general theory already exists in the literature, but the trouble is that its constituents are widely scattered and the whole is considerably less than the sum of its parts. Most, though not all, of what is needed can be located in Clausewitz's *On War*, while Sun Tzu, Thucydides, Niccolo Machiavelli, Antoine Henri de Jomini, Basil Liddell Hart, J. C. Wylie, and Edward N. Luttwak add necessary items and helpful ballast and nuance. However, no one strategic theorist, or mix of the same, ancient and modern, has done the whole job that needs doing. This author is much indebted to the three outstanding classical theorists—Clausewitz, Sun Tzu, and Thucydides—as well as to the 'moderns', pre-eminently Bernard Brodie, Thomas C. Schelling, Wylie, Michael Howard, and Luttwak.[13] But since no one theorist, or even one group of theorists, has provided all that is required, I have no responsible choice other than to set out my own stall with an ambitious general theory. Although the theory borrows unashamedly from here and there, the design and total composition is original.

It is possible that this book will contribute usefully to clarification of basic concepts: definition is a prime duty of the theorist. Recall that this text draws a sharp distinction between strategy and strategies. One is almost tempted to use higher case for the former and lower for the latter. Strategy, singular, refers to a universal challenge and behaviour, whereas strategies mean the actual, specific operational plans at every level of analysis. The latter are context dependent, the former is not.

Clausewitz chose to identify five broad 'elements of strategy'.

> The first [moral] type covers everything that is created by intellectual and psychological qualities and influences; the second [physical] consists of the size of the armed forces, their composition, armament and so forth; the third [mathematical] includes the angles of lines of operation, the convergent and divergent movements wherever geometry enters into their calculation; the fourth [geographical] comprises the influence of terrain, such as commanding positions, mountains, rivers, woods, and roads; and, finally, the fifth [statistical] covers support and maintenance.[14]

Much of what is necessary for a theory of strategy lurks in these five categories, but the design and selection do not speak very helpfully to would-be strategists today. Nonetheless, Clausewitz does speak to the ages when he insists that:

> It would however be disastrous to try to develop our understanding of strategy by analyzing those factors [the famous five itemized in the previous quotation] in isolation, since they are usually interconnected in each military action in manifold and intricate ways. A dreary analytical labyrinth would result, a nightmare in which one tried in vain to bridge the gulf between this abstract basis and the facts of life. Heaven protect the theorist from such an undertaking.[15]

If one leaps forward 147 years from *On War*, one discovers Michael Howard's powerful essay, 'The Forgotten Dimensions of Strategy'.[16] In 1979, Howard was complaining with much justice about the undue fascination with technology with which the United States approached its contemporary strategic problems. He specified just four 'dimensions of strategy': logistical, operational, social, and technological. Whether or not one endorses his choice of dimensions, Howard performed a most valuable task in pointing to the multidimensionality of strategy. Twenty years on from Howard's dimensions' article, the author of this book tested his readers' patience by identifying no fewer than seventeen dimensions of strategy. Clausewitz's four and Howard's five were certainly too few and unduly exclusive, while my seventeen would have had William of Occam cutting himself in anger with his razor. Although Clausewitz's, Howard's, and even my, 'elements' and 'dimensions' stand up quite well under critical investigation, these terms are unhelpfully broad. What is, and what is not, an 'element' or a 'dimension'? Paradoxically, complexity is relatively easy to design. The challenge to the theorist is to achieve simplicity without the surrender of essential content.

Dissatisfied with the packaging, though not so much with the content of my erstwhile dimensions, a new approach is adopted here to meet the challenge of setting forth a general theory. The theory outlined and explained below is crafted

Table 1.2 The General Theory of Strategy: Summary of Dicta Subjects

Nature and Character of Strategy

1. Grand strategy	6. Deception and paradox
2. Military strategy	7. People
3. Strategy bridge	8. Contexts
4. Politics, instrumentality, and effect	9. Permanent nature (strategy), changing character
5. Adversary and control	(strategies)

Making Strategy

10. Strategy-making process	12. Culture and personality
11. Values	13. Strategists

Executing Strategy

14. Difficulties and friction	18. Time
15. Strategy types	19. Logistics
16. Geography	20. Military doctrine
17 Technology	

Consequences of Strategy

21. Tactical, operational, and strategic
    effect

primarily to answer the four questions already identified. It explains a great deal more than the answers to the central questions, but they are the core of the matter. The burden of explanation of the theory is presented in the form of twenty-one dicta, formal pronouncements selected inductively. Each item is well verified historically. Dicta one through nine penetrate deeply into the general nature of strategy, whereas dicta ten through twenty-one pertain primarily to the construction, conduct, and the consequences of strategy in execution. Table 1.2 provides the tersest of subject summaries of the dicta. The dicta deliberately are not labelled elements or dimensions. This text endeavours to stress strategy's holistic nature. To make very much of allegedly distinctive elements or dimensions is to risk encouraging unsound analysis, which is to say unduly exclusive analyses. Dicta *on* strategy inherently are less divisive of the whole subject than are dimensions *of* strategy. All elements, dimensions, and propositions constitute a team that must function as a team on the playing field of conflict. Strictly speaking, this general theory of strategy could label its answers to the driving questions, principles rather than dicta. The dictionary is permissive. However, the principles' label carries too much baggage for comfort. The pronouncements, propositions perhaps, risk erring on the side of undue specificity, but acceptance of this peril seems well merited by the disorganized, somewhat confused, dispersed, and generally unsatisfactory state of the strategic theory extant. Every item in the theory has been discovered from the study of strategic history, not deduced from first principles. In appearance, the theory may read more like a set of maxims rather than as the essential building blocks for construction of the 'whole house' of strategy.[17] Clausewitz notwithstanding, even a holistic view of strategy, such as that taken here by this aspiring strategic hedgehog, is obliged to discuss the parts seriatim. Should some readers believe that the approach to the theory adopted here stands in need of a Clausewitzian benediction, I can offer them some reassuring thoughts from the master.

> If the theorist's studies automatically result in principles and rules, and if truth spontaneously crystallizes into these forms, theory will not resist this natural tendency of the mind. On the contrary, where the arch of truth culminates in such a keystone, this tendency will be underlined. But this is simply in accordance with the scientific law of reason, to indicate the point at which all lines converge, but never to construct an algebraic formula for use on the battlefield. Even these principles and rules are intended to provide a thinking man with a frame of reference for the movements he has been trained to carry out, rather than to serve as a guide which at the moment of action lays down precisely the path he must take.[18]

It is convenient and useful to draw a soft distinction between the core elements of the general theory of strategy and other elements that, though obviously important, do not quite merit A-list status. Core elements can be termed the primary dicta, and the other elements, unimaginatively, secondary. This binary approach is intended to emphasize the more significant features of strategy, while allowing the theory to be comprehensive. As Table 1.2 signals, there are just nine primary dicta that corral what most needs to be understood. The remainder of the theory, presented as dicta ten through twenty-one, is specified and explained in Chapter 2. In no sense are the secondary dicta judged unimportant.

The final word in this discussion of the approach taken here to theory must take the form of a caveat. The general theory of strategy provides an education by explanation of the structure and content-by-categories of its subject. Such understanding is essential, but also it is dangerous. The peril lies in the unstated, but often arguably implied, assumption that strategic happenings can be explained comprehensively in detail by strategic theory. In truth, they cannot. The course of strategic history is a narrative rich in human decision and contingency. Of course, these human decisions and highly contingent events are made and occur within the broad tent provided by the structure of the theory of strategy. But the theory cannot tell its user whether or not, for example, Russia and the United States will fight each other. Structure educates us as to possibilities, even probabilities, founded as it is in careful analysis of historical experience. However, specific strategic happenings do not lend themselves to structural explanation. Such explanation comprises the building that is strategy, but it cannot furnish each room. Having poured a little cold water on structural explanation, it is necessary to balance the argument with the easily supportable claim that those historians who confine themselves to burrowing industriously for the unique, transient detail of events, must always be in grave danger of not comprehending what they uncover. In the timeless words of economic theorist F. A. Hayek, quoted as an epigraph to this book, 'without a theory the facts are silent'.[19] However, it is probably more accurate to claim that without good theory the facts are very likely to be misinterpreted by bad theory.

THE NATURE AND CHARACTER OF STRATEGY

Dictum One: grand strategy is the direction and use made of any or all the assets of a security community, including its military instrument, for the purposes of policy as decided by politics

All strategy is grand strategy. Military strategies must be nested in a more inclusive framework, if only in order to lighten the burden of support for policy they are required to bear. A security community cannot design and execute a strictly military strategy. No matter the character of a conflict, be it a total war for survival or a contest for limited stakes, even if military activity by far is the most prominent of official behaviours, there must still be political-diplomatic, social-cultural, and economic, inter alia, aspects to the war. The effort to coerce an enemy may take military form above all others, but there is near certain to be a diplomatic offensive that seeks to isolate the foe. Also, because the military dimension to the conduct of war is so expensive, governments are compelled to adopt special economic measures to cover those costs, moves certain to require a domestic strategy intended to garner and sustain the necessary political backing.

Grand strategy is an essential level of behaviour in the general theory.[20] When politics have produced a policy, this policy has to be expressed in grand strategy that in a few cases will include active military options. The hierarchy is clear enough in principle, but in practice the traffic among the levels—policy, grand strategy, overall military strategy, joint and single-geography strategies—should be continuous. Feedback—feed-up, feed-down, and feed across—and adaptation are the key terms describing how strategy is designed, refined, and applied in real time. In practice, however, policymakers and generals must frequently choose at several levels of assessment and decision among a shortlist of unwelcome alternatives. Also, no policymaking or strategy-making system can be free of 'friction'.[21] Feedback from the tactical realm of action below can be late in moving up the chain of command, it may never reach beyond the operational level, if such is institutionalized, or it may be received at higher levels and ignored or explicitly rejected in its implications.

Obvious though the logic of grand strategy ought to be, it is surprisingly commonplace for governments to neglect it. The results tend to be policies either over-weighted with supporting military menace, or fatally light in the way of such threats. Whether or not a state or other security community designs a grand strategy explicitly, all of its assets will be in play in a conflict. The only difference between having and not having an explicit grand strategy, lies in the degree of cohesion among official behaviours and, naturally as a consequence of poor cohesion, in the likelihood of success. But even such formal evidence of strategic rectitude can mislead the credulous. Just because a government drafts a document which proclaims the existence of a grand strategy, or a 'comprehensive approach', there is no guarantee that the baronies of officialdom will behave cohesively, coherently, and comprehensively. Strategy, grand or military, is never self-executing.

Dictum Two: military strategy is the direction and use made of force and the threat of force for the purposes of policy as decided by politics

Although this dictum strictly is unnecessary because it is included in dictum one, there are persuasive reasons for strategic theory to strive to be crystal clear in distinguishing between grand and military strategies. The latter is subordinate to the former, just as the former must serve the policy developed by a society's political processes. However, dictum one, absent this specifically military dictum two, might suggest to the unwary a seamlessness that rarely is the case. Frequently, in practice polities do not develop, let alone succeed in effecting, an overarching strategy that manages the military instrument as a team player with assigned roles. Dysfunctional relations between grand and military strategy, not excluding cases of different elements—say, diplomacy, trade, and the military—pursuing incompatible objectives, oblige one to pay close attention to the traffic between the higher and lower levels. Military strategy can dominate grand strategy, while alternatively it may be assigned relatively too limited a role. It is as unusual for high policy to be decided for a single motive as it is for it to be achievable by only one of the polity's grand strategic assets. This theorist is concerned to give grand strategy its due, without inadvertently as a consequence losing the intended primary focus upon military strategy. Clausewitz's definition of strategy is of course a definition of military strategy. He advises that '[s]trategy is the use of the engagement for the purpose of the war'.[22] By contrast, the definition given here as dictum two claims as its domain both peace and war, and it is explicit in characterizing the strategy to which it refers.

Because at least in the Western world today the consideration and employment of the military instrument is beset with historically unprecedented cultural, political, and legal constraints, it is particularly important that understanding of its nature and purpose should not decay. This text by design is targeted to explain military strategy, but to do so in a way that grants due authority to the relevant political and other contexts. In no sense is this analysis of the strategy bridge an exercise in military-strategic advocacy. But, while Clausewitz's definition of strategy was unduly narrow to suit our needs, it is important that one does not overcorrect for that deficiency by allowing military strategy too junior a significance in and for grand strategy. The relevance and exact character of military strategies historically is a highly situational matter.

Dictum Three: strategy is the only bridge built and held to connect policy purposefully with the military and other instruments of power and influence

Strategy has just one function; to provide a secure connection between the worlds of purpose, which contestably is generally called policy, though politics may be more accurate, and its agents and instruments, including the military.[23] To employ the metaphor of a strategy bridge is to offer an effective way in which strategy's function can be explained. Both lower levels of the application of force, arguably operational and unarguably tactical behaviour, ultimately have political meaning through the strategic effect they achieve, but neither are concerned directly with the political consequences of their activity—that is, the mission of strategy. It is the duty of strategy to ensure that operational and tactical behaviour serves political needs. That behaviour is not self-referential.

It would be difficult to exaggerate the importance of strategy. All too often the word is bandied about carelessly. Everyone appears to grasp the point that strategy requires, certainly implies, purposeful behaviour. The charges of having no strategy, or of devising and executing the wrong strategy, are widely held, and are intended to be, serious indictments. However, the concept of strategy is hugely abused by people who know that it comprises heavy metal, but do not understand much more than that. Alexander the Great, Napoleon, and Adolf Hitler, all combined in one person, one charismatic leader, the function of policymaker and sole strategist. There were no strategy bridges except in the minds and bodies of those individuals. With the awesome and awful example of Napoleon, 'the God of War' himself, always before him, it is understandable why Clausewitz could claim, almost poetically, that 'at the highest level the art of war turns into policy—but a policy conducted by fighting battles rather than by sending diplomatic notes'.[24] A few pages further on he wrote as follows:

> Once again: war is an instrument of policy. It must necessarily bear the character of policy and measure by its standards. The conduct of war, in its great outlines, is therefore policy itself.[25]

This is cleverly, even brilliantly, expressed. But also it is apt to mislead. The idea of war, its higher conduct at least, as policy in action, is fundamentally correct. The trouble is that for war to be conducted as an often shifting policy command, someone or some process needs to behave strategically. To wage war in the sense of warfare, fighting, is not automatically to function strategically. This is not to deny that military performance must have some strategic effect—meaning an influence on the course of political events—only that unguided by deliberate strategy it is unlikely to be the effect, or to lead to the political consequences, preferred.

There are always security communities, states, and other entities, wherein the policymaking and instrumental strategic functions are all but fused in the person or persons of a tiny leadership. But in Western democracies, as indeed in most of the world today as well as throughout history, it is unusual for policymaking and strategy-making to be exclusively personal. The political leader may well exercise the right of final decision over strategy, but the choices he or she is offered typically will be generated by an advisory council with a staff.

The metaphor of the strategy bridge is fundamental to the way in which the general theory of strategy is explained, developed, and tested here. The bridge can be in good or poor repair, or may even be destroyed, assuming that it had existed. The necessity for performance of the bridge function is easily illustrated when one asks, in the absence of a strategy bridge peopled by strategists assisted by political and military-technical specialists, who or what guides the war effort? It is true that by accident or design a polity can eschew the strategy function and yet survive or even prosper. Historical experience suggests strongly, though, that higher purpose-free fighting tends to be the path to ruin.[26] If one regards strategy merely as 'a system of expedients', choices driven by operational and tactical success or failure, there will be a lack of political grip upon warfare. In an extreme case war can be literally senseless, waged for its own sake bereft of political purpose.[27] In fact, the author of this oft quoted dismissal of strategy, Moltke the Elder, did not mean to claim that policy initially should not command strategy, but rather that once war began politics should take second place to military considerations. The field marshal insisted that '[s]trategy thus works best for policy, but in its actions is fully independent of policy'. This was lethal nonsense, as Germany's strategic performance in the twentieth century was to demonstrate with exemplary clarity.[28] With respect to the command of actual warfare, which Moltke did try to insist should be a politics-free zone, his reference to experts only meant, sensibly, that flexibility in strategy was required because the tactical narrative dictated on feasibility.[29] While endorsing a prudent expediency in strategy in order to match and direct evolving tactical outcomes in real time, Moltke's Great General Staff always conducted near exhaustive war games, pre-war, so as to prepare as best they could for the contingencies of actual history.

Dictum Four: strategy serves politics instrumentally by generating net strategic effect

The theory of strategy insists that this must be so. There is no denying that much of the violence in today's world menaces and even breaks the definitional barrier between warfare and something else. The something else can be criminal violence on a large scale or simply loosely organized hooliganism. Although there may be political consequences in both cases, the motives for, the sources of, the violence will be personal, criminal, and broadly cultural. Having granted the validity of this breach in the definitional wall that isolates war and warfare from other behaviours, one must not rush to proclaim the death of Clausewitzian theory and the rise of 'new wars' and the like.[30] Despite the caveat just noted, the theory of strategy is correct in nearly all cases when it insists upon the supremacy of politics. In the minimalist, but still valid, employment of the concept of strategy to mean simply a plan of action, one must concede that criminal cartels, terrorists, and tribesmen can and do have strategies.[31] On close investigation, one finds that nearly all extra-state security entities, although their prime motives may be profit, personal salvation, or fun and glory, function with, if not principally for, political consequences. Recall, for example, that for many Moslems there can be no legitimate distinction between the realms of religion and politics. Theirs is a truly holistic view of life.

Although the instrumentality of strategy is absolutely necessary if political guidance is to be translated into operational plans, the relationship between the worlds of politics and of military force is, or should be, one of reciprocal influence. Warfare is not self-referential. It can have no meaning beyond politics, notwithstanding the wide range of motives that animate its human and institutional agents. But, for the warfare that serves war to be used purposefully with a

fair prospect of success, the traffic of information across the strategy bridge must
be two-way. If Michael Howard is plausible when he claims that the means of war
typically exercise more influence than do its political ends, it follows that Eliot
Cohen's 'unequal dialogue' between politicians and soldiers should not be understood too literally.[32] Political leaders may occupy positions of unchallenged
authority over their soldiers, but if the soldiers report that their instrument, at
least with the political constraints placed upon it, is incapable of delivering some
facsimile of victory, the civilians should bow to the unwelcome force of necessity.
Either policy should change, or the political guidance that limits military choice
must be altered.

There can be no doubt that the decision for war today is regarded as far more
fateful than was the case in centuries past. So much is not debateable. The issue
now is not whether Clausewitz was correct in his assertions that '. . . *war is only a
branch of political activity* . . . the only source of war is politics . . .', and '. . . that
war is simply a continuation of political intercourse, with the addition of other
means . . .'.[33] Rather must we consider the proposition that the conduct of war,
certainly by states, is subject to a public moral, perhaps cultural, and legal audit
that did not exist prior to the mid-nineteenth century. The 'war convention', as it
is called, comprising international law and widespread norms, does not approach
decisions for war as though they were a regular part of politics.[34] In addition to
the growing mound of laws and norms that should operate to discourage warfare,
there is the ever more intrusive presence of the now global media, though it is
easy to assign undue significance to its potential to influence events.[35]

The factors just cited do not sink a theory of strategy that has as its centrepiece
a claim for political instrumentality. But the emergence of a significant 'war
convention' and of a mass media with global reach, do mean that war needs to
serve politics rather more carefully than was ever the case in times past. Clausewitz was not wrong, but his most famous dictum is liable to mislead if it is taken
literally, out of historical context. Politics is preferred to policy in the theory of
strategy, because the latter is likely to impart a false impression of coherence, clear
identity, and settled objectives. Because policy is produced by a continuous
political process, it is only prudent to ensure that the theory of strategy incorpo-
rates this vital fact. In common with policy, strategy also should be made in and
by a process. This process needs to be suffused with, though not entirely dominated by, political considerations. History reveals that not all countries have
enjoyed the benefits of a strategy-making process worthy of the name. For
example, Williamson Murray and Mark Grimsley have pointed tellingly to the
stark contrast between the high efficiency of Britain's strategy-making process in
the Second World War and the situation in Germany. 'An almost complete
absence of process marked the Nazi system, as it had the preceding Weimar and
Wilhelmine regimes.'[36] In both world wars, Germany was far better at fighting
than it was at fighting strategically, while the reverse was true for Britain.

Even the strategic level of war can only have instrumental significance. Polities
do not wage war, conduct warfare, for the purpose of achieving strategic effect
upon the course of history. Rather do they use their tactical behaviour to secure a

strongly net positive strategic effect—to allow for the enemy's strategic effect—in order to yield tolerable or better political consequences. Strategy serves politics instrumentally.

If it is to be successful, strategy must be directed to achieve policy goals that command strong domestic political support. But strategic analysis can stray when a focus upon the dependence of a military war fighting effort upon its domestic support is allowed to mislead as to purpose and agent. In 1940, the British war effort was directed on behalf of a policy of no political accommodation with Nazi Germany. Britain's war aims at the time were opaque, so desperate was the country's military situation. However, even though British policy seemed to be geared to the service of the British war effort, both logically and pragmatically the relationship was exactly the reverse of that. That war effort was a massive, all pervading, agent of the policy choice to continue the war. And the determination to continue the war certainly did not reflect any affection for warfare itself. Strategy is instrumental, no matter how dire a community's security context.

Dictum Five: strategy is adversarial; it functions in both peace and war, and it always seeks a measure of control over enemies (and often over allies and neutrals also)

Herein lies the heart of the matter. As Wylie rightly insists, following Clausewitz, the immediate purpose of strategy is to control the enemy's choices.[37] The ultimate purpose, of course, is to exploit that control for our political purposes. Control can be secured by means of physical constraint or by psychological effect, though the latter tends to flow from the former. Victory, success, advantage are secured when the enemy either chooses to comply with some or all of our demands, or he is simply unable to resist our material ability to impose our will upon him. There should be no need to emphasize strategy's adversarial nature, but the historical record illustrates categorically how frequently politicians and soldiers neglect to take due account of the possible choices and probable preferences of the enemy. In this regard, it is worth noting that Sun Tzu's *The Art of War* is greatly weakened by its failure convincingly to treat war as being truly adversarial by nature, notwithstanding his good advice to understand the enemy.[38] In the immortal words attributed not implausibly to Winston S. Churchill: 'However absorbed a commander may be in the elaboration of his own thoughts, it is sometimes necessary to take the enemy into account.[39]

In the face of ignorance about the enemy and his plans, more often than not governments simply assume that he will cooperate and play his pre-designated role as victim-villain. Even when an enemy's plans are known in advance with high confidence, it is not unusual for political leaders and generals to anticipate benign consequences from that hostile behaviour. Such was the case in 1914, for example. France was content to allow the German Schlieffen–Moltke Plan to unroll with its fairly mighty right wing. The French Army's war plan, Plan XVII, specified a furious drive north-eastward through the Rhineland, a move which should neutralize and invalidate operationally a German thrust through central Belgium. Plan XVII proved to direct an operational disaster for France in the Battle of the Frontiers, because at the tactical level—where men fought and died—German firepower defeated high spirited and brightly clad French soldiers.[40] The details of modern firepower were not exactly unknown to French strategists. Indeed, the 'tactical crisis' promoted by military-technological advances had attracted expert analysis and debate since the 1840s.[41] The French defeat in August 1914 was caused not so much by ignorance, but rather by the wilful choice of faulty tactics. As this text has noted already, policy, strategy, operations, and tactics, although hierarchical, also are seriously interdependent, even horizontal in the several capacities of each to harm the others.[42] The élan of the *poilu* was expected to triumph over Krupp steel, albeit at a cost anticipated to be heavy. This approach to the 'tactical crisis' had some merit, but, alas, not enough. If the troops at the sharp end cannot win in combat, then it has to follow that operational art, its directing strategy, strategy's guiding policy, and the politics that created it must be frustrated.

Strategy's adversarial nature is significant in peacetime as well as in wartime. Whether diplomatic démarche or military action is the *Schwerpunckt* agency for policy, the activity is strategic, which means that it must be energized by some measure of enemy identification. Even when no menace is named as dominant threat, strategic planners must select 'enemies', if only for the purpose of enabling rational and orderly planning. Any strategic planning staff worth its salt is able to find a shortlist of possible threats suitable for its guidance. Strategists are clients for threat identification. The 1990s provided a classic example of how well, or otherwise, a very great power copes with the almost embarrassing condition of a security environment free of major near-term threats. The US defence community was politically and strategically rudderless for a decade, from the demise of the USSR in 1991 until 11 September 2001.

Dictum Six: strategy usually requires deception, is paradoxical, and frequently is ironic

This dictum combines the ancient Chinese wisdom of Sun Tzu with the modern American insight of Edward N. Luttwak. The former asserted that 'warfare is the Way (Tao) of deception', while the latter's vision of strategy reveals a content and universal logic that 'was not the prosaic stuff of platitudes, but instead paradox, irony, and contradiction'.[43] These general features of strategy only just succeeded in recommending themselves for inclusion in the primary category. Is it in the nature of all strategy to be deceptive? Sun Tzu's expansive claim could be challenged on the basis of historical evidence of non-deceptive strategy in action. On balance, though, one often discovers that candidate historical illustration of non-deceptive strategy in practice covered cases wherein deception failed. Even when an operational strategy was both transparently obvious and known in detail by the enemy, as, say, was true of the German offensive against the Kursk salient in July 1943 (Operation Citadel), deception was attempted by both sides.[44] Following Sun Tzu, deception for the purpose of achieving surprise is claimed here to be a near universal trans-historical feature of strategy.[45] Rather less universal is the phenomenon of a belligerent thinking through the prospective benefits that should accrue from surprise. Although deception warrants assignment as a primary feature of strategy, albeit only barely so, in practice it can be sought more for its own sake than for any anticipated military reward. Similarly, the achievement of surprise can be treasured for itself as a misidentified value. It is commonplace, but accurate, to observe that even though deception and surprise are valued universally, historically speaking Chinese strategies and strategists have tended to privilege their significance. Sun Tzu's imperial claim for the role of deception in war finds much favour with China's People's Liberation Army (PLA) today.[46] In strategy generally the Chinese must honour the importance of deception and surprise, but in their strategies they choose to repose culturally unique confidence in them. To risk the alleged 'Orientalist' error, it is pertinent to note that the unknown Japanese strategist-author of the *Thirty-Six Strategies* advises, 'Feint east, strike west'.[47] One need not master the classics of strategy in order to recognize both wisdom and banality. In the second half of 1940, Hitler feinted west (Britain), but intended to strike east. Many strategic and military virtues are praised universally, even if skill in their practice varies greatly.

Luttwak is correct to make much of the paradoxical nature of strategy. Strategy may well fail in the future because it succeeds today. The pervasive significance of paradox flows inescapably from the logic of the previous dictum: strategy is adversarial. The adversary should be expected to study one's past and current strategic practice, and on the basis of that analysis make plans to deny one victories in the future. This is rather obvious, but it is necessary never to forget that strategy, expressed in particular historical strategies, is not designed, executed, and, if need be, revised, for the control of an unthinking Mt. Everest. Instead, the adversary is motivated and variably able to take tailored measures for the purpose of defeating our strategy.

In addition to being paradoxical, strategy also is notably ironic, as Luttwak recognizes perceptively. The phenomenon of irony in strategy is best understood as the operation of the so-called law of unintended consequences. To illustrate, the United States, Britain, and a few others invaded Iraq in 2003 in part for the purpose of prosecuting their 'global war on terror' (GWOT, for the delightful acronym, now long lapsed from official favour). Yet, ironically, whatever its benefits to international security, the Western intervention had the hugely unintended effect of providing a rallying focus for violent Islamism. American and British soldiers inadvertently recruited terrorists and other irregular warriors with a mixture of motives—political, religious, and personal. It is probably no exaggeration to claim that every conflict has ironic consequences. Moreover, these myriad ironies are more significant for the general theory of strategy, as well as for the outcomes to actual historical strategies, than is the working of paradox, endemic though that is.

Dictum Seven: strategy is human

The bridge of strategy is constructed, maintained, and trafficked by people. One of the finest books ever written about men in battle, J. Glenn Gray's psychological memoir of the Second World War, *The Warriors*, asserts convincingly that 'for all its inhumanity, war is a profoundly human institution'.[48] In point of fact, every aspect of our study of the strategy bridge is directly or indirectly 'profoundly human'. This should be obvious. However, the literature of modern strategic studies has not always accorded human beings their due. They can appear as mere anonymous numbers, as target-victims, that are 'serviced'—for the revolting euphemism—by deadly weapons, precise and otherwise. Since the professional strategic literature was dominated for nearly fifty years by nuclear issues, it is sobering to recall that the role played by people in nuclear strategy and doctrine was that of hostage to the self-restraint shown by their government. People thus became a huge abstraction. The antiseptic concept of collateral damage neatly captures the ethos of much of strategic analysis. When American theorists and officials spoke of mutual assured destruction (MAD), they meant the assured deaths of civilians and damage to industry. US nuclear strategy in the 1960s was designed to ensure that the Soviet Union would suffer between 20 and 33 per cent fatalities, and lose between 50 and 75 per cent of its industry, in an all-out nuclear war.[49] The capability to inflict this awesome damage was judged to comprise the gold standard that had to be met if Soviet leaders were to be deterred in extremis.

The tortuous logic of nuclear strategy is not of great interest here. Rather are we fascinated by the facts that American strategists coldly could plan to commit a plausible approximation to genocide; the credible threat contingently to inflict this destruction was deemed highly desirable, most especially if it was a mutual menace; and the US government, administration after administration, chose not to hazard the mutuality of the threat to massacre people by the tens of millions by investing in moderately effective, active, and passive population defences. The shorthand we employ to analyse strategic matters at all levels typically under-states, when it does not ignore altogether, the variety among individuals. Speaking on the basis of some personal experience with the commission of this error, I find that strategists can ply their trade with scant recognition of its human meaning. Furthermore, for the professional mistake, strategists frequently proceed without a sensible grasp of the importance of the human contribution to strategy-making and performance.

The significance of individual human beings does not even out in its historical impact, because of the operation of a law of average performance with large numbers: this is why theory or narrative history that is all contextual, which is to say structural, must lose the plot of explanation. To claim that every historical episode is contextual and has contextual significance can only carry understanding so far. Usually, we need to know what was done, by whom, and why, not only what the contexts were for events, treating those contexts as ends in themselves. Of course, there are notable cases wherein individuals melt into the crowd. For a grisly example, a strategist may believe he knows that an opposed amphibious landing will cost upward of, say, 10,000 casualties. But he cannot know in advance precisely who those casualties will be. Fortunately for the morale of those 10,000, nor do they. It is possible, indeed sometimes it is expedient and satisfactory, to write the human 'face of battle' out of policy, strategic, operational, and even tactical analysis.[50] Men and women disappear into governments, sometimes into countries writ large, as in 'France decided . . .', and often into military units which may well not even be characterized by any named human association. But there is grave peril to historical and strategic understanding endemic in such professional practice. The strategic analyst or theorist quite literally may forget that the subjects he explores, assesses, and for which he prescribes are pervasively human; they are all about human behaviour. And this human behaviour, be it most directly political, strategic, operational, or tactical, is not performed by interchangeable automatons. Different people can behave differently. Almost as much to the point, the same people can behave differently from day to day. For example, most probably there are few biologically brave or cowardly people. Human conduct is largely a matter of culture and circumstance, with some unknowable contribution from genetic programming.[51]

The myriad differences between theory and practice, doctrine and conduct, often are persuasively attributable to the personalities of individuals and to the consequences of group dynamics among distinctive mixes of people. Security communities seek such protection as they can find from the incompetence, eccentricity, and other dysfunctional features of individuals, through education, regular process, audit, indoctrination, and some collectivization. Leadership can be charismatically personal, but advice, decision, command, and its execution generally will not be functions exercised by individuals acting alone. As used to be said of Britain's sailing navy, rightly or wrongly, the genius is in the system, lest it should be lacking in the man in charge at sea on the spot at the time. One cannot be certain that a Nelson will always be available when needed. As relevant a thought is recognition that the process of military promotion cannot totally be relied upon to locate and advance the necessary rare talent, genius, when it is required.[52] The history of command in war and warfare typically is a sad tale of human trial and error. There is no law of politics or soldiering to the effect that the circumstances must produce the man who is needed.[53]

When the human element is missing from the theoretical or doctrinal action, so also as a consequence is likely to be due anticipation of the potential power of contingency. Machines and units without individuals would perform as expected by calculation, including measurement of expected technical failure rates, but human beings are apt to distress rational assessment by behaving unpredictably, not only as individuals, but also as groups. For example, sub-communities of soldiers that should cease to fight effectively, if fight at all, when they suffer 25 or 33 per cent casualties, have been known to fight on when their loss rate climbed from 50 to 75 per cent. For another kind of case, most of modern strategic theory, certainly that which purports to predict nuclear related behaviour, assumes the functioning of rational choice by standardized people. 'We know what deters; we know how to limit war in the nuclear era; we know how to control nuclear arms in order to achieve deterrence and arms-race stability; and we know how to manage crises.' Such claims were believed widely in the 1960s and 1970s. I know this to have been the case, because I became a licensed participant-observer in the US-led international strategic studies community in that period. The strategic ideas with which the worst perils of the nuclear Cold War were assaulted were as proudly touted by the mainstream strategic cognoscenti of the 1960s and 1970s, as they were of dubious worth at best, or were dangerously flawed at worst. Poor scholarship by academic economists might trickle down eventually into making an appearance as expensive errors in commercial and official behaviour. But a like scale and quality of error by some strategic theorists, if they have privileged access to civilian and military practitioners of strategy, could literally kill us all. Strategic studies is not just another scholarly discipline.

The general theory of strategy must offer explicit recognition of the ubiquitous significance both of people in general and of named individuals also. Moreover, to cite a major complication for the task of strategic understanding, people are a mix of nature and nurture whose behaviour is influenced, though not reliably determined, by its contexts. Eccentric action is always possible. What one culture regards as peculiar may be standard operating procedure elsewhere. Confusing to those among us who suffer from the malady of acute reductionism, decision making is both highly contingent as well as pervasively structural. As great generalities, neither structures nor personalities determine decision outcomes. Decisions are the product of the synergistic working of both.

The strategic theorist must strive for the general truth that can educate for the purpose of improving particular performance. He needs to remember that sound strategic theory is an equal opportunity enabler; it can aid political interests that he favours as well as ones that he does not. The ancient Chinese may have been wise to regard and handle learned treatises on war and warfare as belonging among the most valuable of secret state assets.[54] Today, advance in information technology is commercially driven and globally available. A book such as this one principally is the result of a theorist-citizen's concern to help protect the society and values that he prefers. However, once a book on strategic theory and ideas is published, it is accessible to readers and users of every political affiliation.

Dictum Eight: *the meaning and character of strategies are driven, though not dictated and wholly determined, by their contexts, all of which are constantly in play*

The general theory of strategy is not contextual, unlike all particular strategies. The pragmatic task of making and executing historically specific strategies au-thoritative for every level of war—grand or national, military, operational, joint as well as single-geography—though a creative challenge, is commanded significantly by its contexts, wherein contingency is always a factor, actual or potential. Strategy, as with war itself, has no inherent meaning or value. This work elects to recognize seven contexts for strategy: political, social-cultural, economic, tech-nological, military, geographical (geopolitical and geostrategic), and historical

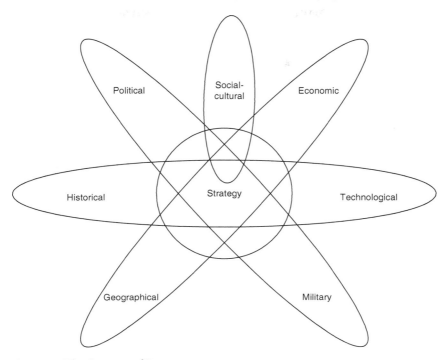

Figure 1.2 The Contexts of Strategy

(see Figure 1.2). If one asks, 'where does strategy come from?'—the answer lies in these seven. Or, if one poses the question, 'where do specific strategies come from?'—the answer lies in the particular details of particular cases unique to time and place. The general theory of strategy applies to all projects in strategy-making and execution, at all times and places. But the content of those strategies and their fates must be individual. Arguably, one could add the human individual as an eighth context. I choose not to do so, preferring instead to regard the behaviour of people as a realm of contingency that functions within the seven contexts.

The political context of strategy is exceedingly broad. It includes the domestic political and bureaucratic processes by which strategy is made and amended, as well as the external or internal conditions which strategy is intended to influence. The will of the enemy that is to be controlled may reside far abroad or close at home. By social-cultural we mean that all strategies are contrived and executed by people and institutions that must be considered encultured by the societies that bred them. Also, all strategies must have an economic context. An extravagantly ambitious strategy will stretch a community's purse and may well mortgage its future to the needs and hopes of today. Every strategy has a technological context, the importance of which will vary widely from case to case. The sources of military prowess in warfare, let alone of success in war as a whole, are apt to be so many that a technological inferiority or superiority cannot be assumed to determine outcomes. The probably dynamic technological context is integral to the military context overall. Strategies should be designed and exercised with close attention to the continuous net assessment that the experience of combat reveals, as well as on the basis of careful prior analysis of the balance of military power.

The geographical, and hence the geopolitical and geostrategic, context of strategy has a pervasive and sometimes even controlling significance. Although warfare increasingly is a multi-environmental, multi-service, which is to say 'joint', activity, the unique qualities of the five distinct physical geographies continue to matter deeply. The information age has yet to obliterate the material and psychological importance of distance and time, even though it has greatly shrunk those factors for some military purposes. Every specific strategy, no matter how particular to armed forces, specialized for, say, air or space warfare, has to contribute to a total strategic effect upon the land, the only geography suitable for human habitation. Finally, the historical context is as noteworthy as it is inescapable, in that it locates a conflict or event in the stream of time, relating it to the past and providing hints about the future. This context yields most of what produces the strategy choices of today. All strategy is indebted to beliefs and possibly legends about what fared well in past strategic practice.

Strategies can have meaning only in their contexts. If a theorist wobbles in his ability to keep blue water between general strategy, singular, and specific strate-gies, plural, the result must be a theory captured by richly textured historical narrative and therefore necessarily failing as general explanation. Appreciation of the eternal nature of strategy will evaporate in the heat emanating from particular historical circumstances. The small book of general strategic theory, cannon lore if you like, exists only to educate the strategist in order to help him design and execute the specific strategies his polity needs.[55] The contexts for strategists require practicable application of the dicta located here.

The general theory insists that context explains what strategy is all about, but such explanation, though necessary, cannot suffice to explain, let alone predict, actual strategic behaviour. The personalities of individual people and the choices they make are not thoroughly predictable from the context, the structure, they derive from society and its cultures. The economical abstraction of general theory may be likened to a skeleton key. It can say nothing about specific contexts for the elementary reason that it has to govern all. One size fits all cases at a high level of abstraction. For another illustration of the point, Johannes Kepler's three laws of planetary motion yield essential education for those who must select specific Earth orbits for particular space-systems missions. What does it mean to insist that strategy is contextual? The answer is that strategy in real-world specificity derives from, and is shaped by and for, no fewer than the seven distinctive kinds of situations specified above. To repeat, these are: political, social-cultural, economic, technological, military-strategic, geopolitical and geostrategic, and historical. The general theory tries to tell the working strategist that none of these contexts should be neglected. Every challenge the strategist must meet can be analysed in terms of these seven. Indeed, every challenge strategists have had to answer in the past and to which they will have to respond in the future, is given meaning by its unique contexts.[56]

Different theorists may elect to slice and dice the intellectual material distinctively, but the subjects to which they apply their methodological skills, once bolted together, have to approximate the items identified here. Strategies must act in these contexts upon them, through them, and with them. Strategy as actual strategies not only derives all its meaning from its multiple contexts, but in addition it is constructed from their matter. Context is not only 'out there', also it is 'in here', contributing to content.[57] Although Clausewitz's dictum concerning the logical dominance of policy plainly merits the distinction he accords it in his theory, a case can be made for replacing that keystone dictum with this one.[58] If the proposition that force must serve political ends unlocks the most significant room in the 'whole house of war', the thesis that all strategy, every strategy, is contextual, can open every door to and within the building. This dictum in the short list of conceptual tools for explanation of strategy's nature has some plausible potential to be a candidate for master status. Indeed, this dictum alone could serve as the framework for an adequate general theory of strategy. That is not the path chosen here, but it may be a possibility worthy of consideration. Because of strategy's complexity, this theorist is unwilling to place all his money on the bet that the authority and utility of a single potent dictum will be able to bear all the diverse traffic that could come its way. Rather is *E pluribus unum* the admittedly rather conservative motto for this venture in theory.

Dictum Nine: strategy has a permanent nature, while strategies (usually plans, formal or informal, expressing contingent operational intentions) have a variable character driven, but not mandated, by their unique and changing contexts, the needs of which are expressed in the decisions of unique individuals

The general theory of strategy is timeless, but grand, operational, joint, and single-geography strategies most assuredly are not. In historical practice, strategies constantly need to be drafted for, and adapted to, dynamic circumstances. This fact should not promote confusion for students of strategy. Each of these dicta that constitute this theorist's general theory of strategy has been expressed and reflected in a richly diverse body of historical practice and malpractice. As claimed already, the theory exposed here is empirical rather than deductive. Statespersons and soldiers have performed with reference to each feature of this litany. Of necessity their performances, however, have been thoroughly specific in detail, dependent as they had to be upon the particular conditions obtaining at their time and place of happening.

Once one grasps the elementary, indeed elemental, distinction between the singular general theory of strategy and the plural historically specific grand, operational, joint, and single-geography strategies, one has to hand the key necessary to unlock much that otherwise would be confused, not to say mysterious. This fundamental binary distinction also holds for war. A great deal of misleading analysis and advice could be prevented, were commentators to understand that war, in common with strategy, has a permanent nature, but an ever variable character.

If the distinction is not recognized, perhaps not understood, as a consequence one all but forfeits the benefits of some education in strategy. The general theory of strategy, the distilled, all-cases, explanation of the nature and character of strategic behaviour, would not be available. Strategists, informed only by their own real-time experience and possibly by what they can glean from the success and failure of near contemporaries, literally could not learn from the performance of Alexander, Caesar, Marlborough, and many, many, more. Without recognition that there is, or can be, a general theory of strategy, episodes of strategic behaviour and misbehaviour are quite disconnected. For the general theory to help educate actual historical strategists, they have to comprehend the true general and generic unity of their duties across time and space.

Absent the boundary separating strategy's nature from its many realities in specifically chosen strategies, the contemporary strategist has no anchor in anything save the ever shifting sands of today. Because strategies are always changing to meet dynamic contexts, the ill-educated strategist and his political masters may succumb to the temptation to believe that their strategic world is all but wholly new. They may be able to persuade themselves, more likely they will be misled into believing by clever briefers that anything and everything is possible and that there are no lessons to be learnt from historical experience. If the fog of war can be dispersed and the enemy stunned, paralysed, into utter ineffectiveness by the tailored military effects of new technology, what can be the relevance of the twenty dicta in my general theory of strategy?

Some people have genuine difficulty understanding why, let alone how, Alexander of Macedon as strategist has relevance for today and tomorrow. They can cure this significant blind spot by appreciating the sense in dictum eight. Each and every historical manifestation of strategic behaviour, albeit unarguably unique, is, indeed had to be, just one case among a plethora of cases that are specific instances of an eternal phenomenon. This is why a general theory of strategy is possible and necessary. Clausewitz made the same point in the following way:

> We wanted to show how every age had its own kind of war, its own limiting conditions, and its own peculiar preconceptions. Each period, therefore would have held to its own theory of war . . .
> But war, though conditioned by the particular characteristics of states and their armed forces, must contain some more general—indeed, a universal— element with which every theorist ought above all to be concerned.[59]

It is necessary to remember that there is a level of general theory specific to each of strategy's instruments, military and other. For example, one can be educated in the general lore of diplomacy or secret intelligence, as preparation for the design and execution of specific strategies in unique historical contexts. Although there are some general truths about, say, sea power and air power, the seeker after general theory for their explanation must sail and fly perilously close to vulnerability to changing contexts. Air power, to illustrate, is ever open to misunderstanding, because the boundaries are apt to be porous among its general theory, service doctrine on contemporary best practice, and specific plans (i.e. strategies).

STRATEGIC EDUCATION

The dicta identified and explained in this chapter comprise the 'A-list', the most defining among all the elements that constitute the whole general theory of strategy. Dicta one through nine specify that military power, force, is a defining characteristic of the domain of military, but not of grand strategy which encompasses all the instruments of power and influence, including the military (dicta one and two); strategy is the bridge that purposefully should connect means with ends, most especially military force with the political purposes for which it is applied (dictum three); the strategic function most essentially is instrumental, only by strategy are a political entity's military and other assets directed to serve policy goals (dictum four); the strategic function necessarily is adversarial, strategy requires an enemy or two, strategy as operational plans cannot be addressed simply 'to whom they may concern' (dictum five); strategy is systemically paradoxical in its logic, it works ironically, and it needs to be served by deception in quest of surprise (dictum six); strategy is a pervasively human project in every aspect, both when approached via the general theory and when applied in plans as historically distinctive strategies (dictum seven); in radical contrast to strategy as general theory, specific historical strategies must be pervasively contextual in meaning and character (dictum eight); strategy has a permanent nature, hence the feasibility and relevant timeless authority of its general theory, but an ever changing character, hence its historical appearance as a wide variety of strategies well suited or not to particular situations (dictum nine). Each dictum offers a distinctive perspective upon the whole nature of strategy and cumulatively provides the necessary minimum core of explanation.

When building a theory, it is easy to lose what should be the plot. Specifically, the general theory must serve principally to help educate those who need an education in strategy and it has to be faithful to history and logic. At least in one important respect theory for the social and the physical sciences share a common standard for excellence. There is beauty in brevity. The leaner the theory, the better the theory, always provided it accomplishes its expressed purposes and is plausibly compatible with such evidence as can be located. To recall Isaiah Berlin, with Archilochus and his fable, the strategic theoretical hedgehog seeks the all encompassing general theory of strategy.[60] This is theory that defines, covers, and explains either all strategic phenomena, or at least the central mystery or mysteries of the strategic realm. General theory must penetrate to the core of its subject. Clausewitz is the closest that strategy's theorists have come to the genius and status of Sir Isaac Newton and Albert Einstein. *On War* offers dicta, singly and in bunches, that approximate the theories of gravity and relativity. Unfortunately, a determination to achieve methodological excellence as currently identified by scholars who lack the genius of Newton, Einstein, and Clausewitz is apt to produce the worst of several possible outcomes. When the theory of strategy comes parsimonious to a fault, it reduces to the simplistic and banal.

The search for evidence in a fairly numerate profession inevitably drives off-road into the bog of inappropriate quantification. Strategic truth, eternal as well as transiently situational, purportedly can be revealed by the magic of mathematics.[61] For a classic example, the military postural requirements of stable nuclear deterrence were supposedly identified numerically, and therefore could be impressively plotted graphically. Such fantasies abound in the minds and computers of strategic theorists who neglect to acknowledge the richness of contingently human strategic behaviour and the significance of strategy's many contexts. To adapt a justly famous Clausewitzian dictum, the meritorious quest either for elegant economy in theory or for comprehensiveness in detail of domain are both likely to exceed their culminating points of victory.[62]

The plot that must never be lost is the educational function of general strategic theory for strategy's practitioners.[63] Theory is a servant of understanding and has to be designed and tested for its educational value. The general theory of strategy should be the prime source of education for the strategist who must do strategy in specific operational strategies expressed as plans produced by a bureaucratic and political process.

To level a charge of reductionism is to be derogatory, yet the theorist has to be a reductionist. The theory exposed in Chapters 1 and 2 is the product of a struggle both to tell no more of strategy's general story than is necessary, yet to tell no less. Tension between the two is unavoidable. Many historians, as well as political scientists of a post-modern persuasion, will be unhappy with the economy in, and expansive claims registered for, the twenty-one dicta identified here. These dicta, these purposefully formal pronouncements, may seem to be advanced with a confidence they do not merit. This author would be untroubled by such a judgement. The general theory of strategy is not akin, say, to the modern theory of deterrence, though it should be permitted to contribute to it. The difference between the general theory of strategy and even the general theory of deterrence is that the latter is highly speculative, while the former rests solidly literally on millennia of historical evidence of varying quality. This history-based general theory of strategy is promoted with confidence because it has been tested by a mountain of historical experience and by the spilling of an ocean of blood. That experience was hard earned, indeed; it has been gathered and organized by reason into the form, and with the content presented here.

This general theory of strategy is a work in progress; it is unfinished, and as such it will remain. I am much attracted to Hew Strachan's overall judgement on Clausewitz's *On War*: 'It is a work in progress. Its unfinished nature should be a source not of frustration but of joy.'[64] But, as Echevarria suggests intriguingly, the obvious fact that it is unfinished does not have to mean that it is incomplete.[65]

NOTES

1. Philip A. Crowl, 'The Strategist's Short Catechism: Six Questions Without Answers', in Harry R. Borowski, ed., *The Harmon Memorial Lectures in Military History, 1959–1987* (Washington, DC: Office of Air Force History, US Air Force, 1988), 377–88. Professor Crowl delivered this brilliant lecture on 6 October 1977.

2. Carl von Clausewitz, *On War*, tr. Michael Howard and Peter Paret (1832–4; Princeton, NJ: Princeton University Press, 1976), 132.

3. John Lewis Gaddis, 'What Is Grand Strategy?' Lecture delivered at the conference on 'American Grand Strategy after War', sponsored by the Triangle Institute for Security Studies and the Duke University Program in American Grand Strategy, 26 February 2009, 7.

4. A sceptical note is sounded in Patrick Porter, 'Good Anthropology, Bad History: The Cultural Turn in Studying War', *Parameters*, 37 (summer 2007), 45–58. See his stimulating book, *Military Orientalism: Eastern War Through Western Eyes* (London: C. Hurst, 2009), for the full charge.

5. Not for the last time in these pages am I grateful to Antulio J. Echevarria II, this time for helping fuel my long-standing unease about the net benefit of the comparatively recent (1982) official introduction to the Anglo–American strategic worldview of the concept of an operational level of war. He writes with masterly understatement: '[t]he invention of the operational level of war—which ostensibly ties strategy and tactics more closely together—has not necessarily improved the conduct of war from the standpoint of linking purpose and means'. *Clausewitz and Contemporary War* (Oxford: Oxford University Press, 2007), 140. I suspect that many of our contemporary soldiers are so encultured by doctrine for an operational level that they are close to unable to conceive of a military universe that is only binary, strategic and tactical. For a full-frontal assault on the concept of the operational level of war, see Justin Kelly and Mike Brennan, *Alien: How Operational Art Devoured Strategy* (Carlisle, PA: Strategic Studies Institute, US Army War College, September 2009). These authors overstate an interesting argument. Their case would be stronger had it rested upon a demonstrated engagement with the rationales favouring recognition of an operational level of war. Carefully considered, it is more sensible to insist upon the primacy of strategy over operations, and to the practice of command for adequate control to that end, rather than to abjure recognition of a command level that is plainly desirable in principle for tactical coherence. Edward N. Luttwak contributed more than marginally to the official American and British decisions in the early 1980s to embrace the concept of an operational level of war. See Luttwak's 'The Operational Level of War', *International Security*, 5 (winter 1980/81), 61–79. Also see his *Strategy: The Logic of War and Peace*, rev. edn. (Cambridge, MA: Harvard University Press, 2001), ch. 7, and 'Errors of Backsight Forethought', *The Times*

Literary Supplement, 16 October 2009, 22–3. Military analyst Stephen Biddle defines operational art as using 'battles to win operations and campaigns'. *Military Power: Explaining Victory and Defeat in Modern Battle* (Princeton, NJ: Princeton University Press, 2004), 253, n. 57. The operational level of war occupies centre stage in Chris Bellamy, *The Future of Land Warfare* (New York: St. Martin's Press, 1987), ch. 4; and Richard D. Hooker, Jr., *Maneuver Warfare: An Anthology* (Novato, CA: Presidio Press, 1993).

6. Bernard Brodie, *War and Politics* (New York: Macmillan, 1973), 452.

7. Edward N. Luttwak has explained that efficiency in the military and civilian worlds has quite different meanings. To be militarily efficient means to function in such a way that an enemy cannot secure high returns for low costs. In order to place him in this situation, one may well need to behave in a manner that may appear grossly inefficient if assessed by the tough accounting standards of commerce. Centralization rather than dispersion frequently is the path to commercial cost effectiveness. But, for the soldier, centralization, say of logistics, is apt to imply severe vulnerability. Civilian business does not usually need to operate in a manner survivable in the face of a malevolent and violent foe. See Luttwak, *On the Meaning of Victory: Essays on Strategy* (New York: Simon and Schuster, 1986), 85–115, 'Why We Need More "Waste, Fraud and Mismanagement" in the Pentagon'.

8. Carl von Clausewitz quoted in Peter Paret, *Clausewitz and the State* (Oxford: Oxford University Press, 1976), 359.

9. Robert Boyle quoted in 'A Deeper Shade of Blue: The School of Advanced Air and Space Studies', *Joint Force Quarterly,* 49 (2nd qtr. 2008), 74. To be true in the physical sciences, theory has to hold good in all cases. If a single apple should decide not to drop all the way to the ground when unimpeded by any countervailing object or force, the theory of gravity would be in serious trouble. By way of contrast, theory in the social sciences is content to predict most case consequences. We social scientists will admit to exceptions, even with respect to our favoured theories. 'There are always exceptions, and sometimes exceptions are very important.' P. C. Bratton, 'A Coherent Theory of Coercion? The Writings of Robert Pape', *Comparative Strategy,* 22 (October-November 2003), 368.

10. Judy Pearsall and Bill Trumble, eds., *The Oxford English Reference Dictionary,* 2nd edn. (Oxford: Oxford University Press, 1996), 1496.

11. Clausewitz, 141.

12. Harry R. Yarger, *Strategic Theory for the 21st Century: The Little Book on Big Strategy* (Carlisle, PA: Strategic Studies Institute, US Army War College, February 2006), 1. See Yarger, *Strategy and the National Security Professional: Strategic Thinking in the 21st Century* (Westport, CT: Praeger Security International, 2009), for an excellent guide to strategic thinking. Athanassios G. Platias and Constantinos Koliopoulos, *Thucydides on Strategy: Athenian and Spartan Grand Strategies in the Peloponnesian War and Their Relevance Today* (Athens: Eurasia Publications, 2006), ch. 1, also is admirably clear and rigorous on methodology.

13. The Brodie canon is long and of exceptionally high quality. In addition to *War and Politics,* his *Strategy in the Missile Age* (Princeton, NJ: Princeton University Press, 1959), is a profound work, notwithstanding its dating detail, while his contribution to Brodie, ed., *The Absolute Weapon: Atomic Power and World Order* (New York: Harcourt, Brace, 1946), 21–69, is strategically stellar. Thomas C. Schelling, a Nobel prize-winning economist, made a unique contribution to the logic of strategy with his book *The Strategy of Conflict* (Cambridge, MA: Harvard University Press, 1960). Most especially he demonstrated how game theory could apply to strategic choice. His

Strategy And Arms Control (New York: Twentieth Century Fund, 1961), co-authored with Morton H. Halperin, laid the intellectual footing for the modern theory and practice of arms control. In *Arms And Influence* (New Haven, CT: Yale University Press, 1966), Schelling wrote a foundation text on the theory of coercion. Michael Howard has not written one or two major works on modern strategy, but rather a stream of outstandingly perceptive essays that captured the issues of the day and subjected them to a historically educated assessment. Given the relatively popular and accessible character of Howard's strategic writings, it is a safe assumption that his name belongs on the shortlist of highly influential theorist-commentators. For a fair sample of Howard's contemporary strategic oeuvre, see *Studies in War and Peace* (London: Temple Smith, 1970); *The Causes of Wars and Other Essays* (London: Counterpoint, 1983); *The Lessons of History* (New Haven, CT: Yale University Press, 1991); *The Invention of Peace and the Reinvention of War* (London: Profile Books, 2001); and *Liberation or Catastrophe? Reflections on the History of the Twentieth Century* (London: Continuum UK, 2007). Alone among the modern theorists and theorist-commentators of war cited in the text, Michael Howard has opened at least a window into his strategic soul in his beautifully written and suitably reflective autobiography, *Captain Professor: The Memoirs of Sir Michael Howard* (London: Continuum UK, 2006). The J. C. Wylie canon offers one contribution, but what a one, *Military Strategy: A General Theory of Power Control* (1967; Annapolis, MD: Naval Institute Press, 1989). Edward N. Luttwak is an outstanding strategic theorist who commands a classical historical reach that even professional historians have been obliged to take very seriously. Beyond his theoretical masterwork, *Strategy*, see his path-breaking studies: *The Grand Strategy of the Roman Empire: From the First Century A.D. to the Third* (Baltimore: Johns Hopkins University Press, 1976), and *The Grand Strategy of the Byzantine Empire* (Cambridge, MA: Harvard University Press, 2009). In addition to his serious historical writing with its partial guidance by some ideas from modern strategic studies, Luttwak is a formidably effective strategic controversialist in essay mode. See his *Strategy and Politics: Collected Essays* (New Brunswick, NJ: Transaction Books, 1980), and his *Meaning of Victory*.

14. Clausewitz, 183.
15. Ibid.
16. Michael Howard, 'The Forgotten Dimensions of Strategy', *Foreign Affairs*, 57 (summer 1979), 975–86.
17. I have borrowed and adapted the house metaphor from T. E. Lawrence, *Seven Pillars of Wisdom: A Triumph* (New York: Anchor Books, 1991), 191. He writes about 'the whole house of war in its structural aspect, which was strategy, in its arrangements, which were tactics, and in the sentiment of its inhabitants, which was psychology'. Lawrence was a strategic 'hedgehog' (see my Introduction), as he revealed even more plainly in his next sentences. 'The first confusion was the false antithesis between strategy, the aim in war, the synoptic regard seeing each part relative to the whole, and tactics, the means towards a strategic end, the particular steps of its staircase. They seemed only points of view from which to ponder the elements of war, the Algebraical element of things, a Biological element of lives, and the Psychological element of ideas', 192. Although Lawrence thus demonstrated a healthy grasp of the holism needed to approach war properly, it is noticeable, alas, that his identification of strategy with 'the aim in war' is not sound. Aims in war are the province of politics and policy. Colin S. Gray, *Modern Strategy* (Oxford: Oxford University Press, 1999), 23–44.
18. Clausewitz, 141.

19. F. A. Hayek, quoted in John Keegan, *A History of Warfare* (London: Hutchinson, 1993), 6.
20. Sophisticated and useful discussion of the concept and practice of grand strategy has rarely been a growth industry among strategic theorists and historians. However, it is worth noting that the challenges posed by insurgencies in the 2000s have sponsored what amounts to a belated mini-boom in grand-strategic studies. The British Government, for example, is quite proud of its newly rediscovered 'comprehensive approach' to counter-insurgency (COIN), an approach that one should be forgiven for labelling grand strategic. This approach is a good idea—and it always was. Alexander of Macedon understood it in the 320s BCE at least as well as do British officials in the AD 2000s. What is more, they both had what we now call Afghanistan very much in grand-strategic view. Consider the message of Director General, Development, Concepts and Doctrine, *Countering Irregular Activity within a Comprehensive Approach*, Joint Doctrine Note 2/07 (Shrivenham: Development, Concepts and Doctrine Centre, Ministry of Defence, March 2007), and Cabinet Office, *The National Security Strategy of the United Kingdom: Security in an Interdependent World*, Cm. 7291 (Norwich: Stationery Office, 2008), in the historical light shed by David J. Lonsdale, *Alexander the Great: Lessons in Strategy* (Abingdon: Routledge, 2007), ch. 3. The theory of grand strategy still leaves much to be desired, in part I suspect because it can appear to be all but synonymous with foreign policy, at least to people who are challenged in their grasp of the key difference between policy and strategy. See Basil H. Liddell Hart, *Strategy: The Indirect Approach* (1941; London: Faber and Faber, 1967), ch. 22; and Luttwak, *Strategy*, ch. 13. Recent productive scholarship from the phalanx of political science is well represented by Colin Dueck, *Reluctant Crusaders: Power, Culture, and Change in American Grand Strategy* (Princeton, NJ: Princeton University Press, 2006). Also, there is value in the essays collected in Paul Kennedy, ed., *Grand Strategies in War and Peace* (New Haven, CT: Yale University Press, 1991).
21. Clausewitz, 119–21.
22. Ibid. 177.
23. The term policy is somewhat problematic, because the products, processes, and people to which it refers are respectively political and necessarily politicians. Clausewitz's German *Politik* is usefully ambiguous. See Hew Strachan, *Clausewitz's On War: A Biography* (New York: Atlantic Monthly Press, 2007), 263–5. On balance, considering his historical context, it is safe to assume that Clausewitz most typically meant policy by his use of *Politik*. For a twenty-first century context, there is much to be said in favour of translating *Politik* as politics.
24. Clausewitz, 583, 607.
25. Ibid. 610.
26. MacGregor Knox, 'Conclusions: Continuity and revolution in the making of strategy', in Williamson Murray, Knox, and Alvin Bernstein, eds., *The Making of Strategy: Rulers, States, and War* (Cambridge: Cambridge University Press, 1994), 614–45, provides exemplary discussion of the costs that tend to accrue to those who do not function strategically.
27. The quoted, though typically much misunderstood, words were written by the most celebrated soldier of the second half of the nineteenth century, Field Marshal Helmuth Graf von Moltke, the victor of the three wars of German unification, and the parent of the modern general staff. Moltke, *Moltke on the Art of War: Selected Writings*, ed. Daniel J. Hughes, Tr. Hughes and Gunther E. Rothenberg (Novato, CA: Presidio Press, 1993), 47.

28. Ibid. 45.

29. This point is argued persuasively in Echevarria, *Clausewitz and Contemporary War*, 142–3.

30. See Colin M. Fleming, 'New or Old Wars? Debating a Clausewitzian Future', *Journal of Strategic Studies*, 32 (April 2009), 213–41.

31. J. C. Wylie defines strategy sparely as 'a plan of action designed in order to achieve some end; a purpose together with a system of measures for its accomplishment'. *Military Strategy*, 14.

32. Michael Howard writes: 'But the strategy adopted is always more likely to be dictated rather by the availability of means than by the nature of the ends'. 'British Grand Strategy in World War I', in Kennedy, ed., *Grand Strategies in War and Peace*, 32. Eliot A. Cohen, *Supreme Command: Soldiers, Statesmen, and Leadership in Wartime* (New York: Free Press, 2002), ch. 7.

33. Clausewitz, 605 (emphasis in the original).

34. On the 'war convention' see Michael Walzer, *Just and Unjust Wars: A Moral Argument with Historical Illustrations*, 3rd edn. (New York: Basic Books, 1997), 44. 'I propose to call the set of articulated norms, customs, professional codes, legal precepts, religious and philosophical principles, and reciprocal arrangements that shape our judgements of military conduct *the war convention*.' Amidst a huge literature, three books merit special mention: Michael Howard, *War and the Liberal Conscience* (London: C. Hurst, 2008); Michael Howard, ed., *Restraints on War: Studies in the Limitation of Armed Conflict* (Oxford: Oxford University Press, 1979), which is somewhat dated in a few of its entries, but overall is most valuable; and A. J. Coates, *The Ethics of War* (Manchester: Manchester University Press, 1997).

35. See Lawrence Freedman, *The Transformation of Strategic Affairs*, Adelphi Papers 318 (London: International Institute for Strategic Studies, 2006), ch. 5; and Rupert Smith, *The Utility of Force: The Art of War in the Modern World* (London: Allen Lane, 2005), 284–9.

36. Williamson Murray and Mark Grimsley, 'Introduction: On Strategy', in Murray, Knox, and Bernstein, eds., *Making of Strategy*, 21. Given the limited quantity of Britain's military assets, especially on land, and the even more modest general quality of its army's fighting power, the country needed every ounce of advantage in strategy that it could contrive.

37. Wylie, *Military Strategy*. This is not to imply that Clausewitz and Wylie stand alone as disciples of control via strategy. See Scott A. Boorman, 'Fundamentals of Strategy: The Legacy of Henry Eccles', *Naval War College Review*, 62 (spring 2009), 91–115. Eccles, in common with J. C. Wylie, a rear admiral in the US Navy, remains underappreciated as a sound strategic thinker. While recognition of Wylie's merit is now proceeding agreeably, Eccles continues to lack the good notice that he deserves. See especially Henry E. Eccles, *Military Concepts and Philosophy* (New Brunswick, NJ: Rutgers University Press, 1965), 45. '*Strategy* is the *art of comprehensive direction of power to control situations* and *areas* in order to attain *objectives*' (emphasis in the original). I must confess that when I first read this book forty years ago, I did not then realize just how good it was.

38. Sun Tzu, *Art of War*, advises that our wisdom and cleverness will ensure our victory. Harassment by an intelligent, capable, and determined enemy is not much in evidence in its pages.

39. Robert Debs Heinl, Jr., *Dictionary of Military and Naval Quotations* (Annapolis, MD: United States Naval Institute, 1966), 102.

40. Terence Zuber, *The Battle of the Frontiers: Ardennes, 1914* (Stroud: Tempus Publishing, 2007); Anthony Clayton, *Paths of Glory: The French Army, 1914–18* (London: Cassell, 2003), chs. 1–3; and Robert A. Doughty, *Pyrrhic Victory: French Strategy and Operations in the Great War* (Cambridge, MA: Harvard University Press, 2005), chs. 1 and 2, are essential additions to the all too thin English language literature on the terrible French experience in 1914 (and beyond). Annika Mombauer has wrought close to assured destruction upon the Zuber thesis that the Schlieffen Plan was not the master plan to win the war in a single campaign that generations of historians have believed it to have been. Terence Zuber, *Inventing the Schlieffen Plan: German War Planning, 1871–1914* (Oxford: Oxford University Press, 2002). See Mombauer, 'Of War Plans and War Guilt: The Debate Surrounding the Schlieffen Plan', *Journal of Strategic Studies*, 28 (October 2005), 857–85. Mombauer's major study of the younger Moltke, the Chief of the General Staff from January 1906 until September 1914, *Helmuth von Moltke and the Origins of the First World War* (Cambridge: Cambridge University Press, 2001), esp. 260–71, tells the German story well, as does Robert Foley, *German Strategy and the Path to Verdun: Erich von Falkenhayn and the Development of Attrition, 1870–1916* (Cambridge: Cambridge University Press, 2005). As for the iconic Prussian military man himself, and most especially for his famous alleged 'plan', see Alfred von Schlieffen, *Alfred von Schlieffen's Military Writings*, tr. and ed. Robert T. Foley (London: Frank Cass, 2003), which provides the notorious memorandum of 1905, places it in historical context, and discusses its significance persuasively.

41. Michael Howard, 'Men Against Fire: The Doctrine of the Offensive in 1914', in Peter Paret, ed., *Makers of Modern Strategy: From Machiavelli to the Nuclear Age* (Princeton, NJ: Princeton University Press, 1986), 510–26; Antulio J. Echevarria II, *After Clausewitz: German Military Thinkers Before the Great War* (Lawrence, KS: University Press of Kansas, 2000); id., *Imagining Future War: The West's Technological Revolution and Visions of Wars to Come, 1880–1914* (Westport, CT: Praeger Security International, 2007).

42. This point is illustrated graphically in Michael I. Handel, *Masters of War: Classical Strategic Thought*, 3rd edn. (London: Frank Cass, 2001), 75. Everything—strategy, operations, tactics—influences everything else.

43. Sun Tzu, 168; Ralph D. Sawyer, *The Tao of Deception: Unorthodox Warfare in Historic and Modern China* (New York: Basic Books, 2007); Luttwak, *Strategy*, xii.

44. See David M. Glantz and Jonathan M. House, *The Battle of Kursk* (Lawrence, KS: University Press of Kansas, 1999); Evan Mawdsley, *Thunder in the East: The Nazi-Soviet War, 1941–1945* (London: Hodder Arnold, 2005), 262–9; Chris Bellamy, *Absolute War: Soviet Russia in the Second World War* (London: Macmillan, 2007); and, for an exciting, but still useful, popular history, Martin Caidin, *The Tigers Are Burning* (New York: Hawthorn Books, 1974).

45. I qualify the claim for the universal appeal of deception, because it appears to be a fact that there are significant differences in its strength among distinctive strategic and military cultures. Stated in the most rough and ready way, as well as in a manner that seems to beg for scholarly challenge, it has been proposed that there is, certainly was, a uniquely 'Western', naturally as contrasted with 'Eastern' (oriental, or Persian), 'way of war', which privileged the stand-up fight in the open between symmetrical battle arrays. See Victor Davis Hanson, *The Western Way of War: Infantry Battle in Classical Greece* (London: Hodder and Stoughton, 1989). Hanson's bold thesis finds much favour in Keegan's *History of Warfare*, esp. 332–3. Keegan argues energetically, imaginatively, and with some good reason that war and warfare are cultural pursuits. The

problems with this argument are that these pursuits are by no means only cultural in character and motivation, and also that some among the cultures in question most probably accommodate more than a single narrow strategic and military style, or at least will be able to adapt somewhat as necessary. Jeremy Black, though friendly to the culturalist thesis, is deeply sceptical of crude binary distinctions that contrast Eastern and Western military practices. Indeed, we need to beware of the danger that a sensible cultural awareness on our part can slip unnoticed into a variant of the alleged 'orientalist' fallacy. See Black's excellent discussion of the cultural dimensions of military history in his *Rethinking Military History* (Abingdon: Routledge, 2004), chs. 2 and 3. 'Fairness is a wonderful attribute, Major Anderson. It has nothing to do with war', Orson Scott Card, *Ender's Game* (New York: Tor Books, 1991), 97, is a wonderfully terse statement of the allegedly tricky, unscrupulous, and dishonourable 'Eastern' way of war. The most energetic challenge to culturalism in strategic history is Porter, *Military Orientalism.*

46. For the 'anything goes' ethos that loves the cunning plan and masterful stratagem, see Qiao Liang and Wang Xiangsui, *Unrestricted Warfare: Assumptions on War and Tactics in the Age of Globalization*, tr. FBIS (Beijing: PLA Literature Arts Publishing House, February 1999). Deceit, treachery, and surprise are prominent themes in the works presented in Ralph D. Sawyer, *The Seven Military Classics of Ancient China*, tr. Sawyer (Boulder, CO: Westview Press, 1993); and id., *Tao of Deception.*

47. Thomas Cleary, *The Japanese Art of War: Understanding the Culture of Strategy* (Boston: Shambhala, 1992), 88.

48. J. Glenn Gray, *The Warriors: Reflections on Men in Battle* (New York: Harper Torchbooks, 1967), 152.

49. See Lawrence Freedman, *The Evolution of Nuclear Strategy*, 3rd edn. (Basingstoke: Palgrave Macmillan, 2003), ch. 16; Henry D. Sokolski, ed., *Getting Mad: Nuclear Mutual Assured Destruction, Its Origins and Practice* (Carlisle, PA: Strategic Studies Institute, November 2004); and Keith B. Payne, *The Great American Gamble: The Theory and Practice of Deterrence from The Cold War to the Twenty-First Century* (Fairfax, VA: National Institute Press, 2008). Payne's is the first study to be written that convincingly connects the parallel tracks of strategic ideas about nuclear weapons to the history of US policy and strategy. His evidence includes archival materials that have been hitherto unavailable. The binding thread for his narrative and assessment is the sharp contrast between the strategic ideas of Thomas C. Schelling and Herman Kahn. The former advocated nuclear deterrence by the fostering of uncertainty, 'the threat that leaves something to chance', while the latter theorist recommended deterrence by certainty of prospective action and outcome. This theoretical and doctrinal debate can be traced from the very late 1950s through to the present. For the most basic contending texts, see Schelling, *The Strategy of Conflict* (Cambridge, MA: Harvard University Press, 1960); id., *Arms and Influence* (New Haven, CT: Yale University Press, 1966); Herman Kahn, *On Thermonuclear War* (Princeton, NJ: Princeton University Press, 1960); id., *Thinking About the Unthinkable* (New York: Horizon Press, 1962). All four books are remarkable intellectual achievements. It is probably fair to say that all of them were highly speculative in character, unencumbered or disciplined by much that warrants the label of evidence.

50. For a potent reaction against the military history and strategic analysis that neglected the human dimension, most especially the fighting man at the sharp end of war, see John Keegan, *The Face of Battle* (London: Jonathan Cape, 1976). Dave Grossman, *On*

Killing: The Psychological Cost of Learning to Kill in War and Society (Boston: Little, Brown, 1995), also is excellent.

51. On physical and psychological cowardice, see Gray, *Warriors*. 'Fear can prey on the mind to the point where it makes a soldier unfit for combat. Usually it rises just high enough to prevent reason, and with it the detachment of self-consciousness, from governing', 105. 'It is necessary to distinguish the person who is an occasional coward in the face of death from the constitutional coward. In almost everyone at times, there is a coward lurking', 111–12.

52. On the contested concept, sparse distribution, and major significance of genius, see Clausewitz, 100–12; and Hew Strachan, *Clausewitz's On War: A Biography* (New York: Atlantic Monthly Press, 2007), 127–9. Also relevant is my *Schools for Strategy: Teaching Strategy for 21st Century Conflict* (Carlisle, PA: Strategic Studies Institute, US Army War College, October 2009).

53. For the challenge and performance of higher command, amongst a literature of forbidding size see John Keegan, *The Mask of Command* (New York: Viking Penguin, 1987); G. D. Sheffield, ed., *Leadership and Command: The Anglo-American Experience Since 1861* (London: Brassey's UK, 1997); Dennis E. Showalter, *Patton and Rommel: Men of War in the Twentieth Century* (New York: Berkeley Caliber, 2005); Andrew Roberts, *Masters and Commanders: How Roosevelt, Churchill, Marshall and Alanbrooke Won the War in the West* (London: Allen Lane, 2008); and Carlo D'Este, *Warlord: A Life of Churchill at War, 1874–1945* (London: Allen Lane, 2009); while Robert Pois and Philip Langer, *Command Failure in War: Psychology and Leadership* (Bloomington, IN: Indiana University Press, 2004), is a fairly successful interdisciplinary (psychology and history) study. For a valuable controversial perspective on civil–military relations, see Cohen, *Supreme Command*. With a main thesis that spoke eloquently to a receptive official civilian audience in Washington, DC, at its time of publication, Cohen's book placed a strong marker for the view that politicians have to be ready to tell generals how to wage warfare. Moreover, if the generals will not listen, then they must be replaced. In the historical context of the national and international debate over a possible US invasion of Iraq, Cohen's work arguably was either the right, or the wrong, book at the right time. The joys of hindsight are apt to induce forgetfulness concerning the opinion one held yesterday. This is all too human, of course.

54. Sun Tzu, 60–1.

55. Clausewitz, 578.

56. See Colin S. Gray, *Another Bloody Century: Future Warfare* (London: Weidenfeld and Nicolson, 2005), ch. 2. My education in the significance of context has been advanced, belatedly perhaps, by Jeremy Black, a historian, of course. Black advises wisely that 'an understanding of war requires contextualization'. *Rethinking Military History*, 243. I have no difficulty adapting Black's dictum to read, 'an understanding of the practice of strategy requires contextualization'.

57. I develop this thesis in my *Modern Strategy*, ch. 5.

58. Clausewitz, 605. But see Echevarria's carefully argued judgement that 'Clausewitz's wondrous trinity, thus, negates the notion of the primacy of policy; it renders policy as purpose, and holds it a priori just as important as chance and hostility. Only when reviewed historically, that is in an a posteriori sense, can we determine the extent to which each of those forces actually influenced the course of events'. *Clausewitz and Contemporary War*, 95. Echevarria's important claim bears on historical practice and malpractice, not really upon the validity of Clausewitz's privileging of the authority of reason as policy (or politics).

59. Ibid. 593.
60. Isaiah Berlin, *The Hedgehog and the Fox: an Essay on Tolstoy's View of History* (New York: Mentor Books, 1957).
61. There is a place for mathematical magic in defence analysis, but its exact location and reliability are contestable. The case for some calculus of combat is well made in David Rowland, *The Stress of Battle: Quantifying Human Performance in Combat* (London: Stationery Office, 2006). Since strategy has the need for qualitative judgement as its required most core of competencies, it is improbable that the mathematical modellers will ever provide very useful tools for its better design and execution. Recognition of the relevant level of analysis is a necessity. There are many problems in defence that lend themselves to mathematical analysis. For a historical example, 'how large should a convoy be, what shape should it maintain, and how many escort vessels would it need?' But performance of strategy's task of translating military deeds into desired political consequences calls for a skill that lies beyond the promise of mathematical support.
62. Clausewitz, 566–73.
63. Ibid. 578.
64. Strachan, *Clausewitz's On War*, 193.
65. The ever insightful and bold Echevarria argues that *On War* contains 'a balanced blend of diverse and ever conflicting ideas, unfinished and perhaps raw in parts, but not necessarily incomplete'. *Clausewitz and Contemporary War*, 7.

2

The Theory of Strategy, II: Construction, Execution, and Consequences

REDUCTION BUT INCLUSION

Every dictum matters profoundly. If I could analyse all twenty-one dicta simultaneously, I would do so in order to show the unity of strategy and strategic behaviour. Because such holistic treatment is analytically impractical, the general theory is divided brutally into two categories of importance, albeit with a soft boundary between them. Chapter 1 posited and explained the more defining of strategy's features, while Chapter 2 examines the rest, the remainder, of the subject. The topics of these remaining dicta are in all cases significant. Indeed, they are so significant that belligerent disadvantage in any one of them, no matter why it obtains, has the potential to hazard the prospects for strategic and political success overall.[1]

It may be useful to recall two methodological caveats. First, a laudable quest for economy in theory is always liable to lead the theorist into the error of undue reductionism. The excellent theoretical proposition that small is beautiful may seduce the theorist into believing that, in this case, strategy 'essentially is about . . .', picking your preference—politics, technology, chance, deception, money, and so forth. Alas, for clarity, and especially for the quality of strategic performance, strategy is not essentially about any single feature. The strategic hedgehog is not to be trusted if he seeks to persuade us that there is but one golden key to strategic excellence.[2] In practice, there are many such keys, and if one or two are severely worn or missing, or perhaps if the locks they should fit are not permissive of turning, the whole project of strategy could well fail. In principle, clarity is a virtue, but it ceases to be virtuous if it is achieved by oversimplification that misleads. Clarity can just be clearly wrong.

Second, endeavours to combat the hazard of unsound reductionism frequently tempt the strategic theorist into an unmanageable comprehensiveness tending towards the malady of encyclopaedism. So rich can be the dish served by the theorist that strategic practitioners would suffer acute indigestion were they ever to be so foolish as to take the theorist and his analytical method as seriously as he does himself. Clausewitz warned admirably against analysis that treats separately and exhaustively what needs to be seen as a gestalt, a whole.[3] But, the fact remains that the strategic theorist somehow must identify an analytical approach able to accommodate a potentially bewildering variety of strategy's features. The twenty dicta proposed in these first two chapters fall perilously close to an injudicious comprehensiveness, even when that is deemed a risk worth running if one is to steer comfortably clear of the hazard of excessive reductionism. For examples of the latter, although this author is a great admirer of both Basil H. Liddell Hart and Edward N. Luttwak, he is more than a little uncomfortable with their approaches to strategy. The former argued for the central significance of what he termed the 'indirect approach', the latter for the authority of paradox and irony. Both ideas are valuable, but even if entirely persuasive on their own terms they are just too austere wholly to satisfy the needs of the general theory of strategy.[4] In order to effect a tolerable marriage between economy and richness, this book opts for a comprehensive approach hopefully rendered non-encyclopaedic in appearance and consequence by means of the provision of deliberately weak internal boundaries. As a result, these two chapters present the general theory of strategy by clusters of dicta attaching, and comprising the answers, to just the four basic questions cited already in Chapter 1: What is strategy? How is strategy made and by whom? What does strategy do?—what are its consequences? And, how is strategy executed?

It is necessary to bear in mind always that theory is in the business of explanation, and that it cannot be tested in the social sciences as it can in the physical. Unfortunately, this unavoidable, indeed existential, truth is not sufficiently discouraging as to prevent the would-be scientific theorists of strategy from seeking an unobtainable metrical measure of certainty. Social scientific theory, addressing human behaviour under uncertainty in unique historical contexts that cannot be replayed, has to satisfy the examining criteria of such factual evidence as there is, plausibility (dare one say it, commonsense), and explanatory power. Efforts to pursue theoretical rigour through application of methods from the much harder sciences are a waste of time and, worse, they can mislead the unduly credulous. It is difficult to locate the right, or right enough, strategic answer when the enemy is able to perform, not as in a controlled experiment, but in a manner constrained only by his imagination, strength of motivation, skill, and capabilities, while also behaviour is ever liable to be the consequence of friction and chance. Strategy is conducted competitively by two, and usually more, contestants, playing by few rules. In fact, definition of the terms of strategic engagement, the rules, constitutes a vital prize, a potentially huge net asset in the struggle of the day. Should readers with a background in the physical sciences venture into this book, they need to accept a degree of social scientific enculturation such that they are willing to relax their understanding of the requirements of testable theory.

Here in Chapter 2, presentation of the general theory of strategy completes the project begun with dicta one through nine in Chapter 1. It advances through clusters of answers, developed in dictum form, to the fundamental questions about strategy. The plan for these pages is to explain: the making of strategy (dicta ten to thirteen, treating strategy-making process, values, culture and personalities, and strategists), strategy in execution (dicta fourteen to twenty, on difficulties and friction, types of strategies, geography, technology, time, logistics, and military doctrine), and the consequences of strategy (dictum twenty-one on tactical, operational, and strategic effect).

MAKING STRATEGY

Dictum Ten: Strategy typically is made by a process of dialogue and negotiation

There have been and will be exceptions to this dictum, but it is a safe, most-case generalization to claim that strategies are developed in an ongoing process of negotiation and dialogue among potent stakeholders, civilian and military. There have been examples of strategies being chosen by a solitary leader, a genius, or otherwise who commands and does not negotiate. Alexander the Great, Napoleon Bonaparte, and Adolf Hitler are the charismatic leaders-cum-strategists who spring most obviously to mind.[5] To focus upon the Second World War, the great-power belligerents offer only one example of the solitary strategist, typically deaf to advice and warnings, and certainly not permitting anything resembling a process of negotiation among stakeholder interests, Adolf Hitler. In Britain, the United States, Imperial Japan, and even Joseph Stalin's USSR, strategy-making was a shared enterprise, though responsibility, glory, and blame usually was not distributed at all evenly.

Also as a general rule, strategy is hammered out and then is near constantly revised in the light of feedback from the several battlespaces. Players in the process of strategy-making seek advantage, as well as the avoidance of disadvantage, for the interests of their particular tribe in the more or less loose coalition of loyalties and cultures that is every government or governing entity. With war frequently waged by rival alliances and coalitions of polities, strategy-making often entails negotiation not only among stakeholders at home, but also among allies.[6] The inductive general theory of strategy cannot claim that the process of strategy-making necessarily is strategically rational; it is not. Certainly there should be a serious effort to identify ways to match military and other means with desired strategic effects in the service of political goals. However, some of the institutional, even just personal, players in the process of strategy-making are sure to promote their own versions of intelligently designed rational strategies. Those versions may well meet a minimal standard of rationality, yet be wholly unreasonable in the assessment of others. In the Second World War, for example, the 'bomber barons' of the Royal Air Force (RAF) and the United States Army Air Forces (USAAF) proposed, quite rationally, that Germany could and should be defeated by bombing alone. Their general theory of air power became doctrine, which directed specific plans intended to achieve victory through (strategic) air power. As recently as 1999, US air force and army generals differed over bombing strategy for the coercion of Slobodan Milosevic's Serbia.[7] Such disagreements, which express contrasting strategic world views and institutional cultures, all held sincerely, are entirely usual. Indeed, they are so usual that it is eminently defensible to argue that strategy is made and revised by negotiation. But this is not to deny the roles both of careful rational planning that tries to match means with ends, and of inspiration, intuition, and—it must be so labelled—occasional genius, as well as the dysfunctional personality.

This dictum specifies dialogue as well as negotiation among strategy-makers in order to ensure that the theory grasps both formal and informal processes. Strategy-makers usually comprise a very small community with a shifting membership. There will be dialogue and negotiation between civilians and soldiers, as well as among civilians and among soldiers. This is what should occur all but continuously on the strategy bridge. In his celebrated controversial book, *Supreme Command*, Eliot A. Cohen asserts with much good reason that 'in fact, the study of the relationship between soldiers and *statesmen* (rather different from the relationship between the soldier and the *state*, as a famous book has it [reference to Samuel P. Huntington, *The Soldier and the State*: CSG]) lies at the heart of what strategy is all about'.[8] Cohen may overreach, but not by much.

The two extremes on the strategy dialogue spectrum are well illustrated by the sharply contrasting performances of American President Woodrow Wilson and British Prime Minister Winston Churchill. The former was so uninterested in strategic matters that he met his newly appointed Commander-in-Chief of the American Expeditionary Force (AEF), General John J. 'Blackjack' Pershing, only once during the war, on 24 May 1917, and resolutely said nothing at all of strategic substance. In the apposite words of one historian:

> Wilson's aloofness had its positive side, as the general realized. 'In the actual conduct of operations,' he would recall, 'I was given entire freedom and in this respect was to enjoy an experience unique in our history.' Yet it also left the army entirely bereft of guidance from its commander in chief: the president of the United States. The country had never fought a war that way before, and never would again.[9]

The sharpest imaginable contrast is to be found in Churchill's efforts to guide and control his country's military effort in the field. For a case more extreme even than Churchill's typically ill-fated forays into military strategy, one need look no further than to Adolf Hitler. Happily for his service chiefs of staff, President Franklin Delano Roosevelt held himself as aloof from military strategy as he was resolutely engaged in the making of policy and grand strategy.

Dictum Eleven: Strategy is a value-charged zone of ideas and behaviour

At least two of the classic texts providing theories of war and strategy, those by Sun Tzu and Clausewitz, are silent on ethical and moral issues. To those theorists, war and its prosecution by strategy were simply facts of the enduring human condition. Neither offers any encouragement to the view that war and strategy have a significant moral dimension. Strategic thinkers in the twentieth century similarly chose not to trouble their readers with ethical dilemmas. Although there was a notable growth of humanitarian sentiment in many countries from the mid-nineteenth century onwards, and especially after the unduly Great War of 1914–18, the explicitly military-strategic literature continued to be all but naked of ethical content. The international peace movement, in the context of the fairly popular beliefs that war should be regarded as either a crime to be punished or a disease to be cured, made little or no impact on the world's strategic theorists and practitioners prior to 1945.

The nuclear age certainly triggered what eventually, by the early 1960s and thenceforth, grew into a large response from those millions of people who were morally outraged by the nuclear facts of life. It is well to recall that this age dawned in the immediate wake of full-frontal public exposure to the facts about the holocaust. Appropriately enough, one might claim, nuclear-age strategic theorizing by defence professionals continued the tradition of value-free strategic analysis, theory, and military doctrine. This theorist, however, believes that the general theory of strategy must accommodate assignment of no small significance to moral judgement and sentiment. It is true that the modern, largely American authored, classics of nuclear-age strategic thought comprise an overwhelmingly value-free zone, explicitly at least. The sub-theories of stable mutual deterrence, limited war, arms control, escalation, and crisis management, for leading examples of modern thought—which inspired and legitimized actual US strategies, please note—by and large were invented through rigorous application of the methodology of rational choice. This was armchair strategy, if ever anything could be so described. It was also deductive theorizing, reflecting American, certainly Western, cultural norms, derived intuitively in a deceptively apparently value-free way. Leaving aside the under-explored issue of hidden values in American rational strategic theory and doctrine, the belief in a value-free, universally rational, strategic theory is fundamentally flawed.

David J. Lonsdale offers an important judgement that simultaneously is empirically correct but which might prescriptively mislead. He claims that

> Strategic studies seeks to present an amoral analysis of military affairs. By doing so, we can objectively assess actions and/or individuals that as moral beings may cause us concern. In the search for best practice in strategic affairs we can, and should, be able to disentangle moral judgements from strategic ones.[10]

Many, indeed most, strategists in all periods have written and behaved as if this were true. But it errs massively because 'moral beings' cannot be separated completely from their strategic persona. Given that moral standards, widely variable as they assuredly are, have been, and will be, integral to all human cultures, and given that all strategists have to be encultured people, there can be no evading a moral contribution to strategy-making and execution.

The effectiveness with which strategies are prosecuted overall, operationally and tactically, always is affected by the attitudes to the conflict and to conflict behaviour of the belligerent parties, and sometimes of neutral, but candidate belligerent, observers. Rarely are these attitudes the product strictly of cold rationality alone. Rather are they shaped, in greater or lesser degree, by people's feelings and preferences, factors that have an inalienable moral, certainly ethical content. When strategists are neglectful of the moral aspect, they are riding for a painful fall.[11] For example, a powerful human motivator is a sense of injustice. To attempt to draft a general theory of strategy, let alone specific strategies for historical application, while being indifferent to the unquantifiable vagueness of such an ethically based criterion as moral authority, would be to commit a most significant error. The general theory cannot be antiseptically dismissive of the potential role of values. The fact that intellectually the two most impressive works among the classics of strategic theory, ancient and modern, have not highlighted the importance of moral beliefs as cultural norms does not legitimize their continuing generic exclusion.

Strategic theorists tend to be rather undisciplined in their use of the closely related concepts of ethics and morals. More often than not they employ them interchangeably, with the choice being more one of literary taste than substantive preference. However, some strategists find value for clarity of argument in the exercise of intellectual discipline over such usage. To that end, these words by former Israeli General Yehoshafat Harkabi are well worth quoting and pondering. He succeeds in nailing two distinctions of high importance, the one plainly so (theory and doctrine), the other arguably.

> The difference between theory and doctrine is comparable with the difference between ethics and morals. An ethics philosopher analyzes what is at the basis of good deeds while the moralist teaches us what to do.[12]

Dictum Twelve: historically specific strategies often are driven by culture and personality, strategy in general theory is not

As general theory, strategy is culture neutral as well as oblivious to the personal traits of individual human player; strategies, however, are anything but naked of such detail. The 2000s registered a long-needed, if eventually probably inevitably overdone, 'cultural turn' in strategy. The concept of strategic culture was first aired in the 1970s with reference to the Soviet Union and nuclear strategy, but the provenance of the sense in the idea is lost in antiquity.[13] The *Strategikon*, attributed to Byzantine Emperor Maurice, leaves nothing much to be desired with regard to the strategic value in understanding the individual character of each of one's foes.[14] There is nothing new about recognizing the merit in cultural awareness as well as some understanding of the personalities and interpersonal dynamics of enemy leaders. In the Second World War, cultural anthropologists were harnessed to the US war effort, though it is less than self-evident that much practical benefit resulted. Cultural ignorance, racial prejudice, ethnocentrism, and the passions of the time were more than a match for the scholarly products of American anthropologists.[15]

Psychological profiling of foreign policymakers is standard practice in Washington today, though it was not always so. Joseph Stalin certainly was fascinated by, and was more than somewhat admiring of, Adolf Hitler.[16] He may not have liked Hitler's policies, but he respected his style and methods. What was novel about the 2000s was that the official American defence community 'went cultural', or, to the more sceptical among us, at least visited culture country. The most formal expression of this unusual and possibly temporary development was the production of a path-breaking and blockbuster joint US Army and Marine Corps doctrine manual on counter-insurgency (COIN) that is, if anything, over abundantly cultural.[17] There is nothing like contemporary crises—Iraq and Afghanistan in this case—for the spurring of theoretical and doctrinal reform, change at least. Raymond Aron was persuasive when he claimed that 'troubled times encourage meditation'.[18] America's greatest strategic theorist of the nuclear age, Bernard Brodie, should have been pleased by the 'cultural turn'. In 1973, he wrote:

> Whether with respect to arms control or otherwise, good strategy presumes good anthropology and sociology. Some of the greatest military blunders of all time have resulted from juvenile evaluations in this department. Napoleon despised the Russians as somewhat subhuman, as did Hitler after him, and in each case fate exacted a terrible penalty for that judgment.[19]

There may or may not be culturally distinctive 'Eastern' and 'Western' ways of war; scholars will debate this exciting, though in this theorist's opinion unpersuasive, proposition endlessly and inconclusively. But it is a certainty that the general theory of strategy is of universal validity. This uncompromising claim is advanced with reference to every enumerated dictum in the theory propounded in these chapters. Nothing here should be culture-bound. On close enquiry, if this claim is found to be incorrect in some respect, the fault lies with the exposition. The theory of strategy that I seek to identify, expose, explain, and examine is both transcultural and transhistorical. This theorist most definitely is not so blessed. China's military strategy and strategies in the twenty-first century assuredly will be drafted and executed in ways unique to Chinese cultures (national, strategic, and military-institutional) and situation. But such overall strategy and its strategies, no matter how Chinese in flavour, must bow to the wisdom in the tenets of the general theory. While it is essential to appreciate that strategies are devised, executed, and revised, by encultured people, in addition they are the product of biologically particular human beings. Individuals differ in their genetic inheritance as well as in some detail of their cultural, or multicultural, programming, as well, of course, in the circumstances in which they find themselves. Cultural influence over strategies is always likely to be detectable and significant, but so too is the stamp of personality as well as institutional (political) context and situation. Sweeping generalizations about the cultural inclinations of the representatives of a particular society may have merit. But such value is nullified if key human players have personalities that prompt them to behave beyond the cultural paradigm that should contain and constrain them. The relations among nature, nurture, and situation or occasion are all too richly variable for terse reductionist explanation.

Dictum Thirteen: The strategy bridge must be held by competent strategists

Is there a Horatius ready and able to serve when he or she is most needed? Formally regarded, a strategist has to be defined as a person who does strategy, either as thought and theory, or in practice as planner or commander–leader (or leader–commander). However, for the special sense required here in strategy's general theory, a strategist is not only a person who plays the role, in addition it is a person who plays the role competently.[20]

Because strategy is uniquely difficult among the levels of war (see dictum fourteen), few indeed are the people able to shine in the role. Their numbers can be increased by education, though not by training, and not at all reliably by the experience of command and planning at warfare's operational and tactical levels. One must admit that so demanding are the intellectual demands for creativity placed upon the strategist, that even previous experience at the strategic level is not entirely to be trusted as a sound predictor of future individual performance. Moreover, the brilliant strategic thinker, the somewhat intuitively gifted strategist, can only be as effective in his job as his logisticians, other planners, operational commanders, and troops permit. To quote Field Marshal Lord Wavell

> The final deciding factor of all engagements, battles and wars is the morale of the opposing forces. Better weapons, better food, superiority in numbers will influence morale, but it is a sheer determination to win, by whomever or whatever inspired, that counts in the end. Fine feathers may make fine birds, but fine battleships do not necessarily make fine sailors or we could never have dominated the Mediterranean against the greatly superior Italian fleet. Study men and their morale always.[21]

The Field Marshal is right, but he could mislead. If the will to win is decisive in warfare, all but regardless of material circumstance, then the Germans might well have won the Second World War. Their morale and sheer determination was not superior, or inferior, to those of the Russians, but they certainly left the Western Allies far behind. The Allies fought hard and well enough; that is the most that can be claimed for them.[22] Without the Russian ally-of-circumstance it would have been a very different story, most probably with a different ending.

Can soldiers and civilians be so educated as to be fit to hold the strategy bridge? Up to a point the answer must be 'yes'. They can be taught the theory of strategy, so that they are, at least, familiar with what the strategic role requires. But can people be so well educated as to ensure that they will perform excellently as practical strategists? The answer has to be a clear 'no'. The principal reason is because strategy is an art not a science, and it cannot be taught as one can teach, say, the principles and methods of engineering or logistics. Napoleon overstated, but made this point plain, when he wrote:

> Generals-in-chief must be guided by their own experience or their genius. Tactics, evolutions, the duties and knowledge of an engineer or an artillery officer may be learned in treatises, but the science of strategy is only to be acquired by experience, and by studying the campaigns of all the great captains.[23]

There is no doubt that experience can help. For example, Frederick the Great's first adventures as a strategist provide rich lessons in how not to do it, but he improved with practice.[24] Not everyone who is called to the practice of strategy is improved by the lessons he should learn from his early defeats. Furthermore, when a would-be strategist is not also simultaneously chief executive and head of state, he is unlikely to be permitted the luxury of repeated learning experiences. This theorist recalls being advised by his colleague, Herman Kahn, that the conduct of several large-scale nuclear wars should greatly improve our strategic performance. There was, however, a systemic problem with his ironic claim, notwithstanding the inherent merit in the argument. Practice may make perfect, but one should not need to study Sun Tzu in order to understand why 'warfare is the greatest affair of state, the basis of life and death, the way (Tao) to survival or extinction'.[25]

Because war is so important to societies, and because strategy is as necessary as it is difficult, it is essential to seek to improve the performance of those charged with holding the strategy bridge. To make the theory of strategy explicit and, one intends, plain, should contribute to the quality of strategy in action as plans and strategies. Unfortunately, it is not only the strategists of a civilized world order who can benefit from the publication of strategic theory, but also those who act for the forces of disruption, disorder, and darkness. Not for nothing did the Chinese Empire treat the better writings on strategy as state secrets.[26] I must hasten to add that this is not to suggest that this text could warrant such limited access and careful handling. It has long been recognized that strategic competence, let alone excellence or genius, requires more than just a suitable education. In addition, the strategist needs physical and moral fortitude, good judgement, and luck. None of these four essentials can be provided by education.[27]

EXECUTING STRATEGY

Dictum Fourteen: Strategy is more difficult to devise and execute than are policies, operations, and tactics—friction of all kinds comprise phenomena inseparable from the making and conduct of strategies

The prime source of difficulty is strategy's instrumental consequential nature. The strategist seeks strategic effect for political effect. To convert the currency of military achievement into desired political results is a task that calls for judgement based more upon intuition, native wit, genius even, to fall back on Clausewitz, than on formal education. Strategy cannot be reduced to mathematics. Contemporary American attempts to provide a quantified basis for deterrence strategy make no more sense than did the official US strategy for a stable deterrence that rested entirely upon untested, indeed untestable, assumptions about the rank ordering and content of Soviet values.[28] Nonetheless, if one is persuaded that targeting is the equivalent to, indeed can substitute for, strategy, then mutual assured destruction (MAD), as well as its earlier manifestation in the theory of strategic bombing to disable or coerce, provided the metrics of a claimed certainty. The fact that such certainty is an illusion has been revealed time and again, but its attractions are more than sufficient to overcome the well-founded objections of critics. Perceived and then assumed intellectual and political, possibly even moral, necessity knows no discipline.

In addition to its political-to-military and vice versa task of currency conversion in the absence of a fixed exchange rate, by definition the strategy bridge has to cope with more traffic of all kinds than must any other relevant behaviour, the political, operational, and tactical. Bluntly expressed, there is far more to go wrong for strategy than there is for the other functions. The strategist must cope with the desires of politicians, the interests and cultures of institutions, as well as the established bureaucratic processes of governance, and that is at but one end of the bridge. At the other, the strategist will be assailed by feedback, reliable and otherwise, from the sharp end of conflict. 'It's a mystery', as the impresario in the movie *Shakespeare in Love* tried to explain how a play would 'come right' on the first night. Somehow, the strategist must provide purpose, drive, and coherence. These achievements should direct the community's war-making behaviours to a favourable political conclusion.

The potential for friction abounds in all aspects of strategy-making and at all levels of execution. The strategist, most typically a professional military person—though not in non-state entities—may well have dysfunctional habits of mind and behaviour in the eyes of his political masters. Those masters, successful politicians, these days are unlikely to enjoy any great understanding of military affairs. As military amateurs, they may find themselves prisoners of their military experts, or, with the arrogance of ignorance, they may insist upon the undertaking of militarily impractical missions. Either way, the personality contrasts between the qualities most characteristic of successful politicians and those of soldiers often yield rich evidence of uneasy and perhaps antagonistic relations. For two major British examples of the point, garrulous and charismatic Prime Minister David Lloyd George and taciturn General Douglas Haig were as perfect a mismatch as one could invent as fiction. While, in the Second World War, the absence of dialogue between garrulous and charismatic Prime Minister Winston Churchill and his supreme Commander in the Middle East in 1940–41, General Archibald Wavell, was costly for British interests. These strategic marriages were failures on a heroic scale.[29]

Even if a strategist holds his bridge as stoutly as did Horatius in Lord Macaulay's apocryphal 'lay', a yet more troubling source of uncertainty is inescapable with respect to the political value of particular military achievements.[30] Specifically, in effect the strategist is a soothsayer. He is predicting the strategic future with his plans. But the future has not happened. Field Marshal Helmuth Graf von Moltke was surely right enough when he said in 1871 that 'no plan of operations extends with certainty beyond the first encounter with the enemy's main strength'.[31] Surprises great and small, agreeable and disagreeable, are bound to occur. Since the strategist seeks to direct his community's military effort in warfare in its entirety, his grander designs are at risk to the unexpected at the tactical and operational levels in every geography. Furthermore, unsteadiness and other pathologies exhibited by politicians and subordinate military commanders, as well as uncooperative behaviour by decidedly flawed foreign allies, are ever ready to reduce strategic effectiveness. Only the most mentally stable, physically robust, best broadly educated, technically sound, and naturally intuitively gifted people qualify fully to be strategists. Unfortunately, the one requirement that cannot be placed upon candidate strategists is the necessity for experience. No experience at a lower level can prepare a person adequately for strategic respon- sibilities. Armies often are inclined to punish those who make serious mistakes at what of recent decades has been known as the operational level of war by enforcing their early retirement. In some cases, those thus discarded instead should be entrusted with further heavy responsibilities, because they should have learnt invaluable lessons from their own past errors. Few military systems operate on such an admittedly risky permissive principle.

Clausewitz can hardly be said to have discovered friction, but he was the first theorist to give a compelling name to all the phenomena that can impede strategic performance. What is friction? The master tells us in these justly much quoted words, that 'everything in war is very simple, but the simplest thing is difficult. The difficulties accumulate and end by producing a kind of friction that is inconceivable unless one has experienced war.'[32] He claims, fairly persuasively, that 'friction is the only concept that more or less corresponds to the factors that distinguish real war from war on paper'. Clausewitz concludes his brief chapter on the subject by advising that 'friction, as we choose to call it, is the force that makes the apparently easy so difficult.'[33]

From what sources does friction stem? Clausewitz fingers in particular the 'climate of war', by which he means 'danger, exertion, uncertainty and chance'.[34] These abstract concepts are broad enough to bear the heavy load that theory requires of them, while also they are sufficiently opaque on specifics as to suggest a suitably unpredictable multitude of detailed possibilities. As always, the actual historical contexts of strategy-making and execution will provide a rich assort- ment of difficulties, universal and in kind eternal, yet unique in detail. It is essential to understand, however, that Clausewitz's warning about the universal play of friction discouraged him neither from advocating careful war planning, nor from reposing confidence in the feasibility of strategy. He believed that the purposeful direction of military behaviour, which is to say strategy, is possible, and that competent or better planning and leadership can succeed despite the inevitable intervention by multi-sourced friction. Friction is a fact of strategic history; it need not be a show-stopper.[35]

There is much to recommend the insight in an inspired aphorism by Lawrence Freedman. He has observed that 'plans may be hatched by the cool and the calculating, but they are likely to be implemented by the passionate and the unpredictable'.[36] True though this is, it is necessary to balance it with the historically well-attested observation that plans developed in the relative calm of peacetime are likely to be far better prepared than are those composed in the context of ongoing hostilities. The latter circumstance will reveal much about friendly and enemy forces that could not be known ahead of actual combat, and the uniqueness of revealed events should guide well-tailored strategic planning, but the pressures of time and the climate of war may well offset those benefits. Strategy 'on the fly' is apt to be more rough and ready than that which is thought through at some leisure.

In his magnum opus, *Strategy*, Edward N. Luttwak makes the following widely underappreciated points:

> The logic of strategy seemed to unfold in two dimensions: the 'horizontal' contentions of adversaries who seek to oppose, deflect, and reverse each other's moves—and that is what makes strategy paradoxical; and the 'vertical' interplay of the different levels of conflict, technical, tactical, operational, and higher—*among which there is no natural harmony*.[37]

The lines just quoted do not reveal anything previously unknown, but they comprise, nonetheless, an intellectual *tour de force*. The words to which emphasis has been added are especially significant. To go beyond Luttwak's persuasive claim, the strategist must somehow succeed in rendering coherent and mutually supporting levels of conflict that have their own natures and characters. Truly, as Luttwak insists, there is no natural harmony among political purposes, strategic objectives, operational goals, tactical aims, and technological achievements. Each level has its own distinctive driving influences. Only the strategist, not the politician, the operational commander, nor the tactician, is obliged to orchestrate behaviour at each level so that the total effort is more than the sum of its disparate parts. When one feeds into this super difficulty the comprehensive problem of a self-willed enemy, it should be easy to appreciate why it is extraordinarily difficult to excel, or even to be barely competent, at strategy.

Dictum Fifteen: strategy can be expressed in strategies that are: direct or indirect, sequential or cumulative, attritional or manoeuvrist-annihilating, persisting or raiding (expeditionary), coercive or brute force, offensive or defensive, symmetrical or asymmetrical, or a complex combination of these nominal but often false alternatives

This possibly unduly rich dictum, with its pairs of specific strategy types, derives in the forms presented here from the writings of five scholars: Sun Tzu and Basil H. Liddell Hart (direct versus indirect); Rear Admiral J. C. Wylie, United States Navy (USN) (sequential versus cumulative); Sun Tzu and again Basil H. Liddell Hart (attritional versus annihilating by manoeuvre); Archer Jones (persisting versus raiding); Thomas C. Schelling (coercive versus brute force); offensive versus defensive has a provenance that is lost in the mists of time; while symmetrical versus asymmetrical, though eternal in practice, if recent in language, also is not clearly traceable to an identifiable theorist.[38] There is no correct type of strategy, because every rivalry and war needs to be conducted with the strategies most appropriate to it. Furthermore, the seven binaries are not exclusive alternatives. More often than not strategists combine these apparent choices, even

Table 2.1 Specific Strategy Types and Their Apparent Opposites

1. Direct or indirect
2. Sequential (linear) or cumulative (non-linear)
3. Attritional or annihilating by manoeuvre (for physical or moral destruction)
4. Persisting or raiding (expeditionary)
5. Coercive or brute force
6. Offensive or defensive
7. Symmetrical or asymmetrical

though they are unlikely to appreciate what they are doing in the conceptual terms presented here. It is plausible to suggest that explicit recognition of the choices, the possibilities, identified in this dictum, could improve strategic performance.

The pairs of strategy types specified are included in the general theory because, viewed collectively, they speak significantly to the nature of strategy (see Table 2.1). They summarize usefully the ranges of choices for strategists. Also, they provide far reaching sets of strategy identities to offer their employers high-octane conceptual fuel for practical exploitation. The pairs are close to self-explanatory.

Although Liddell Hart forever will be known as the father of the indirect approach to strategy, in fact he had to be inspired by the whole body of classical Chinese military literature. It is commonplace to cite and quote Sun Tzu, but really the direct–indirect relationship in strategy is a near universal theme in the Chinese classics. It may be worth noting, as does Ralph D. Sawyer, a recent translator of Sun Tzu, that the Chinese classics invariably write of Ch'i (unorthodox or indirect) and Cheng (orthodox or direct) rather than of direct–indirect as is our practice today.[39] Provided one does not over-egg the theoretical pudding *à la* Liddell Hart, and try to make the indirect approach the all but magical key to victory, there is much to be said in praise of this distinction. Inadvertently, Liddell Hart did his best to kill the utility of the direct–indirect distinction, but we would be wise to include it in the tool-bag for sound practice that is the general theory of strategy.

Inspired both by the distinguished German theorist Herbert Rosinski, and by his own maritime experience and world view, J. C. Wylie is largely responsible for presenting and developing in a helpful way the contestable idea that strategies fall into sequential or cumulative categories. The admiral can speak for himself.

> There are actually two very different kinds of strategies that may be used in war. One is the sequential, the series of visible, discrete steps, each dependent on the one that preceded it. The other is the cumulative, the less perceptible minute accumulation of little items piling one on top of the other until at some unknown point the mass of accumulated actions may be large enough to be critical. They are not incompatible strategies, they are not mutually exclusive. Quite the opposite. In practice they are usually interdependent in their strategic result.[40]

Wylie cites the Central Pacific drive by Admiral Nimitz and the march to the Elbe by Allied forces under General Eisenhower as clear examples of sequential strategies in action. He contrasts these major illustrative examples with the submarine tonnage wars waged by Germany in the two world wars and by the United States in the Pacific against the Japanese Empire. Other examples of cumulative strategy were the strategic bombing campaigns conducted against Britain, Germany, and Japan. To those examples one might add any number of insurgency and COIN campaigns. The sequential–cumulative difference is a vital one. It has been quite common for strategists to direct cumulative military behaviour in the mistaken belief that thereby they would sequentially proceed inexorably towards decisive success. Strategic history is too complex for simple models. Nazi Germany was defeated by the Grand Alliance that had to follow a critical path in a sequential strategy that could succeed only if each step was sufficiently cumulative in its attrition of the enemy. Tersely put, the U-boats had to be defeated, and then the Luftwaffe, for an amphibious invasion to be feasible. Meanwhile, the Wehrmacht had to suffer cumulatively severe enervation on land in the East.

While granting both the theoretical and the historical plausibility of Wylie's distinction, this theorist is not entirely persuaded that the two kinds of strategies thus postulated really are as different as the admiral claims. It is sound to distinguish between actions that follow from those that preceded them and those that strictly do not. However, it needs to be acknowledged that even largely independent engagements can have consequences of a progressive character deriving from the sequence of the behaviours at issue. Therefore, although Wylie's sequential–cumulative distinction between strategies has merit, it does have weaknesses. Most especially might it mislead people into believing that historical strategic performance typically has fallen into one or the other category, when the record suggests that a mixture of the two is frequent. In addition, this distinction encourages an unduly neat and overly simple understanding of how belligerents accumulate strategic effect. To illustrate my caveat: a non-linear character of warfare may well not be recordable either on a map as territory gained, or as a tactically or operationally connected military success. But non-linear tactical victories or defeats can have distinctly linear consequences for the demoralization of soldiers and the relevant publics. To hazard what some may deem to be a proposition too far, one might suggest that the concept of non-linear warfare is essentially ridiculous. In other words, warfare conducted to succeed strategically via the cumulative accretion of positive strategic effect secured by autonomous behaviours—for candidate example, by isolated autonomous engagements in guerrilla warfare—is not really non-linear. Rather will it have a historical strategic narrative where it matters most, in the minds of the people most relevant to the struggle at issue, as well as on the total quality and quantity of assets still available to the belligerents in question. This argument may overreach, but it is important not to be uncritically accepting of a fashionable idea like non-linearity. After all, 'nothing comes from nothing, nothing ever could', as *The Sound of Music* asserts plausibly.

The distinction between strategies of attrition and those of annihilation by manoeuvre is complementary to the other binary sets. Simon Anglim offers a suitable definition of the eminently contestable concept of manoeuvre warfare:

> A term used to describe military operations which happen to defeat the enemy by using superior speed and agility to strike at his vital 'centres of gravity,' dislocating his forces from each other and from their sources of command, control and supply and thereby rendering them helpless, rather than destroy him through weight of numbers and firepower.[41]

In 1914 and again from 1939 to 1942, Germany pursued continental strategies designed to annihilate the enemy's power of military resistance. The campaigns intended to unfold by decisive flank-exploiting manoeuvre failed in action. As a necessary consequence, Germany's strategists were stuck with no practical alternatives. They could pursue an unwinnable protracted war of attrition or seek a negotiated peace that was politically impossible to all parties.[42] Strategies of attrition intend to grind down the enemy's resources and enforce a favourable net loss rate, man by man, asset by asset, a type of strategy that applies also to the psychological dimension of warfare. Belligerents' wills to resist are subject to attrition. Indeed, such psychological attrition is the kind of strategic effect upon which irregular combatants usually must rely. Although strategies of attrition should be fairly reliable in their military promise, it is important to note that they are invariably expensive. Attrition is a two-sided (or more) condition of warfare that delivers victory, when it can, on 'points', via a favourable net loss rate. It should be needless to add that even a highly favourable net loss rate will not deliver ultimate success if one is numerically challenged to a high degree. Crudely expressed, a large army can afford to lose a lot more soldiers and still win, than can a much smaller army. It is worth noting that in theory decisive manoeuvre can work by destruction of the enemy's ability to resist, which is to say by a physically enforced paralysis, or by a severe demoralization of the enemy that paralyses his will to resist, or by some mixture of the two.

The contrast between persisting and raiding or expeditionary strategies are in little need of explanation. The persisting strategy directs its forces to engage the enemy in any or all geographies, and to remain engaged until that enemy is incapable or unwilling to continue the fight. In contrast, the raiding strategist will strike with the intention of effecting a near-term withdrawal. By definition, almost, the raider seeks to alarm and damage, not annihilate. The raiding strategist may function with short, sharp raids of modest scale and immediate purpose, or alternatively by means of a large-scale expedition. Whereas a persisting strategy typically endeavours to seize and hold, the raiding option strives only to 'butcher and bolt', 'burn and scuttle'. Given the unpredictability of warfare, it is scarcely surprising that a raiding mindset and its plans for expeditionary operations not infrequently are obliged to effect an emergency change of course. Expeditions that cannot speedily extract themselves from their missions can become beleaguered garrisons. Raiding tends to be a generically more attractive military option than is a persisting strategy of enduring engagement. But although the raider limits his costs and risks, the downside of the upside of the brief violent encounter is that his short timeline for action is likely to limit his ability to achieve the strategic effect necessary for the benign political consequences that give meaning to the whole strategic project.

Conceptually, it is not difficult to distinguish between coercion and brute force, notwithstanding the theoretically rather awkward fact that the latter can be instrumental for the former. That problem granted, still it is useful to distinguish between an essentially punitive strategy that seeks to persuade its victim to concede under the menace of pain or more pain, and one that strives simply to take or impose what it wishes, regardless of the will of the victim. One can argue persuasively that any application of brute force is potentially coercive, but such a claim were better resisted. It is important to be clear whether one is relying on the enemy to 'cry uncle' at some point of distress of his, admittedly coerced, choosing, or whether one intends to control him physically and deny the power of choice. Because aerial bombardment by its very nature cannot grasp and grip an enemy, when it is advocated as an instrument that is able to inflict much pain it is employed as a strategic tool of coercion.[43]

In common with strategic itself, the adjectives offensive and defensive paradoxically are both meaningless yet useful, depending upon the level of conflict at which they are applied.[44] Tactically employed, the offensive and defensive descriptors do have some integrity. Passive defences such as fortifications and armour of all kinds, and weapons of short range, plainly have little or no reach and striking power. However, those defensive attributes are vital for the protection of military endeavours that, considered overall in the light of their political purpose, can be characterized as offensive. The passive Theodosian triple land walls of Constantinople enabled the Byzantine Empire not only to protect its greatest asset, but also thereby to enjoy some freedom of action in distant parts, for example on and beyond the dynamic Euphrates frontier with Persia or on the Danube.[45] Offence and defence are both matters of strategic context and subject to definition by political choice. If my heart is pure and my policy ends are beyond reproach, my military and other means, though employed for tactical and operational offense, must be serving goals that are defensive of what is right and proper, and so forth.

From June 1940 until the Americans arrived in large numbers in 1943, Britain pursued tactically and even operationally offensive military activity. London conducted small-scale commando raids, long-range bombing, and periodically took the initiatives in land warfare in North Africa. Such offensive military behaviour served the broadly defensive strategic goal of simply staying in the war until better times happened along, which they did, beginning late in 1942. The proposition that particular weapons inherently are offensive or defensive is, by and large, unsustainable. A Roman legionnaire's shield protected his comrade to his left who was enabled thereby to employ his gladius lethally, while his comrade on the right side provided the shield cover for his gladius to stab an enemy warrior. If a soldier can function as a lethal killing agent only because he enjoys some passive protection, there is little sense in terming his shield or body armour defensive.

If one's air defence system so limits the damage that one must suffer that one is granted the time to conduct a long-range bombing campaign, how defensive should it be judged? This is not to deny that if a security community limits its military efforts only to those that are passive or have a very short reach, it would indeed be able to claim credibly that its military strategy was wholly defensive.

The final opposed pair of strategy types, symmetrical and asymmetrical, may be unique in that it embraces explicitly, though strictly does not require, the idea that a strategy can be selected because it is distinctive from the strategy antici-pated to be preferred by the adversary. The distinction need not imply this; it can be simply descriptive of difference. This distinction at least carries some implica-tion of recognition of the potential merit in Sun Tzu's famous dictum: 'Thus, what is of supreme importance in war is to attack the enemy's strategy.'[46] It is worth noting that the defeat of the enemy's strategy is synonymous neither with the enemy's strategic defeat, nor with a victory for the home side. For example, Britain clearly defeated German strategy in the summer and autumn of 1940, but that victory in the air in the Battle of Britain could not itself deliver victory in the war as a whole.[47] Belligerents sometimes change strategy radically in the course of a conflict, while nearly always they are obliged to adapt their plans (strategies) as events unfold in ways that were less than adequately anticipated. In principle, at least, it is possible to generate sufficient strategic effect to win as a scarcely merited consequence of diverse, poorly directed, cumulative tactical success.

It is not unreasonable to regard the symmetrical/asymmetrical distinction just as a way of characterizing the other six opposed strategy pairings. This distinction is, of course, entirely devoid of content beyond the requirement for a difference that may be either purposeful or only expedient to the point of a necessity that might be judged regrettable by its authors and executives. Since all opposed strategies will be in some measure asymmetrical, it is an easy matter to dismiss this distinction as being unduly light in forensic power. On balance, though only on balance, this would be ill advised. The overriding reason to be more respectful of this apparently empty, even rather banal, distinction is that the significance of the enemy and his independent will is so important in strategy that a concept that highlights possible differences between us and them is almost certain to be useful. This is not to deny that in strategically poorly educated hands the concept of asymmetry has some potential to mislead, but one must admit that there is nothing in strategic theory that is entirely proof against folly.

Provided one treats these sets of strategy distinctions simply as ingredients to a strategy mix, their appreciation can only be beneficial. This dictum must be understood in a nuanced way and applied only flexibly to real-world strategic challenges.

Dictum Sixteen: all strategies are shaped by their particular geographical contexts, but strategy itself is not

To understand the general nature of strategy, to have to hand a theory that explains what it is, what it does, and how it does it, is to be well equipped to draft strategies for each of the five geographies (land, sea, air, space, and cyberspace). The geophysical specifics of each geographical environment, together with the shifting technological context, must yield both opportunities and constraints unique to every time and geography. Despite an increasing commonality among armies, navies, and air forces in military capabilities, warfare remains at most a joint undertaking. The age of the all-environment combat or support vehicle, or of the geographically universal soldier, remains a long way off. This is the reason why it remains necessary to respect two levels of general theory. The overall general theory of strategy feeds geographically, sometimes functionally (e.g., for special operations, COIN, or for nuclear-armed forces), partial general theories tailored to specific forms of military power (hence we have, say, air power theory). Today, the geographically specialized armed services typically are far more likely to coordinate, even occasionally integrate, their preparations and actual combat behaviour than was general practice even a generation ago, but the unique geophysical character of each environment continues to matter greatly. The slow process of military transformation, enforced and encouraged by electronic information technologies, enables some sharing of roles and missions between the near-universally still separate armed services. But continuities in distinctive service outlooks or cultures, as well as institutional and personal career interests, thus far are more impressive than are the discontinuities.[48] Security communities tend to wage multi-environment war and warfare, rarely do they fight strictly in a single geography. The rise and yet further rise of air power has meant that no land or sea campaign today can be bereft of an air dimension. Moreover, this dimension is as likely as not to prove militarily decisive, always depending on the character of the conflict. But if the style of warfare is highly irregular, which is to say restricted to guerrilla combat and terrorism, then air power is almost certain to be at a discount, notwithstanding its vital supporting roles.[49]

The geophysical characters of land, sea, air, space, and now cyberspace must shape the character of strategies for their exploitation. Moreover, these specific strategies should be developed by those educated in the general theories that explain how and what the distinctive military instruments uniquely can perform. For example, the many benefits that derive from space forces are in no little measure offset by the high cost of spacefaring, by the predictability of orbits (though intra-orbital manoeuvre and inter-orbital transfer is possible at a price in weight for fuel), by the sheer distance involved, by the limited dwell time permitted, by low orbital passage (in principal, this limitation can be met by increasing the size of the satellite constellation, or by occupying higher orbits, but both options bring their own difficulties), and—last but not least—by the near certainty of tailored harassment by the enemy in many conflicts.[50]

For many years to come, the facts of physical geography will remain critically significant as enforcers of distinctive strategies for the armed services. The services no doubt will become ever more joint in some technical respects, but full multi-service integration, including the emergence of a single military culture, is most unlikely to obtain in the defence establishment of any sizeable security community. What we do know as a part of the general theory of strategy is that because war is a duel, strategy must be attempted in the face of self-willed intelligent opposition. Any geography that a belligerent can exploit to advantage must attract the attention of the enemy. In the twenty-first century, it is a safe prediction that some, eventually many, wars will include space warfare and cyber warfare campaigns. Indeed, such campaigns are likely to open hostilities.[51]

Dictum Seventeen: strategy is an unchanging, indeed unchangeable, human activity in thought and behaviour, set in a variably dynamic technological context

Scholars differ over the relative importance of technology in the waging of warfare. Extreme technophiles argue that technology drives tactics, its influence being both thoroughly pervasive and even close to determining of many, even most, military outcomes.[52] This point of view, though widespread, is not shared here. Fortunately, for the purposes of identifying strategy's general theory it does not matter whether the balance of argument favours technophilia or technophobia, to cite the two extremes on the spectrum of possible attitudes. The general theory must function above and beyond the detail of technological history, a rule that enables it to assert two significant transhistorical facts: first, strategy always has, indeed must have, a technological context (man is a tool-using animal, and he has always made tools for, or usable in, warfare); second, the theory insists that its historical context is dynamic, though at a variable pace. For example, relative to preceding and subsequent periods, military technologies for land and sea warfare registered little advance for the better part of 150 years from the late seventeenth to the early nineteenth centuries. The flintlock musket was a standard issue throughout that era. The armies of the Duke of Marlborough that fought in the 1690s and 1700s would have been almost entirely familiar with the weaponry, and therefore most of the tactics employed in 1815 at Waterloo by the Duke of Wellington. By way of sharp contrast, the British Expeditionary Force (BEF) of the One Hundred Days' campaign of August–November 1918 would have been thoroughly alien to the BEF of August 1914, only four years previously. Technological and tactical change has moved at nothing like a constant rate historically.

The general theory of strategy is content simply to note the vital permanent reality of a technological context to all forms of warfare. However, the theory does insist that strategy is primarily a human activity in a technological context, not vice versa. This is not to demean the role of technology, but it is to claim that in nearly all historical cases the uses made of technology, military and civilian, have had greater strategic impact than has the mere presence of new machines. Improved or even wholly novel weapons do not suffice to effect revolutionary change. Instead, ideas tailored to the potential in combined arms prowess of new technology have been the major engine of radical military and strategic development. The point is well made by Richard O. Hundley of RAND: 'Without an operational concept, the best weapon systems in the world never revolutionize anything.'[53]

The history of warfare demonstrates beyond much room for scholarly controversy that technological possibilities are more likely to be followed, if not always seized with official enthusiasm, than their military, strategic, ethical, social, and political implications are apt to be understood at the time of their introduction. In the twentieth century alone, examples abounded. The aeroplane, radio, television, the atomic bomb, ballistic missile, and the computer, were all easier to invent and develop than they were to understand strategically. In the nineteenth century, to cite but one prominent, even dominant, example among the host of candidates, the dawn of the railway age in the late 1820s and the 1830s was as technologically obvious in most respects, as it was strategically opaque, at least through much of the 1850s.[54] On balance wisely, certainly understandably, Clausewitz devotes no attention to technology, zero.[55] Such lofty disinterest is not inappropriate for general theory. Nonetheless, the drafters of general theory today, as here, do not have the luxury of being able to ignore technology. Instead, while insisting that technology is not and cannot be a defining element in the general theory of strategy, still it is necessary to recognize the permanent importance of machines in the selection and execution of strategies.

The changing technological context does not render strategic practice in chosen strategies any easier. In fact, contra-suggestively perhaps, the reverse is true. A century ago, the strategist had to understand the distinctive strengths and limitations of two geographies only, the land and the sea. Neither the air nor the marine sub-surface environments were the subject of military plans. Today, in contrast, the strategist needs to understand and be able to orchestrate for combined effects, military behaviour in no fewer than five distinctive geographies, perhaps with the underwater world and the nuclear context in addition. Four major problems persist in hampering the ability of technology to serve reliably as the answer to strategists' impious prayers.

First, every technology has inherent limitations that derive from its nature as well as from the particular character of historically transient machines. The machines at issue typically will be (*a*) costly to acquire, which must restrict their number; (*b*) limited in performance; (*c*) difficult to perfect as a useful weapon or for weapons support, because soldiers will need to learn how to operate them, and leaders will have to discover how best to employ them for useful synergistic effect as a component in the combined arms team; and (*d*) subject to their own unique operational vulnerabilities and, therefore, countermeasures and workarounds. Second, within a fairly common cultural space technologically among security communities, no technical development can remain secret for long, certainly not once it is employed in anger. This is not to deny that even when technologically common cultures share approximately the same technical opportunities, they will make some different decisions on operational concepts and therefore on the acquisition of hardware. Viewed overall, however, in modern strategic history technological prowess is shared across cultures and continents. Aside from some cases of colonial warfare, global military history has been marked far more often by conflict among technologically like, rather than unlike, belligerents.

Third, to elevate the argument a little, technology is constrained from enjoying a secure place in the war-winners' enclosure by the inescapable annoying fact that strategy is by definition adversarial. For every technology that seems to promise to retire past and current problems by providing answers via wonderful performance, new problems arise.[56] Fourth and finally, the significance of technology's potential to shape and reshape conflict is limited by the very complexity of strategy. What this means is that a belligerent's technological shortfall, most probably of temporary domain, is likely to find compensation through superiority in other features of grand, including military, strategic performance. For example, excellence in generalship; training; morale; intelligence; brute military arithmetic—numbers or strength in political motivation, vital for morale or in diplomatic skill, can more than offset even a quite daunting level of technological inferiority. As noted already, because strategy is quintessentially, though not entirely, contextual, it is the task of the technologically disadvantaged strategist to seek to alter the military context so that the relative sophistication of machines is at a discount. Most obviously, such a strategist would try to avoid the regular style of conventional combat wherein a technological edge should yield maximum benefit to its fortunate possessor.

Dictum Eighteen: unlike strategy, all strategies are temporal

Time is not a defining feature of strategy, but it is universally so important that it cannot be omitted from the dicta of general theory. Grand and military strategies are all and always time-bounded in their attempted realization in operations and tactics. Every strategy in execution must have vital temporal aspects. Time features in the choices to initiate, continue, or wind down military action. It appears in the form of seasons of the year with their associated weather stories, and itself can signify as a deadly weapon. Belligerents obliged to fight irregularly typically seek to outlast the political will and hence the patience of established authorities, especially if those authorities are assisted notably by a foreign power. There is nothing inevitable about the political victory of an insurgency. At its core, such a conflict is won or lost as a result of one party to the struggle delegitimizing the other irreparably in the minds of the key battlespace, the people. There is a widespread belief that insurgents win by not losing. In other words, what might be termed existential strategy should be preferred. The insurgent employs time as a weapon to frustrate the regular enemy. Since regular armed forces are postured primarily to seek and wage prospectively decisive battle, they are apt to seek operational-level victory despite a thoroughly unaccommodating military context. When an irregular foe declines to stand and fight, there can be no decisive military engagements. This asymmetrical reality was revealed, for example, by the strategic context for the United States both in Vietnam in the 1960s and Iraq from 2003 until 2007. Ironically, it is at least possible that regular armed forces may succeed at COIN just as the domestic political support for the venture vanishes. This is what happened in Vietnam. America's new found prowess at COIN after 1968, guided by a revised doctrine and fresh leadership, was utterly undone strategically and politically by the collapse of political support at home.[57] Time had run out.

Clocks tick for all belligerents politically, strategically, operationally, and tactically. The strategic time frame is longer than the operational, and the operational is longer than the tactical. This is a significant reason why the strategist is in need of greater mental and moral fortitude than is the operational-level commander, let alone the tactician. The strategist has ample time to have the kind of second and third thoughts that are likely to shake his self-confidence. Time is a common property for adversaries to use and abuse, but it is always likely to have a differential meaning. One side will be strengthened by the use it can make of passing time, while the other will find that the balance of advantage slips away with the weeks, months, and possibly years. The closer one looks at strategy as general theory, and at historical strategies and their execution in operations and tactics, the more clearly does one realize that temporal concerns are a pervasively significant reality.

Dictum Nineteen: strategy is logistical

If armed forces cannot be moved and supplied, they cannot fight, and fighting is the most core of their needed competencies. Clausewitz is correct in his insistence that administration in its many forms inherently is dissimilar in nature and purpose from 'the actual conduct of war'.[58] His take on general theory deliberately excludes 'the many activities that are quite different from . . . *the utilization of the fighting forces*'.[59] He distinguishes sharply between 'activities preparatory to battle' and battle itself.[60] However, the master's agreeably neat distinction, though methodologically useful in confining theory's subject matter, is judged here to be unwise. General of the Armies Omar Bradley overstated a potent insight when he claimed pointedly that 'amateurs study strategy, professionals study logistics'.[61] From the other side of the Atlantic, Lord Wavell wrote on 13 August 1944 that

> The more I have seen of war the more I realise how it all depends on administration and transportation (what our American allies call logistics). It takes little skill or imagination to see *where* you would like your army to be and *when*; it takes much knowledge and hard work to know where you can place your forces and whether you can maintain them there. A real knowledge of supply and movement factors must be the basis of every leader's plans; only then can he know how and when to take risks with those factors; and battles and wars are won only by taking risks.[62]

Wavell is unduly dismissive of the difficulties posed at the operational level of war, but he is surely correct in his claim for the significance of logistics, as well as for his Clausewitzian closing flourish.[63] The logistical enabler is so fundamental that it comes close to earning a place in the shortlist of dicta that specify the defining features of strategy. The science of supply and movement, which is to say logistics, is literally essential to strategy at all levels of inclusiveness and of every character. When theorists debate concepts, typically they simply assume logistical feasibility. Just as military doctrine does not feature prominently in the writings of civilian theorists, neither does the subject of logistics.[64] The reason why not is identical in the two cases. Civilians lack expertise in the writing and the use made of doctrine, as well as in the supply and transport of military assets. It must be admitted, though, that Clausewitz's purposeful, explicitly justified, exclusion of logistics from his general theories of war and strategy does not rank high among his more persuasive decisions as a theorist. Of course, logistics can only be a tool of strategy, as the Prussian states, its servant. But, so integral is it to strategic behaviour that in the view taken here it must be included in the general theory.

Dictum Twenty: strategy is the most fundamental source of military doctrine, while doctrine is a notable enabler of, and guide for, strategies

Just as the general theory of strategy shapes and even controls strategies at their several levels and of different kinds (overall military, operational and in recent times usually joint, functional, and single-geography), so also should it shape and control military doctrines at all levels and of all kinds.

What is doctrine? Who writes it? What is it for? And, most pertinent to this text, why does doctrine feature among the dicta that constitute the theory of strategy? The answer to the last question is because doctrine is a vital input to strategic practice. Since strategic theory is developed most strictly for the purpose of educating those who direct and guide strategic practice, it must include an explanation of how it relates to the military doctrine that serves that practice. Theory and practice truly are indissolubly linked for strategy, since strategic thought can have no meaning or purpose if it is divorced from activity that produces the strategic effect generated by actual strategic behaviour. Strategy can have no autarkic significance whatsoever. Regarded in isolation, self-referentially, strategy would be seen as a metaphorical bridge that connects neither with the bank of politics and policy, nor with that of policy's instruments, including the military. Military capabilities and prowess are influenced, and can be driven, by the operational- and tactical-level doctrines chosen and which then are used to train for, and with caution to guide, behaviour.

What is doctrine? Deriving from the Latin, *doctrina*, 'doctrine is what is officially approved to be taught—whether in a service school or an operational unit engaged in training—about what methods to use/carry out [*sic*] a military objective'.[65] David E. Johnson of RAND shows helpful insight when he claims that

> While the services are not unsophisticated, monolithic entities marching blindly to the beat of a rigid set of rules, their 'institutional essence' is defined by their doctrine. In short, doctrine is the frame of reference, derived from its culture, that fundamentally defines the activities of each of the Armed Forces by:
>
> • Prescribing the shared world view and values as well as the 'proper' methods, tools, techniques, and approaches to problem solving within and among the services.
> • Providing a way in which the services view themselves.
> • Governing how the services deal with each other and with other governmental and non governmental agencies.

- Prescribing the questions and the answers that are considered acceptable within the institution or school of thought covered by the paradigm.[66]

The key to answering the question, 'what is doctrine for?', lies in the answer to another question, 'who writes doctrine?'. The answer to the latter question is that only military professionals write military doctrine, and they write it for their piece of the military puzzle. For example, only air persons write air doctrine, only sailors draft naval doctrine, and so forth. The inescapable reason for this apparent parochialism is that it is the nature of doctrine, in contrast to the nature of strategy, to specify how tasks set at different levels of military inclusiveness can best be accomplished. Obviously, only military experts are qualified to answer strictly military questions. Most authors of doctrine owe loyalty to, have careers dependent upon, and are genuinely thoroughly encultured by military organizations with specific geographical foci and bureaucratic interests. It follows that although doctrines typically express what their authors believe to be true, it is near certain to be truth slanted to privilege a particular form of favoured military power, employed in particular service-approved ways. Joint, which is to say multi-service, doctrine should express a judicious melding of beliefs among culturally distinctive institutions, but often it comprises more of a brute force stapling together of unlike elements than a coherent and harmonious whole. So-called joint military plans and performance similarly can have more the character of a shotgun marriage than of anything resembling harmony. The first Gulf War in 1991 was a classic example of a much vaunted, claimed 'jointery' that misrepresented hugely disjointed military practice.[67] To be fair to the strategists and lower level Allied commanders of 1991, the record of military operations by land, sea, air, and recently space and cyber, forces has rarely been shiningly joint. A prominent historical example of a successful truly joint operation, was the *Wehrmacht's* invasion of Denmark and Norway in April 1940 (Operation Weserübung).[68] Historically, it has been more common for different elements of armed forces to wage more or less simultaneously the kinds of warfare that each prefers, than for them to develop and execute plans genuinely calculated to produce complementary, let alone synergistic, military effects.

What is doctrine for? A four-part answer captures the soul of the matter. First, doctrine provides a common basis of understanding of what its issuing organization currently believes to be best military practice. Second, doctrine provides guidance, in some military cultures it provides mandatory guidance, not merely strong suggestions, on how soldiers should proceed on the basis of lessons learnt from historical experience, sometimes on the basis only of deduction from first principles, while occasionally it reflects nothing more solid than the commander's intuition. Third, doctrine both tells a military institution what it wants to believe, and it tells the outside world what it wants that world to believe, about the institution's relative importance, roles, and military behaviour. Fourth, doctrine is essential for the enculturation, truly the indoctrination, of its junior members. Doctrine may not provide a thoroughly reliable guide to probable military practice, but it does provide clues, and more, to understanding the current credo of military institutional stakeholders. It is worth noting that excellent doctrine is at something of a discount if its practical wisdom is ignored by soldiers in combat. For example, Antulio J. Echevarria has made a persuasive case for the proposition that the Imperial German Army possessed a more than adequate tactical doctrine in 1914. The problem proved to be that many formations either ignored it or were ignorant of its precepts when *der Tag* arrived.[69]

Contra-suggestive though it may seem to some, most of the dicta that comprise the framework of the theory of strategy have more or less direct meaning for, and implied practical application to, the writing of doctrine for operational and tactical military behaviour. Strategy and doctrine, doctrine and strategy, are necessary partners. Strategy decides how policy's goals are to be advanced and secured, and it selects the instrumental objectives to achieve those goals. Military doctrine, for its vital part, explains how armed forces of different kinds should fight. Doctrine should be the subordinated party to strategy in their necessary partnership, but such is by no means always the case. The reason is because the doctrines with which armed forces implement strategy must shape the expectations and plans of strategists. For a major classic example, the Anglo-American Combined (i.e. temporally parallel) Bomber Offensive against Germany of 1943–5 was a triumph of 'strategic' air doctrine(s), not of strategy. By default, the strategy, to stretch meaning more than a little, was a decision to implement the theories-as-doctrines of strategic bombardment that were held as sacred tenets by important branches of the RAF and the USAAF. It is worth noting that just as military doctrine can drive military strategy, so military strategy can dominate grand strategy and policy. In an orderly universe, general theory would educate the writers of doctrine, and their doctrinal products would inform strategic, operational, and tactical choices. In the disorderly world of actual history, however, the ideal relations just specified, sometimes are reversed. For example, in the late 1940s and the 1950s the US Air Force first did nuclear tactics and operations for actual strategies, next it developed the doctrine to codify its preferred practice, and finally its endeavours were somewhat blessed by a strategic theory focused on the ways in which the benefit of a stable nuclear deterrence could best be secured. In this case, therefore, the historical order proceeded from practice, though doctrine, to legitimizing theory.

The benefits of doctrine are obvious for military organizations that must strive to produce some order out of the chaos of combat. The costs and risks may be a little less prominently in view. In an inspired short paper on 'Theory and Doctrine in Classical and Modern Strategy', Harkabi suggests, and more, that useful doctrine and strategic theory encourage opposing practices. Whereas on the one hand, the theory of strategy and its expression in planned strategies should privilege creativity, deception, and selection and performance of the unexpected, doctrine, on the other hand, favours quite the reverse. Harkabi advances the caveat that 'doctrine could lead to the trap of stereotyped behaviour which would help the rival to predict and then forestall the commander's plan'.[70] The former Israeli soldier drives home his point by arguing, plausibly enough, that

> Doctrine cannot be kept secret, for doctrines are means to socialization of an army, especially since complying with their precepts is by definition repetitious. Doctrine would thus serve to divulge the commander's plan to the enemy, much as an enemy intelligence agent would. Doctrine may also impoverish thinking and creativity by diverting attention from alternative courses of action.[71]

The military virtues of predictability and order thus can be handicaps, even fatal ones, in the adversarial context of strategy. So much granted, military organizations nonetheless have need of doctrine, despite its downside. Those among us who are sceptical of the value of doctrine can have a hard time explaining how doctrine-free or light forces could function coherently. But there is no denying that the blessings of common thought and practice come with major perils attached. Exhortations for doctrine to be flexible, adaptable, and only discretionary, while nonetheless authoritative, tend to read better than they play in battlespace. What frequently saves doctrine from being fuel for failure because of its privileging of predictability is the pervasive sovereignty of the human factor. Commanders, indeed soldiers typically, will not follow doctrine with which they do not agree. However, Andrew Gordon insightfully offers backhanded praise for doctrine when he advises that it 'is something which we should depart from knowingly, like social graces . . . .'[72]

A basic problem in understanding the roles and importance of doctrine is that, in common with theory, it lacks a single authoritative meaning. Different countries' armed forces employ the term in a variety of ways. Also, it is expedient for doctrine to be ever less compulsory, the higher the level of behaviour it addresses. Tactical doctrine—the sharp end of warfare—typically endeavours to insist upon recognition of, and obedience to, what is believed to be contemporary best practice. But, as one ascends the stairs to the operational level of warfare, it rapidly becomes obvious that although doctrine can educate and advise the commander, it cannot prescribe the particulars of action. Should one venture into the highest reaches of doctrine, the strategic, one will discover that what is on offer is really a broad education in national security strategy. The relations among strategy's general theory, doctrine, and military strategies in plans are intimate and important, yet somewhat opaque. There is much truth in the proposition that the process of planning can be more significant for final military performance, than are the details of the plans produced at any one time. A similar point seems to apply to the development of military doctrine. Without denying that the content of doctrine should matter for military behaviour—if its precepts are followed, of course—the process from which a cascade of doctrine flows, or trickles, is probably more important still. Because warfare is a dynamic and hugely complex reality, it may be more valuable to debate doctrine than to settle firmly upon necessarily temporary answers to the question, 'what is current best practice?'. Needless to add, perhaps, for every level of warfare, even—at a stretch—for the tactical, it is possible and arguably useful to write 'doctrine' that identifies some enduring, though probably not quite eternal or universal, truths for broad gauged guidance.

CONSEQUENCES OF STRATEGY

Dictum Twenty-One: all military behaviour is tactical in execution, but must have operational and strategic effect, intended and otherwise

The theorist can have a hard time defending this essential item. Simply, it asserts that the use of any force or weapon is the realm of tactics, while the net worth of that fighting, positive or negative, belongs to operations and strategy. The reason why one must insist rigorously on this distinction is because if one does not, means and ends will be confused. In that dire, but common, event, the understanding that strategy is an instrumental function is apt to fly out of the silo. There is little difficulty persuading people that patrol clashes or aerial dogfights are tactical business; it is a far greater challenge to defend the propositions that action by a whole carrier battle group or an ICBM wing is tactical in nature.

Unfortunately, the adjective strategic is employed promiscuously as a value enhancing qualifier. Thus, we are blessed with 'strategic air power', 'strategic weapons', and, not to be left out in the devalued tactical wilderness, 'strategic land power', 'strategic sea power', 'strategic space power', and 'strategic cyber power'. The operative principle appears to rest upon nothing more cerebral than either institutional interest or politics, or the conviction that the bigger the bang the higher the horsepower and therefore the more strategic a particular force or weapon must be. It is not unreasonable, indeed it is all too plausible, to view ICBMs, say, as 'strategic' weapons. Since a definition cannot be wrong, merely eccentric and unpersuasive, it is challenging to have to argue that nuclear weapons delivered over long range are tactical in use. But the job must be done. The more significant the force deployment and employment at issue, certainly the bigger the potential bang, as from carrier battle groups, for example, and nuclear-armed ICBMs, the more necessary it is not to confuse action with effect. Even carrier-borne warfare or a strike by ICBMs will not have inherent operational or strategic meaning. As the political and military stakes escalate in a conflict, so it becomes more and more important not to confuse a military tool with its strategic and political purposes and consequences.

The concepts of 'strategic' air, land, sea, space, and now cyber power, are useful only for their merit in pointing to the ubiquity of strategic effect. Any and every action by military forces comprises a smaller or greater driver of the course of a conflict as a whole. Echevarria explains the point in this dictum thus: 'all events in war have weight; even the least can have disproportionate effects'.[73] This is its strategic effect. As soon as one demands an answer to the most vital strategist's question, 'so what?', one should be able to recognize beyond any possibility of confusion why the tactical/strategic distinction insisted upon here is essential.

Confusion over what is and what is not strategic encourages defence professionals to mislead themselves by identifying a strategic, as contrasted with operational and tactical, levels of warfare. Indeed, there is a strategic level of warfare, but it is not as all too frequently it is mis-portrayed. The strategic level is the planning for, direction and consequent exploitation of, action at the operational and tactical levels. It is not action at a higher level. Operations and tactics are action behaviours, albeit ones requiring ideas, doctrine, organization, and plans. Strategy is not itself an action behaviour, it is the translation function, in theory and in practice, of operational and tactical action into (strategic) consequences ultimately for political effect. The immediate product of strategy is strategic effect. This effect is registered in the willingness or ability of the enemy to begin or continue the struggle. Strategy can be thought of as a function which applies at every level of a contest, in peace and in war. Every combatant and combat-supporting person has to function strategically, in the sense that their behaviour has, or at the least can have, meaning and consequences beyond itself. But very few of those people will be professional strategists. The larger and generally more potentially significant the behaviour, tactical and operational, the fewer will be the number of dedicated strategists. There is an obvious sense in which everyone does strategy; at every level of command, plans are made and directed in action, while, to repeat and slightly rephrase the meaning of the Echevarria quotation offered above: all behaviours are tactical, and each and every one has, or might have, some strategic weight, positive or negative.

Explanation of this dictum concludes by quoting one of the clearest of twentieth-century military thinkers, Rear Admiral Henry E. Eccles, USN:

> The fundamental concept of strategy clearly states that strategy is the *comprehensive* employment of power, whereas tactics is the *immediate* employment of forces and weapons. *Thus the immediate employment of any force or weapons is tactical regardless of its name or title.* While the employment is tactical, the *ultimate effect*, considered in conjunction with the employment of other forces and elements of power, *is strategic.*[74]

The admiral was correct fifty years ago when he delivered his dictum, and he remains correct today.

DISTINCTIONS AND UNITY: THE STRATEGIC HEDGEHOG

In a powerful and well-argued indictment, Hew Strachan charges strategic theorists with failing practical strategists. With much justice he claims that 'strategic theory has failed to provide the tools with which to examine the conflicts now being waged [in 2007–08]'.[75] The criticism may be fair, but there is a danger that

Table 2.2 Key Distinctions

Strategy	War
Strategy	Strategies as plans, formal and informal
Strategy	Doctrine
General theory of strategy	Specific general theories of strategy
Politics	Policy
Strategy-making	Strategy execution
War	Warfare
Structure, context	Contingency

his claim could promote confusion. What kind of strategic theory allegedly is in unduly short supply?

To avoid needless opacity, it is essential to recognize no fewer than eight sets of binary distinctions that are vital to understanding. Specifically, there are vital differences between (*a*) strategy and war; (*b*) strategy and strategies, or between strategy's general theory and its historically specific appearance in tailored strategies, or, in other words, between strategy's enduring nature and its ever variable character; (*c*) strategies and doctrines; (*d*) the general theory of strategy and specific general theories (e.g. of sea power, air power); (*e*) politics and policy; (*f*) strategy-making and strategy execution; (*g*) war and warfare; and (*h*) structure or context and contingency (see Table 2.2). The preceding discussion registered these differences, but only to the degree necessary for the purpose of presenting the general theory of strategy. As quoted above, Strachan charges theorists with failing to provide the conceptual tools that practical people require in order to succeed as strategists.

The function of the general theory is to equip the strategists who must do strategy with the conceptual education they need. If the general theory is of no practical utility, then it has no utility at all. It is not the task of the general strategic theorist to understand and explain the character of any particular war, let alone to offer specific guidance for the management of a conflict, at least, not in his role as general theorist. But it is the role of the theorist to explain the nature of strategy and especially the nature of its difficulties, so that the practical strategist understands what to do, what should be expected, and what needs to be avoided if possible. The reason why it is not the responsibility of the general strategic theorist to explain the nature of particular wars is because 'all wars are things of the *same* nature', to quote Clausewitz.[76] In a justly famous dictum, the master tells us that

> The first, the supreme, the most far reaching act of judgment that the states-man and commander have to make is to establish by that test [to try to ensure that the war that is waged is appropriate to the policy goals that inspired it: CSG] the kind of war on which they are embarking; neither mistaking it for, nor trying to turn it into, something that is alien to its nature.[77]

The general theorist educates the strategic planner and commander in the universal and timeless strategic lore that applies to all strategic phenomena.

Because this lore equips all strategists with the basic concepts and understanding that they need, it can be the key to strategic success against all adversaries and in wars and warfare of any character. The dicta of the general theory equip strategists to meet the challenges posed by historically distinctive events. Nonetheless, it is well to remember that just because there may be at hand an adequate general theory of strategy, it need not follow of necessity that those who must behave as practical strategists will choose, or be able, to make good use of it. Sound education in strategic theory may be available, but that guarantees nothing. It is possible that the existence of such a general theory will simply be ignored by strategists who take pride in their operational and tactical pragmatism, much as their political masters may make a virtue of obedience to the maxim that politics is the art of the politically possible, regardless of strategic considerations or logic. Such strategists would fail to appreciate that bereft of conceptual guidance by general theory, their strategies must be akin to sailing a ship without navigation aids. It cannot be done competently, not even by strategic genius, at least not for long. The luck of the ever-improvising pragmatic strategist eventually will run out.

General strategic theory organizes the world for strategists. It is not unlike the basic necessity for mastery of human anatomy for a doctor. One can only make sense of a particular condition in the context of understanding the nature, including the structure and proper functioning, of the subject. And for the general theorist of strategy the subject is not only war or warfare. This is why Strachan could mislead the unwary when he writes, interestingly, that 'of course strategy aspires to create a theory of war'.[78] Clausewitz's theory of war is brilliant and in the main convincing, but it is too restricted in its chosen domain strictly of warfare. It can confuse by its undisciplined slides from time to time among the regions of strategy, operations, and tactics. This general theorist does not aspire to provide a theory of war, not in this book anyway. Strategy and war are not synonymous. A theory of strategy, no matter how mature and refined, cannot serve as a satisfactory theory of war. Just as a theory of war cannot pass muster as an acceptable theory of strategy. The two phenomena differ in their natures. This important issue is pursued in Chapter 3.

It is of fundamental importance to abide by what ought to be the clear distinction between *strategy* as general theory, and *strategies* as plans made and executed to cope with particular contexts. As war has a permanent nature but an ever variable character, so too do strategy and strategies, respectively. The distinction between strategy and doctrine is plain enough in theory, though frequently it is confused in practice. For example, the literature on containment as a concept in official American practice from 1947 until the end of the Cold War has never been able to decide whether its subject was a policy, a strategy, a doctrine, or all three. I. B. Holley seeks to be clear and sharp when he writes

> Military strategy involves the selection of objectives and course of action, the choice of targets, and the selection of forces to be employed. Military strategy is concerned with the ends sought and the means to attain those ends.

> Doctrine, by contrast, has nothing to say about the ends sought, as these can be ephemeral, reflecting the ebb and flow of policy.
>   Doctrine is, however related to means. If strategy is concerned with *what* is to be done, doctrine involves *how* it is to be carried out.[79]

Holley is correct in what he obviously means to say, though this theorist finds that the way he explains the distinction could promote confusion. The view taken here is that strategy in practice provides a 'story arc', probably expressed in a flexible plan, that identifies how what is to be done will be attempted. Tactical doctrine provides instruction in what experience and study reveals to be the best way for today's forces to fight, while operational (today, as noted already, largely joint) doctrine is a mixture of near-mandatory instruction manual and education that leans heavily towards prescription. What matters in this discussion is the insistence that doctrine in its several, indeed many, characters is an important transmission belt connecting strategic theory with tactical performance. But it is necessary to remember also that doctrine is favoured with many meanings, and when formalized in official publications its significance can vary from determinative for good or ill all the way to wholly irrelevant.

The role of specific general theory, as contrasted with the master that is overall general theory, is of crucial moment. At present, for example, there is extant an overall general theory of strategy, and there is military behaviour in space and cyberspace. But because general theory specific to these two unique environments is almost entirely lacking, operational strategies in them are executed bereft of much intelligent grand design. If general theory as developed here performs well as educator, practical strategists and their strategies should improve. Needless to say, since strategy necessarily is adversarial (dictum five), even should the strategists of both, or all, belligerents excel at their tasks, there are still going to be winners and losers. Skill in strategy cannot guarantee victory. As British Colonel Charles E. Callwell wrote in 1906: 'Strategy is not, however, the final arbiter in war. The battle-field decides.'[80] The elder Moltke would have approved of this maxim. This judgement serves as a useful prophylactic against the virus of strategism, the malady of an undue reverence for strategy, that is to say plans. Strategy has to be done by effective fighting at the sharp end of war that is warfare.

There is an important distinction between politics and policy. Politics is the more authoritative of the two, since it provides much of the fuel and most of the process that yields what we call policy. Even when policy has been determined, it can usually be undetermined by a political process that it might be unduly flattering to label as also a policymaking process. Whereas policy cannot emerge save by means of politics, politics can fail to produce policy. Strategists need policy guidance, but often they must contend with a policy paralysis caused by political disagreement. There is merit in acknowledging the distinction between the making and the execution of strategies. The pure light of military-strategic logic easily can be dimmed or doused by a process of planning that moves forward, backwards, and sometimes even sideways, only by compromise. Similarly, as just observed, strategies in execution may be thwarted by the weakness of strategists or the frailties of operational, tactical, and logistical performance.

The vital binary distinction which must be drawn between war and warfare advises military strategists not to forget that they should plan as members of a grand strategy team. Warfare, organized violence for political ends, does indeed distinguish wars from other events, but rivals and actual belligerents pursue their antagonism by means not exclusive to force alone. This point would be banal were it not so often substantially neglected in the historical practice of statecraft.

The final key distinction is that between structure and contingency. A helpful way to appreciate the complex relationship between the two is to appropriate a theatrical simile. A play typically has an abundance of structure, most especially a plot, but how it is performed, by whom exactly, and how the audience and actors interact during each performance, lie in the wonderful realm of contingency. Strategic history is the product of a continuous exchange and tension between structure or context, and contingency. For example, one can identify most of the elements in the structure of the deterrence relationship that may have been the keystone in the arch for non-war between the superpowers during the Cold War. Such an exercise appears to explain why deterrence had to function effectively. Deterrence seems to have been overdetermined, so strong and apparently mutually well understood were the reasons for extreme prudence in statecraft. However, all that glitters is not true gold, particularly when the treasure on offer does not comprise an adversarial process peopled by extra-cultural rational strategic persons. Peace in East–West relations was not structurally predetermined to the degree that human beings merely had to play well-scripted prudent roles. Why was this not the case? Because contingency always can rule over, indeed literally may overrule, structure. Any historical narrative has to be crafted so as to allow for the unpredictable and unpredicted detail: the domain of free will can be exaggerated, but not by much. To return to the Cold War example, the potent political, military, even moral, structures that all but guaranteed that there would not be an East–West nuclear Third World War could not mean that peace was certain. On a particular day, for example, one between 2 and 11 November 1983, to select a brief period not entirely at random, there could have been a few hours on just one day when a sickly and badly misinformed Yuri Andropov might have ordered a would-be pre-emptive nuclear first strike against the West.[81]

For another kind of example of this distinction and for further illustration of why it matters, consider the complex, indeed almost stifling, structures our society has in place for the purpose of road safety. There are structures galore. We have driver training schools, driving tests, a rigorous vehicle inspection system, an over-abundance of permanent road signs as well as real-time adaptable traffic warning message boards, and there is a superabundance of laws, rules, procedures, and cultural norms, reaffirmed by intrusive and aggressive media campaigns. All this diverse overall and cumulatively mighty effort is geared to the holy grail of road safety. And yet, accidents happen. Moreover, accidents will happen no matter what the quantity or quality of the structures for safety. This is so because we are human, and humans, all humans, make some poor decisions.

Furthermore, to quote the occasionally pithily eloquent Donald Rumsfeld, 'stuff happens'.[82] Accidents, some accidents, are normal occurrences. Fatal road accidents are rare when considered in the context of total road use, but their generic happening is entirely unremarkable.[83]

Strategic analysis by professionals as well as amateurs frequently fails to bear this key distinction sufficiently in mind. It is easy to persuade oneself, for a leading example, that peace is robust because of the many structural reasons why decisions for war would be close to absurd. Structures matter. Established institutions, processes, rules, and systems of belief do limit choices and hence purposeful behaviour. But decisions of a contraflow character are made by people, sometimes just by a person, who perceive themselves as being caught in an extraordinary situation, possibly one wherein 'necessity knows no law'.[84] Also, one should not discount the appearance of genius, defined non-normatively: the person who breaks the established rules, ignores old structures, and builds and provides a new paradigm. Structures for peace, or indeed for anything else, are always at risk of being broken. The general theorist of strategy as well as those who should be educated by him dare not lower their guard against the lethal threat of a misplaced confidence that rests on what can be called structural essentialism. Potent, though rather abstract, historical forces, may well explain almost nothing adequately, even though they appear to reveal all. Fortunately, once recognized this peril is eminently controllable. What we do by way of defence is to make generous allowance in general theory for the play of contingency, as Clausewitz insisted so powerfully.[85] This insistence upon appreciation of the role of chance and the variability of human behaviour, in the context of an adversarial relationship, is protected healthily by clear recognition of the distinction between the single general theory of strategy and the plural particular strategies of actual historical record. The contingent decisions of complex and more than a little incoherent individuals, which is to say the exercise of free will, is always more or less constrained by the structures of context.

The general theory provides practical strategists with a distressingly high calorific set of difficulties. It is worth re-emphasizing Luttwak's glittering insight that the levels of conflict enjoy no natural harmony. Policy and politics, grand and military strategy, operations, and tactics each has its unique nature and dynamics. The strategist must conduct an orchestra comprising disparate elements, even though all of the instruments should obey direction from but one interpreter of a common score.

As they are expressed in the dicta specified here and in Chapter 1, the general theory of strategy may have the misleading appearance of a Chinese menu, albeit an itemization from which one is obliged, uncomfortably, to partake of every offering. Nothing could be further from the truth. Strategy is a single subject. The strategic hedgehog rules! Together with Clausewitz, we must condemn any approach that in its analysis gives the impression, or actually advances the proposition, that the many dicta can make sense in isolation: they cannot. Every dictum matters, though admittedly those explained in Chapter 1 matter most. Although relative disadvantage on several counts among the dicta may find compensation in unusual strength elsewhere, still it is possible that any particular weakness among the dicta with reference to particular historical strategies could sink the whole enterprise of a specific war. The twelve dicta added in this chapter to the nine exposed in Chapter 1 provide a rich and complex assemblage that is a single project. In this second tranche of strategic dicta, we have exposed the following important features: the strategy-making process; ethics; culture and personality; the roles of professional strategists; difficulties and friction; strategy types; geography; technology; time; logistics; military doctrine; and tactical, operational, and strategic effect. The strategic hedgehog, unlike the strategic fox, can make sense of the complexity that he cannot avoid. He is able to function coherently and purposefully without undue distraction by one kind of challenge or another. The reason he can do this is because, hedgehog like, he comprehends one big thing, the general theory of strategy that accommodates the diversity of messy looking historical strategic realities.

Strategists of brilliance, or genius, who break the rules of prudence provided by the wisdom of the ages in general theory, are always likely to ride their luck and intuition to destruction. To adapt another inspired Clausewitzian concept, even the true strategic genius most probably will exceed his culminating point of effectiveness if he is permitted to follow his destiny as he perceives it. As all politicians eventually fail, so strategists who function largely on the fuel of individual intuition, when left in charge too long, will fail catastrophically and ruin their army and probably much else besides. In the pertinent words of one of this book's epigraphs: 'Great commanders can lead their countries to calamitous defeats.'[86] It is true that the practice of strategy is a creative art rather than a science, but this significant insight should not be interpreted as an unrestricted licence to experiment with human counters. Having outlined the general theory of strategy itself, this analysis now moves on to explain the complex relations among politics, war, and strategy. This step is an essential contextualization of strategy.

NOTES

1. For an earlier outing of this argument, see Colin S. Gray, *Modern Strategy* (Oxford: Oxford University Press, 1999), ch. 1.

2. See Isaiah Berlin, *The Hedgehog and the Fox: An Essay on Tolstoy's View of History* (New York: Mentor Books, 1957).

3. Carl von Clausewitz, *On War*, tr. Michael Howard and Peter Paret (1832–4; Princeton, NJ: Princeton University Press, 1976), 183.

4. Basil H. Liddell Hart, *Strategy: The Indirect Approach* (1941; London: Faber and Faber, 1967); Edward N. Luttwak, *Strategy: The Logic of War and Peace*, rev. edn. (1987; Cambridge, MA: Harvard University Press, 2001). Both books are packed with insight and are essential items in the travelling library of the strategist. Unfortunately, and probably inevitably, these vibrant and intellectually potent works are so persuasive that they can mislead. They advance such definite views of strategy in action that inadvertently they overreach. Their central strength is also their prime limitation. By advancing

a specific strategic thesis, especially in the case of Liddell Hart, the theorists imperil the authoritative domain of their theories. The general theory of strategy has to be above arguments for a specific strategic thesis, somehow without as a consequence rising as hot air into the intellectual vacuum of banality. J. C. Wylie, with his Clausewitzian insistence that strategy is about planning to control the enemy, just succeeds in being sufficiently general yet adequately particular. It is a delicate balance to seek and sustain. *Military Strategy: A General Theory of Power Control* (1967; Annapolis, MD: Naval Institute Press, 1989).

5. John Keegan, *The Mask of Command* (New York: Viking Penguin, 1987), and Christopher Kolenda, ed., *Leadership: The Warrior's Art* (Carlisle, PA: Army War College Foundation Press, 2001), are usefully complementary, particularly when they disagree, as they do over Alexander, for the leading example. It should be noted that to lead is not necessarily to command, while to command is not necessarily to lead. Scholars need to explore in depth the differences and interdependencies among the roles of the strategist as planner, commander, leader, and charismatic leader. These matters are probed in Chapter 6.

6. The concepts of coalition and alliance often are employed interchangeably. This is an error, though usually not one attendant with grave peril. Strictly treated, alliance refers to a negotiated, agreed relationship, with duties and rewards specified. Coalition, by contrast, is a far looser arrangement that need imply nothing more binding other than agreement upon somewhat coordinated, possibly just roughly parallel, efforts. This is a useful distinction, even though today it is more often honoured in the breach than in observance.

7. See Benjamin S. Lambeth, *The Transformation of American Air Power* (Ithaca, NY: Cornell University Press, 2000), Ch. 6; id., *NATO's Air War for Kosovo: A Strategic and Operational Assessment* (Santa Monica, CA: RAND, 2001); and Sebastian Ritchie, 'Air Power Victorious? Britain and NATO Strategy During the Kosovo Conflict', and Peter W. Gray, 'The Balkans: An Air Power Basket Case?' in Sebastian Cox and Peter W. Gray, eds., *Air Power History: Turning Points from Kitty Hawk to Kosovo* (London: Frank Cass, 2002), 318–29 and 330–44.

8. Eliot A. Cohen, *Supreme Command: Soldiers, Statesmen, and Leadership in Wartime* (New York: Free Press, 2002), xii (emphasis in the original). The reference in the quotation is to Samuel P. Huntington, *The Soldier and the State: The Theory and Politics of Civil-Military Relations* (New York: Random House, 1964).

9. Edward G. Lengel, *To Conquer Hell: The Battle of Meuse-Argonne 1918* (London: Aurum Press, 2008), 19.

10. David J. Lonsdale, *Alexander, Killer of Men: Alexander the Great and the Macedonian Art of War* (London: Constable, 2004), 3–4. In a later book, Lonsdale appears to soften his position a little. He writes: 'We should not conclude from the above discussion that ethics and culture are irrelevant; clearly they have a role to play in the judgement of the strategist. Since ethics may inform political judgements, a simple focus on "military necessity" is inadequate in the world of strategy.' So how does Lonsdale attempt to reconcile the potentially irreconcilable? His brave, but I submit not wholly persuasive, solution is to advise that 'the strategist must devise an approach that achieves the policy objective, does not create such ethical/cultural revulsion so as to undermine this goal, whilst also being tolerant of the nature of war', which is certainly good advice when it is practicable. Lonsdale, *Alexander the Great: Lessons in Strategy* (Abingdon: Routledge, 2007), 155.

11. The *Wehrmacht* provides the plainest illustration of this claim in modern times. The point is well made in Kevin W. Farrell, 'Culture of Confidence: The Tactical Excellence of the German Army of the Second World War', in Kolenda, ed., *Leadership*, 177–203. The dreadful story is told unblinkingly in Wolfram Wette, *The Wehrmacht: History, Myth, Reality* (Cambridge, MA: Harvard University Press, 2002).

12. Yehoshafat Harkabi, *Theory and Doctrine in Classical and Modern Strategy*, Working Papers 35 (Washington, DC: Wilson Center, Smithsonian Institution, 31 October 1981), 20. This long neglected paper truly is a lost gem that merits renewed circulation.

13. Helpful guides include: Lawrence Sondhaus, *Strategic Culture and Ways of War* (Abingdon: Routledge, 2006); Stuart Poare, 'Strategic Culture', in John Glenn, Darryl Howlett, and Poare, eds., *Neorealism Versus Strategic Culture* (Aldershot: Ashgate, 2004), 45–71; Jeffrey S. Lantis and Darryl Howlett, 'Strategic Culture', in John Baylis and others, eds., *Strategy in the Contemporary World: An Introduction to Strategic Studies*, 2nd edn. (Oxford: Oxford University Press, 2007), 82–100; Jeannie L. Johnson, Kerry M. Kartchner, and Jeffrey A. Larsen, eds., *Strategic Culture and Weapons of Mass Destruction: Culturally Based Insights into Comparative National Security Policymaking* (New York: Palgrave Macmillan, 2009); while Patrick Porter, *Military Orientalism: Eastern War Through Western Eyes* (London: C. Hurst, 2009), provides a sceptical appraisal. In addition, two highly ambitious and moderately successful mature studies merit assessment as important contributions to our understanding: Richard Ned Lebow, *A Cultural Theory of International Relations* (Cambridge: Cambridge University Press, 2008); and Martin van Creveld, *The Culture of War* (New York: Ballantine Books, 2008).

14. Maurice, *Maurice's Strategikon: Handbook of Byzantine Military Strategy*, tr. George T. Dennis (ca. 600 BCE; Philadelphia, PA: University of Pennsylvania Press, 1984), Book XI.

15. See John W. Dower, *War Without Mercy: Race and Power in the Pacific War* (New York: Pantheon Books, 1986). For an earlier broader canvas that presaged the appalling misbehaviour of the late 1930s and the 1940s, see Alan Kramer, *Dynamics of Destruction: Culture and Mass Killing in the First World War* (Oxford: Oxford University Press, 2007). The atrocities of the Second World War and of the 1990s are almost overfamiliar for continuing impact upon attitudes. It is less well known that Africa and the Balkans in the years leading up to the First World War do not exactly qualify as zones even of relative decency in quasi-military behaviour. See Isabel V. Hull, *Absolute Destruction: Military Culture and the Practices of War in Imperial Germany* (Ithaca, NY: Cornell University Press, 2005). The bestiality of conduct by all parties in the Balkan Wars of 1912–13 is amply attested in Carnegie Endowment for International Peace, *Report of the International Commission to Inquire into the Causes and Conduct of the Balkan Wars* (New York: The Endowment, 1914). Richard C. Hall, *The Balkan Wars, 1912–1913: Prelude to the First World War* (London: Routledge, 2000), is an accessible introduction to the seemingly ever atrocious Balkans.

16. There is abundant evidence in support of this claim. For example, see Henrik Eberle and Matthias Uhl, eds., *The Hitler Book: The Secret Dossier Prepared for Stalin*, tr. Giles Macdonogh (London: John Murray, 2005).

17. US Army and Marine Corps, *Counterinsurgency Field Manual: U.S. Army Field Manual No. 3–24, and Marine Corps Warfighting Publication No. 3–33.5* (2006; Chicago: University of Chicago Press, 2007). The discussion by Robert H. Scales, Jr. in 'Culture-Centric Warfare', U.S. Naval Institute *Proceedings*, 130 (October 2004), 32–6, was

a noteworthy sign of the times, as is (UK) Assistant Chief of the Defence Staff (Development, Concepts, and Doctrine), *The Significance of Culture to the Military*, Joint Doctrine Note 1/09 (Shrivenham: Development, Concepts, and Doctrine Centre, Ministry of Defence, January 2009). The official American 'cultural turn' is documented in Sheila Miyoshi Jager, *On the Uses of Cultural Knowledge* (Carlisle, PA: Strategic Studies Institute, US Army War College, November 2007). I am indebted to Patrick Porter for the expression 'cultural turn'. See his *Military Orientalism*.

18. Raymond Aron, *Peace and War: A Theory of International Relations* (Garden City, NY: Doubleday, 1966), 1. Aron began his classic work with these words.

19. Bernard Brodie, *War and Politics* (New York: Macmillan, 1973), 332.

20. Carl Builder, 'Keeping the Strategic Flame', *Joint Force Quarterly*, 14 (winter 1996–7), 76–84, says much of what needs to be said.

21. Archibald Wavell, *Speaking Generally: Broadcasts, Orders and Addresses in Time of War (1939–43)* (London: Macmillan, 1946), 79.

22. This argument is advanced and supported convincingly in Max Hastings, *Armageddon: The Battle for Germany, 1944–45* (London: Macmillan, 2004).

23. David G. Chandler, *The Military Maxims of Napoleon*, tr. George C. D'Aguilar (1901; New York: Macmillan, 1987), 81, 'Maxim LXXVII'.

24. Frederick was not always great. See Robert M. Citino, *The German Way of War: From the Thirty Years' War to the Third Reich* (Lawrence, KS: University Press of Kansas, 2005), ch. 2. Apprenticeship in strategy is apt to be costly in blood and money.

25. Sun Tzu, *The Art of War*, tr. Ralph D. Sawyer (ca. 490 BCE; Boulder, CO: Westview Press, 1994), 167.

26. Ibid. 60.

27. As psychologist Norman F. Dixon, *On the Psychology of Military Incompetence* (London: Futura Publications, 1976), has explained, incompetence is not proof positive of stupidity or poor professional education. Some professionally very well-educated soldiers have failed abysmally for reasons that additional years of study and experience could not have prevented. For example, an inclination to indecisiveness is incurable. Similarly, the associated malady of an unwillingness to accept responsibility is a systemic character flaw.

28. This author has had extensive first-hand experience of the never-ending quest by important institutions within the US defence community to make a quantifiable science out of an art. For documented evidence of an American methodological malfeasance which produced and then supported unsound policy and strategy, see Keith B. Payne, *The Great American Gamble: Deterrence Theory and Practice from the Cold War to the Twenty-First Century* (Fairfax, VA: National Institute Press, 2008).

29. The poor relationship between Lloyd George and the Commander-in-Chief of the British Expeditionary Force (BEF) is well handled in Gary Mead, *The Good Soldier: The Biography of Douglas Haig* (London: Atlantic Books, 2007), for example, see 272, 275ff. The Churchill–Wavell antagonism is treated empathetically in Carlo D'Este, *Warlord: A Life of Churchill at War, 1874–1945* (London: Allen Lane, 2009), esp. ch. 46. On the one side, Wavell, albeit brilliant, was uncommunicative and declined to attempt to woo his Prime Minister. On the other side, Churchill needed to be wooed, and insisted on endeavouring to play the role of strategist, sometimes including operational commander, as well as policymaker. D'Este's account of their quite appallingly dysfunctional relationship is dreadfully convincing. Wavell has not exactly been over-examined by biographers, but the recent study by Adrian Fort does the job admirably. In *Archibald Wavell: The Life and Times of an Imperial Servant* (London: Jonathan

Cape, 2009), Fort treats effectively the necessary mixture of personality, culture, and historical context.

30. Thomas Babington, Lord Macaulay, *Horatius Keeps the Bridge* (1842; London: Phoenix, 1996).

31. Helmuth von Moltke, *Moltke on the Art of War: Selected Writings*, ed. Daniel J. Hughes (Novato, CA: Presidio Press, 1995), 45.

32. Clausewitz, 119.

33. Ibid. 121.

34. Ibid. 104.

35. See Barry D. Watts, *Clausewitzian Friction and Future War*, McNair Paper 68, rev. edn. (Washington, DC: Institute for National Strategic Studies, National Defense University, 2004).

36. Lawrence Freedman, *The Transformation of Strategic Affairs*, Adelphi Paper 379 (Abingdon: Routledge for the International Institute for Strategic Studies, 2006), 36.

37. Luttwak, *Strategy*, xii (emphasis added).

38. Sun Tzu; Liddell Hart, *Strategy*; Wylie, *Military Strategy*; Arthur Jones, *The Art of War in the Western World* (Urbana, IL: University of Illinois Press, 1987), esp. 54–7; and Thomas C. Schelling, *Arms and Influence* (New Haven, CT: Yale University Press, 1966), 2–6.

39. Sun Tzu, 147–50, 197–99. For the fairly full story, see Ralph D. Sawyer, *The Seven Military Classics of Ancient China*, tr. Sawyer (Boulder, CO: Westview Press, 1993); id., *The Tao of War: The Martial Tao Te Ching* (Boulder, CO: Westview Press, 1999).

40. Wylie, *Military Strategy*, 24–5.

41. Simon Anglim, 'Manoeuvre Warfare', in the *International Encyclopaedia of Defence Studies*, forthcoming.

42. See Robert T. Foley, *German Strategy and the Path to Verdun: Erich von Falkenhayn and the Development of Attrition, 1870–1916* (Cambridge: Cambridge University Press, 2005). For centuries German military professionals recognized that Germany could not win wars of attrition (*Stellungskrieg*, war of position), only wars wherein annihilation is achieved by swift decisive manoeuvre. See Citino, *German Way of War*, 305, which records the telling fact that on 26 December 1941 the august journal, the *Militar-Wochenblatt*, offered its expert readers the dreadful news of the unwelcome, indeed ultimately fatal, arrival of '*Stellungskrieg* in the east'. In short, the great German manoeuverist gamble had failed. There has long been argument over just what is, or should be, meant by manoeuvre strategy, as contrasted with an attritional strategy. Exceptional conceptual clarity is achieved in US Marine Corps, *Strategy*, MCDP 1–1 (Washington, DC: U. S. Government Printing Office, 1998), 54, 55. 'The goal of a strategy of annihilation is to deprive the enemy of the ability to resist, to make him militarily helpless.' The marines make it plain that the enemy does not literally have to be physically annihilated, only rendered incapable of further resistance. Decisive manoeuvre is the preferred method to secure this highly desirable, albeit ambitious, end. 'The objective of the second approach—a strategy of erosion [i.e., attrition: CSG]—is to convince the enemy that settling the political dispute will be easier and the outcome more attractive than continued conflict.' The attritional strategist erodes the enemy's assets, soldier by soldier and dollar by dollar. But the transaction costs are heavy, since that erosion has to be paid for in like currencies. The manoeuvrist credo is well represented in a large library of not quite sacred texts. These are a good place to begin: William S. Lind, *Maneuver Warfare Handbook* (Boulder, CO: Westview Press, 1985); Richard D. Hooker, Jr., ed., *Maneuver Warfare: An Anthology* (Novato, CA:

Presidio Press, 1993); and, in addition to the marines' *Strategy* already cited, US Marine Corps, *Warfighting*, MCDP-1 (Washington, DC: U. S. Government Printing Office, 1997).

43. See Robert A. Pape, *Bombing to Win: Air Power and Coercion in War* (Ithaca, NY: Cornell University Press, 1996), and the excellent critiques in 'Theory and Evidence in Security Studies: Debating Robert A. Pape's *Bombing to Win*', *Security Studies*, 7 (winter 1997/1998), 91–214, and Patrick C. Bratton, 'A Coherent Theory of Coercion? The Writings of Robert Pape', *Comparative Strategy*, 22 (October–November 2003), 355–72.

44. Stephan Fruhling, 'Offense and Defense in Strategy', *Comparative Strategy*, 28 (November–December 2009), 463–77, is useful.

45. On 'fortress Constantinople', see Edward N. Luttwak, *The Grand Strategy of the Byzantine Empire* (Cambridge, MA: The Belknap Press of Harvard University Press, 2009), 67–77.

46. Sun Tzu, *The Art of War*, tr. Samuel B. Griffith (ca. 490 BCE; Oxford: Clarendon Press, 1963), 77.

47. The most convincing explanation of Britain's vital, if limited (as usual in war), strategic victory in the second half of 1940, is to be found in Stephen Bungay's superb somewhat revisionist study, *The Most Dangerous Enemy: A History of the Battle of Britain* (London: Aurum Press, 2000).

48. Carl Builder, *The Masks of War: American Military Styles in Strategy and Analysis* (Baltimore: Johns Hopkins University Press, 1989), addresses the admittedly exceptionally virulent character of American inter-service differences. The story of sometimes dysfunctionally distinctive service world views truly is a global, though less than grand, narrative.

49. See Philip Anthony Towle, *Pilots and Rebels: The Use of Aircraft in Unconventional Wars* (London: Brassey's, 1989); James S. Corum and Wray R. Johnson, *Airpower in Small Wars: Fighting Insurgents and Terrorists* (Lawrence, KS: University Press of Kansas, 2003); and Alan J. Vick and others, *Air Power in the New Counterinsurgency Era: The Strategic Importance of USAF Advisory and Assistance Missions*, MG-509-AF (Santa Monica, CA: RAND, 2006).

50. Naturally, the lower the orbit the narrower the line-of-sight track and hence the larger the number of satellites required for extensive coverage, as well as the easier it is for an enemy to reach up or across and touch them. A permanently persisting presence in geosynchronous orbit (at 22,300 miles altitude) is agreeably distant from some terrestrial or low-orbit-based threats, but is unduly distant for the resolution needed for terrestrial imaging. Also, since satellites need a particular arc length of separation if they are to use the same frequencies for broadcasting, the number of practicable geosynchronous orbital slots is strictly limited. Martin Libicki, *Conquest in Cyberspace: National Security and Information Warfare* (Cambridge: Cambridge University Press, 2007), 5n3. See Lynn Dutton and others, *Military Space* (London: Brassey's (UK), 1990), and Jim Oberg, *Space Power Theory* (Washington, DC: U. S. Government Printing Office, 1999), for the most basic of basics, especially regarding the physical principles that govern orbital parameters (laws of planetary motion), otherwise known familiarly as 'orbitology'. Contemporary issues of defence, and national security more broadly, are treated controversially in Joan Johnson-freese, *Space as a Strategic Asset* (New York: Columbia University Press, 2007), and James Clay Moltz, *The Politics of Space Security: Strategic Restraint and the Pursuit of National Interests* (Stanford, CA: Stanford University Press, 2008). By controversial, this author means

that these books are helpful, but that he does not agree with the major thrust of their arguments.

51. I am particularly grateful to Colonel 'Coyote' Smith, USAF, and to Dr. Everett C. Dolman of the School of Advanced Air and Space Studies, US Air University, for their advice on space and cyber warfare. Whether or not I have been worthy of their educational efforts, assuredly they will recognize the spore of their expertise in my writing.

52. The most powerful statement of technophile philosophy is J. F. C. Fuller, *Armament and History: A Study of the Influence of Armament on History from the Dawn of Classical Warfare to the Second World War* (London: Eyre and Spottiswoode, 1946).

53. Richard O. Hundley, *Past Revolutions, Future Transformations: What Can the History of Revolutions in Military Affairs Tell Us About Transforming the U.S. Military?* MR-1029-DARPA (Santa Monica, CA: RAND, 1999), 27.

54. Dennis E. Showalter, *Railroads and Rifles: Soldiers, Technology and the Unification of Germany* (Hamden, CT: Archon Books, 1975), Part I, remains essential; as is Edwin A. Pratt, *The Rise of Rail-Power in War and Conquest, 1833–1914* (Philadelphia: J. B. Lippincott, 1916); while T. G. Otter and Keith Neilson, eds., *Railways and International Politics: Paths of Empire, 1848–1945* (Abingdon: Routledge, 2006); and Felix Patrikeeff and Harold Shukman, *Railways and the Russo–Japanese War: Transporting War* (Abingdon: Routledge, 2007), add breadth and depth to the story.

55. See Michael I. Handel, 'Clausewitz in the Age of Technology', in Handel, ed., *Clausewitz and Modern Strategy* (London: Frank Cass, 1986), 51–92.

56. Luttwak, *Strategy*, drives home the pervasive constraints upon strategic choice placed by the need to take prudent account of enemy expectations and behaviour.

57. An especially useful perspective on the later American years in Vietnam is provided by Lewis Sorley, *Thunderbolt: From the Battle of the Bulge to Vietnam and Beyond: General Creighton Abrams and the Army of His Times* (New York: Simon & Schuster, 1992), chs. 14–24.

58. Clausewitz, 129.

59. Ibid. 128 (emphasis in the original).

60. Ibid. 129.

61. Omar Bradley quoted in Thomas M. Kane, *Military Logistics and Strategic Performance* (London: Frank Cass, 2001), xiv.

62. Wavell, *Speaking Generally*, 79 (emphasis in the original).

63. Clausewitz, 190–2.

64. By way of a sample of the logistics literature, see Henry E. Eccles, *Military Concepts and Philosophy* (New Brunswick, NJ: Rutgers University Press, 1965); Martin van Creveld, *Supplying War: Logistics from Wallenstein to Patton* (Cambridge: Cambridge University Press, 1977); George C. Thorpe, *Pure Logistics* (Washington, DC: National Defense University Press, 1986); Julian Thompson, *The Lifeblood of War: Logistics of Armed Conflict* (London: Brassey's, 1991); John A. Lynn, ed., *Feeding Mars: Logistics in Western Warfare from the Middle Ages to the Present* (Boulder, CO: Westview Press, 1993); Ian Malcolm Brown, *British Logistics on the Western* Front (Westport, CT: Praeger Publishers, 1998); and Kane, *Military Logistics*.

65. I. B. Holley, Jr., *Technology and Doctrine: Essays on a Challenging Relationship* (Maxwell AFB, AL: Air University Press, August 2004), 1.

66. David E. Johnson, *Learning Large Lessons: The Evolving Roles of Ground Power and Air Power in the Post-Cold War Era*, MG-405 (Santa Monica, CA: RAND, 2006), 147–8. I have elected to quote Johnson's clear explanation so fully, because many of the

readers of this book who are not military professionals are likely to be relatively unfamiliar with the nature and purposes of doctrine.

67. One of the better histories of Gulf War I did not pull its punches. 'The campaign was "joint" more in name than in fact. Each service fought its own war, concentrating on its own piece of the conflict with a single-minded intensity, and the commanders in Washington and Riyadh failed to fully harmonize the war plans. In this sense, the Gulf War shows that there is much to be done if the American armed forces are to operate in a truly coordinated and integrated manner.' Michael R. Gordon and Bernard E. Trainor, *The Generals' War: The Inside Story of the Conflict in the Gulf* (Boston: Little, Brown, 1994), xiv. The same authors were more impressed by the US Military's 'joint' performance in Gulf War II of 2003. Gordon and Trainor, *Cobra II: The Inside Story of the Invasion and Occupation of Iraq* (London: Atlantic Books, 2006), 499. Unfortunately, the improved jointness in military behaviour in 2003 compared with 2001 was dwarfed in significance by the political and military mistakes of that year and subsequently.

68. Historians appear agreed that Operation 'Weserübung represented the best joint performance of German forces in the war'. Williamson Murray, *German Military Effectiveness* (Baltimore: Nautical and Aviation Publishing Company of America, 1992), 18.

69. Antulio J. Echevarria II, *After Clausewitz: German Military Thinkers Before the Great War* (Lawrence, KS: University Press of Kansas, 2001), 218–19.

70. Harkabi, *Theory and Doctrine*, 19.

71. Ibid. 19–20.

72. Andrew Gordon, 'The Doctrine Debate: Having the Last Word', in Michael Duffy, Theo Farrell, and Geoffrey Sloan, eds., *Doctrine and Military Effectiveness*, Strategic Policy Studies 1 (Exeter: Strategic Policy Studies Group of the Britannia Royal Naval College and Exeter University, 1997), 50.

73. Antulio J. Echevarria II, 'Dynamic Inter-Dimensionality: A Revolution in Military Theory', *Joint Force Quarterly*, 15 (spring 1997), 36.

74. Eccles, *Military Concepts and Philosophy*, 48 (emphasis in the original).

75. Hew Strachan, 'Strategy and the Limitation of War', *Survival*, 50 (February–March 2008), 51.

76. Clausewitz, 606. This declaration by Clausewitz is about as clear as a claim can be. However, the great man, while certainly not speaking with forked tongue, was not beyond being simultaneously apparently on both sides of a tricky issue. With respect to the particular matter of concern here, Clausewitz begins Chapter 2 of Book One as follows: 'The preceding chapter showed that the nature of war is complex *and changeable*' (emphasis added), 90. What Clausewitz would seem to believe is that wars can differ so greatly in their character that they are different phenomena. At least, sometimes he believes that. Happily, we can apply commonsense, agree with the Prussian that wars do indeed vary enormously in their character, while declining to agree with him when he wishes to claim that war can change its nature. The excellent Echevarria elects to endorse Clausewitz's rather flexible, though not wholly unreasonable, two-track view. I disagree, respectfully, I am convinced that war does not change its nature, no matter how disparate the characters of particular wars. See Echevarria's argument in *Clausewitz and Contemporary War* (Oxford: Oxford University Press, 2007), 55–8. One needs to be alert to the danger of theological disputation among theorists. My difference with Clausewitz and Echevarria is not one of substance. All three of us agree that wars differ among themselves widely. Also, we agree that all wars

have potent features in common. The disagreement reduces to a decision on whether or not one is willing to call a great difference in war's character a change in its nature, that is all.

77. Ibid. 88.
78. Strachan, 'Strategy and the Limitation of War', 36, 37.
79. Holley, *Technology and Doctrine*, 2–3 (emphasis in the original).
80. Charles E. Callwell, *Small Wars: A Tactical Textbook for Imperial Soldiers*, 3rd edn. (1906; London: Greenhill Books, 1990), 90. History suggests that almost as often as not the favourable political decision sought through war in warfare is decided neither strategically nor tactically. Rather is it won or lost by the political skill with which politicians play the hand they have extant, or that they can bluff others into believing that they have. Diplomacy has much to learn from poker. The military context must always be important, but it need not be conclusively and exclusively so. That said, unlike poker, skilled diplomacy that relies on a truly hollow military reality will always have its bluff called eventually, usually with fatal consequences.
81. Between 2 and 11 November 1983, NATO conducted a command post nuclear release exercise (Able Archer) that fuelled the suspicions of a highly paranoid and exceptionally anxious ailing Soviet leadership that a US nuclear missile attack was imminent. An authoritative American source, writing with the ever valuable wisdom of hindsight, is Robert M. Gates, *From the Shadows: The Ultimate Insider's Story of Five Presidents and How They Won the Cold War* (New York: Simon & Schuster, 1996), 270–3. See also Christopher Andrew, *The Defence of the Realm: The Authorized History of MI5* (London: Allen Lane, 2009), 722–3. An interesting strategic analysis is Stephen J. Cimbala, *The Dead Volcano: The Background and Effects of Nuclear War Complacency* (Westport CT: Praeger Publishers, 2002), ch. 4, 'A Near Escape? The 1983 "War Scare" and Nuclear Danger'.
82. Donald H. Rumsfeld, then US Secretary of Defense, speaking on 11 April 2003 in response to a journalist's question about the looting in Baghdad.
83. Over the course of a lifetime, the odds on a Briton dying in an air crash are 2,500,000 to 1, in a train crash 50,000 to 1, and on the road 200 to 1. Harvey Elliott, 'Despite Madrid, flying is still safer than ever', *The Times*, 22 August 2008. On the important subject of 'normal accident' theory, see Scott D. Sagan, *The Limits of Safety: Organizations, Accidents, and Nuclear Weapons* (Princeton, NJ: Princeton University Press, 1993), ch. 1.
84. Imperial German Chancellor Theobold von Bethmann Hollweg speaking in the Reichstag on 4 August 1914 excusing Germany's invasion of Belgium. Quoted in Michael Walzer, *Just and Unjust Wars: A Moral Argument with Historical Illustrations*, 3rd edn. (New York: Basic Books, 1997), 240.
85. Clausewitz, 85–6.
86. John Lee, *The Warlords: Hindenburg and Ludendorff* (London: Weidenfeld & Nicholson, 2005), 194.

3

Politics, War, and Strategy

FOLLOW THE LEADER

British journalist and commentator Simon Jenkins writes that 'strategy can go to the wall but not politics'.[1] Although he was indicating only the contestable sins of contemporary British defence planning, his judgement is a potent truth that must figure in the general theory of strategy just as it plays in the course of strategic history. The higher and more consequential the level of real-world strategy-making and execution, the greater is the influence of politics. In a sense this is simply a necessary truth, since the hierarchy from tactics up to grand strategy has politics, or policy—often confusingly—itself as the next step on the ladder. The topmost rung is occupied by vision, the misty realm wherein politics and cultural yearning meet.

This chapter very largely is about politics. Its purposes are to develop, explain, and to some degree apply major ideas identified as belonging in the general theory of strategy; to contextualize the strategy function; and to provide greater depth to the theory. As if those immodest ambitions were insufficient, in addition the discussion provides essential links to the rest of the book. Here, theory meets practice; this is appropriate as well as necessary because it is a vital task of strategies to translate ideas into plans. The ideas key to this analysis are sufficiently obscured by misuse and downright abuse as to merit description as a catalogue of confusion. Clausewitz, for all his brilliance, sometimes contributes to a general lack of conceptual clarity as well as to the reverse. This is the problem when there is one clearly leading text in a field.[2] It leads and it misleads. Were the accidental misleading done by anyone other than Clausewitz, the damage to comprehension would be much less. Respectful though one must be of such a luminous work as *On War*, it is a mistake, at the least it is needlessly costly, to orient strategic theoretical effort today mainly upon and around it. Scholars should be less concerned to demonstrate that they understand what Clausewitz really means, and rather more to be certain that they grasp fully what they themselves ought to think. The former practice rests upon the implicit assumption that the closest we can come to strategic truth is always to be found in *On War* and probably only in *On War*. In effect, this unhealthy degree of veneration elevates *On War* to the inappropriate status of a sacred text. It is wiser to endorse Hew Strachan's sensible view that *On War* was, indeed remains, a work in progress as strategic theory is now.[3] Clausewitz did not construct the definitive conceptual edifice. What is more, it is unlikely that he aspired to do so.

When we claim that the development and articulation of the general theory of strategy is unfinished business, we do not mean to imply that we keep discovering new strategic ideas or new strategic relationships. We do not. What has happened is that we are ever revisiting a stable core of ideas and pressing them in terms comfortable for our times and circumstances. Strategic knowledge is not at all akin to knowledge in the hard sciences. Our grasp of the strategic function may or may not be better than that held by Alexander or Gustavus Adolphus, but if there is a noteworthy difference among us it has nothing to do with further research, or new historical experience. Clausewitz certainly produced by far the most helpful meditation on war and strategy that there has ever been, before or since. But the more significant of the ideas that he articulated so brilliantly could, in principle, though assuredly not in practice, have been written at any time in history. Those who till the field of strategy for the purpose of producing a healthy crop of general theory, must always plough, and plough again, the same field.

This chapter proceeds by clarifying the complex relationship between the theories of strategy and of war; next it unravels the much misunderstood nexi between politics and policy in regard to strategy and war. The analysis then moves on to explain and explore the connections among war, warfare, and grand strategy. This is followed by explication of vital differences between the theory of strategy and its consequences, and their implications for actual strategies as plans and operational behaviour. Finally, the chapter examines the proposition that strategy is prediction as well as aspiration.

THE THEORY OF WAR AND THE THEORY OF STRATEGY

The general theories of war and of strategy must be distinctive because their subjects are by no means synonymous. But despite having drawn that line in the sand, it is plain enough to see that the two share much common ground. More often than not, though, theorists and others who should know better elect to ignore the difference. As an intellectual exercise, one can make cases both for including the theory of war in the theory of strategy and for vice versa. A third option is favoured here, however, one which treats the others as unsound and harmful in their possible practical consequences. This third way regards war and strategy as distinctively definable phenomena that overlap. Even if some strategic theorists do aspire to be general theorists of war, they should not harbour the illusion that the road to the theory of war lies through strategy country.

The condition of war is logically and practically superior to strategy, since the latter is strictly instrumental in the conduct of the former. However, it is commonplace and arguably wise to follow Clausewitz and treat war as an instrument of policy—or politics—while strategy is instrumental in matching warfare to that policy. So, both war and strategy legitimately can be viewed instrumentally. It may be worth adding that as war is instrumental for policy, so too is peace, at least it may be. Instead of being regarded existentially as the natural state of rest of politically organized humankind, peace can be treated as a condition chosen by policy.[4] Since such an attitude appears to legitimize decisions to fight, it is not exactly popular.

Despite the contestably dominant role of war in human history and the depth and extent of the popular desire for peace, it is perhaps surprising to discover how unimpressive is the literature on the nature of war and on the relationships between war and peace and peace and war. There is little theory of war beyond Clausewitz that is worth citing, let alone studying.[5] The general literature on war and peace, as contrasted with studies of specific wars and periods of peace, is unmistakeably short of great works. This is a harsh but unavoidable judgement. The literature is as vast as it is vastly underwhelming intellectually. Given the large quantity and sometimes the high quality of scholarly talent that has been applied to the subject of war, since 1919 in particular, it is surprising that so little of strong merit, let alone obvious practical value, has been produced. Somewhat reluctantly, one is driven towards the tentative conclusion either that the subject inherently is unmanageable, or, as likely, that scholars persistently have so mishandled their mission that they could not deliver a helpful level of understanding. It seems improbable that so many scholars, working so hard, with so powerful a motivation—to rid the world of the scourge of war—for so long a period, could have failed so badly. Lest I be mistaken, I must rush to explain that there are many good books on war and warfare, works full of perception. But none of them save for *On War*, singly or in combination, is even close to being electable as The Book on War. Moreover, for all its insights and structural strengths, even the Prussian's theory falls way short of the necessary inclusiveness. *On War* tells the story of wars underway in warfare, leaving other vital perspectives, causation and consequences for non-trivial examples, barely touched. This is not to criticize Clausewitz for what he did not attempt. But it is to claim that *On War* does not provide a satisfactory general theory of war, though it is the text from which to start.

It is tempting to argue that strategy pertains principally and most significantly to the multidimensional relationship and context known as war, and to the warfare waged in war. Nonetheless, such temptation has to be resisted because not only is strategy relevant to various conditions of non-war, or peace, but its domain can also not be confined to the military. A strategy of deterrence, say, chosen for the purpose of preventing war, can be said to be more important than are plans for the conduct of war, at least until it fails. There is at least one potential trap into which theorists can wander that poses a common menace to the understanding of strategy and of war. The trap may be tagged as definition creep and occasional leap.

As scholarly rigour uncovers ever more aspects to, and complex connections among, the phenomena known as strategy and war, it is apt to threaten to kill the subject through undisciplined over-inclusiveness. To explain: if a theory of war also has to be a theory of peace, surely it needs to be a theory of history also. It has to explain everything in human history. After all, what plainly is not relevant to war and peace? Similarly, if strategy as grand strategy in peace and war orchestrates the threat and irregularly periodic employment of all the assets of security communities as they protect their interests as they define them, which matters should be excluded from consideration? Theories of everything are theories of nothing. They can have no explanatory power. Chapters 1 and 2 provided the general theory of strategy in such a manner as to flag its boundaries. For one leading feature, the theory requires all strategic matters to entail some plausible, perhaps better stated as not wholly implausible, connection to the threat or use of military force. Strachan is useful when he advises that:

> Security concerns are not war, and many so-called security issues are being or will be resolved without a military dimension . . . If we imagine that insecurity itself is war, then we are in danger of militarising issues that would be best not militarised, of creating wars when there do not need to be wars, and of taking hammers to drive in screws.[6]

Amen. Conceptual imperialism promotes an intellectual hegemony that confuses policymakers and threatens to deny them the tools of genuinely strategic thought. Inadvertent conceptual opacity is a self-inflicted wound with potentially catastrophic consequences. How events, actual and anticipated, are defined and thereby conceptually assigned must largely determine how governments choose to respond to them. Readers are recommended to consider the wisdom in the epigraph to this book on the value of strategic concepts that I have borrowed gratefully from Lawrence Freedman. If it is essential to avoid confusion over what is and what is not strategic, it is no less necessary to have a conceptually unimpeded understanding of war. Strachan insists fairly plausibly that 'the most important single task for strategy is to understand the nature [*sic.* should be character: CSG] of the war it is addressing'.[7] This key Clausewitzian point requires augmentation by a like insistence upon recognition of the need to understand war itself in general.

The principal tasks of the general theorist and the practicing strategist are quite different. The former must understand and explain the nature of his subject for the purpose of educating the strategist in how to think about strategy; the latter must strive to devise plans which shape and fit historically unique real-world circumstances. The general theorist identifies eternal truths, objective knowledge, as Clausewitz puts it, and presents them in ways as useful as possible to the practitioner. The strategist as planner and executive does not merely accept the course of history as a bequest he cannot alter. On the contrary, his job, the job of operational strategies, is to effect as much control over the path taken by future history as possible. Strategy as plan constitutes an explicit prediction of events, should all proceed as desired and contingently expected—which it never does, of course. Given that the principal core competency of the strategist is the ability to direct armed forces in war, not necessarily to command and lead them, it is necessary to ask what is known about this phenomenon, or phenomena, we call war.[8] Is there a general theory of war to which the practicing strategist can turn

Table 3.1 Questions for the General Theory of War

Question	Subject
1. What is war?	Nature of war
2. Why does war occur? What is it about?	Causes and origins of, conditions (contexts), and triggers for war
3. Does war lead to peace? Does peace lead to war?	Consequences of war
4. What is war like?	Nature and experience of war
5. How is war fought?	Character of war
6. Why is war won or lost?	Reasons for superior/inferior performance

for the education necessary to equip him to cope with the challenge presented by a particular war?

The general theory of war needs to answer six questions. What is war? Why does war occur, what is it about? Does war lead to peace, does peace lead to war? What is war like? How is war fought? Why is war won or lost? Taken in order, these questions address war's nature; origins, causes and triggers; nature again; consequences; character; and methods (ways and means). Table 3.1 presents this approach.

Although the general theory of strategy and its manifestation in strategies as operational designs apply in times of peace as well as war, armed force must always be a relevant concern. Either it will occupy centre stage as current active hostilities, or it will be waiting in the wings as a fairly plausible possible development. This is why the general theorist of strategy must draw upon whatever he can locate by way of a general theory of war. He is tasked with planning the commitment of some fraction of the security community's assets, pre-eminently the military, to a particular war.

What is war? It is politically organized violence, for the tersest possible definition. To be clearer still, one might prefer to define war as organized violence carried on by political units against each other for political motives. In 1994, John Keegan argued the case powerfully for war to be regarded as a cultural rather than a political phenomenon.[9] He was both right and wrong. War certainly is and has always been a cultural happening. But to acknowledge war's cultural content, even motivation, is by no means to exclude politics. Politics and culture are not alternative explanations for war. Politics always and everywhere is about relative power and is inalienable from human behaviour in a social setting. Furthermore, the social setting of every human being provides more or less cultural programming. It has to follow that war as a tool of politics must be a cultural phenomenon in some measure. In other words, for all his erudition and linguistic charm, Keegan discovered and argued for nothing other than a necessary truth, though assuredly a most important one.

For the heart of the grim matter we have to turn, as usual, to Clausewitz. The Prussian's 'wondrous trinity' reduces the nature of war to an inherently highly unstable compound comprising the combined interdependent effects of 'violence, hatred, and enmity', 'chance and probability', and 'reason'. This primary trinity approximates to 'the people', . . . 'the commander and his army', and 'the government'.[10] While reason (the government) is logically the superior element in the trinity, in historical practice quite often this is not so. In common with Thucydides triptych of 'fear, honour, and interest', the Clausewitzian trinity has to be allowed to serve as the starting gate for a general theory of war.[11]

Next, why does war occur? What is it about? Unlike the relationship between strategy as general theory and strategy as operational plan, thus far there have been apparently insuperable difficulties preventing translation of war's general theory into useful theory applicable to particular wars. In the immediate aftermath of the Great War of 1914–18, scholars, philanthropists, and even some politicians, among a multinational cast of thousands, sought to solve 'the problem' of war.[12] But what is 'the problem'? The trouble was that there were many theories purporting to explain war, none of which held unchallenged intellectual, let alone political, sway. Probably the closest that the activists and scholars could come to a consensus was on the proposition that since wars required armaments, disarmament would be the all cases answer. Even had this theory been highly plausible, which it was not, it failed the strategy test of practicability. Would it work? It may work in theory—disarmed polities cannot wage war—but it does not work in historical practice. The reason is because competitive armaments are only a symptom and expression, an instrument, for what can be a mixture of deep and shallow motives. Polities do not fight because they are armed; rather do they arm because either they wish to fight or they fear that they may be obliged to do so whether or not they welcome the opportunity. Moreover, to cite the disarmament paradox, the greater the inter-communal hostility, the greater the need for disarmament. But, alas, the greater the political and emotional need for disarmament, the less likely is it to be achievable.[13] It is no accident, to use the words once favoured by Marxist determinists, that disarmament proved negotiable in the 1920s, but not in the 1930s, and in the late 1980s and the 1990s, but not in the 1950s, 1960s, or 1970s. Politics rules.

Scholars who seek the Holy Grail of The Great Single Solution to the problem of war are condemned to perpetual disappointment. There is no simple, let alone easy, answer. What is more, the challenge thus framed is falsely conceived. This is a classic case of scholars posing the wrong question or questions, and discovering unhelpful answers. Contrary to the well intentioned assumption prevalent in the wake of the First World War, war is not a phenomenon that can be abolished, cured, or outgrown. Such, at least, is the only judgement one can draw prudently from the evidence both of all of accessible history, and from nearly a century of fairly intense, ever renewed, scholarly and political endeavour.

Where does scholarship stand today on the occurrence of war? Two answers are appropriate. First, the general theory of war is economically, indeed parsimoniously, best expressed in Thucydides' timeless triptych. At a historically unhelpfully non-specific level of generalization, the triptych says it all. Second, every war in history occurred necessarily in unique circumstances and from an individual medley of motives, conditions, and contingent, even accidental, happenings. In other words, scholars can explain war in general—yesterday, today, and tomorrow—with high confidence as always being the outcome of malign interaction among issues of fear, honour, and interest on all sides. But while these three master drives to fight are useful in directing our attention to the particular, this particular must ever be historically distinctive. And the details rule, in the politics. To date, scholars have not sought hard enough perhaps, certainly they have not succeeded, in operationalizing Thucydides. The dominant limitation of the Thucydidean triptych is that it explains too much: at a general level it explains why wars occur. But, alas, it can explain also why peace prevails. As a practical conceptual tool, the triptych does not and cannot explain why on some occasions it propels rivals to war, while on others it does not. Theory for wars, as contrasted with war, must find a persuasive way to render the triptych helpful in specific historical contexts. However, there is no good reason extant to believe that there is another, more fruitful route to the understanding, with a view to the better control, of war. In practice, politics, economics, culture, and therefore strategy, do control war.[14] One would be wise to conclude that war as an institution regarded as a valuable tool for occasional employment, will not be abolished until or unless it abolishes itself through its political inutility. Unfortunately, that day is not on the horizon.

Does war lead to peace? Does peace lead to war? In an obvious sense of historical succession, the answers must be 'yes'. But is it in the nature of war to have consequences that must poison the well for the period of peace, at least of non-war, that follows? Similarly, is it in the nature of peace, or non-war, that it must breed future war?[15] If there is an endless cycle of peace—war—peace, perhaps of war—peace—war, is it sensible even to try to develop a general theory of war? Unquestionably, strategy is best regarded as a perpetual phenomenon, designed and operating in times of peace and war. Even when one focuses upon its military core, the domain of strategy plainly must extend beyond the war zone. Edward N. Luttwak is correct to insist that:

> Because the development and production of increasingly sophisticated modern weapons (and training armed forces in their use) takes years, major powers must also devise peacetime force development strategies that economically build forces for wars they can only anticipate.[16]

Lest one should be misled by the contemporary content of Luttwak's argument, it is well worth noting that peacetime preparation for war is as old as human history. Communities have always required time to acquire weapons and train soldiers. Skill in arms of any kind typically has needed many years to acquire. Even citizen soldiers, part-time and amateur, could not be armed and trained overnight to a level competitive with a competent foe in any historical period. To develop an effective army in preparation for possible, even probable, war, always has entailed a lengthy commitment. This has been true of land and sea forces. The latter could never be achieved near instantly. The rowers for the war galleys needed extensive training and physical conditioning, as did the hoplites (heavy infantry), also of ancient Greece, mediaeval bowmen, knights, and men-at-arms. The story generically is the same in all periods.

It is probable that the seemingly endless quest for a general theory of war has yielded so little fruit beyond the parsimonious but rich harvest of Thucydides, because the mission is fundamentally ill conceived. Since the theory of war also must be the theory of peace, and because conditions of peace and war often are not sharply distinguishable (the terms 'violent peace' and 'phoney war' are not oxymorons), what is required may be nothing less than the complete theory of politics. Particular wars present no basic difficulty likely to frustrate comprehension, but the absence of a refined general theory does limit the range and potency of the analytical tools available to practicing strategists.

What is war like? This vital piece of general theory is in good shape courtesy of Carl von Clausewitz. If *On War* does nothing else comprehensively and in terms fully satisfactory for today's conditions, at least it does penetrate to the eternal nature of both war and warfare—no small achievement. Clausewitz tells us memorably that war has a unique climate comprising 'danger, exertion, uncertainty, and chance'.[17] He proceeds to identify the mechanical concept of 'friction' as the enduring and richly diverse consequence of this climate.[18] Once one has grasped that war, in the sense of warfare, is a uniquely dangerous activity; is exhausting and unparalleled in its testing of body, mind, and character; has a course all but impossible to predict and control because it is interactive as well as sensitive to intervention from its environments; is highly risky in many respects and at all levels; and is permeated with sources of a potential friction that must have enervating consequences, one knows most of what is worth knowing by way of answer to this question. Truly, war closely resembles nothing else. The answer given here, with gratitude to Clausewitz freely delivered, amounts to the inductive claim that for the participants, in key defining respects, warfare is warfare regardless of period and character of combat and notwithstanding the huge variation in relative significance of each of the three elements in Clausewitz's unstable trinity of violence, chance, and reason. This expansive claim does not even require modest qualification in order to allow for the differences in detail wrought by technological, political, and cultural changes. If one polices rigorously a boundary around Clausewitz's climate of war and its implications, one is unlikely to be confused as to what war is like.

How is war fought? If this question requires an answer that explains how war is fought today, or in a particular past period, a potentially endless array of theories must be provided. In the Prussian's words:

> At this point our historical survey can end. Our purpose was not to assign, in passing, a handful of principles of warfare to each period. We wanted to show how every age had its own kind of war, its own limiting conditions, and its own peculiar preconceptions. Each period, therefore, would have held to its own theory of war, even if the urge had always and universally existed to work things out on scientific principles.[19]

In theory, war and strategy have to be approached as sets of explanations that are both singular and plural. Because war's contexts are almost infinitely variable in the conditions they establish through complex interactions, there need to be theories of war adapted and adaptable to cope with them. These are the specific theories of war(s). But although the lore of war-fighting must shift from historical case to case, there is nonetheless 'some more general—indeed, a universal— element with which every theorist ought above all to be concerned'.[20] We note, but are not overly impressed by, Clausewitz's statement in Book Two that 'the nature of war is complex and changeable'.[21] We allow that war is indeed complex and changeable, but not that its nature is so. He claimed to have little respect for purportedly eternal principles. In a famous sentence he warns that 'theory cannot equip the mind with formulas for solving problems, nor can it mark the narrow path on which the sole solution is supposed to lie by planting a hedge of principles on either side'.[22] This is a useful warning no doubt, even though it is not one that he himself heeded habitually. Perhaps true genius functions on a different plane from that inhabited by the rest of us. Nonetheless, despite Clausewitz's expressed disdain for allegedly universal principles of warfare, many military establishments profess to believe that such principles do exist, can and should be taught, and have practical merit.

The widely ridiculed so-called 'principles of war' amount to the barest bones of a theory of best practice in warfare as conducted mainly at the operational and tactical levels.[23] The principles vary in an item or two among military establishments and over time, but their main body has retained its integrity for well over a century. The list of 'dos' is so hard to criticize that one is tempted to join the hostile chorus and condemn the principles as banal and useless. This would be a mistake, because the principles do say vitally important things about good practice in warfare in all periods. The principles comprise the following, give or

Table 3.2 Principles of War

The nine Principles of War as defined in the US Army Field Manual FM-3 *Military Operations*

Principle	Definition
Objective	Direct every military operation towards a clearly defined, decisive, and attainable objective.
Offensive	Seize, retain, and exploit the initiative.
Mass	Mass the effects of overwhelming combat power at the decisive place and time.
Economy of Force	Employ all combat power available in the most effective way possible; allocate minimum essential combat power to secondary efforts.
Manoeuvre	Place the enemy in a position of disadvantage through the flexible application of combat power.
Unity of command	For every objective, seek unity of command and unity of effort.
Security	Never permit the enemy to acquire unexpected advantage.
Surprise	Strike the enemy at a time, at a place, or in a manner for which he is unprepared.
Simplicity	Prepare clear, uncomplicated plans and concise orders to ensure thorough understanding.

take an item, and with some marginal variation in terminology: objective, offensive, mass, economy of force, manoeuvre, unity of command, security, surprise, and simplicity (see Table 3.2).[24]

The principles are helpful precepts for the military strategist to learn and absorb as essential education for the planning and conduct of operations. What they mean in practice must depend upon the historical context and upon the strategist's ability to apply general theory to particular cases.

With great insight Edward N. Luttwak's theory of strategy holds that logically and historically, best, or even just good, military practice can prove to be bad. Because widespread appreciation by strategists of what constitutes best practice is the practice that typically is expected, this best practice becomes bad practice.[25] Good practice for a strategist frequently is the conduct of warfare in ways unanticipated by the enemy. It should be needless to add that although Luttwak's 'paradoxical logic' is persuasive, it is also an idea that can be taken too far. Strategists need to be able not only to surprise their enemies, in addition they have to achieve the surprise effects that should yield decisive advantage. Furthermore, to cite a weakness in Sun Tzu, the enemy may not be the only belligerent vulnerable to the practical implications of the paradoxical logic of war.

To answer directly the question, 'how is war fought', the answer has to be descriptively nuanced for each historical episode, yet general even to the frontiers of banality in order to capture the whole human experience of war and warfare. War is waged by violence, or force; this is a characteristic, indeed it is a necessary defining characteristic. If violence is neither perpetrated nor likely to be used, then the subject at issue cannot be war. War may be much greater than warfare, but warfare lies at its black heart.

Why is war won, or lost? Theories of victory abound. Both Sun Tzu and Jomini, for classic examples, believed that they knew and could teach the way to win. For example, Sun Tzu claims that 'if a general follows my [methods for] estimation and you employ him, he will certainly be victorious and should be retained'.[26] Jomini was less unequivocal, especially if one interrogates the key qualifying adjectives, but still he claimed that one could load the dice heavily in one's favour.

> It is true that theories cannot teach men with mathematical precision what they should do in every possible case; but it is also certain that they will always point out the errors which should be avoided; and this is a highly important consideration, for these rules thus become, in the hands of skilful generals commanding brave troops, means of almost certain success.[27]

The weasel wording is only prudent. Even if one discovers the general theory of war that contains the erstwhile unknown ingredient that should ensure success to those who understand it, a lack of skill by the general or a deficiency in the determination (moral fibre) of the troops, must render the theory inoperable as the key to victory. In the main, one must admit that Jomini is right. There is a general theory of strategy that explains why, meaning how, war can be waged successfully. He is right also in advising that generals need to be skilful and troops valorous. At the level of general theory as well as of specific plans for particular wars, strategy and strategies point to what is known from historical experience to be best practice (general theory) and to what should be good enough practice to get the contemporary jobs done (strategies as operational plans). But as we noted in Chapter 2, best military practice may well not be best strategic practice, because of the paradoxical and ironical nature of conflict. The enemy probably expects us to behave as the manuals of doctrine say we should for best results. Doctrine manuals have a hard time accommodating the inconvenience of a self-willed enemy who insists that warfare is a violent dialectic.

Although the general theory of war is not overly impressive, certainly it is good enough to provide useful direction both to the general theory of strategy and to strategy-making for individual historical conflicts. Some readers who hail from the world of practice rather than scholarship may find this analysis frustrating. The extensive and intensive concern here to define terms and make distinctions is apt to irritate those who set the bar high for tolerable clarity of language and simplicity of explanation. I sympathize with such a view, but do not agree with its implication that a few simple notions, roughly stapled together or wrenched apart, suffice for comprehension of war, peace, and strategy. Not for the first time, and certainly not for the last, I appeal to Clausewitz for my defence. It would be correct to notice that I quote the great man only when it suits me. To repeat, *On War* is by far the richest source of insight available, but not every sentence in it is a god-like utterance. However, this quotation is especially divine in its wisdom and clarity.

> The primary purpose of any theory is to clarify concepts and ideas that have become, as it were confused and entangled. Not until terms and concepts have been defined can one hope to make any progress in examining the question clearly and simply and expect the reader to share one's views.[28]

The theory of strategy must take what aid and comfort it can from what the ages have provided by way of a general theory of war. An elementary diagram explains visually what should be obvious from this text (Figure 3.1).

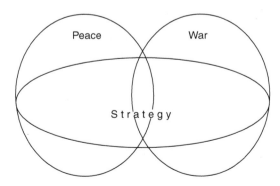

Figure 3.1 War, Peace, and Strategy

War and peace overlap in a fuzzy zone that is a world of both/and, rather than of sharp differences. Strategy must function in all three realms—peace, war, and peace and war (war-like peace, perhaps peace-like war). What is clear enough, though, is that for all their many and complicated connections, war and strategy are sufficiently distinctive concepts, with unique, albeit overlapping, domains, as to require understanding by two general theories, not one.

POLITICS, POLICY, AND WAR

There is no region of and for policy that is beyond politics. What is politics? It is the competition for power and influence among rivals. What is its product? It is the distribution of power and influence. Of course, there are a host of technical matters of deep concern to the strategist, the content, the mechanics, of which are usually utterly non-political; logistics, for example. But the purpose of all logistical planning has to be to enable the execution of operational plans. And those operational plans will be the outcome of strategic deliberation, intuition (i.e. guesswork, inspired and otherwise), and pervasive political judgement. As with most great works, *On War* rediscovers what everyone had known and practised forever. War is a political instrument, which is not quite synonymous with the claim that it is a policy instrument.[29] Before the First World War, at least, the Great German General Staff, following the Jominian canon of military primacy in the actual conduct of warfare, believed that it was the finely tuned source of true expertise in the mechanics of warfare. To be professionally military was to be beyond the practice of mere politics. When the country called, the military machine, directed by the General Staff, would execute the operational plan or plans it had prepared long in advance in meticulous detail, and deliver swift and decisive military victory without real-time political guidance or interference. This pleasing duty and prospect was the epitome of the German way of war under its long-serving Chief of Staff, Field Marshal Helmuth Graf von Moltke, his heirs and successors.

If the conduct of war prudently could be reduced to the waging of warfare, if policy and politics were identical, and if strategy's military choices were not impregnated with political assumptions, hopes, guesses, and purposes, then the Jominian approach to military professionalism would make considerable sense. But, as it happens, each of the three 'ifs' just employed is fatal for the theory of plainly distinctive political and military zones. Moreover, even the arguable Clausewitzian master dictum that 'war is merely the continuation of policy by other means' is not a little misleading.[30] Because of the liberty enjoyed by translators to express *Politik* either as policy or as politics, the inevitable resulting fudge has hindered both theory building as well as the understanding of historical experience. Clausewitz's expedient employment of the inherently non-specific *Politik* has had the accidental consequence of encouraging, indeed all but licensing, lesser minds to be casual about concepts. Politics and policy may be joined like Siamese twins, but they are different behaviours. Whereas politics is about the universal struggle for power—personal, ideological (e.g. cultural), and institutional—policy refers to agreed courses of action or inaction. Policy finds expression in discrete decisions, great and small. What must not be obscured is the ubiquity of the political in and over what academics like to call the policy process. This process is endemically political. Whatever a particular policy process appears to be about, deciding how to allocate scarce British resources for the defeat of Germany, for example, its participants cannot help but function politically. Naturally, a point comes in the policy process when decisions have to be implemented. At that juncture the technicians will be tasked to produce the operational plans. One must add that the linked, and ideally parallel and nearly fused, processes of policymaking and strategy-making should be informed from the outset and then throughout by expert information as to feasibility. This expert input needs to include intelligence on the adversary.

So, are war and strategy policy instruments or political instruments? The answer has to be that they are both. In order to clarify the inspiration for and meaning of strategy, one cannot look initially for enlightenment to its own general theory. Instead, one must distinguish plainly between the concepts of politics and policy. When strategy is regarded strictly as a policy instrument, the implications are significantly different from treating it as a tool of politics. Approached as an instrument of policy, strategy should be able to identify the goals, ways, and means, which ought to deliver the advantage demanded. But when it is viewed as a tool of politics, the implicit suggestion, first, is that strategy is likely to be a dynamic adapting outcome that though settled to some large degree is ever open to amendments of modest and even immodest dimension. The second suggestion implicit in the adjective political is to the effect that strategy is always subject to a domestic, and possibly allied, audit on criteria far removed from strict military-strategic utility.

For example, the large Anglo–Canadian raid on Dieppe on 19 August 1942 (Operation Jubilee) had the ostensible objective of providing education by experience in amphibious assault. Such knowledge, one could argue plausibly, would be invaluable for those who must plan the invasion of Nazi-held Europe on the largest of scales. This was true, but it was not why the raid was conducted. Also, someone ought to have considered the reverse side of the coin; would the Germans learn more from defending against a large raid than would the Allies from its execution? The notably tangled and deliberately obscured historical record shows clearly enough that Jubilee was really all about the ambitions of the newly formed and notably incompetent Combined Operations organization, and particularly about the vaulting ambition of its politically and royally well-connected commander, Lord Louis Mountbatten. One might argue, as some have, that the raid was intended to demonstrate to the Americans just why a major landing on the coast of North-West Europe could not succeed in 1942, or probably in 1943 either. In addition, perhaps as a bonus, the raid was designed to show the Russians that their Western Allies were prepared to shed their blood (Canadian blood, in the main), at least modestly, in some ground warfare on the continent. In practice, serendipity worked expensively. The raid demonstrated the depth of British ineptitude in the conduct of a large and complex amphibious operation, albeit fortunately only a raid. The venture showed the Germans how they could improve their operational design and tactics for coastal defence, but also, inevitably, it bred an understandable overconfidence in the ease with which invasion could be repulsed. The law of unintended consequences showed its iron hand. London certainly had not intended to feed German complacency. Nonetheless, although the British were unhappy with the undeniable failure of the raid, they were more than content with the outcome's unarguably negative verdict on the US Chiefs of Staff's strategic preference for an invasion in the near term. None of these unenthusiastic comments should obscure the importance of the operational level discovery that it was not a sound idea to attempt to seize and hold a well-defended port.

Dieppe illustrates the profound difficulty in currency conversion that is the task of the strategist. The raid mainly was about politics, even though it bristled with military lessons for both sides. Churchill should have tried to calculate, which is to say guess, what the fact of a raid on a substantial scale on a French port would have on British morale; on relations with Canada, which provided most of the troops (more than 5,000 out of 7,000 total); on relations with the United States, whose political leaders and soldiers would judge British will and military performance; and on Stalin, who was likely to be more impressed by the small scale of the continental probe than he would be by the fact of its occurrence. Finally, Churchill needed to speculate as to the raid's impact on the German enemy. For example, would the Germans transfer forces from the Eastern Front in order to bolster *Festung Europa* in the West? The way of the strategist is rarely eased by the discovery of thoroughly reliable signposts and distance markers. Even the best-laid plans can go awry 'on the night'. But, if scholars and other commentators on the Second World War are unanimous on nothing much else, they do agree that the Dieppe adventure is not even a distant candidate for an Allied 'best plan of the war' award, should such exist, although it would be a runner for 'most unsound Allied plan of the war', in tough competition with 'Market Garden' of September 1944 (the 'bridge too far' over the Rhine at Arnhem).[31] Military historian Carlo D'Este offers the plausible assessment that 'Mountbatten had scant grasp of combined operations, and in electing to undertake a raid that had not the slightest chance of success he unwittingly unleashed one of the most ill-conceived operations of the war'.[32] D'Este proceeds to note that Dieppe was one occasion from which Churchill's usual malpractice of attempted military micromanagement by himself would have been beneficial.[33]

Policy frequently is motivated by political considerations that cannot be aired publicly, and which are unlikely to be explained in a paper trail that future archival historians can uncover. Politics produces policy both initially and subsequently when the interpretation of feedback from battlespace makes potent implicit and explicit suggestions for strategic and policy adaptation. Indeed, the more intensely one interrogates strategic phenomena, on the 'bridge' and also on the approach roads on both banks, the more one discovers evidence of political influence. This is neither praiseworthy nor deplorable, it is simply the way things are, have always been, and therefore are likely to continue in the future.

If the erstwhile US Strategic Air Command (SAC) could proclaim proudly and without intentional irony that 'peace is our profession', so also can strategists. Since the concepts that shaped the policy that SAC expressed were rediscovered and adapted by strategic theorists, those theorists could lay some plausible claim to being peace professionals. Modern strategic theory, which is to say—for our purposes—theory developed after 1945, has had more to say about the prevention, limitation, and control of war and its military tools than it has about the conduct of warfare.[34] Pre-eminently this performance reflected appreciation of the nuclear menace, while, in addition, it reflected the fact that the overwhelming majority of contemporary strategic theorists were not military professionals. Perhaps it is surprising that modern strategists so often have abandoned the field of political debate to its occupation by self professing theorists and activists for 'peace'. The concept of peace is at least as opaque and arguable as are the theories for its promotion, but before we address the matter of definition it is necessary to register the claim that to date most strategists have not believed that a discrete general theory of peace could have intellectual integrity. This strategic theorist endorses such a view.

Although modern strategic theorists have differed significantly over, for some examples, nuclear deterrence, limited war, and arms control, they have not argued among themselves explicitly about the requirements of peace. Sensibly or not, strategists have believed that when they addressed the challenges of war prevention, limitation, and control, ipso facto they were tackling the great, if somewhat obscure, problem of peace. Students of modern strategic theory will find scant direct discussion of peace, just as they will find relatively little careful, or even careless, treatment of 'strategic ethics', to coin a subject label. However, the reasons differ between the two cases. The near absence of ethical argument is, in the opinion of this strategist, an example of serious professional neglect and has been, as it remains, a major mistake. But the near silence on peace per se has been intelligent and professionally well judged, though admittedly inadvertently unfortunate in its consequences of public political and ethical debates impoverished or lost by default.

Peace, in common with such other potent notions as love, happiness, and security, cannot be sought directly. It can make no sense to invent peace theory or to adopt a peace policy. Peace is the product of other elements; it cannot be purchased by the yard. Most strategists, most of the time, over most matters, desire and strive to advance peace. The peace they seek may have to be pursued through the travails of war, or it might be achievable through the execution of adroit grand strategy short of the use of force. More often than not, for most modern polities, war and warfare are not interesting live policy options. An absence of bloody hostilities generally is explicable by such conditions as a dearth of vital interests under threat; an acute shortage of military options that plausibly could relieve or resolve any problems that might warrant a decision to fight; and, today in much of EU–Europe for example, even a deep cultural antipathy to use of the military instrument of policy on distinctively military tasks.[35]

In most, though not all, cases, polities can secure peace in the sense of a condition of non-war simply by behaving inoffensively or agreeably towards potential predators. At worst, the truly determined peace seekers will opt for the peace of surrender. There will be occasions when predatory polities cannot be appeased, because they judge the waging of war itself to be in their interest. For a while, at least, war usually unites a divided country. Furthermore, some political cultures hold warfare, and warriors, in high esteem as being socially bracing, manly, and even ideologically necessary. When these conditions hold, the prospects for peace obviously must be desperately slim.

But what is this rather obscure condition called peace? It is essential to recognize the differences among a peace simply of non-war, a political peace, and a peace ensured by the sheer absurdity of war between particular potential belligerents. Taken in reverse order, New Zealand and Finland are at peace with each other because they have nothing to fight about and the very idea of hostilities is frankly ridiculous. Next in reverse, Britain and Germany enjoy a deep, thoroughly comfortable, political peace not only because of joint membership of the European Union (and NATO), but really because of the political reasons why both are able to coexist contentedly in this rather strange political entity. Compared with Anglo–German relations in most, though certainly nowhere near all, of the years from 1871 to 1945, this historical example makes crystal clear what is meant by a political peace.[36] Britain's life-threatening differences with Germany have been settled twice by blood and iron. Finally, India and Pakistan are not at war and hence they must be at peace, if, that is, one grants no authority to the concept of a third umbrella term describing a condition of warlike peace.

It is all too obvious that the theorists of strategy, war, and peace have much hard work to do. As we have admitted already, this work is content to attempt to contribute only to the theory of strategy. Should the discussion here shed some light in dark places of war and peace, that would be a welcome bonus. It is more difficult to devise a convincing general theory of war, and hence of peace also, than of strategy. The theory of strategy lends itself to application in specific circumstances, where it appears in tailored strategies. The theory of war and peace, such as it is, does not, at least as yet it does not. Despite close to a century of often intense, careful, and sometime ingenious scholarship, as well as practical real-world trial and error, we know neither how to prevent war nor how to promote peace, reliably. For a possibly startling thought, we are not even certain of the mission. Should we theorists strive professionally to understand war with a view to its control and alleviation, or do we need to address war as a problem or problems capable of definitive solution? Is war the challenge? Or does the problem lie with the reasons why communities fight? 'Fear, honour, and interest' certainly is a powerful universal formula, but how well does it fit with genetic argument? Are human beings biologically programmed to fight, or only to be willing to fight given suitable stimuli from their several contexts? And do we mean all human beings or only some—and only some of the time? Women as well as men? It is apparent that attempts to penetrate the mysteries of war and peace require the ability to devise theory for unusually murky and deep waters.

Those who aspire to discover and promote a general theory of peace tend to be overwhelmed by the inherent difficulty of their opaque subject. Furthermore, they are harassed by the gratuitous damage apt to be self-inflicted by moral conviction and its consequences in more or less active political promotion. While devotion to peace as a cause is praiseworthy, it is always likely to be perilous to scholarly objectivity. We humans have a way of believing what we wish to believe. If we believe strongly, perhaps passionately, that peace is neces-sary, we are entirely capable of discounting negative evidence and affirming that the peace we seek is possible. Prophets of hope for peace are not only unlikely to be sound scholars, in addition they can be dangerous. They may persuade credulous people in large numbers that a truly unattainable political peace actually is achievable. How can we be certain of failure if we decline to travel the extra mile (to Munich, say)? Being professionally sensitive to voter attitudes and opinions, politicians are quite capable of choosing to pursue, or appearing to pursue, a quality of peace that is beyond attainment. Suffice it to say that modern scholars have yet to produce a general theory of war, of peace, or more sensibly of war and peace, capable of bearing heavy strategic traffic. This is the reason why this strategic theorist keeps returning to the timeless and genuinely useful wisdom of Thucydides' 'fear, honour, and interest'.

As the theory of war must also be a theory of peace, including warlike peace, so the theory of strategy has to embrace grand strategy. Moreover, the peril to the theorist is identical. The danger lies in the unintended consequence that a worthy desire to be sufficiently theoretically inclusive as to corral the subject's true complexity, leads the theorist into a realm without meaningful frontiers. If war and its many contexts are merged, the subject loses distinctive identity. Similarly, if the idea of grand strategy is treated at all carelessly by the theorist, it too melds into its contexts. Because of its intimate proximity to policy and politics, the problem of useful theoretical domain is especially acute for grand strategy. This intimacy was recognized by the grand strategy's conceptual, of course not actual behavioural, parent, Basil H. Liddell Hart. His articulation of the idea remains as authoritative for its topic as is Clausewitz on, say, friction. Liddell Hart explains that:

> While practically synonymous with the policy which guides the conduct of war, as distinct from the more fundamental policy which should govern its object, the term 'grand strategy' serves to bring out the sense of 'policy in execution.' For the role of grand strategy—higher strategy—is to co-ordinate and direct all the resources of a nation, or band of nations towards the attainment of the political object of the war—the goal defined by fundamen-tal policy.[37]

Liddell Hart proceeds to advise that:

> While the horizon of strategy is bounded by the war, grand strategy looks beyond the war to the subsequent peace. It should not only combine the

various instruments, but so regulate their use as to avoid damage to the future state of peace—for its security and prosperity.[38]

There is much good sense in his concluding judgement.

> The sorry state of peace, for both sides, that has followed most wars can be traced to the fact that, unlike strategy, the realm of grand strategy is for the most part *terra incognita*—still awaiting exploration, and understanding.[39]

Since theory should clarify by making clear distinctions and hence establishing recognizable boundaries between phenomena claimed to be unlike, this text is hesitant in pursuing, even briefly, a line of thought whose costs might exceed its benefits. Nonetheless, we shall advance boldly, if possibly recklessly. Given that tactical and operational military behaviour can be regarded as military strategy in action, why should not strategy, especially grand strategy, be approached as policy behaviour? If Liddell Hart is persuasive when he claims that grand strategy is 'policy in execution', does it really differ from policy? More to the point perhaps, even though there is an obvious difference between a policy goal and a strategy to secure it, the intimacy of the connection between them is such that one could argue that insistence upon the distinction does more harm to understanding than it does good. On balance, and it is only on balance, this discussion maintains that the distinction between a policy objective and plans and actions for its intended achievement is valid, necessary, and sustainable under critical fire. However, we admit that policy and its execution should be so closely interwoven and continuously in dialogue that some apparent fusion of, and confusion between, the two is always likely. This is a classic example of the ironic truth that a belief (in the distinctions among ends, ways, and means) may work well in theory, but far less well in practice. If we insist with undue scholarly rigour upon the theoretical separation of purpose from the methods and tools for its attainment, we risk losing essential grip upon the need for aim and action to be constantly coordinated, matched, and, if need be, reconsidered fundamentally.

Whether or not a political entity consciously produces some approximation to a definite overall plan for the distribution and employment of all its assets, the historical effect of its sundry behaviours will be as if it had indeed operated according to a plan. To explain: can one tell the difference between a state that functions with an explicit grand strategy and one that does not? The one that does may have a poor grand strategy or, as likely, might mismanage what in theory is a sound grand design. Grand strategy can be regarded both, or either, as a function of central political invention and management, and, perhaps or, as a definite plan with a distinct intellectual and physical existence. In a basic functional sense, political authorities have no choice other than to conduct their statecraft, including their wars, grand strategically. They are in greater or lesser command of a society's assets. It should be the case that a polity will generate more strategic effect on behalf of its policy goals if it works hard to design, execute, and constantly interrogate an explicit grand strategy. However, as we shall explain in later chapters, even the best-laid plans of more than averagely competent and typically sober people can go terribly wrong in practice.

Domestic political influence on high policy and strategy is likely to be determinative over grand strategy, especially in peacetime. When a government makes decisions on the deployment of many national assets—manpower, financial reserves, and wealth in general, public utilities, for example—it must engage across the whole board of domestic political life. Even when a country is conducting a very limited conflict, a context more akin to warlike peace than to sustained warfare, hard choices may need to be made. For a case in point, the British armed forces were severely stretched both in personnel and equipment in the 2000s, a period of intense and varied activity, including combat.[40] The reason is attributable to inadequate financial allocation to defence functions by the British government for many years. The general theory of strategy must include recognition of the enduring central significance of money (or its contemporary equivalent). If society through its political agents is not willing to buy military means, then military plans, the strategies they express, and the foreign policy they should advance must have no more actuality than dreams. States and other security communities compete, and occasionally fight, grand strategically, not just military strategically. This is not a theorist's opinion; for once it is a statement of objective reality. When some of the non-military aspects of grand strategy are neglected, the military pursuit of political goals is ever likely to find itself inadequately supported. Diplomacy may fail to garner allies, intelligence can be lacking on adversary intentions and capabilities, and political determination at home may be gratuitously fragile.

If the concept of grand strategy is to have intellectual integrity it has to admit a necessary connection to military force as a, not the only, defining characteristic. Only by applying such a test can one stake out a meaningful boundary to what is, and what is not, grand strategy. Absent a requirement for the force connection, grand strategy becomes simply any purposeful behaviour by a political authority in pursuit of any kind of policy. The military force need not be applied, it may merely be threatened, explicitly or implicitly. But that force is one of the signatures that has to be on any behaviour for the activity to be termed grand strategic. Some readers might wonder whether theoretical clarity thus insisted upon constitutes an avoidable own goal scored against the understanding of real political life. They should be reassured by the argument that in the absence of acceptance of the concept of grand strategy, and of explicit effort to devise one, official activities are apt to proceed uncoordinated. There will be inadequate appreciation of the scope of the domain relevant to the community's competitive performance. The overall competitive performance of Germany in the first half of the twentieth century yields a textbook example of what can happen to an exceedingly powerful country that does not have even the semblance of a grand strategy.

POLITICS RULES

Four major arguments were presented in this chapter. First, the general theories of strategy and of war were judged sufficiently distinctive as to mandate separate development. This position was maintained despite the considerable overlap between them. War is a complete relationship among adversaries; it is a legal, political, and social institution, notwithstanding the many unpleasant varieties in which it is manifested. But, to cite the second main argument, tight definitions of war and peace are as theoretically expedient, possibly necessary, as they affront the fuzziness and untidiness of historical reality. The international laws of war, particularly in the sharp distinction they draw between combatants and non-combatants, even as recently modified for greater inclusivity, do not capture satisfactorily the true complexity of conditions. It was suggested above that in addition to the familiar concepts of war and peace, there needs to be recognition of a third concept, warlike peace. The second major argument insists that the theory of war must also be a theory of peace, all the while it needs to develop the analytical tools suitable to cope with conditions that are neither plainly of war nor of peace, but rather are both.

The third main point has been to insist that the all but magical term, policy, needs to be humbled somewhat in favour of greater recognition of the pervasiveness of politics. As best today's scholars can tell, Clausewitz did not intend to imply a notable domestic political content to his *Politik*. His usage meant what we understand by policy.[41] This choice of words was understandable for a strategic theorist whose inspirational icons were absolute monarchs (Frederick the Great and the Emperor Napoleon), but it is less appropriate for a policymaking context characterized by powerful contending interests and therefore distinctive perspectives and preferences. Although we have to respect the differences between the concepts of politics and policy, unless we are careful we can slide innocently into the serious error of discussing strategic choices as though they were wholly the objective products of a strategically rational process. Politics, and especially the politics of public finance, money, ensures that the Rational Strategic Person, should such exist, would be hugely frustrated by the character of the policy guidance he received.

The last of the four major arguments presented here has been an insistence upon treating all strategy within the nest of grand strategy. No matter how military the behaviour, and regardless of its geographical focus, all strategy is grand strategy. To move from the general to the particular, all specific strategies should be components, when they are not the entirety, of a grand strategy. Of course, as we cited above with respect to Nazi Germany, an explicit grand strategy is only a desideratum, it is not an inescapable necessity. A polity can function without a grand strategy because it is structurally incapable of designing and effecting one, as was the case with Hitler's Germany. Alternatively, thinking of the

United States in some, but only some, periods, a country may be so confident of its ability to produce military capabilities that it appears to have little need of an explicit grand strategy. I will go further and claim that in the German and American cases not only was grand strategy missing from the action, so also was overall military strategy. Both countries functioned fairly effectively at the operational and tactical levels of war, but not really at the strategic. Germany was overconfident in its ability to wage and win wars by decisive operational manoeuvre, while the United States repeatedly felt so secure in the material footing for its war effort that it was under no great pressure to make difficult strategic choices. On a personal note, I can report that in the course of writing this book a distinguished American strategic thinker and defence analyst told me that strategy was needed only by the relatively weak.[42] America is strong and therefore does not really need strategy. Strategy is about making choices. If you do not have to make choices, certainly not painful ones, what is the role of strategy? If the first question for the strategist has to be 'so what?'—another assuredly is 'what are the alternatives?' Some Americans who should know better appear to believe that the United States is sufficiently wealthy that it has no requirement to identify and decide among alternatives. I must hasten to add that I do not endorse this view of the United States as being in a post-strategic condition.

For the concluding thought to this three-chapter venture in theory building, it is helpful to note that strategy is an exercise in highly contingent prediction. The strategist seeks to give his political masters some control over future events. In particular, as Clausewitz and Wylie argue convincingly, the strategist aspires to control the enemy.[43] Such control can be either of his will to resist or of his ability to do so. In practice, the two forms of control generally are mutually reinforcing. The tolerably rational enemy will conduct a net assessment and decide that his means and his ends need to be rebalanced so as to privilege less ambitious policy goals. In practice, though, the enemy may well be unreasonable in his rationality and believe that something miraculous will turn up to save the day. Adolf Hitler in 1945 was not the sole exemplar of such unreasonable rationality. Winston Churchill in the summer of 1940 was another case of a statesman promoting hope masquerading as strategy.

Strategy as a plan is really a prediction of how one intends to shape and conclude hostilities, or the course of a rivalry, to one's own advantage. The strategist, grand or military, predicts the future of a competition. Of course, the prediction has to be contingent. Everyone is familiar with Moltke the Elder's all too accurate claim that the integrity of pre-war plans of war do not long survive first contact with the main body of the enemy's strength, to amend a little the Field Marshal's words, though not his meaning. Moltke's timeless wisdom sounds the tocsin for the necessity to be alert to war's, and rivalry's, adversarial nature.

NOTES

1. Simon Jenkins, 'Lovely new aircraft carrier, sir, but we're fighting in the desert', *The Sunday Times*, 16 February 2008.
2. Carl von Clausewitz, *On War*, tr. Michael Howard and Peter Paret (1832–4; Princeton, NJ: Princeton University Press, 1976).
3. Hew Strachan, *Clausewitz's On War: A Biography* (New York: Atlantic Monthly Press, 2007), 193.
4. 'War appears to be as old as mankind, but peace is a modern invention', Michael Howard's quotation of these words from the nineteenth-century jurist, Sir Henry Maine, may well have shocked, certainly surprised, many of his readers. *The Invention of Peace and the Reinvention of War*, 2nd edn. (London: Profile Books, 2001), 1.
5. The causes of war and the nature of war tend to merge as subjects for scholarly investigation. In part this phenomenon is attributable to the unhelpful narrative impulse that cannot help but attend scholarship in this case. Scholars are apt to leap early from some understanding to policy prescription, even though their theory of war is immature and eminently contestable. Alas, good intentions have yet to bequeath us a dominant general theory of war sufficiently plausible as to merit translation from education to policy, let alone strategy. By way of a light sample of the literature, see: Julia G. Johnsen, ed., *Selected Articles on War—Cause and Cure* (New York: H. W. Wilson, 1926); Quincy Wright, *A Study of War*, 2 vols. (Chicago: University of Chicago Press, 1942); Kenneth N. Waltz, *Man, the State and War: A Theoretical Analysis* (New York: Columbia University Press, 1959); Geoffrey Blainey, *The Causes of War* (London: Macmillan, 1973); T. C. W. Blanning, *The Origins of the French Revolutionary Wars* (London: Longman, 1986), ch. 1; Stephen Van Evera, *Causes of War: Power and the Roots of Conflict* (Ithaca, NY: Cornell University Press, 1999); Dale C. Copeland, *The Origins of Major War* (Ithaca, NY: Cornell University Press, 2000); Azar Gat, *War in Human Civilization* (Oxford: Oxford University Press, 2006); Niall Ferguson, *The War of the World: History's Age of Hatred* (London: Allen Lane, 2006); David Sobek, *The Causes of War* (Cambridge: Polity Press, 2009); and John A. Vasquez, *The War Puzzle Revisited* (Cambridge: Cambridge University Press, 2009). War is so large a subject that it invites, even tempts, the bold theorist to overreach and fail. Somehow, the larger the book and the more shiny the grand hypothesis, the more obvious is likely to be the inadequacy of the offering. For the theory of war there should be a Chinese proverb, 'deep thought, great theory, small book'. Sun Tzu is terse to a fault, but manages to provide a high calorific approach to the understanding of war. His understanding is couched as definite nuggets of advice specifying proven best practice, all but guaranteed to be such by the author. *The Art of War*, tr. Ralph D. Sawyer (ca. 490 BCE; Boulder, CO: Westview Press, 1994).
6. Hew Strachan, 'Strategy and the Limitation of War', *Survival*, 50 (February-March 2008), 37; Clausewitz, 88.
7. Hew Strachan, *The Changing Character of War* (Oxford: Europaeum, 2007), 27.
8. A strategist may be required to command and to lead, but the three functions and roles are different. Appreciation of the distinctions among them, and understanding of the different qualities needed for competence, let alone true excellence, in each, is not as widespread as it ought to be. There is no subject that begs for more careful complementary treatment by historians and social scientists. One thoughtful author with considerable military experience draws an interesting, but in my opinion erroneous, distinction

between leadership and charismatic leadership. I believe that all leaders, as opposed to commanders, require some charisma. John C. 'Doc' Bahnsen, 'Charisma', in Christopher Kolenda, ed., *Leadership: The Warrior's Art* (Carlisle, PA: Army War College Foundation, 2001), 259–75.

9. John Keegan, *A History of Warfare* (London: Hutchinson, 1993), 387.
10. Clausewitz, 89. I prefer Antulio Echevarria's translation of *wunderliche* as 'wondrous', to Michael Howard and Peter Paret's 'remarkable', or, in their 2nd edn., 'paradoxical' (Clausewitz, 1832–4, 1976; London: Everyman's Library, 1993), 101. See Echevarria, *Clausewitz and Contemporary War* (Oxford: Oxford University Press, 2007), 81, n.40.
11. Thucydides, *The Landmark Thucydides: A Comprehensive Guide to the Peloponnesian War*, ed. Robert B. Strassler, rev. tr. Richard Crawley (ca. 400 BCE: New York: Free Press, 1996), 43.
12. See Johnsen, ed., *Selected Articles on War*.
13. I have delved into these rather depressing and murky waters in my book, *House Of Cards: Why Arms Control Must Fail* (Ithaca, NY: Cornell University Press, 1992).
14. See Colin S. Gray, *Another Bloody Century: Future Warfare* (London: Weidenfeld and Nicolson, 2005), ch. 9.
15. Despite their central importance, these most vital of questions have not attracted much productive scholarship. However, we do have Stephen R. Rock, *Why Peace Breaks Out: Great Power Rapprochement in Historical Perspective* (Chapel Hill, NC: University of North Carolina Press, 1989); Matthew Hughes and Matthew S. Seligman, *Does Peace Lead to War? Peace Settlements and Conflict in the Modern Age* (Stroud: Sutton Publishing, 2002); and Williamson Murray and James Lacey, eds., *The Making of Peace: Rulers, States, and the Aftermath of War* (Cambridge: Cambridge University Press, 2009).
16. Edward N. Luttwak, 'Strategy', in John Whiteclay Chambers, ed., *The Oxford Companion to American Military History* (Oxford: Oxford University Press, 1999), 683.
17. Clausewitz, 104.
18. Ibid. 119–21.
19. Ibid. 593.
20. Ibid.
21. Ibid. 90.
22. Ibid. 578.
23. See John I. Alger, *The Quest for Victory: The History of the Principles of War* (Westport, CT: Greenwood Press, 1982); Robert R. Leonhard, *The Principles of War for the Information Age* (Novato, CA: Presidio Press, 1998); Anthony D. Mc Ivor, ed., *Rethinking the Principles of War* (Annapolis, MD: Naval Institute Press, 2005); and Colin S. Gray, *Strategy and History: Essays on Theory and Practice* (Abingdon: Routledge, 2006), 81–7.
24. US Army, *Operations*, FM 100-5 (Washington, DC: Headquarters, Department of the Army, 14 June 1993), 2–4-6.
25. Luttwak: 'Strategy', 685; id., *Strategy: The Logic of War and Peace*, rev. edn. (Cambridge, MA: Harvard University Press, 2001), passim.
26. Sun Tzu, 168.
27. Antoine Henri de Jomini, *The Art of War* (1838; London: Greenhill Books, 1992), 323.
28. Clausewitz, 132.
29. Echevarria, *Clausewitz and Contemporary War*, ch. 4, is an outstanding analysis.
30. Clausewitz, 87.

31. The mixture of political skulduggery for personal and institutional gain, and—above all else—plain incompetence on a heroic-scale, that yielded the small but appalling disaster of the Dieppe raid, is almost too implausible to be credited. The most searching analysis of this sorry episode conducted to date is Brian Loring Villa, *Unauthorized Action: Mountbatten and the Dieppe Raid* (Oxford: Oxford University Press, 1994). Lord Louis (then Captain) Mountbatten's career in very high command ought to have been terminated in August 1942. Admittedly, he was a military leader and political operator of some genius, but as a military commander he was an unqualified disaster. True incompetence can be a career disadvantage, but obviously it is not always fatal for advancement.

32. Carlo D'Este, *Warlord: A Life of Winston Churchill at War, 1874–1945* (London: Allen Lane, 2009), 661.

33. Ibid. 662.

34. There is as yet no competent history of the rise and maturing of the modern strategic studies profession. Necessarily, it follows that there is extant no half-way adequate critical analysis of the consequences for policy and international security of this historically novel profession of largely civilian strategic thinkers. Of course, the specific strategies of the nuclear age have been devised and adapted by soldiers, but, probably for both good and ill, those military functionaries contributed relatively little to modern strategic thought. Readers should find the following books useful, if dated in two cases (Gray and Kaplan). Colin S. Gray, *Strategic Studies and Public Policy: The American Experience* (Lexington, KY: University Press of Kentucky, 1982); Fred Kaplan, *The Wizards of Armageddon* (New York: Simon and Schuster, 1983); Lawrence Freedman, *The Evolution of Nuclear Strategy*, 3rd edn. (Basingstoke: Palgrave Macmillan, 2003); Bruce Kuklick, *Blind Oracles: Intellectuals and War from Kennan to Kissinger* (Princeton, NJ: Princeton University Press, 2006); Alex Abella, *Soldiers of Reason: The Rand Corporation and the Rise of the American Empire* (Orlando, FL: Harcourt, 2008); and Keith B. Payne, *The Great American Gamble: Deterrence Theory and Practice from the Cold War to the Twenty-First Century* (Fairfax, VA: National Institute Press, 2008).

35. Post-military EU–Europe is analysed perceptively in two robustly controversial short texts by Robert Kagan: *Paradise and Power: America and Europe in the New World Order* (London: Atlantic Books, 2003); and *The Return of History and the End of Dreams* (London: Atlantic Books, 2008).

36. See Paul Kennedy's solid study, *The Rise of the Anglo–German Antagonism, 1860–1914* (London: George Allen and Unwin, 1980).

37. Basil H. Liddell Hart, *Strategy: The Indirect Approach* (1941; London: Faber and Faber, 1967), 335.

38. Ibid. 336.

39. Ibid.

40. See Jeremy Black, *The Dotted Red Line: Britain's Defence Policy in the Modern World* (London: Social Affairs Unit, 2006), for a characteristically hard-hitting analysis.

41. Echevarria's discussion should be regarded as essential reading, *Clausewitz and Contemporary War*, ch. 4. Wherever one comes down in the somewhat misconceptualized debate over Clausewitz's use of *Politik*, it is tempting to observe that the Prussian ought to have been rather more careful than he was with his linguistic choice over a matter so central to his argument. Of course, it is possible that he was ambiguous by design. More likely, though, the great man simply did not realize that in a domestic political context radically different from his own, the distinction between politics and policy would be significant.

42. Name withheld to protect the guilty. I have chosen to break the rule, certainly the convention, of scholarship that obliges one to provide checkable references. The reasons are because the claim I report in the text is so important to the argument of this book, and that the opinion was expressed informally, notwithstanding the careful thought behind it and its evident sincerity. Although the claim that America does not 'do' strategy because it does not need to is a deliberate exaggeration, it is neither obviously false nor is it implausible. Whether or not one agrees with the judgement, there is no doubting its value for the promotion of constructive thought.
43. Clausewitz, 75; Wylie, *Military Strategy*, 152.

Part II

Practice

4

Problems with Strategy: Often a Bridge Too Far

THE ART OF THE POSSIBLE: MOLTKE WAS (PARTLY) CORRECT

'Like politics, strategy is the art of the possible, but few can discern what is possible.'[1] Typically, it is difficult for the strategist to know what is possible. Similarly, it is challenging for the policymaker to know what to require of the strategist, while it can be hugely painful for the tactician to discover by bloody trial and error just what is feasible and what is not. The modern German school of warfare has been much criticized for its real, certainly its apparent, subordination of strategy to the authority of unfolding tactical events. The criticism has been well merited with reference to actual German strategic malpractice, but nonetheless it has been overdone, certainly it has often been discussed inaccurately. The principal German solution to the problems with strategy discussed in this chapter essentially was to permit the flow of tactical events and their operational consequences to drive strategic history. Apostasy on this theorist's part, though it may seem to some readers, I believe that there is more value to the German approach than often is granted. In fact, it can be argued that that approach had a great deal of merit, even though it failed catastrophically through repeated German malpractice. So, what was the German way in warfare as expressed in a dominant approach to strategy?

The German way in warfare developed in the seventeenth century, matured in the eighteenth, attained its apogée in the late nineteenth, and failed miserably in the twentieth.[2] Necessarily it was the product of German, which is to say substantially Prussian, geography and the strategic history played out upon and from that geography. Success and failure depended upon a host of factors, as the theory of strategy specifies, not least among which were the relative competencies of key individuals functioning of necessity in the contexts of their days. Stated at its tersest, Prussia/Germany always needed to win its wars swiftly, because it lacked the material resources, including the space, the geographic depth at home, to conduct long wars successfully against enemies certain to be better endowed with physical assets. This meant that the German style in warfare had to be manoeuvrist in quest of the rapid destruction of the enemy's ability or will to fight on. But, how could this necessary outcome best be accomplished? By sound strategy, of course, one can reply. What is the sound approach to strategy? The difficulties already cited in Chapter 2, together with others explained here, may suggest to some people the necessity for extreme care in strategic planning. Further thought may suggest the high virtue in prudent selection of the strategic concept that gives birth to, and animates, the strategic plan or strategy. These would be appropriate judgements. Unfortunately, their merit is so self-evident and imperial in apparent domain that they are likely to cause the incautious among us to lose the strategic plot. And the plot, as we must emphasize time and again, is that of a 'duel...on a larger scale', or a wrestling match, to which Clausewitz likened war.[3] Because conflict, war, and actual warfare is akin to a grand duel, strategy in all its facets cannot be developed and applied as a solitary pursuit. The enemy matters deeply. Indeed, the enemy matters so deeply that his presence must be reflected in everything that we decide and attempt strategically. Even when one elects to ignore believed enemy preferences as a potential influence upon friendly behaviour, one should do so consciously. To return to the main theme, what was it about the German way in warfare that was right, even if it foundered badly in historical practice when misapplied by incompetents and other unfortunates in the twentieth century?

In a much-quoted, but also frequently misunderstood passage written in 1871, Field Marshal Helmuth Graf von Moltke, military victor in the three brief wars of German unification (1864, 1866, 1870–71), advised as follows:

> [S]trategy affords tactics the means for fighting and the probability of winning by the direction of armies and their meeting at the place of combat. On the other hand, strategy appropriates the success of every engagement and builds upon it. The demands of strategy grow silent in the face of a tactical victory and adapt themselves to the newly created situation.
>
> Strategy is a system of expedients. It is more than a discipline: it is the transfer of knowledge to practical life, the continued development of the original leading thought in accordance with the constantly changing circumstances. It is the art of acting under the pressure of the most difficult conditions.[4]

All too often Moltke is criticized unfairly by scholars and others who seize upon his apparently dismissive formula, '[s]trategy is a system of expedients', while neglecting to appreciate its context. This context is provided with what seems to this armchair strategist to be high clarity. The remainder of the Field Marshal's sentence at issue makes what should be unmistakeable reference to 'the continued development of the original leading thought in accordance with the constantly changing circumstances'. What Moltke was claiming, unexceptionally one would think, is that one needs to be flexible in adapting to the dynamic reality of tactical circumstances, anticipated and other, all the while holding 'the original leading thought', the dominant strategic concept, plainly in view as a guiding light that may well have to be trimmed, and more, under the pressure of events.

Even the Field Marshal's assertion that 'strategy is a system of expedients' is by no means as deadly to good strategic practice as one might choose to argue. After all, the claim is exactly correct. He did not say, and certainly he did not mean to say, that the strategist does what he can do, simply because he can do it and regardless of consequences. Rather did he try to explain that warfare is an uncertain and notably unpredictable project that should be prosecuted flexibly as to ways, means, and sometimes ends also. Moreover, the necessity for flexibility is imposed by the semi-independent will of the enemy. Moltke did no more, nor less, than speak a vital truth about the nature of warfare and strategy. The former proceeds to manifest itself with unpredictable particulars, while the latter has need to adapt to what is revealed through its education by events. Moltke was seeking to bolt together the actual tactical reality of warfare and a sensible strategic direction to that project. His great conceptual failing was that although he recognized the supremacy of high policy over the decision for war, he insisted that the conduct of the war chosen by the politicians must be left wholly in the hands of the military professionals of the general staff. Antulio Echevarria has explained convincingly how, in Moltke's view, tactical success should pull strategy close behind it, albeit guided overall by a dominant strategic concept.[5] By contrast, his successor as chief of the great general staff, Alfred von Schlieffen, the author of the great plan whose operational authority has been contested by historians, had no difficulty with the proposition that military strategy should push tactical behaviour, rather than the reverse. But Schlieffen, unlike Moltke, did insist that a war's political purpose should not be permitted to overrule the military logic of strategy.

What appears to have happened in the strategic literature is that the succession of great German misadventures in strategy in the twentieth century have been at least partially misunderstood in strategic terms, a matter of historical judgement that transcends the scope of this chapter. More to the point of our text, unsound criticism of Moltke's writing on strategy has been stimulated, understandably enough, by the great soldier's iconic authority over Germany's subsequent military malpractice. Moltke can be presented as the apostle of an operational opportunism unbridled by the discipline of anything worth calling strategic grip for control. A classic expression of this view was offered in the British Official History of the Great War, with reference to General Erich Lindendorff's conduct of the five offensive thrusts against the Allies on the Western Front between 21 March and 15 July 1918. Official historian Brigadier General Sir James E. Edmonds was critical on what he judged to have been Ludendorff's astrategic performance of operational art, loss of strategic plot perhaps. It is worth noting that notwithstanding the contestable and still much contested judgements that abound in the official histories, this view of German performance in 1918 has, if anything, gained in scholarly favour over the years. Edmonds' 'Reflections' on Ludendorff's command performance includes this passage:

> His original plan—like the Schlieffen-Moltke plan of 1914—was far too ambitious and took too little account of the enemy. He was certainly right to change it radically when the operations failed to take the course he had forecast. He started with an elaborate plan on paper for the *Second Army*, the central one, to break through and, wheeling north with the *Seventeenth*, to

roll up the British front, whilst the *Eighteenth* kept off the French. Possibly from the outset he had something less completely strategic in his mind; for all depended on a tactical-breakthrough. At any rate, he soon dropped this plan, and when, in the course of the battle, Crown Prince Rupprecht of Bavaria enquired what the strategic objective was, true to Moltke the elder's teaching that strategy is made up of expedients, he answered on the telephone, 'I forbid myself to use the word *strategy*. We chop a hole. The rest follows. We did it that way in Russia' . . . He [Ludendorff: CSG] has been blamed by some post-war German writers for putting tactics before strategy, but according to the accepted view in Germany before the War strategic victory follows from tactical success.[6]

Edmonds, among many others, has judged Ludendorff guilty of 'lack of determination, and . . . taking counsel with his fears of an Allied counter-stroke . . . [in stopping operation after operation probably prematurely: CSG] . . . when a little more persistence might have given him Amiens, broken the railway communication between the Allies, and left the British on "an island" so that they could be dealt with at leisure without weakening the tactical situation . . .'.[7]

Hindsight, the rear-view mirror, is a magical tool for the student of strategy. Nearly all that was obscured by the fog of war appears to be revealed. The temptation to play 'what if . . .' can be irresistible. Ludendorff failed in 1918. But did he fail because the die were loaded too heavily against Germany, which is a contextual structural explanation, or because he made poor choices while his enemies made better ones? Were the difficulties for German strategy just too many and too severe in 1918? If strategy is the art of the possible, as must be true, did the strategic history of 1918 reveal what was and was not possible, or did it simply register what happened along one of several historical paths that could have been pursued? How great were the difficulties that denied Imperial Germany victory in 1918? Were they impossible to overcome or evade?[8] This chapter seeks to identify the principal reasons why strategy is difficult to do well. In addition, this discussion explains why strategy can be done well enough, the problems notwithstanding. This is a classic bad news and good news presentation. In principle, and often in practice, the sources of difficulty for the strategist, any strategist in any period, are appallingly legion. But one can hardly fail to notice that despite the problems some belligerents do succeed strategically. How is this possible, given the difficulties that lurk in strategy country? This chapter argues the case for the feasibility of successful strategy. At this juncture, it is appropriate to venture the proposition that individuals can matter. Without wishing to encourage pointless 'what ifs . . .', it is nonetheless sensible to note that Germany in 1918 was not utterly bereft of highly experienced soldiers who might well have conducted a desperate offensive with far greater operational skill than did First Quartermaster General Ludendorff. And who can be sure that one among Generals Hoffman, Kuhl, Lossberg, and Seeckt might not have triumphed over Germany's contextual weaknesses.[9] As argued in the Introduction, one should strive to understand strategic theorists as best one can on their own terms in the several relevant contexts of their times. It is important that we comprehend accurately what a theorist was seeking to explain. But this particular book is more interested in identifying usefully the logic of strategy, and the nature of its connections with policy and tactics, than it is in being strictly faithful to any one, or several, classics of strategic ideas. This effort recognizes that it must climb on the shoulders of those who have gone before on the theory trek, but the prime loyalty of my venture is to truth, not to history as an end in itself. It is essential for us to try honestly to grasp what Clausewitz sought to explain, but even should we achieve high confidence that we have done that, our most important mission remains to be completed. Specifically, we are committed to the effort to understand strategy in such a way that its complex working can be explained to those who must try to do it on our behalf in actual command performance. The core of the tangle that needs to be sorted out lies in the difficult connections among policy, strategy, and tactics. The German example offered here serves to illustrate this historical reality. As we have emphasized already, there is no natural harmony among policymaking, strategic direction, and operational field command.

The critical path pursued here traverses the diverse badlands of the bandit country of strategy's difficulties. The concluding section presents some offsets to the difficulties examined and offers the possibly apostate proposition that one can overvalue strategy. Perhaps strategy can be over- as well as underappreciated. This analysis helps contextualize the main body of the chapter. It may help protect against the raising of unusually optimistic expectations concerning the relative value of measures to arrest or avoid the problems with strategy. As a bold, possibly foolhardy thought, we deploy the most quintessential of the strategist's questions, 'so what?', in order to challenge the relative significance of strategy itself.

PROBLEMS

Existential Understanding

Before plunging into the specific problems with strategy, it is necessary to record a few fundamental facts, appreciation of which should help explain the approach chosen. First, there is a basic existential problem. Strategy is so ill understood as a function that its absence can pass unnoticed. Videos record leaders stating policy goals, and they show military hardware impressively in motion, but they have great difficulty showing strategy. Since strategy is not well understood, unlike policy and tactics, it is scarcely surprising that the difficulties which harass its creation and performance are rarely considered competently. Second, even when the meaning of strategy is grasped securely, indeed because it is so grasped, theorists and practitioners alike can be appalled into a paralysis of will born of an all too human, and not unreasonable pessimism. When one considers much, certainly not all, of what could go wrong, how dare one make a major strategic choice and aspire broadly to adhere to its requirements? We shall strive to immunize theorist and practitioner alike against the malady of inappropriate pessimism.

Third, it is important to recognize that there is a most vital sense in which a polity must do strategy, at least behave strategically, whether or not it invents and pursues definite plans purposefully, even if adaptably. Like breathing by individuals, security communities in conflict behave strategically. What they do and do not do, and how they do it, produces net strategic effect by belligerent interaction. All that can be at issue are the degree of explicitness to strategic direction and the quality of strategic performance. Functionally regarded, participation in strategy and strategic behaviour are not discretionary.

Fourth and finally, the realm of problems for strategy presents itself to the theorist, certainly to this theorist, as a potentially unmanageably target-rich environment. The remainder of this chapter locates and addresses strategy's problems by convenient cluster, all the while recognizing that the list could be endless. We armchair strategists should enhance our empathy for action strategists by contemplating how wide and deep are the traps, accidents, and other impediments to excellent, or even to just good enough, strategic performance. It is advisable to close this section of the discussion with the proposition that among the phalanx of difficulties for the strategist none looms so formidably as does the enemy with an independent will. Given that the strategist needs an enemy, or simply a rival, in order to have a professional function at all, the implications of this proposition plainly are unavoidable. Cunning plans to evade the very fact of an unruly enemy frequently fail.[10] But fortunately for the strategist, both his—The Other's—and our, paradoxical and ironic logic can help save us from strategy's worst dilemmas.[11] Although we must confront awesome problems with strategy, so too must our enemies. Moreover, the difficulties are not truly activated save in a context of actual conflict, most especially though not exclusively of warfare itself. It has to follow that we can count absolutely upon the problems with strategy afflicting The Other as well as ourselves. There should be much comfort in this recognition. When politicians and military commanders focus unduly, even exclusively, upon their own problems at the expense of appreciation of the enemy's difficulties, their strategic performance is certain to be impaired. However, when it comes to problems, enemy behaviour must be a principal worry; indeed, as a general rule it should be the major concern.

Three kinds of difficulty can frustrate the strategist: these pertain to the basic inherent challenge of strategy; to the scarcely less demanding need to shape what can be a highly resistant, indeed directly contested, course of future history; and to the frequently near impossible task of actually getting strategy 'done' from beginning through to the end game (see Table 4.1). To explain: first, the core function of strategy is to convert assets into benefit. Military power may provide a useful yield simply by the fact of its existence. It is perceived and interpreted by those whom its images principally concern. In explicit, as contrasted with merely latent, menace, as threat, and in action, armed force is expended by the strategist

Table 4.1 Three Kinds of Problem with Strategy

1. Understanding—what should be done?
2. Difficulties—how can we do it?
3. Performance—can we get it done?

in return for desired military and then political consequences. This is the theory. It should be needless to add that currency conversion from cause into effect is a hazardous and inherently uncertain enterprise. The transaction costs are usually high and the rate of exchange may prove unfavourable.

The second source of generic difficulty for the strategist is the necessity to predict how his assets will be rewarded when deployed to secure a desired political future that enemies will resist. To repeat a familiar refrain, strategy is not a game played against a mindless nature, lethal though nature can be. Rather is strategy pursued in a context wherein paradox, irony, and a skilled or lucky enemy assuredly will line up in independent, actually somewhat interdependent, opposition. Finally, it is always difficult to ensure that strategy is done 'in the field', as it were.[12] The reason why this should be so can be explained by thinking of a country at war as an incredibly complex system of systems. For a state to function well enough grand strategically, most of its interconnected parts need to do at least a minimum of what they have to do at a tolerable level of competence as contributors to a single war effort—when the grand strategy key is turned. Moreover, someone, actually several people, processes, and enforcers, are required if a war effort is to be maintained in the face of surprises. Descending from the level of grand strategy down to the plateau wherein generalship is needed, once a military commander launches an operation, he and his staff have to ensure the continuous functioning of all the components essential to completion of the action. Often it has been observed that the key difference between great and not-so-great generals is not a gap in knowledge of the science and art of war, but rather is a gulf in the ability to make happen what is intended.[13] It is all very well to claim plausibly, as does Harry R. Yarger, that 'planning makes strategy actionable', but 'actionable' is not synonymous with effective action. The strategic function requires more of a strategist than just planning.[14] Also it mandates competent command for control of implementing behaviour against an actively resisting enemy.

Table 4.2 summarizes the problems with strategy. By and large, each of the items listed as a problem truly is a category of problems. This analysis is placed in Part II of the book as 'Practice', despite the generality of the presentation. What follows here is general theory, but its potential applicability to any and every strategic historical happening is so close that the author prefers to explain the problems with strategy in the context of 'Practice' rather than 'Theory'. In truth, theory and practice are so entwined that they need to be regarded as a strategic whole, the gestalt to which this text has referred already.

Table 4.2 Problems with Strategy

Existential understanding
The inconvenient, but necessary, enemy
Currency conversion without a stable exchange rate, from assets and prowess–
    with transaction costs–into net benefit
Lack of expertise and process
Culture, personality, biology, and circumstance
Complexity, disharmony, and range of domain
Friction, the climate of war, and prediction
Culture clash: civil–military relations

It is useful to consider this chapter as an exercise contrapuntal to the general theory as presented in Chapters 1 and 2. Much as the theory of war must include the theory of peace, so the theory of strategy has to accommodate the theory of strategic failure. The latter is not strictly essential to the integrity of the positive theory, because it ought to be implicit in, and signposted by, that theory. Nonetheless, given that the general theory of strategy must be theory for practice, it is desirable and eminently defensible to approach the realm of problems for the strategist as the flip side of the positive strategic theory coin. One side does not function without the other. To understand strategy's difficulties in practice, first one must understand strategy. On the same logic, in order to grasp properly the function of strategy, it is literally essential to have some comprehension of the harassments that impair practice.

It may be no exaggeration to claim that for many a government and more than a few generals, strategy is one of Donald H. Rumsfeld's unjustly infamous 'known unknowns'.[15] It is relatively easy, albeit perilous, to fail to notice that one lacks a strategy. Perversely perhaps, it is not hard to sympathize with the outlook of astrategic practical people. They comprehend policy goals and military threat and action. Military professionals charged with the mission of winning will devise and execute military plans for the purpose of beating the enemy. If the purpose of the war is the enemy's overthrow, then total military victory should secure all of the strategic effect necessary to satisfy policy. But if the political purpose is modest, then military strategy cannot be guided wholly by military considerations. Historically, even when the complete downfall of the enemy had been the initial goal, the course of events will reveal what is and is not possible at bearable cost.

As was explained in the previous section, the strategic function cannot be evaded. Behaviour has consequences. A polity may not have an explicit grand or overall military strategy, but it will perform strategically, probably poorly, through the effects of its strategies-as-plans in action. The professional strategist in this author rebels at the thought, but he is obliged for the ethical reason of full disclosure to concede that a polity may perform well without strategic guidance of an explicit purposeful kind. Armed forces can be mobilized, committed to battle when and where it is expedient, prudent, or necessary. The enemy also may fight bereft of anything worthy of the strategy label above the operational level of warfare. Success in battle may bring its own strategic and political reward. If one can meet the enemy and slay or otherwise neutralize him, what need is there for strategy? This is not the occasion to answer the question, but it is not hard to see why the benefits claimed for strategy may elude understanding by those uneducated in the holistic reality of conflict, war, and warfare.

This author has yet to be convinced that there is, or even could be, a plausible case for disdaining strategy. However, it can be instructive for a relatively unselfcritical strategist to be challenged, confronted even, by a sceptic who will dare to ask, 'so what?'. The sceptic could try to argue that a neglect of strategy is of little or no importance. To return to a point made earlier, Moltke (the elder) did not demean strategy, he insisted only that it should be flexible in the light of unfolding events, because tactics must drive the actual course of strategic history. The existential difficulty for the would-be strategist is to secure appreciation for the importance of his mission. This is unlikely to be achievable if policymakers, soldiers, and others fail to grasp strategy's vital bridging role.

THE INCONVENIENT ENEMY

On 16 September 2008, the American general then commanding in Iraq, Raymond T. Odierno, issued a commander's 'counterinsurgency guidance' document that contained the following admirable, if obvious, points: 'We have made great gains, but much remains to be done. *The enemy still has a vote*, and progress may sometimes be slow.'[16] Obvious though it should be to insist upon recognition of the reality of the independence, actually the interdependence, of the enemy, neglect of his nature, of his role and of the historically unique detail of his being, has been commonplace by belligerents throughout the ages. The reasons have been many, including unsound cultural assumptions and unavoidable lack of information. Each case is different, at least in detail, though not so much in kind. Strategic theorists differ in their rank-ordering of the factors that promote strategic success and failure. However, inadequate understanding of the enemy, often truly The Other in psychological terms, should score heavily in the negative column.

When asked why his eponymous 'charge' with 14,000 men failed to break the federal line along Cemetery Ridge on the third day at Gettysburg, Major General George Pickett replied with grimly humorous understatement, 'I think the Union army had something to do with it'.[17] It should be difficult to ignore, neglect, or thoroughly discount the role of the enemy in strategy, but many strategists have succeeded in so doing, despite the formidable obstacles to such error. Consideration of the enemy, the 'Other' if you will, is as central to the subject of this book as any theme can be. The fact that such consideration so often is inadequate and is a prominent source of weakness in strategic performance adds potent fuel to the necessity to privilege its analysis here.

Since the primary purpose of strategy is to control an enemy's behaviour, it is challenging to contrive strategies when foes are absent. Both logically and practically, the designation of a particular enemy or enemies is not strictly essential for strategy. Typically, security communities can, indeed need to, 'do strategy', as manifested in peacetime defence preparations even when either plausible enemies cannot be located, or their precise identity is uncertain. In such historical cases, defence plans, which is to say strategies, have to be adaptable and flexible so as to provide hedges against at least a short range of possible future dangers.[18] Literally, it is not feasible to abjure strategic behaviour, no matter how strongly averse one may be to planning. All communities do strategy functionally; they manipulate a complex compound process of applied ways, means, and ends, even if they do not do so with steady purpose coherently. Armed forces, existentially and in action, must have strategic effect, whether or not generals, admirals, and their staffs have developed specific plans. As we have observed already, there is more than a mere element of truth in the belief that success in fighting the enemy, more or less whenever he can be brought to battle, will take care of the challenge of strategy. Alas for such a pragmatic view, though, its undoubted merit is dangerously limited in domain. War is about more than warfare, and warfare is about more than battles. An enviable record of victory in warfare, duly tabulated as a string of battlefield triumphs, is entirely consistent with defeat in war as a whole and in the end. Witness the enviable combat career of Hannibal Barca in the ultimately catastrophic Second Punic War, or the even more disastrous consequences of the initial successes of Adolf Hitler's magnificent Wehrmacht. In most wars, the losing belligerent does not receive an attractive prize for coming in second after competing well, if not necessarily honourably.

So, although 'war is nothing but a duel on a larger scale', the purpose of which has to be 'to impose our will on the enemy', the foe's identity need not be absolutely certain.[19] It is necessary, therefore, to approach the subject of threat identification in strategy by treating it as a spectrum ranging from the all but unknown to the transparently and all but unarguably certain. Strategy is much easier to design when the enemy is known rather than only suspected. In the 1900s, the 1930s, and yet again in the 2000s, for some examples, the British army has been obliged to divide its attention between enemies who wage warfare in a regular style, and those who must adopt irregular practices. Does one plan to control revolting insurgents, or the regular military prowess of ambitious, aggressive, proud, and fearful states, or both? When strategists cannot, or are not permitted politically, to designate a prime enemy, they have to invent plausible virtual adversaries. In principle, it is entirely possible to raise and sustain armed forces while remaining in a condition of near, even total, strategic ignorance and innocence. Indeed, it is common for states to maintain a military instrument that is not purchased according to any discernible strategic logic. However, even if the political process functions astrategically in the exercise of its responsibility for community defence, it is unlikely that professional soldiers would follow that example. As a general rule, armed forces acquired, sustained, and occasionally modernized for non-strategic reasons on the part of political resource providers, nonetheless will be more or less strategically rational in design and preparation. Whatever the size of the defence budget, and regardless of political constraints upon certain kinds of military capability (e.g. land mines, cluster bombs, poison gas, nuclear weapons), professional soldiers will do their best to match what they can build to what they believe ought to be achievable for 'Case X' against enemy 'Y'. Strategy, and the making and doing of strategies, always is the art of the possible, as we have sought to insist.

As a general though not invariable rule this book prefers to refer to the enemy rather than to the adversary, opponent, rival, competitor, or foe. These are certainly alternatives, but they are not quite synonymous. Enemy carries suitable menace as a concept for the theory of strategy; helpfully it exudes more than a hint of violence. Unfortunately, though, enemy is so strong an idea that it suffers from the sin of over-designation. In many, probably most, historical circumstances of inter-communal relations short of actual war, adversary is more appropriate a concept than is enemy. Both may well be correct. The former risks understating the enmity, while the latter all but guarantees some measure of exaggeration. As for the other alternatives cited: opponent is unduly bland and uncommunicative, rival is insufficiently hostile in suggestion, while foe is becoming archaic and hence can sound rather precious. Despite these quibbles, this text will have occasional resort to the less-favoured terms, if only for the sake of literary variety or to reduce the horsepower of antagonism implied by unvarnished reference to the enemy. Although adversary is an anaemic term for a participant in such a sanguine activity as warfare, it is preferred in dictum five because the dictum covers contexts of both war and peace. Not least among the challenges for a strategist is the difficulty of knowing whether a polity in question truly is an enemy, as opposed to an adversary or merely a rival: American strategists today confront this conundrum when they consider China and Russia. It may be needless to add that one's choice of designation—enemy, adversary, and so forth—is both liable to subjective influence, and may itself alter the designated state's policy and strategic behaviour, and hence the character of the political relationship.

Clausewitz is clear enough on the centrality of the enemy to the problems of war, strategy, and warfare. Nonetheless, his treatment of the duelling feature, even arguably prime dynamic, of war leaves much to be desired. Generically, at least, we know why states duel on a grand scale in warfare, but the Prussian does not offer much of substance on how they do it. The general theory of strategy has long been in need of historically well-attested amplification on the subject of the ways and means by which antagonists pursue their more or less deadly quarrels. In point of fact, strategic studies in all periods betrays a systemic weakness in treatment of the enemy, The Other. More often than not, only one side in strategic history's bloody conflicts receives its due, and probably more, from historians. Despite the unavoidable, indeed necessary, centrality to strategic affairs of antagonistic relations between political entities, truly holistic two-sided-plus narratives are not as common as they should be. Advancing relentlessly with the apparently lethal precision gifted by hindsight, analysis proceeds in reverse using the marvellous tool of the rear-view mirror. Beginning with the end condition of victory and defeat, we like to work backwards, demonstrating 'why Germany lost', 'why the Allies won', 'why deterrence succeeded', and so forth. The synergistic biasing effects of the historian's unavoidable foreknowledge of outcomes, and of his chosen master question, all but guarantee notably unsafe assignment of causation.

The general theory of strategy requires that scholars at least attempt to approach strategic history—past, present, and future—holistically, as a duel, as an inalienably adversarial project wherein the enemy is permitted to play a role that although interdependent also has independent content. When one belligerent loses, the other wins, or at least fares better on some assay. It is dangerously easy to slide inadvertently into the mode of all but autarkic analysis. Explanation of the course and outcome of a complex historical episode, say the American Civil War, reduces to the quest for reasons why the South had to lose or the North had to win.[20] The question itself is not so much the methodological problem, rather does the trap lurk in the systemic bias in the approach, a quality not always obvious to its users and clients. The careless scholar seeks and finds Confederate limitations, contingent and structural deficiencies and errors, rather than Union strengths and competencies. As George Pickett so wisely observed in the words quoted already, when one side loses in warfare it is more likely than not that the other had performed at least creditably. For a minimal claim, the enemy must have fought well enough to win, no matter how far short of an absolute standard of combat excellence the performance fell.

Bifocality is as necessary for strategic effectiveness in historical reality as it is rare. It should be no great comfort to practicing strategists to discover that their autarkic bias is a malady shared with the authors of the classics on strategy. There is no denying that although an enemy, actual or virtual, is necessary for strategy, in practice he is an inconvenience for the strategist. Indeed, he is likely to be so inconveniently uncooperative as to shred the merit in one's strategic plans. Self-consciously or not, often the most practicable solution to the open-ended potential challenge to our wishes and intentions posed by the enemy effectively is to ignore him as an independent actor.

Seemingly, every feature in the theory of strategy comes with an intellectual health warning; so it is with dictum five. Strategy is indeed adversarial by nature and the character of adversaries must be distinctive from historical case to case. But while neglect of the enemy as a self-willed actor is often a fatal error, so too can be an undue respect for his believed strengths. By way of illustration of this point, we can quote General William Tecumseh Sherman on the subject of his friend, General Ulysses S. Grant, as a commander. Sherman wrote:

> I am a damn sight smarter than Grant. I know a great deal more about war, military history, strategy, and grand tactics than he does; I know more about organization, supply, and administration, and about everything else than he does. But I tell you where he beats me, and where he beats the world. He don't care a damn for what the enemy does out of his sight, but it scares me like hell.[21]

Respect for the implications of strategy's adversarial nature is a virtue only when it does not foster and license a paralysing or panicking anxiety over possible, exaggerated to probable, enemy strengths and options.[22] Not for nothing is 'the initiative' hailed as a vital principle of war. The enemy must not be regarded as a passive and option-less victim, but neither must his potential for harm be permitted too easily to deny otherwise attractive looking options to us.

CURRENCY CONVERSION

Strategy as currency conversion is inherently problematic. To secure particular political goals, how great a threat is required, perhaps how large a bribe? To win a war for limited purposes, how substantial a military defeat must be inflicted? Or, to influence, if not necessarily control, the political will of an enemy, how heavy need the costs be that we impose upon him? How much pain need we inflict? As much if not more to the point, with respect to each of the abstract questions just posed, in actual historical practice is a particular enemy deterrable, bribable, and coercible? Only a process of trial, error, and honest learning on the bloody job can tell us. Culturally speaking, Western civilization appears to have great difficulty thinking holistically about war, peace, and strategy. Television journalists are addicted to referring to combat aircraft as 'war planes', though they might with as much reason be called 'peace planes'. I admit that such an unusual term would be ill-received politically, because it would certainly be misinterpreted as revealing a cynical irony rather than a praiseworthily rigorous strategic logo. One recalls with some pleasure the unintended irony in the organizational logo of the US Strategic Air Command, 'Peace is our profession'. The fact that the logo was accurate, strictly revised, did not save it from negative assessment. Western culture(s) continues to make a fairly sharp distinction between war and peace, even though a condition of more or less warlike peace is common for some communities. The drawing of a clear legal, ethical, and political distinction between conditions of war and those of peace has much to recommend it— obviously so, hence its cultural popularity. However, the distinction can have injurious consequences for strategic performance.

The whole point of strategy, after all, is to bridge a divide between politics and (military) action 'in the field'. Military behaviour naked of political purpose is meaningless in our culture. We are Clausewitzians. Warfare, the exercise of organized violence, is only allowable for political purposes. Indeed, to be truly Western and contemporary, one must insist that warfare is, or at least is more, an instrument of international law than it is of politics/policy as *On War* asserts and argues.[23] No longer should polities fight for glory and profit. Warfare is not to be regarded as a healthy self-referential activity, an expression of a society's manliness in pursuit of fame and gold. Such is supposed to be the case today, though on close examination Thucydides' triptych of 'fear, honour, and interest' continues to hold a steely grip on human behaviour and misbehaviour.

The nature of war matters deeply for the difficulty of strategic performance. Warriors enjoy warfare; they are social deviants only saved from perdition because they place their personal drives at the political service of the community.[24] Since warfare necessarily entails the killing of people and the damaging of property, the challenge is, and has always been, to employ those horrors for net political benefit at socially tolerable cost. The trouble is that there is a radical difference in nature, in kind, between violence and political consequence. War, even warfare, is not a science, but even if it were, how would one attempt to calculate the conversion rate for death, destruction, and fear, into political reward? If there can be no general metric conversion table, applicable to all belligerents at all times, every project of war is a journey on the dark side into the unknown and the unknowable. Whatever one's cause, whether one is regarded by future historians as mainly villain or victim, this dilemma of currency conversion is central to the difficulty of strategy.

EXPERTISE AND PROCESS

There is a sense in which everyone is a strategist in their daily lives. Each of us trades the temporary or more commitment of our personal assets for emotional-psychological, financial, or other material returns. Muscle power, brainpower, and power of emotional attraction becomes money or some other currency— love, happiness, security, physical well-being, and so forth. This exchange partly of like for unlike provides some unsystematic education, even training, for the would-be professional strategist. However, professional strategists are few and far between. The nineteenth-century Italian poet, Gabriele D'Annunzio (1863– 1938), wrote the much-quoted line, 'happy is the land that needs no heroes'. He might have written, to the same effect, 'happy is the land that needs no military strategists'. Unfortunately, the polities that need no such strategists are rare. Despite the richness of demand for strategic performance, the supply of excellence, or even just competence, more often than not is lacking.

In practice, several deficiencies combine malevolently to produce a great compound difficulty. Specifically because the strategic function frequently is not well understood, there is a lack of institutional provision for its performance. It follows that the lack, or dysfunctional character, of a workable institutional context has to mean that there is little demand for warm bodies to people them and perform as strategists. Strategy is made by strategists in a process by an organization.[25] Process requires organizational engineering. The metaphor of the strategy bridge highlights the historical reality that strategy, both grand and military, cannot prudently be entrusted to individual genius or even to presumed or anticipated divine inspiration. Both could be useful and are usually welcome, but when they do not turn up to play on the days of decision there needs to be a practicable alternative. This alternative is a staff, it is an organization, it is a process, and it is a routine, without entirely excluding inspiration, of course. And as history records, strategic inspiration is near certain to be the product of a single brain, not a committee. Nonetheless, the truly inspired strategist, the person with a genius for war in the full meaning of the concept, cannot perform alone. He must have a staff with a competent chief, as well as subordinate commanders worthy of trust. The adequate and better strategist, most likely in some good measure self-educated and instinctual, must have a team if his ideas are both to be translated into actionable plans, and then if those plans are to be effected adaptably in battle.

Polities need access only to a thin trickle of strategists. Of course strategy is 'done' by a cast of thousands, perhaps millions, as tactical behaviour of all kinds, and that behaviour is guided in plans-as-strategies by operational artistry with some science (logistical expertise, for a leading example), by a team of tens. But, the overall direction of military, let alone total societal, effort, is a function assigned to few people indeed. Because strategy is so difficult, for all the reasons and more deployed here, excellence in its performance is rare rather than standard. Fortunately, strategic excellence is not usually a requirement, if it were then few of history's great victories would have been achieved. In practice, polities tend to win despite the fragility of their strategies or even the plain incompetence of their strategists. So multifaceted is conflict, war, and warfare that there are usually potential sources of compensation for weakness in strategy: wealth, numbers, technological superiority, ideology, enemy error, among many others. The list of possible, though unreliable, aids for the strategically challenged is a long one.

As a strategist, this author is uncomfortable writing this, but it must be admitted that polities can win without a purposeful strategy, with no orderly process for developing strategy and strategies, and without competent strategists. By analogy, (a very few) people have been known to fall from high buildings and survive uninjured. Strategy, strategists, and bureaucratic routines to produce strategies are not strictly essential. There is no law of strategic history that mandates strategic competence, let alone excellence, as a necessary condition for strategic success. However, the gods of war are not to be mocked with impunity. Strategy-free, strategy-light, and strategy-distinctly poor, belligerents eventually, and usually sooner rather than later, are punished by events for their incompetence. One thinks immediately of Hannibal Barca, Julius Caesar, Christian Outremer (the Kingdom of Jerusalem) in the Middle Ages, Napoleon, and Imperial and Nazi Germany. But people inclined to rush to the judgement that a strategy fix is the elixir that must convert the base material of raw assets into the precious metal of advantage, success, and victory, would be well advised to restrain their enthusiasm. Strategic competence is not a panacea, though assuredly it is always a major, and sometimes a decisive, benefit. Probably it is historically accurate to claim that the strategic incompetence of the enemy more often is a crucial advantage than is the quality of the victor's strategy. Both world wars in the twentieth century illustrate this claim amply.

Can strategists be trained or rather must they be educated, and can education be reliable?[26] Staffs as staffs do not usually conceive strategy, but they are necessary if the strategic concept, should there be one, or more, is ever to find itself in action. Because strategy is difficult to do in all senses—to conceive, render actionable, and do in battlespace—there is never an abundance of suitably gifted potential strategists. Many countries strive to train strategists, in part because they do not grasp fully just what the strategy function requires, while a few endeavour earnestly, if rarely rigorously, to educate strategists. It is the view of this book that the excellent strategist should be theorist, planner, charismatic leader, and commander. If strategy frequently is a bridge too far, so also is superior competence in each of the roles just itemized. Some great commanders have been short of charisma as leaders, while a host of excellent planners and a few outstanding theorists—Clausewitz for one, Friedrich von Paulus (of Stalingrad notoriety) for another—did not shine when entrusted with operational command.

It is probably not true to argue that as in poker the superior player-strategist will always win ultimately, regardless of the value of the hands that are dealt. On balance, this rule for poker does not apply reliably to conflict and war. Context can triumph over personal attributes. Strategists can only be educated, they cannot be trained. By contrast, staff officers can and must be trained.[27] Excellent staff officers do not necessarily make first-rate strategists. By analogy, superior skill in operations analysis does not indicate a high talent for systems analysis. The latter requires imagination, lateral thinking, the former typically does not. This is not to suggest that systems analysts, even the greatest among them, necessarily bring to their analysis the breadth and depth of understanding needed for strategic judgement.[28] We can train tens of thousands of people to be expert in application of the quantifiable methodologies of operations research. We cannot train many people to be expert in judging how much, and what kinds of military leverage should be exercised in order to secure the political rewards we seek. It is necessary to establish appointments with defined strategic responsibility, and also to establish staffs and routines for their operation to support the strategists. However, the mere existence of a position that requires strategic thought and judgement does not guarantee anything. The people appointed may not be highly capable, neither may they be sanctioned by political authority to perform the strategic function, notwithstanding their job description. The practice function may not follow form, to mistreat le Corbusier's famous dictum ('form follows function'). A proposition that runs throughout this text holds that the quality of practice of strategy in strategies always is driven by the character of key unique people's performance both as individuals and as members of a group.

Organizations certainly can be designed rationally, so that in principle they should be fit for strategic purpose. Talented individuals can be educated by exposure to the classics of strategy, to military, and other histories, and by reflection upon their own and others' experience. But ultimately the quality of practical strategy is governed significantly by the highly variable quality of unique people's strategic aptitudes and actual performances 'on the day', day after day—and those people include the enemy, and sometimes one's friends and allies also. It is important never to forget that one's strategic performance can only be as good as the enemy, inter alia, allows. Happily perhaps, the enormous difficulty with strategy that is the result of somewhat dysfunctional individuals, supposed team-groups, flawed institutions and processes, has to be a bilateral phenomenon. Not only does the enemy have a vote, but he too is certain to find his overall strategic performance more or less enervated by dysfunctional elements. Strategy is a duel, as the great man wrote unarguably.

He may be guilty of promoting a counsel of perfection, but the ever estimable Harry R. Yarger has words of wisdom to offer as a suitable capstone to the discussion of the absence of true strategists as a difficulty.

> Strategy formulation is not a domain for the thin of skin or self-serving. Detractors stand ever ready to magnify a strategy's errors or limitations. Even success is open to criticism from pundits who question its role, methods, or continued validity. Furthermore, strategy achieves strategic consequences by the multiorder effects it creates over time—always a point of contention in a time-conscious society that values quick results and lacks patience with the 'long view.' In the end, it is the destined role of the strategist to be underappreciated and often demeaned in his own time. Consequently, strategy remains the domain of the strong intellect, the lifelong student, the dedicated professional, and the invulnerable ego.[29]

CULTURE, PERSONALITY, BIOLOGY, AND CIRCUMSTANCE

Strategy is a human endeavour in all of its interlocking, mutually influencing phases. Moreover, lest one forgets, opposition to our strategy also is a human effort on the part of the enemy. In preparing to write this book, and then in the real-time performance of composition, this author has come to see more and more clearly that Ralph Peters is right to insist that 'in this age of technological miracles, our military needs to study mankind'.[30] Unfortunately to be right is not necessarily to be useful. It should be helpful to understand just how pervasively human is the project of strategy in historical experience. But of what exactly does strategy's human dimension consist, indicated as it is to be vital in dictum seven of the general theory? For a dangerously unscholarly thought, this author suspects that strategy's human dependency is easier to accommodate in the realm of practice than it is in theory. The subject of this chapter is the problem of performing the strategic function well enough for reasonable and acceptable political consequences to be earned. Probably one should not say that the challenge is to secure competent strategic performance, because to do so would imply strongly that only competent strategists succeed, which is not always true. One of the messages of this work is that strategy is important, but another is that it is not all important. If strategy is difficult, is assailed by problems that are plainly human, which assuredly is so, it is only logical as well as plausible to insist that when strategy succeeds there must have been human hands on, or off, the tiller. Lest some readers are misled by the litany of bad news about the way of the strategist recounted here, it is essential to recognize that both failure and success with strategy comprise but one subject. The logic in this claim applies also to war and peace. Any theory of war has to be a theory of peace, and vice versa. A university department of War Studies is really a logical, historical, and practical nonsense, as must be a department of Peace Studies. To explain the sources, causes, and triggers for strategic failure, also has to be to explain the sources, causes, and triggers for net positive strategic achievement.

When one endorses the commonsense proposition that strategy is human, to what, specifically, does one refer? Everything that contributes to strategic performance is created and conducted by people functioning as individuals and as groups, including somewhat competing groups, within institutional structures and via processes of more or less orderly, or disorderly, interaction. So we must begin by recognizing the strategist or strategic aide—staff officer—as *fonctionnaire*. People must function in and through organizations in order to do strategy in any sense whatsoever. There is always a distinctive organizational setting, a structured social context. Next, we have to understand the materials from which human strategic performance is fabricated. Principal among these are an individual's biology, psychology, culture, and particular circumstances, institutional and historical (e.g. right man, wrong time, and so forth).

One should not need to penetrate deeply into the scholarly jungle pertaining to strategic performance before a great epiphany becomes unavoidable. Specifically, scholars tend to dissect when they ought to combine; fission should be fusion. Strategy and strategic performance is nothing if not a gestalt, a subject or phenomenon that needs to be approached and conducted as a whole. Of recent years, scholars belatedly have recognized the pervasive significance of culture for strategy.[31] This is praiseworthy. However, unfortunately for the would-be parsimoniously elegant theorist of strategy, as well as for the practical strategic executive, strategy is by no means wholly cultural. The encultured strategists for a security community are indeed the social inheritors of assumptions and preferences that they learn. But alas for simplicity of comprehension and predictability in behaviour, they carry also a genetic inheritance, as well as a psychological character largely attributable to individual life experience, and they must function in a unique and dynamic historical context of menace and opportunity. As if these elements were insufficiently complex, we must never forget that every kind of element that contributes to 'our' human performance of the strategic function contributes also to 'their's', the enemy's. No belligerent is personed by featureless, interchangeable *fonctionnaires*. Everywhere, in all places, at every level of analysis of concern to the strategist, there are people, and those people are individuals.

It is just about possible to write strategic history that is innocent of the acknowledged presence of actual human beings. The actors can be France and Germany, or the Wehrmacht's Sixth Army, or technology duly reified, or B-17s, with scarcely a named individual in sight, nor even explicit recognition that strategic performance has to be done by real human bodies. It is a cliché to assert that morale is the most important element contributing to fighting power.[32] However, this historically amply attested fact is apt to be forgotten when theorists focus unduly upon the potency of ideas, or emphasize the skill or clumsiness of commanders. My argument is not intended to laud 'the face of battle' and its close associates allegedly as comprising some true nature of strategy in tactical action as the field performance of plans and strategies.[33] But, it is to alert theorists—sometimes mea culpa[34]—to recognize the necessity for what one can term the human enabler. Strategy as concept, as plan, and in action in the form of operations and tactical behaviour is enabled, and frequently disabled, by the quality of human performance. This performance has to be considered not only rationally in military terms, but also as a product of culture, psychology, organizational setting, and historical circumstances. And, inconveniently for understanding and prediction, the performance of every belligerent must be shaped by these factors, a shaping of what rolls out as a net dynamic outcome of a grand interaction. These thoughts are mighty daunting to the theorist or historian who seeks humbly, but honestly, to explain strategy. Simple explanation is as easy to do as it must be wrong. Strategy as theory and in practice is complex.

The general theory of strategy can only indicate the key elements and some of the more significant interactions that combine as strategy and are made manifest in specific strategies. The theorist's role is so constrained by poor methodology that while a positive science is way beyond reach, even understanding strategy regarded as a fairly creative art is a notably challenging stretch. If we can understand how strategy should work, in other words how to do it well enough, we will understand why strategy frequently is done less than well. This chapter seeks to provide at least the minimal bare bones of a theoretical explanation of the problems with strategy. Because the subject is so complex and social science is decidedly less than impressively scientific, it is helpful to return again and again to the main story arc, or plot line, of the book, which is the provision of theory for practice. In his path-breaking study of *War and Human Nature*, Steven Peter Rosen offers a powerfully persuasive, almost elemental, explanation of a vital distinction between theory and practice. Rosen grants that biomedical and pharmacological data on individual political leaders must nearly always be inadequate for high confidence prediction of behaviour, when it is not missing altogether. However, he proceeds to claim that 'an understanding of the factors investigated in this book [human biological inheritance in relation to decision making for, and behaviour in, war] could still be useful, in specific situations.'[35] Then he offers the following important judgements:

> As Isaiah Berlin noted many years ago, practical political judgment is not the same as political science. Political scientists seek general explanations that, on average, use a small number of factors to predict behaviour across a wide range of causes, and across time and space. Political leaders do not wish to be right, on average, about hundreds of cases. They wish to be right about one case, the case that they are faced with.[36]

The general theory of strategy has to be shallow but wide, while historically specific operational plans as strategy and strategies must be deep and relatively narrow. General theory will provide persuasive explanation of why strategy is difficult, but it cannot yield detailed prediction as to precisely which problems will occur. By analogy, we can predict the behaviour of crowds (communal ecstasy, or communal panic, say), but not of individuals. Unfortunately, perhaps it is not safe, as the legal wording has it, to treat a particular country, government, or even an army as a crowd, readily predictable as a collective.

Theory advises, indeed instructs, that strategy is extremely difficult to do well. This may seem to be a banal truth, but in historical practice many overconfident strategists could have benefited from the reminder. Also, the insistence of theory upon recognition of the problems with strategy should serve usefully as cues to those who need educating about the virtues of the strategy function.

It has to be admitted that the constraints upon good enough, let alone best, practice in strategy design and execution are truly formidable. In point of fact, they can appear so formidable as to incline one to judge strategy an impracticable function altogether.[37] To illustrate this claim, consider what these paragraphs have argued. They explained that among the many reasons why strategy is difficult is the multi-forked set of interpenetrating factors that we summarize expediently as human. Strategy always is done by people, as individuals and in groups, but the behaviour of the one is rarely identical to the behaviour of the other, notwithstanding their common total biological content. Biology tells us that all persons are not the same, biological inheritance varies as it must for evolution to operate. Similarly, we know that people differ psychologically, in what we call their personality, for reasons of biology, life experience, cultural learning, and circumstance. Moreover, personality can and does shift with age, context, and mood changing chemicals (e.g. caffeine, alcohol, Prozac).[38]

Since strategy essentially is about the control of enemies (and often allies also), and typically is more about the control of their will to compete, including to fight, than it is about their physical ability to resist, how serious is the human factor? For a historically specific example, consider how difficult a challenge Winston Churchill as Britain's prime minister posed for Germany in the summer of 1940.[39] Hitler expected to be able to dictate a highly advantageous peace to a partially defeated Britain. But Churchill was an all too human difficulty; he was a fatal roadblock on the pathway to a German-authored peace (for a 'new world order', in much tainted words). Possibly not unreasonably, Hitler expected Churchill, or if not Churchill then a successor, to behave in a politically and strategically rational manner. With historical hindsight, we can find a rational actor in the Winston Churchill of 1940, but it was difficult for some people to do so at the time, not least in the prime minister's own Conservative party. Hitler had the unenviable need to judge what Churchill was about, why, and with what degree of determination or downright obstinacy. The new British prime minister was known to be culturally more than a little anachronistic—in his attitude towards the British Empire, for example—to be senior in age with some health problems, to drink heavily, to be prone to fits of severe depression, and to be none too secure politically, and so on. Admittedly, Churchill is an extreme example on the spectrum of strong complex characters that have been a source of profound difficulty for enemies to influence. Nonetheless, extreme or not, his case does illustrate usefully the scope and intensity of the problems that the human factor poses for the strategist. Strategy always is done by people, and those people are not stable in their moods, their medical condition, or indeed much else, at least not to the point where they can be profiled with certainty. Individuals are not reliably interchangeable and nor are they predictably ruled by events in their decisions.

The rather pessimistic analysis developed here should give one pause if one nods approvingly when rereading Sun Tzu's most famous dictum: 'One who knows the enemy and knows himself will not be endangered in a hundred engagements.'[40] Is the enemy, say, 'Britain' or is it Churchill? If one is confident of knowing him at 2 a.m., is that to know him at 6 p.m.? How well can we know a personal enemy who thinks, or fails to think, differently when he is drunk (how drunk? Depressed drunk, elated drunk, combative drunk?), or on mood modifying medication? Is it safe to assume that the enemy can be regarded as a collective that performs on average in ways governed by stable preferences? It is not hard to see how the newly fashionable emphasis among Anglo-American strategists upon cultural information may yield disappointing results in practice. Enemies are not only cultural beings, they are also psychological and behaviour self-modifying beings. And different circumstances will likely trigger somewhat unlike decisions or actions. A political leader who seems wise, thoughtful, and competent in deep peacetime may fall apart psychologically and medically when under acute pressure from unanticipated events.

Nonetheless, rather grim though this analysis has to be, it is a fact that strategy has to be done. What is remarkable is that purposeful centralized strategy actually is done quite often tolerably well. The historical performance of strategy can be regarded as something of a miracle, even a mystery, given the problems that its design and conduct must overcome. To repeat a vital refrain, the strategist is likely to be aided significantly by the problems that his enemy's strategist has to resolve or somehow work around.

COMPLEXITY, DISHARMONY, AND SCOPE OF DOMAIN

Occasionally, though only occasionally, it is necessary to state and restate what ought to be transparently obvious. It should be self-evident that a prime source of the problems with strategy is the sheer complexity and scope of the responsibilities inalienable from its function. As the bridge between often shifting political purposes and variable military and other behaviour, strategy cannot avoid being potentially harassed, it will certainly be challenged, by difficulties on both banks and by the problems that each bank's activities pose for the other. The strategist must hold the bridge between political thought and decision and their implementing expression in behaviour in the field or battlespace. Whether or not a strategist is confined to a desk in Washington DC, his intentions must be implemented, enabled, by an assembly of thousands or more, functioning well enough in the face of accident, error, and a variably motivated and uncertainly competent, and materially endowed, enemy. Willingly following Clausewitz, we must note that friction is unavoidable and in detail is generally unpredictable for reason of history and geography's known unknowns and even unknown unknowns.[41] So complex is the most senior military strategist's relevant universe of concern that it cannot helpfully be modelled. Happily, just as 'stuff happens' that creates the friction that impedes, enervates, and frustrates, so also 'stuff happens' that oils the wheels of complex operations. And, recall, negative stuff happens to all belligerents. However, the objective strength of a military effort, in all its aspects, will decide whether friction is merely an annoyance that hinders, or a lethal show-stopper.

The cliché that quantity has a quality all its own applies generously to the high stress realm of the strategist in action. Strategy should work adequately as central direction for, say, military operations, but any of the many relevant dimensions to those operations contains the potential to reveal a disabling dysfunctionality. For example, strategy can be frustrated by logistical failure, unexpectedly severe weather, faulty intelligence, enemy cunning, low morale, technological shortfalls bereft of compensating workarounds, and almost any number of specifically unanticipated occurrences, major and in and of themselves even minor. Such is the complexity and scope of strategy's domain that there is no meaningful limit to the difficulties with which the strategist may need to cope. These difficulties pertain to the bridge itself, naturally enough, as well as to the quality and quantity of behaviour on both banks. Even in the rare event that political ends and military and other means appear to be near perfectly aligned, a purposeful connection between them has to be effected by the work of the strategist and his staff. Wise policy, good troops, and lethally incompetent plan is a flawed trinity that in principle is always waiting to betray the unwary.

The problems with strategy comprise a subject that easily could occupy a whole book, not merely a single chapter, as here. As an issue area, strategy's problems are potentially as extensive as one has time, space, energy, and reader tolerance, to pursue. It is not hard to understand why this should be so. Whereas the policy-maker must decide what should be done, and the principal executive agent, which is to say the army and its commanders, must provide the quality and quantity of fighting power to do it, the strategist with his bridge between the two has to try to match violence with political wishes. To illustrate: how much damage must one wreak upon the enemy by way of threat or actual death and destruction in order to secure the necessary control over his policy? In truth, one cannot know, given the impossibility of exact prediction. So, one must guess, with a prudent bias privileging conservative estimation, and be able to adapt in real time to the education provided by unfolding events.[42]

Of course, politics is the master narrative of strategic history; it provides the story arc. But, no less obviously, policy is only hot air and a waste of ink if the troops cannot do what they are tasked to attempt—but how can one be certain, short of the attempt? On close inspection, it soon becomes obvious that the problems with strategy are by no means confinable to strategy and its bridge. As massive and complex challenges to the strategist, there are the problems *for* strategy that flow, or stutter, down from policy and up from tactics. Because the strategist must match purposes with assets and provide centralized direction for that matching in action, the bridge cannot sensibly be regarded as the whole of his domain. It is obvious to this strategic theorist that the strategist must hold bridgeheads, at least, on both the policy and the operational–tactical banks that he is required to keep well connected. It is never appropriate for the strategist and his staff simply to take direction from the political bank, render them actionable as operational plans, and deliver the enabling orders to the soldiers and others who must perform in the battlespace. And yet this is what often happens, actually it is what always happens in some measure. In theory, there should be continuous dialogues among policymakers, strategists, and operational artists-tacticians.[43] Policymakers will need to adjust their political guidance to the dynamic evolution of the 'big picture'; tacticians and operational commanders must report on what is proving militarily feasible and what is not, as events reveal; and strategists have to translate a shifting political guidance into operational plans that need to be practicable for combat. Table 4.3 expresses the basic triadic construction of the strategist's world, and suggests perilously that strength at one level of contribution sometimes can compensate for relative weakness at the others.

Table 4.3 The Strategist's Triad: A Matrix of Compensation?

	Poor	Average	Superior
Policy (political skill)	G,I		B
Strategy (creative management of assets)	G,I		B
Tactics (fighting power)	I	B	G

Key:
G is for Germany in the Second World War.
B is for Britain in the Second World War.
I is for Italy in the Second World War.

Notes:
1. The purpose of this matrix is to explain in the simplest possible terms the vital truth that belligerents vary in their relative competence in the intimately interconnected, but distinguishable, realms of policy, strategy, and tactics.
2. The examples given in this simple form, of Britain, Germany, and Italy, 1939–45, conceal a myriad of important detail. This reductionism is necessary in order to present the thesis that the strategist's triad of policy, strategy, and tactics, though interdependent as mutual enablers, also provides scope for fungibility to work its magic.
3. It is rare for a polity to score 'superior' at all three levels. Happily, to survive, even succeed, three 'superiors' are not essential, two should suffice. However, there is no doubt that three 'poor's and a polity is out of the game for a while, if not permanently.
4. Performance can vary significantly in the course of a conflict. For example, the British Army shifted from being poor in 1940–41 to average by 1944–5. A similar score, for 1942–3 to 1944–5, holds for the US Army. The US Army Air Forces (USAAF) began poorly but became 'superior', while the US Navy and US Marine Corps were always 'superior'.
5. I admit to the crudity and ambiguity of the performance ratings. As a strategist I mean poor, average, or superior, with reference to the needs of the moment against a particular enemy, not with reference to an absolute standard.

If the title to this subsection seems unduly imperial—complexity, disharmony, and scope of domain—so be it. Each of the three elements are important. Because a strategist seeks to control the direction and character of military operations overall, flaws in the military machine, its assets, and its performance in action are certain to be many. It is true to claim that complexity can be a benefit as well as a burden. While there will be more that can go wrong in a highly complex enterprise than in a simple one, also there should be many ways to compensate for error, accident, and the skill or luck of the enemy. Large, well equipped and trained armies are not proofed against defeat by virtue of their mass and complexity, but they should be more able to tolerate mistakes and bad luck than would a much smaller force. Similarly, in large-scale military enterprises, good generals can carry some poor ones, just as the warriors in a military unit will carry the rest.

To venture a dangerous thought, although competence and better in strategy can and should be held to require both sound policy guidance and high combat effectiveness, this need not be the case. I am unhappy with this argument, but in the interests of honesty I cannot suppress it. Most strategic theorists—admittedly, not a populous profession—defence analysts, and officials incline to believe that their particular level of concern, their functional focus, is the most essential. Specifically, it is possible to argue fairly persuasively that policy is the master and must matter most; or strategy is key, it is the only bridge that connects political intention with military capability and behaviour; or that operations and tactics are 'where the rubber hits the road', and that is what decides whether or not strategy succeeds and if policy is mere vanity.[44] On the basis of historical evidence, as well as the persuasiveness of rigorous logic, one has to admit that there is no natural harmony among the levels of conflict—to simplify: policy, strategy, tactics—as Edward N. Luttwak, in particular, has pointed out.[45] Indeed, it is precisely because of the distinctive natures of the three levels that it is necessary to insist upon the keystone role of the strategist holding his bridge. But, for a hazardous caveat, the levels can function well enough even in a condition of severe disharmony. Moreover, one has to insist that some degree of disharmony among policy, strategy, and tactics is the natural state of affairs. This seemingly apostate argument by a strategist plainly is in urgent need of explanation.

Although in theory belligerent excellence might appear to require high competence in policy, strategy, tactics, and in the dialogues among them, the actual narrative of the past is not like this. The grand narrative of strategic history always is one of some disharmony. It is rare for a belligerent to be equally excellent, or, one must add, equally impoverished, in policy, strategy, and tactics. It is possible, indeed it happens, that poverty on one or even two of the three levels finds adequate compensation on the single level of excellence. Because politics rules, it is appropriate to recognize that extraordinary skill in the political arts should have the result of requiring only a modest, or less, performance by strategy and tactics.[46] The outstanding politician would not burden his strategists and tacticians with tasks beyond their capacity. However, if the army, its commanders, and the strategists who guide them, truly are incompetent to the point where an enemy need not demonstrate genius in order to succeed militarily, any ambitious policy is likely to be challenged and duly punished by defeat in the field.

Strategic history is not usually a tale of either/or's. The purposefully reduced universe, here of policy, strategy, and tactics, appears in the narrative of history on three spectra of absolute excellence, set in an adversarial context. It is tempting to argue that policy, strategy, and tactics can only be assessed relative to enemies, fit for specific purposes at particular times over particular issues. This temptation should be resisted. It is true that policy, strategy, and tactics need only be good enough to succeed against an adversary's policy, strategy, and tactics. However, it is necessary to recognize that policy, strategy, and tactics need to be assessed for their internal as well as their external integrity. Although the three functions of policy, strategy, and tactics have meaning only in terms of the enemy, and only he can reveal how good one really is, still it is possible to be better or worse in performing the three functions, objectively assessed.

This text may have ventured perilously close to making the dangerous suggestion that political, strategic, and tactical performances are all of them fungible, possibly sometimes to an astonishing degree. To translate the suggestion into a specific claim: a talented politician–policymaker may be able so to succeed by the black arts of his profession-trade that major weaknesses in his military instrument, which he knows about or suspects strongly, do not count heavily against him. Next, a strategist may be so skilled in making optimum use of the threat and carefully tailored employment of a distinctly flawed military instrument that his polity as a consequence of his brilliance (and adversary incompetence) should derive a political return that less than stellar political guidance, and a poor-to-average military establishment, would not have been expected to garner. Finally, even when politicians are indecisive and weak, and strategy is hard to find, a superb fighting force may win anyway. It may not win what politicians perhaps should have intended, but success in the field may well suffice. Purposefully or not in political and strategic sense, victory in battle can shape strategic history decisively.

Whereas normatively and logically, though not always actually, policy is the master in the trinity of policy, strategy, and tactics, it must be the tactical-level struggle that decides whether or not policy and strategy can be successful. This does not reduce the weight of the point that tactical success can prove to be fool's gold when it enables strategy to advance poor policy. In the battlespace, as elsewhere, the enemy might well have the marginal vote that delivers the verdict. Always bearing in mind the need to respect the role and potential of the enemy, though not too much lest one demoralizes oneself, the argument here points to the basic structure of the problem with strategy. Through continuous dialogue with policy, strategy can and should influence what it is required to deliver, while what it cleverly commands to be produced by way of strategic effect may or may not be achieved by a variable potency in battle. With the enemy always in mind, that requirement admittedly should be hard to fail to meet, since he provides an ongoing interactive reality check. Strategy ought to provide ever adjusting central direction to multifaceted effort. It is an exercise in asset management. Nonetheless, the historical record demonstrates a permanent structural disharmony, great and small, among policy, strategy, and tactics. Policy can ask too much or too little; strategy may be unduly demanding or too modest; and tactical effort, the fighting, may produce more or less success than one needs politically. Disharmony, perhaps one should say disharmonies, are normal. It is a mission of the strategist to keep overall strategic performance within the net positive zone despite the potential dysfunctionalities, so that the ship of state effort can proceed, flawed but working well enough in the face of nature and a sentient, but blessedly also flawed, enemy.

FRICTION, THE CLIMATE OF WAR, AND PREDICTION

Clausewitz wrote eloquently, briefly, and creatively about the reasons why it is difficult to perform well in war.[47] For the purpose of this study, it is necessary to extend his intended domain from war, with its 'fog', to peace, which also can be murky.[48] Not least is peace often murky with respect to the prospects for war. No one has improved upon the terse but brilliant Clausewitzian discussion of friction, but this is not to say that his analysis is fully satisfactory for our needs. Since the theory of war cannot be synonymous with the theory of strategy, and given that the text of *On War* is strictly obedient to its title, it is not surprising that the Prussian needs to be augmented, though most certainly not replaced. He tells us that war has a distinctive climate, composed of 'danger, exertion, uncertainty, and chance'.[49] This climate frames systemically what happens in war. It provides an unwelcome context of harassment that impairs human and institutional performance.

For the theory of strategy, Clausewitz can be more than a little too rich. Because we must insist that strategy is a peacetime as well as a wartime function, there is need to demote danger and the extremity of exertion from its 'climate'. Even during a time of warlike peace, it is highly unusual for strategists to have to perform in a context characterized by acute personal danger or literal exhaustion. However, there is no denying that the strategist, a person professionally charged to locate and plan against threats, is likely to function with a sense of peril unusual in his society, possibly to or beyond the point of sharply diminishing returns to personal effort because of exhaustion and stress.

Although friction is well appreciated as a general compound truth, in common with the climate of war, typically it is not usefully predictable in precise detail in advance. Nonetheless, by so shaping the actual climate of particular hostilities that there ought to be less scope for adverse happenings to thwart him, the strategist can strive to reduce the occurrence of events that produce friction. For example, if one succeeds in staging a surprise attack, the enemy's independent will may be all but deleted as a major source of friction. Clausewitz, alas, did not offer much education on the subject of the enemy as a challenge for strategy. This is not to deny, though, that he did say enough, with sufficient clarity, for us to avoid confusion. For another example, a strategist can choose to try to minimize the exertion required of his soldiers—for example, how rapidly must they climb a range of hills?—and he may be able to choose to wage a style of warfare that should be economical on his casualties.[50] However, as we must keep repeating, the enemy will always have a vote. Both war and strategy are adversarial in nature, not just in variable historical character. This means that the uncertainty and chance so powerfully identified by Clausewitz as components of the climate of war can never be reduced to insignificance. To put the matter thus is to risk overstatement, but the point is so important that it is a hazard well worth accepting.

Clausewitz was both right yet possibly unduly discouraging when he claimed that 'friction . . . is a force that theory can never quite define'.[51] Similarly, he is surely correct to insist that 'war is rich in unique episodes. Each is an uncharted sea, full of reefs.'[52] These and cognate assertions are unarguably true. Indeed, truly 'action in war is like movement in a resistant element'.[53] No doubt it is valuable to be told or reminded that 'everything in war is very simple, but the simplest thing is difficult. The difficulties accumulate and end by producing a kind of friction that is inconceivable unless one has experienced war.'[54] Nonetheless, it is not unfair to comment almost rhetorically, 'so what?' and 'what is your point?' Of course, war, and strategy in war and peace, is difficult. The future is not foreseeable, the strategist cannot predict reliably how his clever designs will fare in practice against an enemy with an independent will. 'Stuff happens', and the strategist, necessarily a pragmatist, must cope with both the anticipated and the unanticipated. Because the future is not foreseeable it cannot be predicted with certainty. It has to follow that it is the strategist's mission to strive to shape the future that he prefers in accordance with the political direction he receives, insofar as the net effectiveness of his assets in combat, or rivalry, with the enemy permits.

Friction is always a fact, though it need not be fatally debilitating. The climates of war and of strategy simply are what they are. Danger, exertion, uncertainty, and chance beset the Roman and the Byzantines, just as they beset the Americans, Russians, and everybody else today. Friction cannot be eliminated, the generic climate of war cannot be changed, and the future will never be predictable in sufficiently useful detail. However, all is not lost; there is hope for the prudent strategist, as the final section of this chapter reveals.[55] But before we collect and display such good news as may be found, it is necessary to register concern over the persisting troubles for the strategist that flow from the nature of civil–military relations.

CULTURE CLASH: CIVIL–MILITARY RELATIONS

Hew Strachan claims uncompromisingly that 'the principal purpose of effective civil–military relations is national security; its output is strategy'.[56] He is right. But what are effective relations and how difficult is it to establish and maintain them? As usual, the problems are not hard to identify and define; it is only the practicable solutions that frequently pose what can be insuperable challenges. To locate a problem certainly is a necessary step to its solution or alleviation, but it is not synonymous with that step. More often than not, civil–military relations are dysfunctional with respect to their ability to operate a genuine strategy-making process. The reasons why this unhappy condition should be so prevalent are many and frequently more than transient for the security communities in question.

The essential first step in understanding civil–military relations is recognition that the civilian must be the master. This injunction holds even if the highest political office is occupied by a soldier. In a military regime, the soldier as chief executive embodies the civil power, no matter that the army may have assumed control of the polity. The point is that politics must rule over the military instrument, regardless of who or what controls politics and policy at the time. The senior soldier may well rule in the army's interests, but in that fairly familiar situation it is a near certainty that the military leaders of a country will be reasoning politically and will equate the national with military institutional interests. Clausewitz's discussion of civil–military relations is extremely well targeted, though his brilliant analysis is not fully adequate for the needs of today. Still, no one should emerge from *On War* confused as to the proper relationship between politics and war, politician and commander.

> No major proposal required for war can be worked out in ignorance of political factors; and when people talk, as they often do, about harmful political influence on the management of war, they are not really saying what they mean. If the policy is right—that is, successful—any intentional effect it has on the conduct of war can only be to the good. If it has the opposite effect the policy itself is wrong.
>
> Only if statesmen look to certain military moves and actions to produce effects that are foreign to their nature do political decisions influence operations for the worse. In the same way as a man who has not fully mastered a foreign language sometimes fails to express himself correctly, so statesmen often issue orders that defeat the purpose they are meant to serve. Time and again that has happened, which demonstrates that a certain grasp of military affairs is vital for those in charge of general policy.[57]

Clausewitz proceeds to explain that a civilian representing the policy function to the military establishment—he cites 'a minister of war'—should be a person of 'distinguished intellect and strength of character. He can always get the necessary military information somehow or other.' This is true enough, for today as well as the 1820s, but the admittedly profound discussion in *On War* needs augmentation, particularly with respect to potential dysfunctionalities in the relations between politicians and soldiers.

Because war should never be self-referential, let alone simply a purposeless existential tactical reality, the political policy function must always be in charge. As noted, it does not really matter for this principle whether the person or persons in political charge are civilians or soldiers, their role is political. However, in practice it does tend to matter greatly whether policy is dominated by soldiers out of uniform who have usurped the top political function, or by civilian professional politicians. A military background must ease communication for a political figure with the soldier servants of the state. However, facility in dialogue is not the only requirement for a constructive relationship. It may well be the case that a former soldier is so confident in his own military judgement that he is unwilling to listen to his senior military advisors. The medium need not be the message. Strategy should emerge from an institutionalized dialogue between the civilian and military agents of government, with the former firmly in the saddle. But dialogue, though vital, needs to be a genuine process of interaction. The upside for strategy of a militarily somewhat expert president or prime minister rapidly becomes a strongly negative factor if that expertise leads the policymaker to misuse the strategy-making process as a one-way transmission belt for inappropriately sourced command.[58]

The obviously complementary nature of the agents in civil–military relations in practice can be contrasting to the point of dysfunctionality. The political science literature has made much of the theory of bureaucratic politics, a theory which has as its centrepiece the commonsense proposition that 'where you stand depends on where you sit'.[59] Ergo, soldiers seek rationally to protect their institutional, which is to say their bureaucratic, military interests. In general terms, looking to our topic, the several responsibilities of every player in the civil–military process of strategy-making will be reflected in their substantive positions on nearly all controversial issues. Unfortunately for the theorist, and hence the practitioner in need of assistance from his ideas and way of thinking, strategy-making is not only the product of rational choice reached through debate over the strategic merit of alternatives. Instead, it may well express the balance of power in an exercise in bureaucratic politics.

Strategy is made by negotiation, and the negotiators will express the interests of their organizations as they and their staffs perceive them. So much so rational, even though the negotiated compromise outcome may well not be strategically so. But complexity truly does reign and often it rules dysfunctionally, because a fairly orderly and identifiable process of strategy-making may not reveal much of value about how strategy is constructed. This is not to deny that the roles played by individuals, as dictated by their formal responsibilities, must be significant. However, in practice the negotiated outcome of human dialogue can depend more on culture, biology, personality, and historical context or the accident of circumstance, than on nominal wiring diagrams specifying information flows and decision gateways. For example, a study by Dale R. Herspring of American civil–military relations from the late 1930s to the 2000s demonstrates the wide range of possibilities that the US 'unequal dialogue' can accommodate.[60] Herspring argues convincingly that personalities differ and matter. He shows how, of the twelve most recent presidencies, three registered 'high' civil–military conflict, five saw 'moderate' conflict, while only four achieved 'minimal' conflict.

The potential for conflict in civil–military relations must be fuelled by particular challenges, for example, gays in the ranks or strategy for a particular mooted or actual campaign. In addition, however, conflict is always apt to be promoted by the contrasting cultures of professional political, and similarly professional military, life. Soldiers hold some words to be sacred and they are educated and trained to be guided in their deeds by a code of honour. Politicians tend to regard words as the malleable and expedient tools of their trade. Whether or not a politician–policymaker is honourable, on a widely acceptable standard, is a matter for the person in question to decide. For example, there is no strict requirement for politicians to tell the truth or to accept responsibility for their decisions. By way of contrast, the professional military person signs on, and typically though naturally not universally, is obedient to a code that mandates a high standard of personal behaviour, and which obliges the acceptance of responsibility.

Strategy-making is not facilitated when soldiers despise political superiors. By way of illustration, President Bill Clinton was a civilian policymaker whose personal misbehaviour would have had terminal career consequences had he been a soldier. The military profession is apt to be strict in its honour code, the political one is not. In addition to the contrast in cultures with respect to personal behaviour, to standards of acceptable conduct, civil–military relations are systemically harassed by the consequences of the characteristic differences in personality profiles between politicians and soldiers. Politicians and soldiers are distinctively self-selecting communities of professionals. There are always outlier, even roguish individuals, people who somehow become and succeed as soldiers when they would have been better suited to politics, and vice versa. The exceptions granted, politics and the military favour their own, culturally viewed. One can hypothesize with little fear of scholarly, though not historical anecdotal, contradiction that the personal characteristics most advantageous to career success as a politician or as a soldier differ significantly. While institutional cultures will insist upon some measure of professional cultural conformity, it should not be forgotten that by and large the people most likely to seek either political or military careers will have some biological—yes, genetic—and psychological predisposition to prosper in these contrasting milieus. One may overstate the obvious, but an effort to probe why strategy is difficult must bear in mind the cultural, biological, and psychological asymmetries that tend to characterize distinctively the professions of politician and soldier. These considerations obviously do not preclude competent strategy-making and conduct, but they do point to an important source of problems. And, to add a vital layer to the general level of this analysis, one should never forget that particular soldiers and particular politicians may be extreme exemplars of their professions, almost self-parodies.

For example, consider the typically sound, but inarticulate, though scheming, Field Marshal Douglas Haig, in dialogue with the brilliant, but verbose, glib, and—by Haig's Presbyterian standards—rampantly immoral Lloyd George. The commander-in-chief of the British Expeditionary Force (BEF) from December 1915 until April 1919 and his political superior did not exactly comprise a human partnership for strategy made in heaven.[61] History provides any number of colourful examples of more or less dysfunctional civil–military relationships between highly competent people who differed not only in their responsibilities—for example, the future security of the country, contrasted with soldiers' lives now—but also, sometimes crucially, in their personalities. It is not uncommon for the process of strategy-making to be hindered by the consequences of potent personal animosities.

It has to be recorded that strategy can be difficult to make, let alone conduct resolutely if adaptably, should neither civilian nor soldier be willing to give what the other requires. Specifically, the soldier will demand clear political instruction as to the mission assigned, its purpose, and the rules of engagement. Furthermore, the soldier will require the civilian policymaker to be ready to stand up and accept his large share of the blame if the mission fails undeniably. For his part, the policymaker is likely to wish to be somewhat ambiguous, which is to say flexible or even vague, as to the mission assigned, lest hope and achievement do not march in lock step. It is worth noting the systemic point that because strategy in action often results in failure, a possibility of which all players are sharply aware, civil–military relations vis-à-vis strategy always are prosecuted with the paying of some attention to the crucial issues of the apportionment of blame as well the claiming of credit. The civilian political leader and his senior military servant are natural antagonists in the practical realm of attributable responsibility for strategic failure. Each is obliged by institutional and personal interests, as well as by culture, biology, and psychology, to perform in ways conducive to the plausible placing of most of the blame upon the other in the event of strategic disaster. When failure occurs, the civilian is almost certain to claim that his military instrument did not perform as it should. Scapegoats will be sought, found, and, in some political cultures, executed. The soldier, for his part, will argue either that his mission was impossible of achievement, or, more likely, that it would have been achieved but for civilian political interference with military operations. I confess to reducing a complex historical reality to an over-simple binary issue—policymaker and soldier—for the purpose of highlighting a general challenge to strategy-making. In practice, the politics of strategy-making frequently will see cross-cultural alliances of convenience among civilian and military organizations, as well as sometimes severe conflict, certainly tension, among different levels of command and responsibility.[62]

One size in detailed theoretical explanation of strategic difficulty does not even begin to fit all cases. The subject of strategy, its making as well as its unmaking by military practice and malpractice in the field, is too complex and historically rich to allow for theoretical explanation more helpful than that offered here. By way of a closing negative observation on the myriad problems with strategy, this strategic theorist is moved to record the judgement that frequently, all too frequently, although a strategy bridge exists in assigned roles and procedural architecture, in actuality the forms are hollow. There may appear to be people charged with the making of strategy, and there can seem to be committees and staffs toiling away over the details of strategies as plans, but often in practice there will be no civilian–military strategic dialogue worthy of the name. It is one thing if this strategically pathological condition is the product of malign intent by one side or the other, but it is quite another when the neglect of strategically purposeful civil–military relations is the result mainly of ignorance or indifference. On the one hand, it is commonplace for politicians or policymakers to craft words that they present as policy, but as Strachan has noticed, they may well mistake those words for strategy.[63] On the other hand, again to quote the perceptive Strachan, the military contribution to civil–military relations is rarely inclined to favour strategic considerations. As he writes convincingly, 'the operational level of war appeals to armies: it functions in a politics-free zone'.[64]

Strachan suggests that politicians knowingly confuse policy with strategy. He argues that 'the consequence of politicians pretending that policy is strategy and of soldiers focusing on operations has been to leave strategy without a home'.[65] The strategy bridge may appear intact, but often there will be no strategically constructive traffic upon it. Probably more often than not, a polity's strategy bridge in effect will be closed for repairs that can be a long time coming.

AND YET, PURPOSEFUL STRATEGY IS POSSIBLE

The strategist's mission is fraught with peril. Whether or not he is accomplished, pathologies, maladies, disharmonies, cunning enemies, and sheer bad luck lurk to ambush him. Moreover, the strategist's contexts for thought and action fundamentally cannot be evaded. He may select one strategic path over another, he may shift paths, effect the strategic equivalent to a 'Hohmann transfer' move from one strategic orbital path to another, and he may even perform utterly innocent of any centralized purposeful strategy whatsoever, but he cannot avoid behaving to strategic effect.[66] Conflict behaviour has strategic consequences, which is to say effect, whether or not the effect achieved was intended. Restated in basic functional terms, it is accurate to claim that strategy is unavoidable.

This chapter has not sought to spare the reader exposure to the hazards for strategy and strategists, though there has been no endeavour to present the dangers encyclopaedically. By way of the tersest of summaries, this discussion pointed to, and analysed, eight clusters of problems for strategy. These were: (*a*) lack of understanding of the strategic function; (*b*) enemy behaviour; (*c*) the challenge of currency conversion of threat and military (and other) action into desirable strategic, and then political, consequences; (*d*) the shortage of strategic expertise and the poverty of the strategy-making process; (*e*) a complex product of culture, personality, biology, psychology, circumstance, and poor human performance; (*f*) the complexity and disharmony among all the levels of behaviour that comprise strategy's domain; (*g*) the realities of friction in the uniquely stressful climate of war, and the inherent impossibility of reliable prediction; and (*h*) the culture (inter alia) clash integral to the very nature of the civil–military relationship that must develop strategy and perform strategically.

So much for the bad news. But if the strategist is so variously and seriously harassed, how can he ever succeed? In a justly celebrated analysis, Richard K. Betts posed the question directly, 'Is Strategy an Illusion?'[67] He answered convincingly that it is not. Furthermore, there is no doubt that Clausewitz would have agreed with Betts' argument, notwithstanding his major contribution to registration of the perils that impede strategic performance. Since the strategic function is literally inescapable, even though explicit purposeful strategy is not, it is fortunate that somehow, seemingly against mighty odds, the strategist can succeed. How can this be so?

There appear to be four broad and mercifully potent reasons why purposeful strategy is feasible. First, the greatest of all problems for the strategist is also the reason why the strategic function can be performed successfully. This glorious paradox lies in the fact that the enemy too is beset by potentially unsolvable problems, by far the most significant among which should be us, his enemy. Thus, both calamity and salvation lie in the adversarial nature, not merely character, of strategy and the strategic function performed sometimes by people explicitly charged to develop and execute strategies. There is something deeply satisfying, certainly reassuring, about this paradox.

The second source of relief for the strategist lies in the complexity, diversity, and sheer scope and number of behaviours that when compounded comprise strategic performance for overall strategic effect. Yes, the difficulties are large and various, great and small. However, there is, or should be, extensive potential for compensation in complexity and diversity. For any among an awesomely substantial list of reasons, some important components of a highly complex military enterprise are certain to underperform when they are needed. But there are likely to be other elements that overperform. Prudent planning should be able to ensure that few items in the total strategic project literally lack for compensating substitutes. For example, excellent artillery may support an only average at best quality of infantry. The substitutes need not even be close in character. Competent strategy will find alternative means and methods, different people to command, and uses for machines that their inventors and initial military operators had not intended, in order to adapt in near real time to the challenge of necessity. This is not to claim that all military, or grand strategic, assets are fully fungible; of course, they are not. But the strategist needs to be a creative person, selected in part for his ability to conceive of different routes to an objective.

Third, while strategists cannot be trained to deliver strategic performance at the genius level, they can be educated in schools, by wide independent reading, and by experience. Biology and experience, which is to say genetic inheritance and personality, as well as culture, preclude most people from being educable even to a zone close to outstanding. This fact should not be fatal for a polity's strategic performance, since a whole cohort of strategists is not required. A thin trickle of naturally gifted, but also purposefully educated, strategists will suffice, always provided they are contextually enabled to demonstrate their outstanding qualities.[68] For example, the exceptionally able strategist is certain to require the implementing skills of subordinate commanders and leaders who must perform competently as operational artists. People cannot be trained to be strategists, but they can certainly be educated so as to improve their prospects of functioning adequately or better in the strategic role. Recall the point made repeatedly above to the effect that the almost grotesque number and quality of difficulties for our strategy, in principle should be matched by the enemy's problems. To gain advantage, to succeed, to achieve victory, we do not need to be superb in strategy or anything else. Instead, we just need to outperform the enemy in the production of net positive strategic effect. If the enemy is poor, all that is required of us is that we be less poor, overall, and therefore better. Any duel is a relative venture. The better player on the day wins, not the best player assessed according to some objective assay. For example, the British army in 1940 was not exactly one of history's finest, but it was much better in North Africa than was the Italian, and that was all that it needed to be so long as the enemy was wholly Italian. Polities as belligerents, even only as probable belligerents, are learning institutions. For example, American strategists and their staffs can learn, actually relearn, how to conduct a counter-insurgency (COIN) mission. If properly educated and trained, materially supported, and encouraged to adapt, armies, indeed any agency, can learn from experience, including from books (the experience of others, preferably), what tends to be good practice in COIN. Moreover, this learning can be codified with temporary authority in doctrine, and tested in the field of practice.[69] General COIN theory always needs to be tailored to particular situations, and there are crucial political and strategic requirements for success in COIN that the COIN manual itself cannot provide. It is one thing to recognize the essentiality of political legitimacy, but it is quite another to be able to achieve it. Of course, many organizations are incapable of learning what they need to, but the point is that historical experience as well as deductive logic is able to educate those who are educable, should their military and other cultures permit.

Fourth, when possible the prudent strategist hedges against some of the negative consequences of the difficulties that are unpredictable in detail, by providing apparently redundant capabilities. Mass will not always substitute for missing qualities, but it will often help. The strategist needs to be flexible and adaptable over means and methods. Often he will find that the assets nominally adequate, if tautly calculated, for mission performance, will be so damaged, paralysed, or misused by bad luck or incompetence that he must scramble to find gap-fillers or workarounds. Large armies are no less accident and error prone than are small armies, but they tend to be more tolerant of accident, error, and even incompetence. Armed force tends to be a blunt instrument, despite the precision with which some weapons can be targeted today and the care with which special operations forces can apply leverage. The doing of strategy in military performance is not akin to keyhole surgery. As a general rule, it is strategically prudent to employ much more force than a particular mission is expected strictly to require.

To summarize, this text argues that the problems with strategy paradoxically can be, and frequently are, alleviated critically by the options for compensation that lurk in the fungibility of its many diverse elements. Again paradoxically, as well as ironically, the problems of strategy are vastly reduced by the systemic reality that its adversarial nature requires the presence of an enemy who also must face many problems. The challenge of strategy can be met, sometimes well enough, by strategists educated in the mysteries of their calling; while, finally, the default position against nasty problems that cannot be anticipated exactly is to provide mass as insurance against an absence of quality in performance. With respect to the last claim noted, the historical record suggests that the deployment and employment of forces apparently disproportionately large for their tasks, frequently is rewarded by the suffering of casualties on a scale disproportionately small to the scale of their missions. The historical evidence for this proposition is overwhelming and can be expressed convincingly by mathematics, for once. Inevitably, though, there have been exceptions to the rule that the way to minimize friendly casualties is to apply hugely superior mass. Incompetence, bad luck, and strategic excellence on the part of the enemy are capable, in principle, of producing any measure of disaster for friendly arms.

Perversely perhaps, it is prudent to provide caveats that should help counter any tendency towards the overvaluation of strategy, even of superiority in strategy. The central thrust of this book obviously is to argue for the importance of strategy and, *ab extensio*, for the vital role of the strategist. However, without contradicting those assertions, it is necessary to state that purposeful deliberate strategy is not always an essential prerequisite either for strategic or for political success. Polities in conflict generate strategic effect; they must perform strategically, whether or not they design and execute an explicit strategy or strategies. Logic, commonsense, and historical experience suggest that polities should perform better with explicit strategy than without, but this will only be true if the chosen strategy is sound and if the enemy does not perform better as an adaptive adversary.

For a final caveat, it is distinctly possible for a polity to rely overmuch on strategy, at the expense of the contributions needed at the operational and especially the tactical levels of conflict. It is useful to recognize a condition of 'strategism', which is defined here as a pathology prone to afflict those overimpressed by the potential rewards of strategy. 'We need a strategy', 'we need a better strategy', are not unfamiliar mantras. The thought behind such laments is fundamentally sound, but in practice such *cris de coeur* reflect nothing much more than a conviction that there is a simple functional solution to some complex challenge, and the attractively simple solution must be strategy. Those demanding strategy, or a new strategy, commonly would be hard pressed to define the term and explain precisely what it should do. Strategy may be a great hammer, generically viewed, but are there nails available to be hammered, and can hammering be an effective answer to the challenge? The strategic theorist has to beware of enthusiastic disciples who seize upon the portentous sounding idea of his product and regard it as a panacea. Not every problem for national and international security can be resolved by superior strategy, let alone by superior strategy not much enabled by only average, or worse, competence in operations and tactics. And are politics and policy alive and well at their end of the strategy bridge?

NOTES

1. Williamson Murray and Mark Grimsley 'Introduction: On Strategy', in Murray, Mac-Gregor Knox, and Alvin Bernstein, eds., *The Making of Strategy: Rulers, States, and War* (Cambridge: Cambridge University Press, 1994), 22. Murray and Grimsley highlight the familiar fact that many of the great great truths about strategy are singularly unhelpful to the problem-solving strategist. To recognize the validity in the vitally important maxim that strategy is the art of the possible is about as helpful as grasping the general good sense in Carl von Clausewitz's caveats about what he calls 'the culminating point of victory'. *On War*, tr. Michael Howard and Peter Paret (1832–4; Princeton, NJ: Princeton University Press, 1976), 566–73. How can the strategist recognize the true warning signs that more (e.g. territory gained) actually is less? Military maps do not come marked conveniently with 'culminating point of victory' plainly indicated. When the scale of victory or defeat is registered in coinage far less specific than physical geography—in influence over minds, for example—the judgement necessary for the strategist may need to be based more on an educated intuition than any metric.
2. See Robert M. Citino, *The German Way of War: From the Thirty Years' War to the Third Reich* (Lawrence, KS: University Press of Kansas, 2005). The excellent Citino canon also includes significantly his *Quest for Decisive Victory: From Stalemate to Blitzkrieg in Europe, 1899–1940* (Lawrence, KS: University Press of Kansas, 2002), and *Blitzkrieg to Desert Storm: The Evolution of Operational Warfare* (Lawrence, KS: University Press of Kansas, 2004). For a short course on the subject of German obsession with the operational level of war, see Samuel J. Newland, *Victories Are Not Enough: Limitations of the German Way of War* (Carlisle, PA: Strategic Studies Institute, U. S. Army War College, December 2005).
3. Clausewitz, 75. Justin Kelly and Mike Brennan, *Alien: How Operational Art Devoured Strategy* (Carlisle, PA: Strategic Studies Institute, U. S. Army War College, September 2009), also is useful.
4. Field Marshal Helmuth Graf von Moltke, *Moltke on the Art of War: Selected Writings*, ed. Daniel J. Hughes, tr. Hughes and Gunther E. Rothenberg (Novato, CA: Presidio Press, 1993), 47.
5. I am pleased to acknowledge my debt to Antulio J. Echevarria II for his masterly unravelling of the tangled skeins of German military thought and practice. With respect to the differences between Moltke and Schlieffen, see his book, *Clausewitz and Contemporary War* (Oxford: Oxford University Press, 2007), 142–3.
6. James E. Edmonds, *History of the Great War, Military Operations, France and Belgium, 1918: 2, March-April, Continuation of the German Offensive* (London: Macmillan, 1937), 463–4.
7. Ibid. 464.
8. For the finest analysis and most balanced scholarship of which this author is aware, see David T. Zabecki, *The German 1918 Offensives: A Case Study in the Operational Level of War* (Abingdon: Routledge, 2006). Zabecki finds fatal fault with Ludendorff's misdirection of the tactics–operations transition zone. He writes: 'This prejudice ["against the operational level and operations (*Operative*) as opposed to tactics"] comes through again and again in his own words and writings. Each of the six great offensives planned aimed to produce a large-scale tactical breakthrough, with the follow-on action being ad hoc and determined by the situation. This is the very antithesis of the operational art', 327. Zabecki's concluding judgement on Ludendorff is as damning as it is persuasive: 'I have to conclude that in many ways he was a reflection of the German Army as a

whole in the first half of the 20th century: tactically gifted, operationally flawed, and strategically bankrupt', 328.

9. Ibid. 328, plants this speculative thought effectively. The fairly glittering credentials of Generals Hoffmann, Kuhl, Lossberg, and Seeckt for high command are presented in David T. Zabecki, ed., *Chief of Staff: The Principal Officers Behind History's Great Commanders, Vol. i: Napoleonic Wars to World War I* (Annapolis, MD: Naval Institute Press, 2008).

10. Surprise, sought through deception and stratagem, is the leading source of the cunning in the strategist's plans. But, notwithstanding Sun Tzu's (over)confident endorsement, such plans have an undeniably spotty historical record of strategic success. See Sun Tzu, *The Art of War*, tr. Ralph D. Sawyer (ca. 490 BCE; Boulder, CO: Westview Press, 1994), 168, 'Warfare is the Way (Tao) of deception'.

11. Interesting discussion of enemies as 'The Other', alien and hostile, is provided in Alexander Wendt, *Social Theory of International Politics* (Cambridge: Cambridge University Press, 1999), 21–2, 187, 262, 327.

12. For those among us who are attracted to maxims, I commend this gem from Michael Clarke: 'It is easy to think strategically, it is hard to act strategically.' The first claim is distinctly challengeable, but it serves usefully to set up the austere wisdom of the second. Professor Clarke was speaking at the conference, 'Defence in the Round', Royal United Services Institute, London, 27 November 2008.

13. Prominent among the better scholarly discussions of how outstanding commanders frequently 'got it done' well enough, despite the multitudinous frictions of warfare, is Martin van Creveld's assessment of Napoleon in *Command in War* (Cambridge, MA: Harvard University Press, 1985), ch. 3. Van Creveld goes so far as to describe the Emperor, admittedly challengeably, as 'the most competent human being who ever lived', 64. Fortunately for Europe, the Emperor's competence did not extend into the strategic realm. On Napoleon's lack of gifts as a strategist, see Charles J. Esdaile, 'De-Constructing the French Wars: Napoleon as Anti-Strategist', *Journal of Strategic Studies*, 31 (August 2008), 515–52.

14. Harry R. Yarger, *Strategic Theory for the 21st Century: The Little Book on Big Strategy* (Carlisle, PA: Strategic Studies Institute, U. S. Army War College, February 2006), 47.

15. See Nathan Freier, *Known Unknowns: Unconventional 'Strategic Shocks' in Defense Strategy Development* (Carlisle, PA: U. S. Army War College, Strategic Studies Institute, November 2008); and US Office of the Secretary of Defense and others, *Anticipating Rare Events: Can Acts of Terror, Use of Weapons of Mass Destruction or Other High Profile Acts Be Anticipated? A Scientific Perspective on Problems, Pitfalls and Prospective Solutions* (Washington, DC: November 2008), http://redteamjournal.com/papersU_White_Paper_Anticipating_Rare_Events_Nov2008rev.pdf (accessed 20 June 2009).

16. Raymond T. Odierno, 'Multi-National Force-Iraq Commander's Counterinsurgency Guidance' (Baghdad: HQ Multi-National Force-Iraq, 16 September 2008), 2.

17. George Pickett quoted in George Walsh, *'Damage Them All You Can': Robert E. Lee's Army of Northern Virginia* (New York: Tom Doherty Associates, 2002), 349. In truth, the 14,000 unfortunates were not all from the three brigades of Pickett's division of Virginians; six brigades from A. P. Hill's division charged also, while there were a further two ready in immediate reserve. See James M. McPherson, *Battle Cry of Freedom: The Civil War Era* (New York: Oxford University Press, 1988), 661–3; and particularly Joseph T. Glatthaar, *General Lee's Army: From Victory to Collapse* (New York: Free Press, 2008), 279–81.

18. Since the end of the Cold War, Western defence establishments have found it expedient to make a virtue of necessity and proclaim a shift in defence planning methodology from 'threat based' planning to 'capabilities' planning. In practice, capabilities planning can be very largely self referential. In the absence of a plausible dominant threat, one develops the military power that one favours doctrinally, that is to say substantially culturally, and which—hopefully—should be useful across a wide band of future warfare possibilities. In practice, a technologically obsessed defence community like the American is apt to proceed to indulge its love affair with machines without much consideration of how mechanical and especially electronic advances should contribute to enhance operational or strategic performance. The whole principally Western, largely American, history of debate in the 1990s and very early 2000s about a revolution in military affairs, and then 'transformation', in essence was an enemy-naked, strategy-light, endeavour. Helpful commentaries include the following: Andrew F. Krepinevich, 'Cavalry to Computer: The Pattern of Military Revolution', *National Interest*, 37 (fall 1994), 30–42; id., *The Military-Technical Revolution: A Preliminary Assessment* (Washington, DC: Center for Strategic and Budgetary Assessments, 2000); Lawrence Freedman, *The Revolution in Military Affairs*, Adelphi Paper 318 (London: International Institute for Strategic Studies, 1998); id., *The Transformation of Strategic Affairs*, Adelphi Paper 379 (London: International Institute for Strategic Studies, 2006); MacGregor Knox and Williamson Murray, eds., *The Dynamics of Military Revolution, 1300–2050* (Cambridge: Cambridge University Press, 2001); Colin S. Gray, *Strategy for Chaos: Revolutions in Military Affairs and the Evidence of History* (London: Frank Cass, 2002); id., 'Technology as a Dynamic of Defence Transformation', *Defence Studies*, 6 (March 2006), 26–51; Tim Benbow, *The Magic Bullet? Understanding the Revolution in Military Affairs* (London: Brassey's, 2004); Frederick W. Kagan, *Finding the Target: The Transformation of American Military Policy* (New York: Encounter Books, 2006); and Thomas G. Mahnken, *Technology and the American Way of War Since 1945* (New York: Columbia University Press, 2008). Especially constructive scepticism is offered in the brief analysis by Antulio J. Echevarria II, *Challenging Transformation's Clichés* (Carlisle, PA: Strategic Studies Institute, U. S. Army War College, December 2006). It is well to remember that American national, as well as its partially derivative strategic and military, culture(s) privileges change as a value and effectively equates it with progress. The desirability of change, let alone its strategic purpose, can be slighted with neglect when a community deems it inherently advantageous.

19. Clausewitz, 75.

20. The question of winning or losing is a matter of vital importance. It is both appropriate and natural that historians and soldiers should seek to understand the reasons for victory or defeat. My point simply is that the methodological choice to explain either the one or the other all but inevitably biases research and judgement. With reference to the example cited in the text, see Richard E. Beringer and others, *Why the South Lost the Civil War* (Athens, GA: University of Georgia Press, 1986); and Gary W. Gallagher, *The Confederate War* (Cambridge, MA: Harvard University Press, 1997).

21. William Tecumseh Sherman quoted in Harold R. Winton, 'An Imperfect Jewel: Military Theory and the Military Profession', paper presented to the Society for Military History Annual Meeting, Bethesda, MD, 22 May 2004, 22. The high plausibility of Sherman's claim is amply illustrated in John Keegan's outstanding study of Grant as commander, *The Mask Of Command* (New York: Viking, 1987), ch. 3.

22. A pathological respect for the enemy is examined in Michael C. C. Adams, *Our Masters the Rebels: A Speculation on Union Military Failure in the East, 1861–1865* (Cambridge,

MA: Harvard University Press, 1978). Neither in sport nor in war do teams fare well who disbelieve in their ability to win.

23. Although Clausewitz appears to be clear enough in his insistence upon war's nature as an instrument of policy, *On War* does leave much of high importance underexplored in the crucial policy–war nexus. Antulio J. Echevarria II, *Clausewitz and Contemporary War* (Oxford: Oxford University Press, 2007), ch. 4, is especially rewarding.

24. These truly murky waters are penetrated to some contentious effect in Norman Dixon's extraordinary, overstated, yet strangely still classic, *On the Psychology of Military Incompetence* (London: Futura Publications, 1979). Also useful are J. Glenn Gray, *The Warriors: Reflections on Men in Battle* (New York: Harper Torchbook, 1967); Dave Grossman, *On Killing: The Psychological Cost of Learning to Kill in War and Society* (Boston: Little Brown, 1995); Joanna Bourke, *An Intimate History of Killing: Face-to-Face Killing in Twentieth-Century Warfare* (London: Granta Books, 1999); and Michael Evans and Alan Ryan, eds., *The Human Face of Warfare: Killing, Fear and Chaos in Battle* (St. Leonards, Australia: Allen and Unwin, 2000). The concept and reality of the warrior is shown history's door in Christopher Coker, *Waging War Without Warriors? The Changing Culture of Military Conflict* (Boulder, CO: Lynne Rienner Publishers, 2002). But see his later book, *The Warrior Ethos: Military Culture and the War on Terror* (Abingdon: Routledge, 2007), which finds much value in the warrior ethos. In addition, Rune Henrickson, 'Warriors in Combat—What Makes People Actively Fight in Combat? *Journal of Strategic Studies*, 30 (April 2007), 187–223, is important.

25. See Murray and Grimsley, 'Introduction: On Strategy', 20–2.

26. See Colin S. Gray, *Schools for Strategy: Teaching Strategy for 21ˢᵗ Century Conflict* (Carlisle, PA: Strategic Studies Institute, US Army War College, October 2009). Strategists cannot be trained because too much creative thought is necessary. But strategists can be educated by their own and others' experience, as well as by reflection upon the meaning in the general theory of strategy. However, education has its limits because strategy has to draw upon much intuitive wisdom. In common with everyone else, the strategist is the product of his genetic inheritance and his life experience. Personality can be critical.

27. The roles and importance of staff officers varies from army to army, period to period, and from individual commander to individual commander. On the significance of chiefs of staff see Zabecki, ed., *Chief of Staff*, 2 vols. The Prussian, then German, armies invented and developed the modern military staff system. See two classics: Walter Goerlitz, *History of the German General Staff, 1657–1945* (New York: Frederick A. Praeger Publishers, 1953); and T. N. Dupuy, *A Genius for War: The German Army and General Staff, 1807–1945* (London: MacDonald and Jane's, 1977). Robert T. Foley explains that '[t]he German army of World War I relied upon its network of staff officers to communicate not just official orders, but also the real intentions of those orders'. He elaborates on this point usefully by proceeding to note that '[i]n addition to formal means of communication, staff officers relied on an informal system, one based on personal relationships built up over years of working together, to transmit ideas and opinions'. *German Strategy and the Path to Verdun: Erich von Falkenhayn and the Development of Attrition, 1870–1916* (Cambridge: Cambridge University Press, 2005), 98. For some more historical depth see Annika Mombauer, *Helmuth von Moltke and the Origins of the First World War* (Cambridge: Cambridge University Press, 2001); while for German command performance in the return fixture, see the excellent study

by Geoffrey P. Megargee, *Inside Hitler's High Command* (Lawrence, KS: University Press of Kansas, 2000).

28. See Edward S. Quade, ed., *Analysis for Military Decisions: The RAND Lectures on Systems Analysis* (Chicago, IL: Rand McNally, 1964); E. S. Quade and W. I. Boucher, eds., *Systems Analysis and Policy Planning: Applications in Defense* (New York: American Elsevier Publishing Company, 1968); and Alain Enthoven and K. Wayne Smith, *How Much Is Enough? Shaping the Defense Program, 1961–1969* (New York: Harper and Row, 1971). For a much more recent entry from approximately the same school of analysis, see the ambitious comprehensive work by Richard L. Kugler, *Policy Analysis in National Security Affairs: New Methods for a New* Era (Washington, DC: National Defense University Press, 2006). For a leading case, the godfather of modern American quantitative defence analysis, Lt. General Glenn A. Kent, for all his genius as an analyst, persistently displayed little comprehension of the wider implications of, certainly of the crucial political dimension to, his work. He illustrates my claim all too amply in his book, *Thinking About America's Defense: An Analytical Memoir* (Santa Monica, CA: RAND, 2008).

29. Yarger, *Strategic Theory for the 21st Century*, 75.

30. Ralph Peters, *Fighting for the Future: Will America Triumph?* (Mechanicsburg, PA: Stackpole Books, 1999), 172. By way of supplementary gems from the same stable, consider these; 'But machines, no matter how magnificent, do not of themselves constitute a revolution. True revolution happens, above all, in the minds of men', 18; and, for my personal favourite, '[t]echnologies come and go, but the primitive endures', 171.

31. Lawrence Sondhaus, *Strategic Culture and Ways of War* (Abingdon: Routledge, 2006); Jeannie L. Johnson, Kerry M. Kartchner, and Jeffrey A. Larsen, eds., *Strategic Culture and Weapons of Mass Destruction: Culturally Based Insights into Comparative National Security Policymaking* (New York: Palgrave Macmillan, 2009); and Patrick Porter, *Military Orientalism: Eastern War Through Western Eyes* (London: C. Hurst, 2009), are particularly helpful.

32. But it is a cliché that is a universal and eternal truth whose importance can scarcely be overstated. See John Baynes, *Morale: A Study of Men and Courage* (Garden City Park, NY: Avery Publishing Group, 1988); and Richard Holmes, *Firing Line* (London: Penguin Books, 1987). Examples of high and low morale abound in every war. Simply to illustrate what is meant by high morale, I will quote a telling short passage from Howard R. Simpson's history of the siege and battle of Dien Bien Phu in 1954. Simpson was a US war correspondent present at Dien Bien Phu in the opening phase of the battle. He records this vivid impression of the counter-attack by two weak companies of the First Foreign Legion, Parachute Battalion (1BEP) in defence of the fortified position known as 'Eliane' 1 on 10 April 1954. 'At this point one of those rare events occurred that remain in men's minds long after the blurred memories of horror, victory, or defeat. The recollection still causes a catch in the voices of Dien Bien Phu veterans. Lieutenant (now Colonel) Lucciani of the First BEP, speaking of the move up the slope of 'Eliane' 1, recalls without dramatics, "Our Legionnaires sang the song of the First BEP." In the midst of a night battle the flying tracers, yellow explosions, and the hellish roaring of the flame-thrower, the deep resonance of the slow-paced, cadenced marching song "Contra les Viets" ("Against the Vietminh") could be heard. The chant broke through the din in disjointed waves of sound and died as the Legion paras closed with the enemy.' *Dien Bien Phu: The Epic Battle America Forgot* (Washington, DC: Brassey's, 1996), 125. Needless to say, perhaps,

Vietminh soldiers required exceptionally high morale in order to overcome French élite troops in protracted close battle. The small bloody event just described was repeated generically by both sides for weeks on end.

33. I allude to the deservedly iconic modern text that launched, perhaps relaunched, scholarly appreciation of the human dimension to military history. See John Keegan, *The Face of Battle* (London: Jonathan Cape, 1976). This was the book that launched a fleet of imitators, one or two of them worthy successors.

34. In my own research and writing over many years I have been as guilty as anyone, and more guilty than many, of neglecting the human dimension to strategic affairs.

35. Stephen Peter Rosen, *War and Human Nature* (Princeton, NJ: Princeton University Press, 2005), 182.

36. Ibid. 182–3.

37. This most vital of questions is answered persuasively in strategy's favour in Richard K. Betts, 'Is Strategy an Illusion?' *International Security*, 25 (fall 2000), 5–50.

38. The scholarly literature on psychology and strategy, and psychology and command, is both intriguing and frustrating. It is intriguing in that unquestionably it is rich in insight. It is frustrating in that it always threatens to explain too much. Also, dare I say it, this literature evokes, in this strategist at least, the response 'so what?'—intended as a scholarly challenge, not to be dismissive, I must hasten to add. With major caveats necessary bearing on the quality of his strategic historical research, and the utility of psychological insight for understanding the world of strategic practice, readers should make what they are able of Dixon's incomparable book, *On the Psychology of Military Incompetence*, and Robert Pois and Philip Langer, *Command Failure in War: Psychology and Leadership* (Bloomington, IN: Indiana University Press, 2004). Dixon's pioneering study is by far the more original, as well as wide ranging, of the two, but Pois and Langer have brought far more convincing military historical scholarship to the plot, as well as a more nuanced psychological approach. This strategic theorist is in debt to Dixon for his many insights, is deeply respectful of the scholarly boldness and coherence of his analysis, and is hugely approving of the reminder that strategy is made and done by people. 'People are policy', as a popular American saying has it (see 'Running the World', *The Economist*, 14 February 2009, 52). But Dixon's potent exposé of the roots of military incompetence is far too reductionist to satisfy this author. Dixon admits to the reductionism and defends it (18). However, notwithstanding the Occamite privileging of parsimony, Dixon's admission, indeed defence, of reductionism ultimately does not persuade. Not only is the concept of the authoritarian personality unduly opaque, in addition the idea of military incompetence is analytically unsatisfactory. Simple dominant explanations for highly complex phenomena are almost invariably seriously misleading. The problem for we strategic theorists is to know what use to make of psychological research, even when it appears to be well rooted in evidence. As noted already, overexplanation is a significant challenge to the theorist. The problem is akin to that posed by the work of a careful scholar who claims, not unpersuasively, that 'geography is destiny' in historical matters great and small. Or, for an example of the threat of overexplanation by a very Big Idea, the proposition that all strategic behaviour is cultural is a necessary truth, and hence can verge upon banality: its recognition mandates applied scholarship in local detail.

39. See Carlo D'Este, *Warlord: A Life of Churchill at War, 1874–1945* (London: Allen Lane, 2009).

40. Sun Tzu, 179. Some readers may prefer 'the modern Chinese interpretation', the translation by Yuan Shibing for General Tao Hanzhang of the People's Liberation Army. His version of this famous maxim of Sun Tzu proceeds thus: 'Know the enemy and know yourself; in a hundred battles, you will not be defeated.' Tao Hanzhang, *Sun Tzu's 'Art of War': The Modern Chinese Interpretation*, tr. Yuan Shibing (ca. 490 BCE; New York: Sterling Innovation, 2007), 36. The excellent translation by Samuel B. Griffith offers this slight variant on the above: 'Know the enemy and know yourself; in a hundred battles you will never be in peril.' Sun Tzu, *The Art of War*, tr. Samuel B. Griffith (ca. 490 BCE; Oxford: Clarendon Press, 1963), 84.

41. Clausewitz, 119–21; Barry D. Watts, *Clausewitzian Friction and Future War*, McNair Paper 68, rev. edn. (Washington, DC: National Defense University, August 2004). Among the under-reassessed major concepts in *On War*, friction ranks high. None among the small crowd of first-rate recent studies of *On War* devotes the close critical attention that it should be obvious this strategically central idea requires.

42. For an approach to strategic issues thoroughly at odds with that expressed in this text, see Kent, *Thinking About America's Defense*.

43. Eliot A. Cohen, *Supreme Command: Soldiers, Statesmen, and Leadership in Wartime* (New York: Free Press, 2002), is a powerful examination of what is termed the 'unequal dialogue' between politicians and soldiers. A rich case study of this dialogue is Andrew Roberts, *Masters and Commanders: How Roosevelt, Churchill, Marshall and Alanbrooke Won the War in the West* (London: Allen Lane, 2008). It should be noted that in the text I emphasize the need for dialogue not only between policymaker and general, but also between general as strategist and general as operational commander and tactician.

44. In the immortal words of Charles E. Callwell, '[s]trategy is not however the final arbiter in war. The battlefield decides, and on the battlefield the advantage passed over to the regular army', *Small Wars: A Tactical Textbook For Imperial Soldiers*, 3rd edn. (1906; London: Greenhill Books, 1990), 90. Callwell contrasted the strategic advantages of irregular warriors with the tactical superiority of regular soldiers.

45. Edward N. Luttwak, *Strategy: The Logic of War and Peace*, rev. edn. (Cambridge, MA: Harvard University Press, 2001), xii.

46. An overenthusiastic reading of Sun Tzu might convince would-be cunning politicians that statecraft in its extensive political domain can succeed even when the iron fist is brittle. One thinks of Italy in both world wars for example. Still thinking of Italy, though in a more positive vein, the political context for strategy and tactics is treated masterfully in Niccolo Machiavelli, *The Prince*, tr. Peter Bondarella and Mark Musa (1532; Oxford: Oxford University Press, 1998).

47. Clausewitz, 119–21.

48. See Talbot C. Imlay and Monica Duffy Toft, eds., *The Fog of Peace and War Planning: Military and Strategic Planning under Uncertainty* (Abingdon: Routledge, 2006).

49. Clausewitz, 104.

50. For example: Field Marshal Bernard Montgomery chose to orchestrate his battles so as to allow maximum effect to be achieved by his superior firepower (he had been a staff officer under General Herbert Plumer in 1918); General Douglas MacArthur in the South West Pacific, and Admiral Chester Nimitz in the Central Pacific chose to bypass many well-defended Japanese garrisons; and as a general observation, a style in warfare that privileges air power, though sometimes costly in the lives of airmen and civilians, tends to be casualty light for friendly forces overall.

51. Clausewitz, 120.

52. Ibid.

53. Ibid.
54. Ibid. 119.
55. Michael Fitzsimmons strikes a blow, albeit not a wholly convincing one, against the evil authority of uncertainty, in his valuable article, 'The Problem of Uncertainty in Strategic Planning', *Survival*, 48 (winter 2006–07), 131–46.
56. Hew Strachan, 'Making Strategy: Civil–Military Relations after Iraq', *Survival*, 48 (autumn 2006), 66.
57. Clausewitz, 608.
58. An egregiously awful example was when a former corporal in the Sixteenth Bavarian Infantry appointed himself commander-in-chief in practice as well as in principle, and, naturally, sole strategist. The outstanding, most wonderfully nuanced study is John Keegan's portrait of Adolf Hitler, the ex-company runner (a very dangerous duty that Hitler consistently performed well), as military commander, *The Mask of Command* (New York: Viking Penguin, 1987), ch. 4. Many detailed studies of Hitler at war have been published since Keegan's book appeared, but none match his empathy, grasp, and persuasiveness. That said, Megargee's *Inside Hitler's High Command* successfully contextualizes Hitler's exercise of the command function. Most especially, Megargee offers the essential point that '[t]ry as he might he [Hitler] could not work without a command system, a collection of individuals bound together by common values, ideas, and practices', 230. In other words, even Hitler as unchallenged warlord had no practicable alternative to dependence upon the General Staff that he so distrusted.
59. See Graham Allison, *The Essence of Decision* (Boston: Little, Brown, 1971), for the modern foundation text.
60. Dale R. Herspring, *The Pentagon and the Presidency: Civil-Military Relations from FDR to George W. Bush* (Lawrence, KS: University Press of Kansas, 2005).
61. From a large literature, see these fairly recent entries: David French, *The Strategy of the Lloyd George Coalition, 1916–1918* (Oxford: Clarendon Press, 1995); David R. Woodward, *Lloyd George and the Generals* (London: Frank Cass, 2004); Gary Mead, *The Good Soldier: The Biography of Douglas Haig* (London: Atlantic Books, 2008); and J. P. Harris, *Douglas Haig and the First World War* (Cambridge: Cambridge University Press, 2008).
62. To cite but one historical case, consider the still quite lively American question, 'who lost us the Vietnam War', in the light of the argument and evidence in H. R. McMaster's bold classic study, *Dereliction of Duty: Lyndon Johnson, Robert McNamara, the Joint Chiefs of Staff, and the Lies that Led to Vietnam* (New York: Harper Collins, 1997), and C. Dale Walton's no less scintillating, or controversial, study, *The Myth of Inevitable U. S. Defeat in Vietnam* (London: Frank Cass, 2002).
63. Strachan makes this vital argument powerfully in his article, 'Making Strategy'.
64. Ibid. 60.
65. Ibid. 61.
66. A satellite can change orbit by accelerating out of its existing orbit into an elliptical orbit from which it will effect the deceleration needed to reach the desired new orbit. I show this graphically in Colin S. Gray, *Another Bloody Century: Future Warfare* (London: Weidenfeld and Nicolson, 2005), 298.
67. See Betts, *Is Strategy an Illusion?*
68. There is no commanding literary authority either on how to teach strategy, or how to perform well enough as a strategist. With regard to the latter, the best advice one can give is to read the classics of strategic theory. This theorist has attempted to teach

strategy for more than forty years, a mission which by unavoidable implication must include some preparation for functioning as a strategist. Those readers in search of useful literature on the teaching of strategy may find some value in a noticeably dated book, Gene M. Lyons And Louis Morton, *Schools for Strategy: Education and Research in National Security Affairs* (New York: Frederick A. Praeger, 1965), while Ken Booth and Eric Herring, *Keyguide to Information Sources in Strategic Studies* (London: Mansell Publishing, 1994), is a fund of useful facts of more recent vintage. Also, one should not neglect the better student textbooks. David Jordan and others, *Understanding Modern Warfare* (Cambridge: Cambridge University Press, 2008), and John Baylis, James Wirtz, and Colin S. Gray, *Strategy in the Contemporary World*, 3rd edn. (Oxford: Oxford University Press, 2009), are highly recommended, even for advanced students of strategy, academic and military professional. David Auerswald, Janet Breslin-Smith, and Paula Thornhill, 'Teaching Strategy Through Theory and Practice', *Defence Studies*, 4 (spring 2004), 1–17, and Gabriel Marcella, ed., *Teaching Strategy: Challenge and Response* (Carlisle, PA: Strategic Studies Institute, U.S. Army War College, March 2010) also are helpful. For tools in higher military education that still find favour, see David Ian Hall, ed., 'The Relevance and Role of Military History Battlefield Tours and Staff Rides for Armed Forces in the 21st Century', *Defence Studies*, 5, Special Issue (March 2005). In the opinion of this theorist-educator, there is no fully satisfactory substitute for physical acquaintance with a remote bowl-shaped, fog-prone valley (i.e. the location of Dien Bien Phu), to educate students of strategy on the significance and unreliability of risk assessment, even when it appears to be calculated conservatively. I am grateful to Dr James Kiras of the US Air Force's School of Advanced Air and Space Studies (SAASS), and to some of his students, for first-hand testimony on the value of the modern staff ride. See my *Schools for Strategy*.

69. See John A. Nagl, *Learning to Eat Soup with a Knife: Counterinsurgency Lessons from Malaya and Vietnam* (Chicago, IL: University of Chicago Press, 2005), and US Army and Marine Corps, *Counterinsurgency Field Manual: U. S. Army Field Manual No. 3–24, and Marine Corps Warfighting Publication No. 3–35* (Chicago, IL: University of Chicago Press, 2007). Although good doctrine matters, it is not a panacea. Some contexts of complex insurgency, civil wars, tribalism, and large-scale criminality defy even the soundest of Western COIN wisdom. On the important subject of the need for humility, see Adam Roberts, 'Doctrine and Reality in Afghanistan', *Survival*, 51 (February–March 2009), 29–60. Also see David Kilcullen, *The Accidental Guerrilla: Fighting Small Wars in the Midst of a Big One* (London: C. Hurst, 2009), which is the COIN book of the decades of the 1990s and 2000s.

5

The Product: Strategic Effect

CONSEQUENCES FIT FOR PURPOSE

The function of strategy is to bridge the gap between purpose and action, while its role is to generate the effect necessary to shift enemy behaviour from the path it was on. The primary role of the strategist on his bridge is so to manage his polity's assets that some useful measure of control over enemies and rivals is achieved. Rephrased, the strategist seeks to secure the consequences necessary for political success. These consequences have to be fit for purpose. It is not the strategist's professional duty to select political aims, but he is obliged to contribute to the making of policy by virtue of the needs of his bridging function. He must advise policymakers, which is to say politicians, as to what should be possible and at what probable cost. The strategist must strive to keep policy ambition within the bounds of strategic feasibility. Also, naturally enough, the strategist must advise, though not recommend, when policy is asking less of the polity's military and other assets than they have demonstrated the ability to deliver. Effect is the concept key to comprehension of the importance of the strategy bridge; it is the strategist's product.

To risk muddying the water more than a little, it must be admitted that one need not have an explicit strategy in order to win or lose in the contest for net strategic effect. Given that we choose to define military strategy functionally as the direction and use that is made of force and the threat of force for the ends of policy, it has to follow that strategic effect can be the product simply of the events that happen, by and large unplanned beyond the immediate context. This book insists that even when the strategy bridge is broken or acutely dysfunctional, military, inter alia, events have consequences. For a historical example, as Charles Esdaile among other scholars has suggested persuasively, for all his gifts and achievements, Napoleon Bonaparte does not appear to have designed and followed strategy, grand or military.[1] But we need to append to Esdaile's opinion, recognition of the fact that Napoleon's episodic and typically massive military effort assuredly did have strategic effect. It had a cumulative as well as a sequential impact upon the course of events.[2] The reason why an education in strategy is important, and why polities are well advised to strive to design and conduct strategy and strategies explicitly, is for the purpose of enhancing, not simply enabling, net positive strategic effect. Strategic effect per se can be secured with no special, tailored strategic effort. Just deploy forces and fight opportunistically and, who knows, the end result may be a strategic success that promotes political success. And it would all have been achieved without the benefit of the coherently and centrally directed victory that explicit strategy should have provided. However, the historical record of wars and warfare suggests strongly that belligerents who neglect to recognize the merit in providing a strategy bridge between their political wishes and their military behaviour, tend to fail badly.[3] One might get lucky and win without choosing, and then determinedly applying, a strategy, but war inherently is so risky an enterprise that it must be foolish to lengthen the odds against success thus gratuitously. Of course, failure to devise and implement a strategy may not be gratuitous and easily avoidable. Many have been the belligerents who genuinely just did not understand the need for strategy. Even in the modern world, a lust for plunder and delight in the joy of battle can suffice to send legions marching who knows where. The embarrassingly hopeless situation in which Friedrich von Paulus found himself with his Sixth Army, trapped at Stalingrad on the Volga in the winter of 1942–3, is an abiding testament to what can happen even to tactically superior armies when they are commanded without strategy or moral courage.[4] In November–December 1812, the sad remnants of Napoleon's once truly very Grande Armée, though amazingly and paradoxically still loyal to their emperor, also might have reflected on the consequences for them of their leader's disdain for strategy and, for once, his discounting of physical geography also.[5]

Although this chapter moves the story along ever deeper into the realm of strategic practice, it needs to be read as a thickening of the theoretical discussion. In this respect it serves a common goal with the analysis of the difficulties of strategy presented in Chapter 4, and with the treatment of command performance in Chapter 6. Before we plunge into consideration of the thus far undergoverned space of strategic effect, it is probably useful, some readers might claim it is necessary, to restate the basic structure of our subject. To this necessary end, we claim that the strategy bridge is

1. An eternal and universal *function* with a permanent nature
2. A particular *plan* for action with a unique character
3. A *distinctive theory* of victory

Strategy, a creative function, has to be rendered actionable by the managerial functions of planning and programming.[6] Then it is expressed in threat and combat by commanders at all levels who need also to be leaders. As Sherlock Holmes was wont to observe perceptively, 'these are very deep waters'.[7] To penetrate these deep and murky waters, this chapter proceeds to explore and explain the nature of strategic effect as the product of strategy; then it moves on to examine the story arc of strategy; next it considers pathologies characteristic of undue enthusiasm for the concept of effect, or should 'it' be plural as effects?; while finally it discusses ways in which the strategically necessary focus upon consequences, which is to say effect, can be rescued from the clutches of some of its less well educated devotees.

THE PRODUCT OF STRATEGY

Chapter 1 defined strategic effect as the cumulative and sequential impact of strategic performance upon the course of events. I have deployed the concept of strategic effect on many occasions for many years, but have yet to be challenged as rigorously as I deserve. The meaning of the general idea of strategic effect is obvious enough. It makes the existential claim that what we do, including what the enemy fears we may do, generates a composite compounded strategic performance that can shift the course of events, outcomes, hopefully in our favour. Never forgetting for one moment the necessarily adversarial context of all strategic behaviour, the most basic meaning of strategic effect is the net consequence of thought and action upon the single and only course of history that the laws of physics known to us allow. The concept is thoroughly admirable for its essential truth. When a person appreciates the meaning and implications of the concept he is a good way along the path to achieving understanding of strategy. However, strategic effect, though certainly not a poisoned chalice, is by no means as straightforward a masterful idea as one might be forgiven for believing.

To perform competently as a strategist, or to pass fair judgement upon those charged to function as strategists, it is necessary to climb beyond the theoretical base camp that is registration of the central importance of strategic effect. At least a firm grasp on the concept should mean that the strategist knows what he needs to do. In the admirable words of Harry R. Yarger in an outstanding and admirably brief treatise on strategic theory, 'the purpose of strategy is to create strategic effect'.[8] Fortunately, Professor Yarger is not content to leave the matter thus. When one probes, as one should, to explore the ways in which this necessary, if substantively still rather mysterious, product, strategic effect, can be obtained, he tells us that 'objectives are selected to create strategic effect'.[9] Read properly, Yarger has penetrated to the heart of the matter. Of course, he is right when he notes that 'objectives too seldom receive the depth of thought and reflection they merit'.[10] Similarly, he is surely correct when he risks giving offence to William of Occam with his razor, by advising as follows:

> Strategy reflects a comprehensive knowledge of what else is happening within the strategic environment and the potential first-, second-, and third-order effects of its own choices on the efforts of those above, below, and on the strategist's own level.[11]

This magnificent sentence should send a ripple of fear through the ranks of would-be strategists. Yarger has just complicated life for strategists by making three claims that either can, or plausibly could, frustrate purposeful strategy altogether. What has Yarger done? He tells us that although strategy generates strategic effect (singular) as its product, this holistic output is the consequence of contributory effects, plural; that these effects are of three kinds—first-, second-, and third-order; and that the burdens and rewards of these first-, second-, and third-order effects, shape the performance of those functioning politically, operationally, and tactically. It is tempting to suggest that Yarger overintellectua-lizes what really is a rather simple matter, the generation of this marvellously undifferentiated currency of strategic effect. But, alas, Yarger is all too right. Unfortunately, there is a great deal more to the concept of strategic effect than meets the eye at first, or even second and third glance.

It would be a most serious error were one to dismiss the concept of strategic effect as a banal truism of no practicably actionable value. This abstract noun refers to a compound of quality and quantity in consequence that must be imprecise and metrically incalculable. As was observed earlier in this text, a systemic problem with strategy is that there is no evading the necessity for human judgement. Elevation, even coronation, of the concept of strategic effect as the master key to unlock the potency of strategy does not, itself, have the leverage to resolve the challenge to strategy. However, the concept does serve the vital purpose of pointing correctly to the core purpose of the function of strategy. So, just what is this alchemical brew that we know as strategic effect? Can we buy it? If so, where and from whom? A moment's reflection tells the theorist that strategic effect cannot be purchased directly. In a world designed for the content-ment of strategists, the polities they serve would be able to purchase strategic effect directly, 'by the yard or metre' as it were, in their defence budgets. Instead, in common with love, happiness, fear, well-being, and security, this concept refers to a near-end state that is the compound product of lesser effects. Strategic effect cannot be the end state for strategy, because the whole strategic function and its product can only be politically instrumental.

Reluctantly, one is obliged to admit that although there is everything to be said in praise of the concept of strategic effect, its recognition alone, though valuable, leaves the strategic heavy lifting still to be done. By analogy, Clausewitz contri-butes hugely to understanding, as well as some misunderstanding, though that tends to be our fault rather than his, when he advances the concepts of friction, centre of gravity, and culminating point of victory. In common with these potent ideas, strategic effect has only limited educational, and zero operational, utility. The point is easily illustrated by posing the simple question, granted that the enemy will be defeated by the net strategic effect of our overall effort—a circular definitional truth—exactly which effects, achieved how, by whom, what, when, and in what quantities will produce the strategic effect that wins? One can concoct similar questions that demonstrate the operational vacuity, yet near brilliance, of several such ideas as, for example, those cited immediately above: friction, centre of gravity, and the culminating point of victory.

The challenge to the strategist, first, is to be open to education by the general theory that tells him that he needs to generate strategic effect; that is the purpose of his function. But, second, the strategist well educated by theory needs to be able to employ the conceptual tools that are strategic ideas in order to produce the effects that must be orchestrated in pursuit of strategic advantage, success, and possibly victory.

Regretfully, one must confess that to understand a strategic concept, to recog-nize its truth and its purpose when translated into strategic behaviour, is by no means synonymous with knowing exactly, or even imprecisely, how to do it, how to render it actionable. Furthermore, for yet more bad news, even if one thinks one knows how to bring an enemy down, this desirable fact, should it be such, can only be of limited value if one lacks the means to achieve it. By way of illustration, let us suppose that the theory of strategic air power in its several major variants, as developed, preached, and officially adopted in the 1930s, had been correct. Perhaps so-called strategic bombing of civilian 'morale' targets, or of the 'vital nodes' in the 'industrial web', would have deterred those who needed deterring and, *in extremis*, would have delivered victory in war on its own with little or no direct assistance from armies and navies.[12] Alas for the testing of air power theory, in practice a strategic air power instrument arguably capable of securing Germany's defeat, built at huge multidimensional costs by Britain and the United States, did not exist until late 1944 and 1945. My point is not to claim that the Royal Air Force (RAF) Bomber Command and the heavy bombers of the US Army Air Forces (USAAF) could have won the war substantially unaided by maritime and ground operations. I do not believe this. Rather is the point that even when there is a reasonably explicit and unambiguous body of strategic thought endorsing a particular source of military effect for overall strategic effect, in this case victory through air power over Germany (and Japan), the strategist cannot exploit such understanding by performing his function as the strategy bridge unless he can design and execute actionable plans with a military instrument tactically.

The bad news from strategic theory is that there is no conceptual insight that can negate or even noticeably offset the hazards for strategy that lurk systemically in the nature of war. The better news is that by recognizing the central purpose of the function of strategy to be the generation of sufficient net strategic effect, one is at least heading in the right direction towards practical value. Recall, yet again, that the strategy bridge employs theory for practice. We can close this opening section by resorting to a mixture of general theory, historical experience, and commonsense to answer the questions that should lead down the path of pragmatic utility. And such utility, we ought never to forget, remembering Bernard Brodie's dictum, is what strategic theory is all about.[13]

Now for the questions: first, just what is strategic effect? It is the net result of our largely coercive behaviour of any and all kinds upon the behaviour of the enemy. What is strategic effect, precisely? It is control over enemy thought and behaviour on a spectrum of possibilities. Strategic effect is never what we do; by definition it can only be in the consequences of what we do. These consequences ultimately will not be material. People, not machines or buildings (e.g. the White House, the Kremlin), wage war. With the important partial exception of a war conducted to achieve the total military overthrow of the enemy, the strategic effect of primary interest is manifested in the perceptions, judgements, and behavioural choices of a human enemy: his political leaders, military commanders, and probably his general public also. Furthermore, the strategic effect of our efforts will be felt and should be identifiable in the attitudes and behaviour of our allies and of neutral polities. Given the complex mixture of influences upon human thought and behaviour, it should be obvious that prediction of strategic effect must be guesswork, it has to be an art, it cannot be a science. As Clausewitz and J. C. Wylie asserted, control is the object of strategy.[14] The political use that is made of control is, of course, the zone of the policymaker, not of the strategist. At least it is not the role of the strategist functioning as strategist. This is not to deny that strategists should always be prepared to challenge the wisdom in policy on the grounds of strategic feasibility.

Next, how do we measure strategic effect? Can we measure it? Since such effect must always exist, be it net positive or negative from our point of view, how can we locate it and assess its ever dynamic condition? 'By their deeds shall ye know them' has to be the basic answer to this question. Inadvertently yet necessarily the enemy must tell us what effect we are having upon his thought and behaviour. He will speak with his actions, or inaction, as well as in words. This is not very satisfactory to those among us who have difficulty accepting ambiguity as an existential reality. Strategy is always an effort to seek some measure of control over an enemy by means of actionable plans that are, by intent, hopefully more or less reliable predictions of the course of future tactical and hence operational events. It is unsurprising that the strategic quest for a predictably favourable future is ever liable to mislead the unwary into unsound methods.[15] Methodological pathologies have abounded throughout history. For example, Clausewitz waged merciless intellectual combat against those among his contemporary theorists who advanced what he regarded, all too plausibly, as nonsensically geometrical and stylized formulaic theories of warfare. The same challenge that he recognized and conceptually eviscerated exists today. Truly there are no new ideas pertaining to strategy, neither the sound nor the unsound. Both good and bad strategic ideas reappear irregularly but cyclically on the metaphorical conceptual carousel. The commonplace English saying, 'a good idea whose time has come', needs to be augmented by two closely associated sayings: 'a bad idea whose time has come', and 'a good, or bad idea whose time has come around yet again'. Also, need one add that the merit in almost any strategic idea always is heavily contextual. Sundry pathologies seemingly are inescapable from strategic studies. Most especially there is need to recognize the fact of an intellectually central mission impossible; the ever recurring effort to remove chance, uncertainty, and hence high risk from war. Before addressing the challenge of prediction in the strategist's worthy search for control, it is necessary to pursue the source of strategic effect more deeply than has been attempted here thus far. This narrative must seek a firm grip upon the whole project from which the wonderful consequence collectively termed strategic effect derives.

STRATEGIC EFFECT AND THE 'STORY ARC' OF STRATEGY

It is helpful to think of strategic performance as having a 'story arc'.[16] A specific strategy can be conceived both as a theory of, and a journey to, victory. Policymakers functioning primarily politically should develop a policy which provides guidance for the strategist holding the strategy bridge. These strategists conceive creatively the particular theory of victory, the actionable plan or plans, which in their turn are executed tactically under the direction of operational level commanders. This neat orderly journey has its Jerusalem, whatever the policy bank of the strategy bridge decides is a satisfactory outcome in the context of a duel with a living self-willed enemy. By way of useful illustration of an invitation to error, it would be difficult to improve upon Scott Sigmund Gartner's view that '[w]e can think of strategy as a policy implemented by organizations to pursue desired goals'. Indeed we can, but we should not. Gartner innocently, quite gratuitously, all but invites confusion between the realms of policy and strategy.[17]

The complementary ideas of strategic effect and a strategy story arc are far from immaculate. But they do share the priceless quality of holism: together they are a potent duo. One would need to search long and hard to unearth substitute terms that offered superior explanation of what should happen. Of course, in the ever inventive realm of contingency that is actual strategic history, anything and everything can, and sometimes does, go wrong. The decision to position the chapter on the problems with strategy ahead of this one on strategy's output was not taken casually. However, nothing in the preceding detailed discussion of the speed bumps on the strategy road, or along strategy's arc, contradicts the analysis here. But, as the next section highlights, strategic performance, including the performance of would-be strategists, is open to harassment by pathologies fairly specific to a focus upon effect and effects. For a somewhat cynical comment, this theorist is convinced that we humans will always find ways to make mistakes in the adversarial context of war and warfare. The necessarily more or less flawed behaviour of those who hold the strategy bridge derives from the typically underrecognized facts of biology, psychology, culture, and sociology regardless of the approach to strategic challenges currently held officially in most favour. The creation of a staff system can help mitigate the potential to cause harm by truly eccentric leaders and other commanders, but staffs acquire and protect cultures of their own that can impede prowess at the sharp end of war. These cultures are entirely capable of adopting and promoting dysfunctional ideas and practices. Naturally enough, staffs take their cultural cues as well as their orders from their commanders, and the latter can deny them a creative role. Napoleon depended upon his chief of staff, Marshal Louis Alexandre Berthier, but he did not share the command function with him in any meaningful sense.[18] That necessary delegation, rather reluctantly and erratically, applied to the emperor's relations with the others in his marshalate.[19]

It is unfortunate, but commonplace, for blameless concepts to be abused by those who, in need of practical help, seize upon a potent strategic idea and require of it a pragmatic utility that it cannot deliver, no matter how expertly crafted the methodology of implementation. For an analogy *à l'outrance*, no matter how expertly it is practised, astrology cannot help be anything other than a nonsense. Paradoxically, strategic effect is a concept as useful, powerful, and, if deployed with care, unchallengeable as it is open to misuse. Indeed, it may be a law of strategy that every dominant, at least plainly major, concept bears matching promises to promote both benefit and harm. Stated thus, what we suggest here is the operation in strategy of some approximation to physics' law of the conservation of energy. The principal ideas that comprise the general theory of strategy, and then their specific application as adapted and adopted in historically specific strategies, carry a capacity to advance or hinder strategic performance. If a fashionable idea is not rewarding in execution, it is likely to be harmful. More likely, the idea at issue, say deterrence, escalation, crisis management, or (strategic, operational, tactical) effects, will play both positively and negatively for a net outcome.

The concept of strategic effect is an idea that assembles, unifies, packages, translates, and propels forward, everything that a belligerent does and attempts in an adversarial context. Strategic effect is a common currency that converts bombs delivered, threats received, troops moved, soldiers forcibly retired from life or current duties, and so forth into their consequences compounded into a single master, though unquantifiable, metric. Obviously this effect has a dynamic quantity. The inconvenience of immeasurability for those in need of demonstrable evidence of the consequences of action is simply a fact of human behaviour, and warfare is nothing if not such behaviour. At the killing and dying tip of a polity's spear, men will be devoted to the twin, if often conflicting, duties to fulfil military tasks and to stay alive to fight tomorrow. The latter goal is not only an instrumental one, at least it is not for the soldiers whose lives are most at risk. They will value their lives as an end worthy in itself. The strategist who holds and seeks to control the spear needs to know what the performance of the tip of his spear means for the willingness and ability of the enemy to continue the struggle. The strategist does not strive to win a war tactically. His mission is not to pile up a succession of tactical or even operational level victories. Rather is it his function so to direct his disparate assets that their total net (remember the enemy) effect contributes strongly positively to the securing of whatever it is that policy demands. Alternatively, it can be the function of a strategist so to orchestrate his side of a struggle that a war is lost slowly rather than rapidly and, if not gracefully, at least in such a way that the successful enemy is powerfully motivated to settle for an advantageous, rather than a triumphally punitive, peace.

If one dismisses the concept of strategic effect as too nebulous, a judgement that would not be wholly unreasonable, one is left with the need to locate a superior substitute. Pragmatically regarded, at the highest of levels a polity needs to approach a conflict, any conflict, with a view to gaining advantage and avoiding disadvantage; in short with a view to achieving some control over the course of events. Strategists performing for a security community typically will have to provide direction to the military behaviour of a wide variety of forces, and those forces will fight singly, most often jointly (inter-service), and generally 'combined (inter-nationally)'. Nonetheless, the strategist most in command on the strategy bridge cannot allow his attention to be entirely consumed by the progress of warfare in any, or even all, of strategy's five geographies (land, sea, air, space, and on the electromagnetic spectrum (EMS)), to the degree that these contests are prosecuted as self-regarding combats at an arguably operational level of war. The most senior strategist and his political masters must wage warfare as a whole, not warfare on land, at sea, and so forth. By way of poignant, but happily only fictional, illustration of this vital point, a cartoon from the Cold War era said it all. Sitting relaxing in a café in occupied Paris, a Soviet officer asked a fellow officer, 'By the way, who did win the air battle?'

Notwithstanding its vagueness, strategic effect is existential. It is reality, and it is expressed in thought and behaviour. By analogy again, this time from astrophysics, strategic effect can be thought of as a purposeful Δ; it is the propulsion that moves strategic history onwards and is the dynamic product of events as human actors choose, or are compelled to interpret them. For example, the Third Reich was defeated by the cumulative and sequential strategic effect generated by its enemies in all ways, by all methods, and in all geographies. How much effect was required for the allies to win? The answer, alas, was 'enough to beat Germany militarily'. Most of the strategic effect was achieved by the Soviet defeat of the main body of the *Wehrmacht* in the east. But, that plausible claim granted, Soviet continental victory was greatly assisted by the Western Allies' defeat, first, of the Kriegsmarine's U-boat campaign in the spring of 1943, and then of the Luftwaffe in the late winter and spring of 1944. The Allies' expeditions to North Africa, Italy, and finally across the channel into France and beyond contributed, though only arguably as to relative significance, to the attritional defeat of German fighting power overall. It is easy to the point of banality to assert the tautology that Germany was defeated by the net strategic effect generated by all its enemies.[20] Paradoxically, what is a banal tautology happens also to be a vital truth about the nature and historical practice of strategy. Despite its apparent undue simplicity, the concept of strategic effect points with high accuracy to the most essential duty of the strategist. This duty must always be to design and adhere to the plot in the contexts of superordinate guidance by policy and feasibility as revealed by the course of contingent events.

Most histories of every conflict register historians' judgements on the question of why one belligerent was more successful than another. How important was Persian gold to the final defeat of Athens in the Peloponnesian War? Did the Roman Empire in the West mainly decline and fall, or was it pushed into extinction? How important was the overambitiously titled Anglo-American Combined Bomber Offensive to the conquest of Germany? Every war has but a single course, a story arc or narrative, from ever debateable origins, through alleged causes, to probable or certain triggers, to active hostilities, through to an often untidy and not entirely conclusive conclusion. This arc comprises military and other behaviours that strategists, and particularly politicians (functionally policymakers), seek to direct to net single unified strategic effect. This is reality. It is the past, as contrasted with history, the product of contending historians.

How is strategic effect generated? An answer is that it is the cumulative net output, compounded in consequences, of the effects of every variety of effort committed to a struggle. This is not especially helpful an explanation if one is seeking methodological assistance to do strategy. But nonetheless it is crucial to understand the nature of the basic plot. At its tersest, the concept of strategic effect explains what strategy does and how it delivers its value. Its output is strategic effect. But strategists and their planning staffs need to move from their theoretical education in strategy and perform in real-time for specific contexts. After all, education has its limits. Strategic theory only educates, it cannot train, let alone specify unique solutions to unique problems. For example, theory arms the strategist with the contestable, but vital sounding, concept of centre of gravity; it does not identify the centre of gravity of a particular historical enemy. In the historical realm of practice, strategy in action is thoroughly contextual. In common with many of Clausewitz's and others' big strategic ideas, the more closely one examines 'centre of gravity', the less self-evident is its exact meaning and pragmatic value.[21] Debateable translation from the original, not modern, German is an ever present source of friction for today's strategist who needs clarity rather than an intellectually fascinating ambiguity.[22]

On the positive side, the concept of strategic effect is a necessary aid to combat the tendency for warfare's complexity to overwhelm the human brain. To repeat, when confronted with the actualities of combat in battlespace in five geographies, in the context of war's non-military, but strategically essential, dimensions, with the complication of diverse enemy behaviours, it is not hard for policymakers or a strategist to miss his way and lose the strategic plot. As already suggested, to help focus attention upon what should be the single design of concerted, more or less integrated, certainly cooperating, performances by any and every asset employed and employable, one can borrow profitably from the world of creative writing the attractive metaphor of the story arc.

By employing the concept of the arc to explain strategic phenomena overall, one should be helping those apt to be perplexed. After all, in practice strategy is done more or less purposefully as contrasted with merely contingently and opportunistically, by dozens of politicians, by staffs of hundreds and even thousands, and by military forces in the field and off that can number tens or hundreds of thousands (and beyond). If one embraces grand strategy as well as its subordinate military strategy, the sheer complexity and diversity of agents, agencies, processes, and happenings, all influenced by enemies, friends, and neutrals, is apt to amount more to chaos than to order in any sense. Strategic theory acknowledges complexity, diversity, contingency, the unwelcome influence of the enemy's efforts, and so forth. But also it must insist upon the primary existential significance of an actual story arc to the course of strategic history. For example, despite its awesome complexity, the Second World War did proceed from pre-war context, through crisis-times with early, mid, and late phases, to a definite conclusion, and then into a post-war era. There was a unique historical journey. It is true that no one could orchestrate the grand sequence of happenings, but also it is true that there was an actual passage from peace, through warfare, to victory and defeat, to an eventual de facto political settlement in 1947–9.

Strategic effect has to be understood temporally and analytically by function. The strategist must think in time in order to understand how his plot, his theory of victory, should be made manifest in deeds. This means with respect to a control over the enemy achieved at a bearable cost proportional to the political stakes at risk in the struggle. The journey from peace, through war, to victory cannot be planned reliably, because of the many problems for strategy discussed at length in Chapter 4. However, the strategist knows that he must mobilize his assets and his liabilities for a journey to whatever policy destination politicians choose. His strategy in action should be conceived as a journey, with its vectored arc selected to produce such harmful effect that the enemy either is weakened for the next stage of the contest, or decides to try to bring play to a close by accepting a measure of defeat deemed tolerable, given his unfavourable circumstances and even less promising prospects.

What happens along the story arc of strategy? While it is analytically useful, even essential, to distinguish among policy, grand strategy, military strategy, operations, and tactics, in practice each function in war happens simultaneously though hierarchically in quality of effect. To explain, from day one of a war every belligerent generates strategic effect. Military engagements, actual, anticipated, and predicted, produce local tactical effects which, managed at every level of military effort by operational commanders, yield operational—typically campaign—effects with more, or less, consequence for the overall course of the conflict. It is the function of the strategist to assess this overall course and adjust plans and assets to fit well enough, including efforts to alter, unfolding historical reality. He is striving to pursue his preferred story arc temporally from the here and now to a situation in time, place, and friendly imbalance of power that can serve as sufficient success to be called victory, or at least to satisfy his political masters. Judgement as to what is necessary and desirable by way of the specific definition of victory in a particular case is not the professional duty of the strategist, save only in his role as strategic advisor to the policymaking process.[23]

Strategy might be viewed holistically, if erroneously, as necessarily embracing the realms of operations and tactics that must carry it into effect in the field, which comprise one bank to the strategy bridge, as well as the zone of policy that must tell strategy what it has to try to achieve through action on the other bank to the bridge. Alternatively, as here, one might prefer to treat strategy much more restrictively as the behaviour by its guardians who hold the strategy bridge. In this second view, strategists, probably episodically, deliver a theory of victory as a central concept expressed in the form of operational plans for execution by operational commanders who must command and lead men into contact with the enemy. The first, fully holistic, approach is in error because it conflates improperly the different realms of policy, military (inter alia) guidance and direction, and action. Nonetheless, so much granted for the satisfaction of definitional purists, I am concerned that the placing of heavy emphasis upon the undeniable distinctions among the functions and activities of policy, strategy, operations, and tactics, though philosophically correct, is likely to discourage recognition of the need for unity of thought and behaviour in war and warfare.

Yes, policy should guide strategy, which should command, certainly direct, operations which need to be executed ultimately by men with guns. However, the essential accuracy of this statement of a neat logical hierarchy must not be permitted to hide the reality that every level, every function represented in this hierarchy, performs its duties simultaneously, ideally in concert though frequently unharmoniously.[24] This strategic gestalt in historical motion proceeds along a temporal arc navigated by the light of a variably purposeful strategic story.

OF CONCEPT AND METHOD: ANALYTICAL PATHOLOGY

This chapter argues that strategic effect is the concept most suitable to explain the nature and most proximate purpose of strategy's output. If defence professionals can remember that in any and all circumstances, and by any and all means, strategy generates strategic effect, they should thereby have inoculated themselves against several maladies potentially deadly to a polity's security.[25] Without the concept of strategic effect, one must flounder in a confused sea of words that do not quite penetrate to the heart of the matter. If the plot of national and international security is not to be lost amidst the complexity and volume of disparate events, there has to be a binding idea. Strategic effect is the most powerful such idea and conceptual tool that many generations of strategic theorists have discovered to date. Fortunately, the concept is simple. Less fortunately, unless it is treated with great care and respect this admirable simplicity can deceive the unwary, both as to the meaning of the concept and with regard to the reach of its utility. It is common for fundamentally sound strategic ideas to be employed in unsound ways by pragmatic people who do not understand the limitations of the concept they employ. One thinks of the 'indirect approach',[26] of 'asymmetric conflict', and for our topic here, of strategic effect. The recent (late 1980s and 1990s) rediscovery of effect(s) singular and plural, was hired by some American and other Western officials to provide the intellectual engine that could power 'Effects-Based Operations' (EBO). Basil Liddell Hart's much favoured 'indirect approach' to warfare has in common with EBO an essential high value, but in addition, alas, a value easily lost when the concept is misappropriated for missions beyond its competence. The EBO controversy of the 1990s and 2000s is reviewed later in this chapter with reference to analytical pathology. The problem with the indirect approach as a means to deceive is that it cannot be operationalized as a universal and eternal key to victory, as the all circumstance theoretical tool to unlock the mysteries of strategic history, or even as a concept that has an identifiable meaning for historical practice. But, those major limitations duly noted, it is usually a good idea to endeavour to deceive the enemy by taking action indirectly, translated as not from a direction or in a manner that he anticipates.

As for 'asymmetric conflict', another popular concept cited here, the problem, as with the indirect approach, is that it has no definable meaning. To be asymmetrical simply is to be different. Since nearly every belligerent in the entire course of strategic history has differed from every other belligerent in some significant regard, what possible utility can repose in the concept? The answer is that because strategists somewhat ignorant of their enemies are wont to make the unsound assumption that their enemies are very similar to themselves, it is beneficial for the notion of asymmetry to have some authority. Although it must lack inherent specific meaning, its currency alerts the defence planner to look for, perhaps anticipate, the unusual.

As with the indirect approach, however, the concept of asymmetrical conflict becomes a blight rather than a minor blessing when people assume that there is, or can be a distinctive form of warfare that is asymmetrical. In common parlance in the 1990s and 2000s, asymmetrical conflict came to refer, all too loosely, to what a century ago Colonel Charles E. Callwell referred to as 'small wars' conflict between regular and irregular forces.[27] Historical context creates a demand for useful concepts. America's strategically unipolar moment following the demise of the Soviet Union meant that those who would oppose American hegemony have needed to locate styles of conflict in which US military primacy is at a heavy discount. This goes a long way towards explaining the attractions of such asymmetrical—to US regular conventional military power—modes of conflict as terrorism and insurgency in its several complex forms. Unfortunately for those who like simple binary distinctions, careful defence analysis reveals what has always been the case, that many, certainly most of our contemporary conflicts are of a complex hybrid character. Conflicts do not separate neatly into regular or irregular, rather do they register a range of belligerent behaviours, ranging from terrorism to regular stand-up conventional combat.[28]

However, it is ironic and paradoxical that the almost pure gold of the concept of strategic effect is all but valueless at best, actually has negative worth, when sincere and rigorous efforts are made to translate it from idea to practical military planning method. Because this book is not a work with a prescriptive purpose, the discussion has only a limited interest in controversy over the merit in analytical methods developed to implement so-called EBO. We are interested in EBO largely for the purpose of illustrating the perils in strategic theory and analysis, and because of its conceptual and pragmatic proximity to the entirely sound idea and practical goal of strategic effect.

Lest there be any misunderstanding, this book has no interest in pursuing the largely American and rather vicious inter- and intra-service debate over the merit in EBO, approached as a planning methodology for tactical and operational purposes.[29] However, given the intellectual proximity of the EBO controversy to the argument here, it seems advisable to offer a few words on the debate. Accepting the risk of undue reductionism, it is fair enough to claim that in the 1990s, in the immediate wake of the air power-led victory in the Gulf in 1991, the US Air Force was emboldened to argue that technology and associated tactical prowess had caught up with the traditionally dominant doctrine of strategic air power. Specifically, some vociferous air-minded persons had always claimed that wars could and one day would be won from the air.[30] The first Gulf War and the subsequent decade—certainly through the defeat of the Taliban regime in Afghanistan in 2001, and just possibly through the spring of 2003 with the prompt demolition of B'aathist Iraq—did witness a cumulatively dramatic improvement in the potency of (US) air power. Indeed, one could almost argue that the 1990s and early 2000s comprised an, really the first, air power decade.[31] The key to this transformation was precision targeting, and the key to precision was the full operational arrival and exploitation of the twenty-four-satellite constellation of the Global Positioning System (GPS).[32] The new and improved technologies of stand-off aerial bombardment encouraged development of the EBO approach to military operations. Essentially, EBO promised to take an enemy apart, certainly paralyse him by means of exceedingly precise kinetic effects, bombardment. As a whole approach to warfare, it should be needless to add, the EBO philosophy reduced to an exercise in targeting, which is to say in the application of fire-power.[33] This approach, one that heavily privileged air power, met with most determined, and eventually successful, opposition from the practitioners of ground warfare. With respect to a definition of EBO, this attractive claim can suffice: 'EBO, stated simply, is a disciplined way to first understand the strategic objective, take a comprehensive look at possible courses of action, and then link tasks (through the effects they create) to that objective.'[34]

On balance, EBO advocates in the 1990s and 2000s can be judged to have taken a most important, indeed critically significant, valid idea a step or two too far. The leading modern air power school of thought is absolutely correct in pointing to the recent transformation in its instruments' ability to strike ever smaller and more elusive targets with unprecedented precision. Furthermore, these theorists and practitioners of air power are surely sound in demanding a focus upon military, and then political, consequences—in another word, upon 'effects'. However, the waging of warfare, let alone war, is so complex a project that it cannot sensibly be reduced to a quantifiable targeting exercise, no matter how precise. War cannot be a science because it is a human activity subject to control by incalculable determination as well.[35] As one proceeds from the analysis of first-order tactical effects, to speculation about second-order operational, and then to third and beyond order strategic—let alone political—effects the methodological impracticality of the EBO enterprise rapidly is revealed to those with open minds. But the theoretical and practical official demise of EBO must not be allowed to cast a shadow over the importance of the concept of strategic effect. Bathwater may be safely drained away, but not the baby of strategic consequences.

To summarize, it has long been believed by some military theorists that wars can be won if strategists take the time and trouble to understand what kinds of, and how much, damage they need to inflict on the enemy. Once they are able to specify, and we mean specify (with enemy assets identified in detail and the quality and quantity of necessary damage similarly identified) the damage that has to be wrought, strategists should be able to calculate the effort required to achieve that effect.[36] Of course, there must be practical difficulties with enervating contingencies (e.g. bad weather reducing sortie rates for aircraft or reducing bombing accuracy), but EBO can cope with those by allowing generously conservative margins for error. If the analysis shows a need for forty sorties, plan to provide sixty, for example; or, if an enemy's ICBM in a superhardened silo is calculated to be only 78 per cent vulnerable to attack by a single warhead on a multiple-warhead missile with conservatively assumed performance characteristics, plan to send two or three warheads, cross-targeted from other ICBMs in order to drive the expected vulnerability percentage up into the 90s. An effects-based approach to the conduct of warfare is commonsense. Decide what needs to be done and then calculate prudently, but precisely, how it can be done. Since strategy is all about consequences, surely a focus upon effects is quintessentially strategic? Was not Clausewitz a prophet for an effects-based approach? When he wrote, 'strategy is the use of the engagements for the purpose of the war', what could this mean other than the 'use' of the effect or effects of the 'engagement'?[37] Stated thus boldly, Clausewitz is indeed heading the column of enthusiasts for the proposition that effect has to be understood as the product of strategy in action, and perhaps even of action in the calculable currency of firepower for assessable damage of known value.

One can suggest with high confidence that the great Prussian would be appalled were he able to read the previous paragraph. Far from licensing what today commonly is understood as an effects-based view of strategic behaviour, he was instead a merciless critic of such an approach. What has happened is that problem-solving defence analysts simplemindedly have wrenched an unexceptionable high concept, strategic effect, out of its natural orbit of comfort. The idea has been misapplied as method with an ambitious domain. The claim has taken some root because strategic effect is what wins wars, the way to plan to win is to calculate the effect that one must achieve. Exactly what the enemy will be doing while one imposes the necessary effect ought to be a concern, even a potentially show-stopping concern of some significance. Also, need one add, it is always possible that the enemy will not interpret the consequences of the effects from which he is made to suffer in a way that we should judge rational. He may just be reasonable in his own lights, but not rational for EBO analysis according to ours. These should be troubling thoughts.

The lethal problems for those who seek to reduce warfare, let alone war writ large, to calculable metrics of largely kinetic damage, is that their subject is too complex, too dynamic, too human, and too interactive in its functioning to be usefully measurable. Most aspects of war are not subjects for calculation. Educated guesswork based upon some empirical evidence, yes, but quantifiably correct solutions to definable contained problems, no.[38] Strategy is not a science, it is an art with some scientific features. No planning staff, regardless of the excellence of its professional skills is literally able to calculate, even approximately, how a war can be won. Naturally, the strategy or strategies as actionable plans must be supportable by calculated quantities: numbers abound. Time, distance, logistical provision of all kinds, anticipated combat loss and other sources of human wastage as well as machine replacement—all of these and many more important matters both lend themselves to calculation and indeed must be calculated. It follows that once one decides what is to be achieved and broadly how to achieve it, the means and methods selected, or that happen to be available, should be applied for the desired effects. Unfortunately for elegance and economy in theory, however, everything I have just written, though I believe it to be true as stated, carries a deadly virus.

War is so densely complex, eternally and universally, that its 'climate'—danger, exertion, uncertainty, and chance—must frustrate the would-be scientific strategist.[39] For a pertinent aside, although this author has been variously described over the years as a political scientist and a social scientist, the noun is not merely wrong, rather is it impossible for it to be right. Strategy, and strategic studies, cannot be a science in any meaningful sense. This is not a matter of opinion only. Possibly because many defence professionals, military and civilian, have been educated in the physical and mathematical sciences, understandably they reach for the analytical tools with which they are familiar. Effect and effects would seem to many of those trained in the sciences, properly so-called, to be just the approach needed to reduce or eliminate the uncertainty and chance with which Clausewitz unerringly harassed overconfident strategists. Let mathematics solve the problems of warfare; indeed, why not of war itself? If we know what has to be done in order to win, or simply to avoid defeat, it should be possible to measure the effects required and therefore the effort needed to secure those calculated effects. If only.

I admit to insisting here upon a restrictive understanding of what is and what is not science. Of course, from its Latin root *scientia*, science simply means knowledge. By the restrictive definition of scientific knowledge—of warfare and strategy, for our case of interest, one would have to mean knowledge 'conducted on objective principles involving the systemised observation and experiment with phenomena'.[40] This translates as thoroughly reliable knowledge that can be checked by anyone, anywhere, anytime. By and large, though not invariably, such science lends itself to, indeed requires, quantitative expression. There are other definitions of science of a far more relaxed character, for the social sciences for example. That granted, there is a significant distinction between approaching war as an art or as one of the harder sciences. It is unhelpful to blur the difference, as in the relaxed definition of science. The social science of strategy could attempt to justify the scientific label by claiming that it identifies most case, perhaps just some case, truths, hardly laws. The dicta that constitute the general theory of strategy might qualify as social science according to the relaxed understanding. They do comprise 'a systematic and formulated knowledge' and they are certainly 'organized'. However, I resist making the claim for science, even for a relatively undemanding social science, because such a position is apt to mislead. Strategy inherently is difficult enough to do well, given its active, competitive dimension as a duel, its complexity, and its pervasively human aspects. It is not sensible, or appropriate, to seek an unattainable certainty to be reflected in objective replicable universal truths. The search for a (harder) science of strategy is a hunt for a chimera.

The dazzling concept of strategic effect is pure gold as a general intellectual master, but as a concept for methodical, calculated application as intended effects, it is and can be nothing more than fool's gold. US Army Air Corps war planners believed that they could calculate well enough how many bomber sorties would be needed in order to defeat Nazi Germany. The product of this belief was Air War Plan 1 (AWPD-1) of 1941.[41] The doctrinal fallacy expressed in AWPD-1, reflecting unsound strategic theory, was that Germany could be defeated by the correct aerial bombing campaign. At the level of theory, the logic is circular. Germany is envisaged as a system, a mechanical entity with interacting parts, some of which, and some of whose interactions, are far more vital than are others to the functioning of the whole. Rephrased, if we assume that (*a*) we can understand how Germany as a country at war 'works' and that (*b*) we are able to strike effectively from the sky to inflict critical damage on the key 'links', most useful 'nodes', or 'chokepoints' in the 'industrial web' that keeps Germany functioning, then (*c*) Germany would be defeated. Admittedly this is an extreme historical example of the calculable approach to the conduct of war. It does, however, happen to be an actual historical case, not a hypothetical one. One can never know beyond all room for argument, whether or not victory through (so-called strategic) air power alone could have been achieved by the USAAF and the RAF, but there are large and persuasive grounds for doubt.[42] In practice, on the course that strategic history meandered from 1939 to 1945, Germany eventually was defeated jointly by all practicable forms of power, military and other, though primarily military, and through the combined, if understandably self-privileging, efforts of most of humankind. The jury will be out forever on the much contested issue of the relative contribution of Allied strategic bombing to the defeat of Germany. In the opinion of this author, the contribution was considerably greater than currently it is popular to grant, but that it fell short, though possibly not far short, of meriting a credible claim to have been the Allies' military leading edge for victory. The bombing needs to be appreciated in its joint contexts, and even as a contributor to combined arms warfare. There can be little doubt that Nazi Germany was defeated primarily in its great continental struggle with the Soviet Union. Nonetheless, the Western Allies played both direct, but also some largely indirect roles of some significance for the course and outcome of that titanic contest within a contest. An important point to remember is that although air power is subject to its specific general theory, in historical practice the utility of air power always must be contextually shaped and frequently driven, notwithstanding the role played by contingency.

Strategic effect is too difficult to the point of utter impracticality to serve other than as the brilliant single currency descriptor of all kinds of strategic consequences. Let us plunge into the realm of potential application, so as to be satisfied, really satisfied, that effect and effects cannot be converted from a core idea into a methodologically all weather paved highway leading to calculable and therefore predictable victory. By way of a vitally needed caveat, I must register my determination to separate the useful from the useless and harmful in our subject. Strong critics of EBO have been apt to shoot on suspicion and association, presumably on principle that it was better for nine innocent ideas to be slaughtered rather than that one guilty one should survive. Strategic effect is not merely a good and useful idea, it is literally the essential and master concept that expresses the product, the very output of strategy. It is useful to state boldly the barest of bare essentials of the structure and functioning of effects and effect in and for strategy.

1. Every level of effect, orchestrated more or less centrally or not—tactical, operational, strategic, political—influences every other level.

2. In aggregate, tactical and operational effects must have a compound net strategic effect.

3. Strategic effect has to be a net value, since it applies friendly or unfriendly leverage on the course of strategic events, depending upon enemy performance. Effect and effects at every level are net, given that conflict, war, and warfare are adversarial enterprises.

4. The course of strategic events will have political consequences, intended and otherwise.

This logical outline, though plausible both empirically and logically, beckons to deceive the unwary. The real historical world with its multiple contexts and untraceable relations of influence among and within them cannot be modelled thus. There are analysis-stopping problems everywhere. Most especially, there are awesome difficulties for judgement, let alone for quantified calculation. The military strategist as most senior commander cannot work backwards from strategic effect to tactical effects in order to plot anticipated best practice for the securing of victory. The reasons why he cannot do so are irremovable from the nature, not merely the ever changing character, of war and warfare. The events the strategist seeks to orchestrate and guide to the desired conclusion are potentially too variable in outcome, even when they can broadly be anticipated at all. It is popular to think in terms of first, second, and third-order effects of action. I suggest that one cannot ignore three sets of complication that render quantifiable analysis absurdly impractical. The three orders of effects certainly apply simultaneously to the levels of conflict horizontally, vertically, and both horizontally and vertically.

If one speaks rapidly and the audience is unprepared, a speaker might survive presenting a briefing which simply states the most essential truths about effect and effects, the ones we have made explicit as enumerated points 1–4. The tactical level of behavioural consequences yields net operational effects, which fuel the single strategic effect that is the totality of a belligerent's achievement at any one time upon the course of history. Alas, this straightforward, though not exactly elementary, reasoning leaves some deadly traps untouched. What are these traps? First, there are first, second, and probably third and beyond order effects at every level of conflict, and the confidence with which they can be predicted diminishes at least logarithmically from order to order. Second, the deeply uncertain tactical effects of tactical behaviour must have operational level consequences, which in their turn will have first, second, and third (plus) effects. And the identical challenge to precise understanding pertains to the relationship between the operational and the strategic levels. Third, there has to be constant complex interaction, multiple generally unpredictable feedback loops, among each level of conflict. In other words, for example, a tactical success can have an operational consequence in that the enemy answers his bad tactical news by means of an operational, or even strategic, level adjustment. As we keep trying to insist, the key to the master plot that is war, warfare, and strategy in peace and war, is the unavoidable reality of their nature as a gestalt. In some respects it is praiseworthy to seek to reduce the potential chaos of war by controlling its course through the execution of plans calculated to deliver the quantity and quality of overall strategic effect necessary for victory. But the effort is bound to fail. It is mission impossible, and that has to mean that it is an unsound approach to strategic performance.

I may appear to overstate the problems with what I recognize is the valid concept of strategic effect. Unfortunately, if anything, I understate them. There is a danger of over-analysing the challenges of strategy. If a strategist methodically took explicit note of every difficulty mentioned in this and the previous chapter, even a person of extraordinarily robust character could be excused for falling into a professionally fatal depression. Somehow, and it can be close to a mystery, commanders at all levels process what they think they know about events extant and to come, possibly from first through several more orders of effects, and make decisions. Education, training, experience, and a competent staff must contribute to decision making that more often than not benefits significantly from intuition exercised via some approximate to Clausewitz's *coup d'oeil*.[43] It is, and has always been, a fact that some practising strategists have been able to perform well enough strategically. Strategy is not mission impossible. Given that strategy's product for political leverage is strategic effect, obviously sufficient effect is generated in conflict after conflict, albeit not invariably, for there to be a political settlement satisfactory to the military victor, should there be one.

What has been explained, to some people perhaps just suggested, in these pages is why the effects achieved tactically and operationally cannot reliably be predicted, are unable literally to be calculated, even at their own levels, let alone when transformed alchemically into overall strategic effect. For example, in 1944 the Allied Combined Chiefs of Staff could not be certain even what the immediate, first-order, tactical effects would be of the aerial and naval bombardment they programmed to help enable the D-Day landings.[44] How would the German High Command, effectively meaning Adolf Hitler personally, respond to Allied tactical success or failure on the beaches of Normandy? What were Germany's tactical, operational, strategic, and political options? The invaders had to guess as to how well their forces would do, and how the enemy most likely would respond. But the role of contingency, including blind chance, and the pressure of uncertainty, provided the most living proof imaginable of the soundness of Clausewitz's insistence that war is more of an art than a science.[45] Strategy is human and it delivers effect through tactical behaviour that has operational consequences that shape the strategic context, whence flows the leverage for policy to achieve, or fail to achieve, its political goals.

Effect thinking becomes strategically pathological when it misleads people into an attempt to achieve a quality of reliable control of events that simply is not attainable. The error, the huge error, lies in believing that the concept of strategic effect can be harnessed and driven to conquer the chance, uncertainty, and friction of war. Of course strategists must try to control events, of course they have to try to anticipate enemy moves and countermoves, and of course they are obliged to try to prepare against the multitudinous sources of potential friction. But strategically well-educated strategists should know that Moltke the Elder was correct when he said, as we quoted in Chapter 4, that 'strategy is a system of expedients', albeit a system whose systemic integrity requires constant awareness of the central plot and the need for a coherent story arc connecting here with there, wherever 'there' may lie.

KILLING THE VIRUS AND SAVING THE PATIENT

We have sought to demonstrate that strategic effect is both a valid and an important concept. In addition we have striven to explain why ever repeated efforts to treat warfare as a quantifiable science rather than an art are doomed to fail. The problem is not lack of methodological sophistication. Rather is the challenge the complex, adversarial, human, contingency prone, nature of conflict, war, warfare, and strategy.[46] More to the point, the practical problem is that defence communities are vulnerable to seduction by the purveyors of strategic alchemy and astrology. Strategists with difficulties to overcome or evade often are insufficiently suspicious of the conceptual and analytical patent medicines that purportedly will deliver certainty out of uncertainty, or at least that carry a promise to reduce markedly the risks of conflict. As often as not the same idea can be both sound and unsound, depending upon the historical context for its particular application and the skill with which it is employed; so it is with the baseline concept of effect for the strategist. While this chapter has suggested how truly indeterminate the course of history has to be, the argument developed here is anything but uncertain in its conclusion. Four broad thoughts bring this discussion to rest.

First, this analysis should have settled some doubts concerning the validity of the concept of strategic effect, and even of an effects-focused approach to strategic performance. In addition, the discussion ought to have cast significant doubt upon the wisdom in attempting to apply the concept with a rigorously numerate methodology. But because strategy can have only instrumental purpose and meaning, recognition of the importance of effect—and effects—is not merely appropriate, it is close to being a tautology. The patient must be saved. If the concept of strategic effect lacks authority in the minds of those who should be strategists, then the strategy bridge cannot be held, it will not function. The trouble is that although they are existential historical realities, strategic effect as a master concept, and the idea of tactical and operational effects also, suffer in analytical legitimacy by obvious association with the often repeated endeavours to use the concept and idea inappropriately as a means to treat warfare as an exactly quantifiable science. An excellent textbook on strategic studies offers a fully defensible definition of EBO, one that should not mislead its readers.

> Rather than prioritising the destruction of enemy forces through the application of military power, this [effects-based operations] is an approach that focuses first on establishing the broad end states that need to be delivered (the 'effect') and then choosing the most appropriate range of instruments to achieve it (of which military power may be only one). It is a process designed to produce better strategic performance.[47]

So far so good. So high in ambition, so good. It is only when strategic performance is stapled to the concept of strategic effect via pseudo-scientific methodologies that problems arise.

Second, strategic effect and the tactical and operational effects that are its fuel are historical realities. Only rarely will it be entirely obvious exactly which lower level effects have precisely which higher level consequences. Just occasionally, cause and effect can be determined with complete confidence. A besieged garrison can literally be starved into submission. But when one applies measured violence for influence, especially if the coerced party is assailed by several military as well as other instruments of leverage, exact apportionment of responsibility for cause and effect must be contestable. For example, just why did Serbia concede to NATO over Kosovo in 1999? Was it because of NATO's air campaign?[48] Perhaps it was the threat of invasion on the ground? What role did domestic unrest in Serbia play? And so on and so forth. Explanation is speculative. However, we do know that NATO anticipated that its coercive air campaign would deliver Serbian submission in four days, but that it had to be extended to seventy-eight. Strategic history is like that. Nonetheless, grand overall strategic effect and its lesser contributors exist. Behaviour has consequences, though frequently not precisely predictable ones, and certainly not ones predictable out to the second and third orders.

Third, lest the point has been understated thus far, there are strategically relevant, even vitally enabling, activities that are in some respects measurable and that need to be measured. The entire realm of logistics is a prime example. However, even logistical calculation can mislead. The variable human factor sometimes is able to find non-predictable and therefore non-measurable compensation for, say, supply interruption. Furthermore, predicted negative logistical effects upon tactical performance and hence operational achievement, may be rendered irrelevant if operations can be redirected to evade the problem. Calculation is not the proper issue here. Rather is the vital issue the persisting urge by defence analysts of a scientific persuasion to measure the unmeasurable.

Fourth, every effect has its value determined by the contexts within which it is felt. Effect is pervasively situational. Hardly any effect we can specify, deriving from any item in a polity's grand strategic basket of assets, has an absolute consequential value. For example, as a physical instrument, long range conventionally armed air power may be the same in warfare that is largely regular or mainly irregular, but its probable contribution to strategic success is likely to differ markedly as between the two broad categories of organized violence. The instrument is not the effect. This is why one ought not to refer to 'strategic' air power, for a leading example of the error. Every element in the armed forces ultimately contributes to overall strategic effect. No single kind of force inherently can be more effective than another. The identity of the leading edge in delivering effectiveness in warfare depends upon the context.

Strategic effect requires rescue from its guilt by association with a deeply flawed pseudo-scientific approach to war. Not infrequently, a critically important concept and some body of theory is unjustly tainted by its false association with some derivative bastard offspring of ideas. Geopolitics is a major example of this phenomenon. The political implications of spatial relationships have always been significant. But German *Geopolitik* in the 1930s and early 1940s, not all of which was infected by a biasing ideology, certainly not a racist one, succeeded inadvertently in retarding geopolitical scholarship for more than fifty years.[49] The geopolitical postulate insists wisely that geographical relationships have a powerful influence upon statecraft. Similarly, the idea, indeed recognition of the reality, of strategic effect and tactical and operational effects, opens a window of understanding that is essential for the strategist.

NOTES

1. Charles J. Esdaile, 'De-Constructing the French Wars: Napoleon as Anti-Strategist', *Journal of Strategic Studies*, 31 (August 2008), 515–52. MacGregor Knox agrees with Esdaile. Knox judges that 'Napoleon incarnated operational brilliance—and strategic lunacy'. In a note he explains that 'Napoleon, like his German successors in the "thirty years war" of 1914–45, resolved strategic issues by battlefield virtuosity and harboured apparently unlimited aims. The outcome in both cases was defeat by a "world of enemies."' 'Conclusion: Continuity and Revolution in the Making of Strategy', in Williamson Murray, Knox, and Alvin Bernstein, eds., *The Making of Strategy: Rulers, States, and War* (Cambridge: Cambridge University Press, 1994), 616.

2. J. C. Wylie emphasizes the distinction between cumulative and sequential strategies. The former accrues its strategic effect by amassing largely independent gains, while the latter proceeds to secure strategic advantage via a 'series of visible, discrete steps, each dependent on the one that preceded it'. *Military Strategy: A General Theory of Power Control* (1967; Annapolis, MD: Naval Institute Press, 1989), 24. Wylie's distinction is arguably useful, but it could mislead the unwary. While one can distinguish independent from interdependent acts of war, it seems to me that even independently cumulative strategic effect is secured in a sense sequentially. At the very least, I am not entirely convinced that Wylie's admittedly clear binary may not do as much harm to understanding as it delivers benefit.

3. The analysis and judgments in Murray, Knox, and Bernstein, eds., *The Making of Strategy*, are awesomely damning of those who have been contemptuous of strategy.

4. See Robert Pois and Philip Langer, *Command Failure in War: Psychology and Leadership* (Bloomington, IN: Indiana University Press, 2004), ch. 8; and Horst Boog et al., *Germany and the Second World War: vol. VI, The Global War* (Oxford: Clarendon Press, 2001), pt. VI. While Hitler's strategic ineptitude had a lot to answer for, the

fact is that the Sixth Army lost at Stalingrad because it was outfought by the initially less-than-élite Soviet Sixty-Second Army under Lt. General Vasily Ivanovich Chuikov. See Michael K. Jones, *Stalingrad: How the Red Army Survived the German Onslaught* (Philadelphia: Casemate, 2007).

5. Harold Winters, *Battling the Elements: Weather and Terrain in the Conduct of War* (Baltimore: Johns Hopkins University Press, 1998), 176–87, is geographically grim; Carl von Clausewitz, *The Campaign of 1812 in Russia* (1832–7; London: Greenhill Books, 1992), is a neglected minor classic; while Adam Zamoyski, *1812: Napoleon's Fatal March on Moscow* (London: Harper Collins Publishers, 2004), is both lively and scholarly.

6. Planning is about deciding what to do. Programming is about doing it. Not infrequently, officials are so busy behaving as programmers that they cannot find time to perform adequately as planners. Needless to add, perhaps, planners require, at the least, broad conceptual guidance. Carl H. Builder and James A. Dewar, 'A Time for Planning? if Not Now, When?' *Parameters*, 24 (summer 1994), 4–15, is exceptionally clear in its explanation of the vital distinction between the two functions.

7. Arthur Conan Doyle, *The Adventures of Sherlock Holmes* and *The Memoirs of Sherlock Holmes* (1892 and 1894; London: Penguin Books, 2001), 166.

8. Harry R. Yarger, *Strategic Theory for the 21st Century: The Little Book on Big Strategy* (Carlisle, PA: Strategic Studies Institute, February 2006), 14.

9. Ibid. 52.

10. Ibid. 53.

11. Ibid. 66.

12. See Malcolm Smith, *British Air Strategy Between the Wars* (Oxford: Clarendon Press, 1984); Charles Griffith, *The Quest: Haywood Hansell and American Strategic Bombing in World War II* (Maxwell AFB, AL: Air University Press, September 1999); and Tami Davis Biddle, *Rhetoric and Reality in Air Warfare: The Evolution of British and American Ideas about Strategic Bombing, 1914–1945* (Princeton, NJ: Princeton University Press, 2002). For the history of the Allied strategic bombing offensive in Europe, see Richard G. Davis, *Bombing the European Axis Powers: A Historical Digest of the Combined Bomber Offensive, 1939–1945* (Maxwell AFB, AL: Air University Press, April 2006). Donald L. Miller, *Eighth Air Force: The American Bomber Crews in Britain* (London: Aurum Press, 2008), is a compelling combination of narrative drive and scholarly precision.

13. Bernard Brodie, *War and Politics* (New York: Macmillan, 1973), 452. 'Above all, strategic theory is a theory for action.'

14. Carl von Clausewitz, *On War*, tr. Michael Howard and Peter Paret (1832–4; Princeton, NJ: Princeton University Press, 1976), 75; Wylie, *Military Strategy*, 124.

15. A leading modern example of a methodological pathology was the endeavour to identify by quantifiably calculable analysis 'stable', as contrasted with 'unstable', states of the Soviet–American strategic nuclear 'balance'. As I have noted earlier in these pages, the truest father of unsound American defence analysis on the nuclear age has been Lt. General Glenn A. Kent, a person whose undoubted analytical brilliance and professional patriotic devotion has, unfortunately, rested almost completely upon a thorough misunderstanding of politics and strategy. The generation of 'vulnerability studies' of strategic nuclear forces was a cottage industry whose artisans took themselves and their well-calculated products—seemingly endless numbers of drawdown curves—far too seriously. Much of US vulnerability analysis during the Cold War was

innocent of a plausible, indeed of any, political dimension, and relied upon highly unreliable technical and tactical assumptions about the enemy's forces and prospective behaviour. See the criticisms that I levelled in my *Modern Strategy* (Oxford: Oxford University Press, 1999), chs. 11 and 12. For a prime example of the kind of defence analysis that should give the profession a bad name, and which must have caused Clausewitz to turn in his grave, see Glenn A. Kent, Randall J. Devalk, and D. E. Thayer, *A Calculus of First-Strike Stability (A Criterion for Evaluating Strategic Forces)*, N-2526-AF (Santa Monica, CA: RAND, June 1988). In addition to Edward S. Quade, ed., *Analysis for Military Decisions: The RAND Lectures on Systems Analysis* (Chicago: RAND McNally, 1964), and Glenn A. Kent, *Thinking About America's Defense: An Analytical Memoir* (Santa Monica, CA: RAND, 2008), the RAND school of defence calculation is explained revealingly in some of the contributions to A. W. Marshall, J. J. Martin, and H. S. Rowen, eds., *On Not Confusing Ourselves: Essays on National Security in Honor of Albert and Roberta Wohlstetter* (Boulder, CO: Westview Press, 1991). The latter book sank without trace, which was a shame, because it contained some entries of outstanding merit (the short chapter by Fred Charles Iklé, for example). It may seem to some of my fellow strategists that I am guilty of serious apostasy. I must confess that I myself used to take numerical 'vulnerability analysis' more seriously than I should have done (including a willingness to demonstrate my prowess in manipulating the mini missile vulnerability calculators—one by RAND—that were popular in the mid 1970s). It was with some reluctance, and even some professional and personal embarrassment, that I came to recognize the essential folly in RAND-style vulnerability and stability calculations. Some key metrics for Soviet forces were not known, the variable political velocity of motivation was absent, and human elements were off the board. By way of illustration, see the period piece by this author, *The Future of Land-Based Missile Forces*, Adelphi Paper 140 (London: International Institute for Strategic Studies, winter 1977). Notwithstanding my unhappiness with RAND-style numerate defence analysis, I find that some scholars, who are not strategists, have written critiques of the strategic advisory industry on a basis of insufficient empathy for the mission and its difficulties. For examples, see Bruce Kublick, *Blind Oracles: Intellectuals and War from Kennan to Kissinger* (Princeton, NJ: Princeton University Press, 2006), and Alex Abella, *Soldiers of Reason: the RAND Corporation and the Rise of the American Empire* (Orlando, FL: Harcourt, 2008). Writing more than thirty years ago, Bernard Brodie, formerly a star at RAND, aired criticism of his more numerate former colleagues with which I have long associated myself. It is a little ironic that Brodie cited me, critically though justifiably, in the pages of *War and Politics* (453), given that I agree with him today, as really I had always. See his highly personal, powerful Chapter 10. Brodie's charges are broadly compatible with critiques of American strategic analysis delivered a decade apart by an Australian and a British scholar, respectively, Hedley Bull, 'Strategic Studies and Its Critics', *World Politics*, 20 (July 1968), 593–605, and Michael Howard, 'The Forgotten Dimensions of Strategy', *Foreign Affairs*, 57 (summer 1979), 975–86. Contrary to appearances, most probably, I am not at all hostile to numerate defence analysis or generally to the use of mathematics as a tool. My criticism is only of attempts to employ quantitative analysis to derive knowledge that is utterly beyond its domain. Political communities do not go to war because the strategic balance is calculated by the general staff to be 'unstable', or any similar notion. Military calculation, if an input at all, is only ever one contributor to decisions to fight, and typically it is minor relative to broad, and some deeply personal human, reasons of fear, honour, and interest.

16. A 'story arc' is a term-of-art used in the design and production of television series. It refers to a programme that is a part of a series where the narrative plot carries over from one episode to those that follow. This idea fits strategy well, because it emphasizes a holistic approach to what should be regarded as a joined-up project. Strategy's story arc needs to connect engagements as battles, with campaigns, with the war treated in its entirety as both a cumulative and sequential dynamic episode. I am grateful to the entertainment industry for provision of this useful metaphor.

17. Scott Sigmund Gartner, *Strategic Assessment in War* (New Haven, CT: Yale University Press, 1997), 163.

18. See Martin van Creveld, *Command in War* (Cambridge: Cambridge University Press, 1985), and Samuel J. Doss, 'Louis-Alexandre Berthier', in David T. Zabecki, ed., *Chief of Staff: The Principal Officers Behind History's Great Commanders, i: Napoleonic Wars to World War I* (Annapolis, MD: Naval Institute Press, 2008), ch. 1.

19. David G. Chandler, ed., *Napoleon's Marshals* (London: Weidenfeld and Nicolson, 1987), is a fine comprehensive compendium.

20. The literature on this inherently contestably comparative subject is vast and still growing. Given the *embarras de richesse* of scholarship, I shall recommend just four exceptional studies: Gerhard Weinberg, *A World at Arms: A Global History of World War II* (Cambridge: Cambridge University Press, 1994); Richard J. Overy, *Why the Allies Won* (London: Jonathan Cape, 1995); Williamson Murray and Allan R. Millett, *A War to be Won: Fighting the Second World War* (Cambridge, MA: The Belknap Press of Harvard University Press, 2000); and Chris Bellamy, *Absolute War: Soviet Russia in the Second World War* (London: Macmillan, 2007).

21. Clausewitz, 595–7, set the ball rolling among theorists and practitioners. As usual, Michael I. Handel's comparative analysis is useful, *Masters of War: Classical Strategic Thought*, 3rd edn. (London: Frank Cass, 2001), ch. 5. Also see Antulio J. Echevarria II, *Clausewitz and Contemporary War* (Oxford: Oxford University Press, 2007), ch. 8, who characteristically is constructively thought provoking, even if he is apt to muddy waters that some of us, incorrectly apparently, hoped and thought were clear.

22. Jan Willem Honig, 'Clausewitz's *On War*: Problems of Text and Translation', in Hew Strachan and Andreas Herberg-Rothe, eds., *Clausewitz in the Twenty-First Century* (Oxford: Oxford University Press, 2007), ch. 3, is valuable.

23. Victory has an ancient history as a contestable concept in practicable historical application. Contemporary meditations on the theory and practice of victory include Robert Martel, *The Meaning of Military Victory* (Boulder, CO: Lynne Rienner Publishers, 2006); William C. Martel, *Victory in War: Foundations of Modern Military Policy* (Cambridge: Cambridge University Press, 2007); and Colin S. Gray, *National Security Dilemmas: Challenges and Opportunities* (Washington, DC: Potomac Books, 2009), ch. 2.

24. See Edward N. Luttwak, *Strategy: The Logic of War and Peace*, rev. edn. (Cambridge, MA: Harvard University Press, 2009).

25. See Colin S. Gray, *Weapons for Strategic Effect: How Important is Technology?* (Maxwell AFB, AL: Center for Strategy and Technology, Air War College, January 2001).

26. Basil H. Liddell Hart, *Strategy: The Indirect Approach* (1941; London: Faber and Faber, 1967). The concept of the 'indirect approach' is immaculate as a basic idea. Indeed, it can be regarded as an application of Sun Tzu's somewhat overstated maxim, '[w]arfare is the way (Tao) of deception'. *The Art of War*, tr. Ralph D. Sawyer (ca. 490 BCE; Boulder, CO: Westview Press, 1994), 168.

27. Charles E. Callwell, *Small Wars: A Tactical Textbook for Imperial Soldiers* (1906; London, Greenhill Books, 1990).

28. Stephen Biddle and Jeffrey A. Friedman, *The 2006 Lebanon Campaign and the Future of Warfare: Implications for Army and Defense Policy* (Carlisle, PA: Strategic Studies Institute, US Army War College, September 2008), draws out clearly the complex character of a contemporary campaign, while Frank G. Hoffman explains the most relevant concept admirably in 'Hybrid Warfare and Challenges', *Joint Force Quarterly*, 52 (1st qtr. 2009), 34–9.

29. The high aspirations of those who drove for Effects-Based Operations (EBO), are well explained in David A. Deptula, *Effects-Based Operations: Change in the Nature of Warfare* (Arlington, VA: Aerospace Education Foundation, 2001), and US Joint Forces Command (JFC), Joint Warfighting Center, *Commander's Handbook for an Effects-Based Approach to Joint Operations* (Norfolk, VA: US Joint Forces Command, 24 February 2006). Ironically, two and a half years later a new commander at JFC, Lt. General James N. Mattis, USMC, explicitly condemned and rejected EBO and most of its analytical trappings in language that greatly upset some of the residents in EBO's Air Force homeland. For this blunt repudiation, see James N. Mattis, 'USJFCOM Commander's Guidance for Effects-based Operations', *Joint Force Quarterly*, 51 (4th qtr. 2008), 105–8. Not merely did Mattis subject EBO to an intellectual firing squad, he dispatched the unfavoured victim concept and methodology personally with maximum analytical violence. In the general's uncompromising words: '*Effective immediately, USJFCOM will no longer use, sponsor, or export the terms and concepts related to EBO, ONA* [Operational Net Assessment], *and SOS* [System of Systems Analysis] *development, and support of JPME*', 108 (emphasis in the original). This was a declaration of interservice war upon those air power analysts who believe in victory through precision strike from the sky. The US Air Force's Chief of Doctrine was obliged to publish a semi-official reply, as follows: Tomislav Z. Ruby, 'Effects-based Operations: More Important than Ever', *Parameters*, 38 (autumn 2008), 26–35. The sharpness of the EBO controversy of the 2000s, true to the American tradition of few-holds-barred interservice rivalry, may be gauged from the content and tone of these collector's items: Milan N. Vego, 'Effects-Based Operations: A Critique', *Joint Force Quarterly*, 41 (2nd qtr. 2006), 51–7; P. Mason Carpenter and William F. Andrews, 'Effects-based Operations: Combat Proven', *Joint Forces Quarterly*, 52 (1st qtr. 2009), 78–81; and Paul K. Van Riper, 'EBO: There Was No Baby in the Bathwater', *Joint Force Quarterly*, 52 (1st qtr. 2009), 82–5. The scholar observing such debate is struck both by the healthiness of an American defence community that allows such vigorous disagreements. But, also, one is impressed, less favourably, by the near theological intensity with which apparently reasonable and equally well-informed professionals hold their beliefs. When those beliefs conform closely to the tenets of geographically distinctive service cultures, notwithstanding the formal commitment to 'jointness', one is inclined to interrogate an idea not only for its merit, but in addition for its institutional provenance. This is not to deny that some very sound notions cannot help but privilege especially the capabilities and military culture of one service over another. To shift focus for some useful overseas perspective on the American EBO dispute, as well as for a helpful example of theory turned into doctrine for the instruction and guidance of practice, see (UK) Assistant Chief of the Defence Staff, 'Development, Concepts and Doctrine', *Campaign Planning*, Joint Doctrine Publication 5-00, 2nd edn. (Shrivenham: Development, Concepts and Doctrine Centre, Ministry of Defence, December 2008).

30. Giulio Douhet, *The Command of the Air* (1921; New York, Arno Press, 1972), is the most classic of the air power classics. For fairly recent theory on air power as war-winner, see John A. Warden III, *The Air Campaign: Planning for Combat* (Washington, DC: Pergamon-Brassey's, 1989). Empathetic, but not uncritical, assessment of Warden's ideas and career is presented in the superb intellectual biography, John Andreas Olsen, *John Warden and the Renaissance of American Air Power* (Washington, DC: Potomac Books, 2007). Two excellent overviews of air power ideas and practice are presented in Phillip S. Meilinger, ed., *The Paths of Heaven: The Evolution of Airpower Theory* (Maxwell AFB, AL: Air University Press, 1997), and John Andreas Olsen, ed., *A History of Air Warfare* (Washington, DC: Potomac Books, 2009).

31. See Benjamin S. Lambeth, *The Transformation of American Air Power* (Ithaca, NY: Cornell University Press, 2000), and Richard B. Andres, 'Deep attack against Iraq', in Thomas G. Mahnken and Thomas A. Kearney, eds., *War in Iraq: Planning and Execution* (Abingdon: Routledge, 2007), 69–96.

32. See Michael Russell Rip and James M. Hasik, *The Precision Revolution: GPS and the Future of Aerial Warfare* (Annapolis, MD: Naval Institute Press, 2002). The US armed forces have been less than swift in recognizing the military value of GPS, while today they are equally reluctant to take precautionary measures to hedge against the deeply unpleasant possibilities that lurk rather obviously in their newly created pervasive dependence on the system.

33. Giulio Douhet made the point that 'the selection of objectives, the grouping of zones, and determining the order in which they are to be destroyed is the most difficult and delicate task in aerial warfare, constituting what may be defined as aerial strategy'. *Command of the Air*, 50. Frederick W. Kagan, *Finding the Target: The Transformation of American Military Policy* (New York: Encounter Books, 2006), is useful for providing historical context to narrowly military controversies.

34. Carpenter and Andrews, 'Effects-based Operations', 79. This is reasonable, indeed it is close to compelling as well joined up strategic thinking.

35. No matter what the leading theorists of China's People's Liberation Army may claim at length and with asserted, including ideological, authority. See Peng Guangqian and Yao Youzhi, eds., *The Science of Military Strategy* (Beijing: Military Science Publishing House, 2005). Science requires certain knowledge and, as a logical consequence, thoroughly reliable predictability. Because military strategy in most of its aspects is a thoroughly human project, pervaded by uncertainty, it must follow that it cannot usefully be approached as a science. (Clausewitz, with his 'wondrous trinity', which includes chance, is crystal clear on this point, at least).

36. Gartner, *Strategic Assessment in War*, offers interesting case studies of the use made by organizations of analytically derived information in wartime.

37. Clausewitz, 177.

38. Judy Pearsall and Bill Trumble, eds, *The Oxford English Reference Dictionary*, 2nd edn. (Oxford: Oxford University Press, 1996), 1297. The concept of science in modern usage carries a dominant meaning, considerable authority, and much baggage that are likely to raise false expectations among those who are insufficiently aware of just how undemanding of certainty are some no less valid among our contemporary definitions.

39. Clausewitz, 104.

40. Pearsall and Trumble eds., *The Oxford English Reference Dictionary*, 1297.

41. For a monumental lack of realism it would be difficult to top the calculated beliefs of America's air war planners in 1941. 'So extensive and detailed was the Americans'

target information that the War Plans Division [of the U. S. Army Air Forces, USAAF: CSG] planned the precise basis of 66,045 sorties [a sortie is single mission by a single aircraft: CSG] needed to destroy the nine major German target systems, and 51,480 sorties for the selected Japanese targets.' R. J. Overy, *The Air War, 1939–1945* (New York: Stein and Day, 1985), 310. The frenetic activity and products of the Air War Plans Division, especially with respect to the creation and fate of AWP-I, are well described in Haywood Hansell, Jr., *The Air Plan That Defeated Hitler* (New York: Arno Press, 1980), and James C. Gaston, *Planning the American Air War: Four Men and Nine Days in 1941, An Inside Narrative* (Washington, DC: National Defense University Press, 1982). The historical record of strategic bombing, with particular reference to the American performance in the Second World War, is reviewed critically, though carefully, in Gian P. Gentile, *How Effective Is Strategic Bombing? Lessons Learned from World War II to Kosovo* (New York: New York University Press, 2001). In the 1980s and 1990s, John Warden developed his 'five rings' theory of victory through air power. He conceived of an enemy polity as a single complex target system with centres of gravity that 'can be laid out in the form of five concentric circles. The most important element—the enemy command—is in the centre circle; essential production is second; the transportation network is third; the population is fourth; and the fielded military forces—the shield and spear—are fifth. The most critical ring is the enemy command structure, because it is the only element of the enemy—whether a civilian at the seat of government or a general directing a fleet—that can make concessions.' Warden, 'Employing Air Power in the Twenty-first Century', in Richard H. Shultz, Jr. and Robert L. Pfaltzgraff, Jr., eds., *The Future of Air Power in the Aftermath of the Gulf War* (Maxwell AFB, AL: Air University Press, July 1992), 57. Thus the enemy is perceived as a dartboard. Writing in the immediate wake of air power's triumph in the first Gulf War of 1991, Warden felt no need to be modest about his instrument's leading role in the future. 'This victory provides the strategic model for American operations well into the twenty-first century', 57. For good and for ill, Warden was somewhat correct in that claim. See Olsen, *John Warden and the Renaissance of American Air Power.*

42. On the history of strategic bombing, see R. Cargill Hall, ed., *Studies in Strategic Bombardment* (Washington, DC: U.S. Government Printing Office, 1998); and Gentile, *How Effective is Strategic Bombing?* For a study of air power in the Second World War that is unusually wide while remaining tolerably deep, see Horst Boog, ed., *The Conduct of the Air War in the Second World War: An International Comparison* (New York: Berg, 1992).

43. Clausewitz, 100–12. Also see Echevarria, *Clausewitz and Contemporary War*, ch. 5.

44. Andrew Roberts, *Masters and Commanders: How Roosevelt, Churchill, Marshall and Alanbrooke Won the War in the West* (London: Allen Lane, 2008), ch. 18, is very much to the point.

45. Clausewitz, esp. 86. 'The art of war deals with living and with moral forces. Consequently, it cannot attain the absolute, or certainty; it must always leave a margin for uncertainty, in the greatest things as much as in the smallest.'

46. See Alan Beyerchen, 'Clausewitz, Nonlinearity, and the Unpredictability of War', *International Security*, 17 (winter 1992/3), 59–90; id., 'Clausewitz and the Non-Linear Nature of Warfare: Systems of Organized Complexity', in Hew Strachan and Herberg-Rothe, eds., *Clausewitz in the Twenty-First Century* (Oxford: Oxford University Press, 2007), 45–56. But, note well Betts, 'Is Strategy an Illusion?'

47. David Jordan et al., eds., *Understanding Modern Warfare* (Cambridge: Cambridge University Press, 2008), 344.

48. See Benjamin S. Lambeth, *NATO's Air War for Kosovo: A Strategic and Operational Assessment* (Santa Monica, CA: RAND, 200).

49. For a first-rate analysis of *Geopolitik*, see Holger H. Herwig, '*Geopolitik*: Haushofer, Hitler and Lebensraum', in Colin S. Gray and Geoffrey Sloan, eds., *Geopolitics, Geography and Strategy* (London: Frank Cass, 1999), 218–41.

6

Strategy, Strategists, and Command Performance: Joining Up the Dots

THE HUMAN FACE OF STRATEGY

Strategy as theory and even as plans has no inherent value. Theory and practice need to be approached as a whole. Books of, let alone about, strategic ideas necessarily run the risk of appearing to undervalue the significance of action. The cerebral and the physical are likely to be disconnected, as if each zone of concern might lend itself to distinctive analysis. Whatever may be possible in other fields, it is surely incontestable that in the strategic realm thought and behaviour must be treated as a unity. In the world of strategic concerns thought disconnected from behaviour must be without intelligent purpose, as also must be strategic behaviour apparently bereft of thought. The purpose of this chapter, metaphorically expressed, is to join up the dots; to ensure that the text of this strategic exposition succeeds in reaching the battlespace, and that the battlespace is tautly connected to its strategic and political consequences, inter alia. As the greatest strategic theorist of them all expressed the matter:

> But in war more than in any other subject we must begin by looking at the nature of the whole; for here more than elsewhere the part and the whole must always be thought of together.[1]

Strategic behaviour is command performance writ large. Previous chapters have presented the general theory of strategy; explored the relations among politics, war, and strategy; considered the awesome problems that make strategy so difficult to do well enough; and have sought to explain strategy's output, strategic effect. What has not been pursued in any depth thus far is the human agent of strategy, the strategist, and how he or she 'gets it done', or fails so to do. Although strictly distinctive from the theory of strategy, that theory cannot be understood, let alone used constructively, in the absence of some grasp of the subject of this chapter. The 'dots' must be connected among strategic ideas, strategists in their several roles, and the enablers of strategic performance via command and its associated functions and duties.

Because primarily this is a work of theory, and because this author is a civilian academic, again primarily, it is essential that damaging skill and purpose biases on my part should not be permitted to mislead. To this end let me emphasize the point that strategic theory has but one purpose, to help educate the practicing strategist. For contemporary timbre, we can raid the arsenal of jargon and buzz-words and add the aspiration to help educate stakeholder communities.

So, this book ultimately has to be all about the practice of strategy. But who practices strategy? Exactly who holds the strategy bridge?—and how do they hold it? It may assist understanding of the purpose and ethos of this discussion if I state my dislike of a common dictum. Specifically, frequently it is asserted that 'one has a strategy, but one does tactics'. The dictum is not entirely wrong, but its uncritical deployment runs a serious risk of misleading the unwary. History and commonsense, for once in accord, suggest strongly that the admittedly vital conceptual distinction between strategy and tactics threatens to conceal the intimate interdependence of the two. Probably we should not go as far as did T. E. Lawrence in his assertion that strategy and tactics 'seemed only points of view from which to ponder the elements of war....'.[2] Lawrence risks losing appreciation of the key difference between behaviour (tactics) and its purpose and consequences (strategy). However, it is necessary for strategic educators to recognize that the actual doing of strategy is not a function that can just be assumed to be performed somehow, by somebody. As a matter of good practice, there should be umbilical links between the individual soldier and the grand strategist, as well as between the grand strategist and the politician as policy-maker.

The essential unity of strategy and tactics is illustrated helpfully by what is known as the tactical paradox, though more accurately it might be called the strategy–tactics paradox. There is no doubt that strategy is both more important to conduct well than are tactics, if only because the latter has to derive its meaning and purpose from the former. Also, as Chapter 4 elucidates, the strategic function inherently is more difficult to perform competently than is the political or the tactical. However, for the paradox, while strategy can be corrected in a matter of hours or days, tactical performance typically takes months, if not years, to improve markedly—should the enemy be so obliging or to allow the time. And, need one add, if indeed tactics must take time to correct—an army may have to be retrained—the strategic function as command performance must be greatly impaired.

The theory of strategy is, and can only be, about the doing of strategy. The many dicta of the general theory are not self-referential, accountable only to some abstract array of ideational merit in a great audit for objective truth. At this late juncture in the narrative, arguably belatedly, it is necessary to reinforce recognition that the strategy bridge needs to be held by people who have to ensure that strategy is done by way of implementing behaviour. As general theory, the doing of strategy has to be explained with reference to roles, functions, missions, tasks, organizations, and processes. But the historical doing of actual strategies must be performed by particular people functioning both as individuals and in groups. Civilians are apt to forget, if they ever knew, that it can never suffice simply to have a strategy. Strategy must be performed, hence the title of this chapter. Civilian scholars of strategy usually inhabit an academic world wherein ideas both reign and rule. It follows that they are vulnerable to the fallacy that ideas rule the world of strategic practice. More properly appreciated, strategic ideas are vitally important, but they have meaning only for strategic practice. If scholars are vulnerable to being overimpressed by the apparent authority of ideas, of theory, they are joined in the phalanx of the credulous by those many commentators, as well as scholars, who confuse military doctrine with actual military behaviour in the field. Sensibly understood, theory and practice, ideas and behaviour, truly are a unity. No matter how pragmatic a general may believe himself to be, he cannot help but act upon some theory, singular or plural, of strategy. His practical behaviour must express convictions and hopes that purposefully connect actions with intended consequences. Every pragmatic general is a theorist, but that is another matter. Nature, education, experience, and circumstances, including quantity and luck (e.g. the size and quality of his enemy), will determine how well he performs. To risk a distinctly contestable proposition, the quantity of a general's human and material assets relative to those of the enemy can help greatly to decide how well he needs to perform.

Among the classic authors of strategic theory identified in the Introduction, three were devoid of substantial personal military experience: Machiavelli and the contemporary theorists, Thomas C. Schelling and Edward N. Luttwak;[3] the other seven—Sun Tzu, Thucydides, Carl von Clausewitz, Jomini, Basil Liddell Hart, J. C. Wylie, and Bernard Brodie—except Brodie, were military persons in some sense, but even he had served in the US Navy in the Second World War, albeit briefly (1943–5).[4] Military professionals and civilians, with intense first-hand military exposure (e.g. Thucydides, Liddell Hart),[5] know that strategy is about command performance. Also they know that people matter more than does materiel and that strategy as, and in, command, can succeed or fail depending upon the personal qualities of individual strategists. It is true that the classical canon of strategic theory treats command and leadership more than adequately, but it is also true to claim that many of our modern strategists do not read those classics in ways that highlight the relative importance of people.

Because this book is intended as a work of strategic theory, rather than a work about strategic theory or strategic theorists; I have not and will not devote space and risk diverting attention to people and ideas that are merely interesting, but are not central to the plot. Nonetheless, this theorist does feel some regret over a few of his omissions from the honour roll. For the leading example, it has been hard to decide to admit Liddell Hart to the hall of strategic theoretical glory, yet to omit his unquestionably brilliant contemporary, also British military theorist and historian, Major General J. F. C. Fuller (1878–1964). I have no serious doubts about the wisdom of excluding Fuller from my shortlist of all-time contributors to the general canon of strategic theory, but I admit that my judgement is not beyond plausible challenge.[6] Most other challengers for inclusion in the front rank of paladins of strategic theory either did not write with sufficient wisdom in the opinion of this author, or were unduly focused upon a single geographical environment—one thinks of Giulio Douhet (1869–1930), Julian S. Corbett (1854–1922), and Alfred T. Mahan (1840–1914)[7]—or were unduly dated historically by time, place, and culture. I admit to the suspicion that many years from now the controversial contemporary Israeli military historian, Martin van Creveld, may well be deemed widely to merit elevation to the status of classic theorist, to cite but one case.[8] One definition of a classic book that this theorist finds attractive holds that '[a] classic is a book (hence a race, building, human activity) about whose value it is assumed that there can be no argument'.[9]

Modern strategic studies were founded for the pre-eminent purpose of making sense of atomic, then thermonuclear, weapons.[10] The intellectual leaders of what became, in effect, a new profession by and large were profoundly civilian scholars.[11] Although some had had a brief military career during the Second World War, their commitment to the study of strategic matters was not an inevitable consequence of the growing responsibilities attendant upon military career progression, given that they had been in uniform only briefly in wartime. The inevitable result of a Western defence community drawing intellectually most heavily upon civilian scholars, was a literature, including a new canon of would-be authoritative ideas and theories, that reflected the comparative advantage, and disadvantage, of non-military experts upon strategy.[12] Hence, 'modern strategy' after 1945 had as its centrepiece the trinity of theories purporting to explain the mysteries of (largely nuclear) deterrence, limited war in the shadow of nuclear menace, and arms control. Beyond this trinity, civilian theorists professed theories of crisis management, escalation (control) and coercion, and arms race dynamics, inter alia. None of these topics, at least as they were defined and treated by American officials in the 1950s and 1960s, depended upon much, if any, professional military understanding of warfare, and neither did they hold high attraction to soldier-scholars. It is important to appreciate that the founding fathers—sightings of female strategic theorists have been rare, though not quite unknown—of modern strategy, meaning modern strategic theory, most typically were scientists of one persuasion or another, which is to say truly theoretical, physical—experimental, or social. Historians, for example, as well as cultural anthropologists, were not thick on the professional ground. The professional enculturation of a fairly distinctive cohort of theorists with their distinctive skill biases bequeathed us the intellectual core of modern strategy. Almost as much to the point, the classics of general strategic theory necessarily were written by particularly encultured and skill-biased authors. And it is no less the case that these great books have been read and interpreted, again necessarily, by modern theorists and analysts who tend to find in them both what they are looking for and what cultures and personalities enable, perhaps allow, them to find. The corpus of nuclear-age(s) scholarship, (excluding Wylie, Luttwak, and some of Brodie's and Schelling's writings), genuinely much of the best and the brightest Western strategic intellectual responses to the challenges of the nuclear age, now appear, to this rather late nuclear-age theorist at least, to suffer from notable deficiencies.

What are among the more prominent weaknesses in modern Western strategic theory and analysis? One looks almost in vain for careful and deep studies of the roles of the commander, with particular attention to the human dimension right down, or up, to the level of the individual. Similarly, modern strategic theory has said little, to be polite, about the nature and many functions of military doctrine, or about that most vital of enabling agents, logistics (supply and movement). Also, strategy itself, its nature, adaptable character as historical strategies in plans and other schemes, has not exactly been the subject of a brilliant modern literature. Much of the substance of this critique was offered by Bernard Brodie towards the end of his life. Indeed, his final book contains passages, especially some potent, almost toxic, footnotes, that are exceptional in the forthrightness of their condemnation of his peers.[13] The purpose in venturing briefly into the history of the modern profession of strategic studies is not to refight old battles, settle old scores, or any other such pettiness. Rather is the intention to explain that for systemic reason of professional skill bias, strategic studies applied to defence issues that had a massively technological dimension, conducted pre-eminently in an American cultural milieu—the nuclear age, Cold War and beyond—has been notably light in recognizing the human face of strategy.[14] Had the profession been dominated by military historians, civilian or military, it is near certain that this human deficit would not have occurred. Good military historians know that people, even individuals, make history happen the way that it does. Physical and social scientists can be short on understanding of this reality. Here we will endeavour to help correct what this theorist perceives as an imbalance in the modern strategic literature, one which privileges purported rational choices by universal strategic persons or systems or political entities such as 'France' or 'The United States'. John Keegan warns that strategic theorists have neglected both the individual and his context: 'Rarely is either [Marx or Clausewitz: CSG] subject to the rigour of contextualization. Yet context, when theories as powerful as theirs are at stake, is all.'[15] A little earlier he eviscerated depersonalized theorizing in the following matter:

> In ignoring the particularity of leadership, social scientists have been encouraged by unlikely allies, the strategic theorists. Social science conceives itself as a benign discipline, one of whose purposes is to rob strategy of point by reasoning the causes of struggle away. But strategic theorists are, in their way, social scientists also. For their aim—and the aim is a recent one, since strategic theory in its pure form was unknown before the eighteenth century—is to reduce the chaotic phenomena of warfare to a system of essentials sufficiently few for an ordered mind to tend to its purpose.[16]

Unfortunately, Keegan's keen and important appreciation of the neglect of the human dimension in modern strategic studies, and in strategic theorizing in particular, leads him into the grievous error of devaluing strategy per se. If, as I insist, strategy applied as strategies is both highly desirable and feasible, it has to follow that general strategic theory also must be regarded positively. Keegan performed a useful role as a critic of undue abstraction, and indeed as a sceptic of the Clausewitzian paradigm—in company with Martin van Creveld—but his value is limited by the overwhelming strength of the argument which finds him in error.[17] In very short, strategic theory is important, and Clausewitz is worthy of the esteem in which we theorists hold him.

Because strategy is a practical endeavour, works of strategic theory, especially works of theory keyed to derivative theories-as-advice, which neglect the human element in all its variety, are potentially dangerous to our security. It is a challenge to the theorist of strategy to strike the right balance in explanation between emphasizing mighty, if somewhat abstract, factors which provide the context for human effort, and the significance of what particular groups and individuals bring to that context. For a classic historical example of this problem in explanation, a recent biography of Field Marshal Sir Douglas Haig has this to say about his contribution to victory in 1918:

> In recent years, many historians of the War have tried to shift the focus of attention away from personalities to technology, social forces, or the respective underlying economic strength of the powers involved, all of which are relevant but, ultimately, are controlled by human hands and guided by human minds; personality inevitably reasserts itself, despite the understandable desire to focus on matters open to more rational examination. Those who take against Haig have done everything to destroy his reputation, while his uncritical admirers, whose ranks have inevitably been thinned by the passage of time, have lost no opportunity to assert his unique, personal contribution to winning that appalling war. The truth is that Field Marshal Haig, or someone equally resolute, was necessary. The British and French Allies, together with their American associates, did not purposefully march to victory in the final one hundred days of war with a clearly elaborated or carefully constructed plan: they stumbled along in their advance, sometimes blindly, sometimes mistakenly, occasionally cleverly and always courageously, often surprised to find that first pockets, then whole swathes of the German army crumbled, burdened as they were by a growing sense that all was utterly lost. It was in a very real sense a victory; but one that took everyone, including Haig, by surprise. Haig's greatest contribution in mid-1918 was, finally, to delegate, and let others get on with their specific tasks. His contribution prior to that had been his own unflappable character—leadership, of a sort.[18]

A little earlier the author of these quoted words, journalist-turned-historian Gary Mead, hazarded the judgement that in the hundred days' campaign of July–November 1918, 'Haig's role was largely that of a figurehead'.[19] Quite evidently, Mead does not write this in order to demean Haig. He explains that 'he now had little choice but to watch as his branch managers [army and corps commanders] pushed ahead on their own momentum'.[20] Haig's command style from his chateau in 1918 was about as far removed from the heroic as one can imagine.[21] Nonetheless, obviously it sufficed and, one can argue persuasively, it was thoroughly appropriate. The fact that Haig was obliged to command in the only way that his personality permitted is true, but beside the strategic point. A commander only has to do, perhaps to be, enough, he need not score high on all possible counts of excellence. Furthermore, it is difficult to find in the literature adequate treatment of the several roles of the commander, or indeed of the relations between strategist and commander. It is to these topics that we turn now.

Strategists

The Introduction to this book presented and defended the bridge metaphor as the most appropriate statement of the function of strategy. However, it also offered the vital caveat that whereas a material bridge is a passive structure, albeit one needing to be flexible so as to withstand high wind velocity and other hazards, the strategy bridge should be anything but passive. The keepers of the strategy bridge are not merely clerks running a two-way postal service, at least they ought not to be so limited in their role. A bridge is a bridge is a bridge, but in historical reality the strategy bridge can perform its function in a wide variety of ways. Here, as throughout this text, our subject must be approached with respect to the elemental contrast between strategy in general and specific historical plans and strategies. It may be necessary to add the explanation that although all strategies are plans, no matter the form in which they appear, not all plans warrant title as strategies. At the least, a strategy must strive to connect means purposefully with ends, whereas a plan may fail this basic test.[22] A plan that is short of clear—not necessarily precise, let alone detailed—purpose does not deserve to be considered a strategy. We can and do explain the function of the strategist with a view to enriching general theory. The purpose of this exercise is to provide a framework that can accommodate all historical examples of the behaviour of strategists. However, while we weave our general theory we are ever mindful of the contextual and human particularities of each historical case. To understand, what the strategist must and might need to do as a general matter, most emphatically is not to understand what any particular strategist actually does or how he does it. General theory can only educate. It should help equip us to comprehend; it cannot yield solutions to specific questions that it is unqualified to answer.

In order to avoid needless confusion, it is useful, actually it is probably essential, to make three sets of binary distinctions when we endeavour to sort categories of strategists. First, it is necessary to distinguish between the strategist as conceptualizer-executive and the strategist as intellectual. This theorist's Anglo-American culture is not entirely comfortable with the intellectual tag, but it is difficult to locate a superior alternative. This binary sorts the makers and doers of strategies, actually of real historical strategies, from those who think about, analyze, and comment upon strategy and strategies. Conceptualizer-executive lacks linguistic elegance, but it has the overriding virtue of accuracy. The official military strategist, almost always a soldier, must both make strategy in the sense of conceptual invention, and also do strategy as a managing executive. Hence the admittedly somewhat clunky descriptor, conceptualizer-executive. It is necessary to recognize both of the roles most essential to performance of the strategic function.

For our second distinction, it is necessary to recognize that conceptualizer-executive strategists for military strategy are almost entirely military professionals, while strategy intellectuals these days, indeed since 1945, most often are civilians, at least they are civilians in the societies with which this theorist is most familiar (i.e. American, British, and Canadian). The civilianization of strategic thought and commentary has been an unmistakeable characteristic of the nuclear age. As one would expect, the closer the subject under investigation is to live military experience, the heavier the intellectual contribution by serving or retired soldiers. For example, whereas the theory of nuclear strategy, especially the theory and doctrine of stable nuclear deterrence, was dominated intellectually by civilians, the theory of counter-insurgency has always been authored primarily by military professionals, typically with field experience.[23] Such experience mercifully has been absent from the nuclear zone of strategic theory, hence the absence of a comparative advantage for the soldier over the civilian. It is convenient to refer simply to strategists, but the distinction between the strategic executive and the strategic intellectual is both real and important. When the latter strives to educate, let alone advise or instruct the former, cultural differences and contrasting personality profiles can impede communication.[24]

The third distinction—in addition to those between the strategist as executive and the strategist as intellectual, and between civilian and soldier strategists—is between what this theorist elects to identify as the executive strategist's primary and secondary functions. In the primary category, the executive strategist must be a theorist-planner and a commander. In his role as commander, the strategist should be both a manager-bureaucrat and a leader. The secondary function of the executive strategist obliges him to be able to play the roles of politician-diplomat and educator-persuader. These secondary roles can be of the utmost importance, to risk an only apparent oxymoron. A soldier strategist certainly needs to explain military realities, broad as well as narrowly specific, to a political leader who these days is unlikely to bring much prior military understanding to what should be a dialogue. In addition, the strategist as expert military adviser typically requires some comprehension of, possibly even empathy with, the political values and concerns of civilian policymakers. Although it is essential that policy and strategy should not be confused, it cannot be denied that the strategist is obliged to be able to function politically and diplomatically if he is to do his job. Clausewitz is correct when he advises that 'at the highest level the art of war turns into policy—but a policy conducted by fighting battles rather than by sending diplomatic notes'.[25] This advice he repeats as the dictum, 'the conduct of war, in its great outlines, is therefore policy itself, which takes up the sword in place of the pen, but does not on that account cease to think according to its own laws'.[26] However, the great Prussian theorist oversimplifies perilously with those thoughts.

Carefully read, Clausewitz as quoted is accurate and brilliantly succinct. But, in careless, ignorant, or malevolent hands, his apparent fusion of policy for war with war itself, though admittedly only its higher conduct, is extremely dangerous. It may be likened to equipping soldiers in the field who have a reading age of fourteen with weapons that require exquisitely careful handling and maintenance. Strategists as planners and commanders must be able to communicate a sufficient understanding of strategic matters for civilian policymakers to perform their functions on the basis of adequate knowledge.

If war is not to serve itself, with policy as its servant, there can be no argument over the primacy of the political over the military. Nonetheless, so close should be the dialogue between policy and its military agent that the strategist can hardly help but function to some variable degree both in a political or diplomatic role and to political effect. Similarly, the politician-policymaker, canonically a civilian, certainly the authoritative representative of the civil power, cannot help but play as military strategist in his or her conduct of the 'unequal dialogue'. As Eliot A. Cohen is quoted as arguing unanswerably at a meeting in the White House on 11 December 2006: 'Generals disagree, sometime profoundly. Civilian leaders need to discover these disagreements, force them to the surface and probe them. This is what Lincoln and Roosevelt did. LBJ's failure in Vietnam was not micro-management, but failure to force serious strategic debate.'[27]

For a clear contemporary illustration of the phenomenon of the strategist theorist and commander functioning also as politician, consider the bureaucrati-cally subversive behaviour of Lt. General Raymond Odierno (US Army) in late 2006. Odierno was appointed as deputy commander in Iraq on 20 November 2006. He discovered a thoroughly astrategic, really dysfunctional, command structure in place. In the words of a careful and detailed study of his situation and solution:

> Ironically, it was only after Odierno stepped outside that [military command: CSG] structure, rejecting the views of his superiors [including the Chairman of the Joint Chiefs of Staff, General Peter Pace: CSG] and lobbying the White House on his own, that policy formulation began to work effectively, produc-ing a workable strategy. Arguably, his actions amounted to insubordination.[28]

Not only did Odierno tackle the politics of the war in Iraq with policymakers in Washington, in addition he did so behind the back of his military chain of command. Thomas Ricks, the author of the words just quoted, is unduly coy when he adds 'arguably' to the issue of the general's insubordination. The truth of the matter is that in most countries and other security communities, not exclud-ing the United States, it is not at all unusual for soldier strategists to function in a political role. Of course, one can try to insist that it is one thing for a general to treat with politicians and civilian officials over the strategy judged best suited to deliver success; it is quite another for that general to debate strategy with those policymakers in such a way that, in effect, he is trying to reshape policy goals.

There should be no escaping the fact that if a strategist is convinced that the extant strategy is failing, or missing from action, his message to his political masters has to be that their policy must alter. In other words, it is not possible for a responsible military strategist to confine his judgement strictly to the military sphere. If that sphere is unduly discordant with the political demands that equate to policy, then either the military or the policy plot must be changed if success is to be achieved. All of the greater commanders, at all times and places, not excluding the contemporary United States, have been obliged to function across the line of civil–military relations as politicians and policymakers, as well as generals. It is in the very nature of war and strategy that this should be so; it is not a case of systemic malfunction when it occurs. Indeed, in most of the world's lengthy record of strategic history, it has been quite routine for politics, policy, and the conduct of strategic duties, to be substantially indistinguishable. At the least, even when societies have maintained some structure of distinctive civil and (subordinate) military command, each party has been expected to penetrate the other with demands and influence. And this is the way that strategic history should proceed. The conduct of statecraft, including its strategic dimension, needs to be a fully 'joined up' project in the interests of a tolerable civil–military harmony of endeavour, or only a tolerable level of disharmony. The single illustration provided here of a senior general stepping off the strategy bridge onto the political bank is simply one recent example amidst an historical forest of cases. Referring to one of the finest operational artists and battlefield generals of all time, Julius Caesar, a scholar has observed that 'Caesar was a politician with the brain of a strategist'.[29]

Before discussing the roles of the strategist in some detail, it is necessary for the human and functional domain of this discussion to be specified with as close to crystal clarity as may be achieved. The basic questions are 'who is the strategist' and 'what does he do?'. For the purposes of this exercise in theory for practice, we must insist that the executive military strategist is a person with responsibility for making, or for conducting, military strategy or strategies designed to shape the course and outcome of an entire conflict. Loose linguistic usage refers to theatre strategy, while the literature, and common parlance, frequently refers to strategy and strategies with respect to plans at the tactical and operational levels.[30] For this discussion, we must deny the validity of such employment. Tactics are performed by tacticians, while operations are conducted by operational artists, as standard terminology will have it. The strategist, in sharp distinction, 'does', or conducts, the strategy that he makes and adapts through the tactical and operational performances of his enabling agents. There is an obvious, if somewhat mislead-ing, sense in which all actual military behaviour, tactical performance, is strategy in action. Certainly, all tactical and operational behaviour must have the potential to register ultimately as strategic effect. That granted, strategy and tactics, to keep matters truly simple, are qualitatively different. One cannot deny that it makes some sense to argue that the strategic function is, or should be, active at every level of conflict. Such a plausible view finds potent support in Edward N. Luttwak's marvellous study of strategy. It is true to argue that the strategic function that connects purpose with outcome via tailored behaviour is all too relevant at every level of military effort. Nonetheless, this logic, though unde-niably sound, needs to be disciplined lest the more important plot line is mislaid. The plot in question is the making and execution of highly purpose-specific plans for the conduct of a whole conflict. To claim, correctly in several senses, in effect that 'everyone does strategy', risks sacrificing a monstrously important truth for an understanding of lesser significance.

Of recent years, it has been fashionable in some Western defence communities to recognize the high significance of some very small unit military behaviour in irregular warfare by referring to 'the strategic corporal'.[31] Such a label is correct in

Table 6.1 (Military) Strategists' Roles

A	*Binary distinctions*	
	Conceptualizer-executive	Intellectual
	Soldier	Civilian
B	*Roles of soldier-conceptualizer-executive*	
	Primary	*Secondary*
	Theorist-planner	Politician-diplomat
	Commander manager-bureaucrat trainer leader	Educator-persuader

Notes: These shortlistings cover only the people who, as designated strategists, must hold the strategy bridge. Politician-policymakers and operational-level commanders and soldiers of all kinds who do tactics are excluded.

its implicit claim that mere handfuls of soldiers can behave in ways of high importance, especially in warfare conducted against insurgents and terrorists. The term is unfortunate, though, in that inadvertently it hides the facts that corporals have always been of strategic significance, because all tactical military behaviour has strategic meaning, be it ever so slight and be it net positive or negative. Unhappily, if one refers to 'strategic corporals', one is likely to encourage that confusion of action with consequence that so harasses and impedes strategic understanding. To be absolutely clear, as politicians are fond of saying, though admittedly ironically in their case, the corporal, no matter what he does, can only be an instrument of strategy, he is not strategy itself.

The argument developed thus far is presented summarily in Table 6.1.

An all too rich historical mixture of broad context, contingency, and circumstance explains who play the roles of strategist as theorist-planner and as commander. There is no universal and eternal template that can educate far beyond the austere outline in Table 6.1. The value in approaching the awesome variety of historical experience as general theory is to ensure that the structure of the subject of strategy and the strategic function is appreciated as fully as can be useful. Table 6.1 seeks to cover all examples of strategy and strategist in all periods at all times. In the wider contexts of politician-policymakers on one bank, and soldiers on the other, strategists on the strategy bridge must play the roles here specified. These roles are functionally discrete, though more than a little mutually dependent, and they can be performed more or less collectively or by a single person. Precisely who does what, and how he does it, must vary hugely from situation to situation. The situations, or contexts, of relevance include pre-eminently the details of political system (including organization of government) and culture, the flow of events, and the accidents and lottery that gift individuals to particular moments in history. The point is that every role identified here always needs to be performed by someone, more or less explicitly and purposefully, either on the strategy bridge by a person or person designated as strategist(s), or by people and organizations on the political or military agency banks.

The general theory of strategy identifies what needs to be done if strategy is to be performed. There has to be a master strategic concept, grand or otherwise, to inform the drafting of strategy(ies) as plans which, in their logical turn, guide the behaviour of soldiers who have to be commanded in action. For these soldiers and their units to be fit for the strategist's purpose, he must ensure that they are trained to fight effectively. Different commanders, though facing command constraints, often will disagree on the tactical doctrine which they will strive to instil. Also they may well differ in their understanding of current best operational practice. The strategist, with his function strictly understood, performs as such when he locates the North Star for the guidance of operational plans, and in a more, or less, personal sense commands all that follows from master plan through to the last enemy soldier still in the field appearing with his hands up, willing to surrender (or die). In practice, we know, the strategist is obliged frequently both to slip across from his bridge to engage in dialogue with his political superiors, and also, moving in the other direction, to impose his intentions upon his military subordinates and perhaps to insist that they train the troops in a manner that he favours strongly. These qualifications duly noted, it is essential not to lose the main thread of the plot. The function of the military strategist, his unique *raison d'être*, is to ensure that policy and the military instrument are purposefully connected. This function obliges him to conduct unequal dialogues with the distinctive occupants on both the banks upon which his bridge should be robustly anchored.

Contrary to the sense conveyed by much of the literature on military history and strategic studies, the functions and roles of strategy and generalship, and strategist and general (or admiral), plainly are distinctive, at least in principle they are easily distinguishable. The strategist must understand the whole nature of a conflict, including war and its warfare if antagonism has escalated thus far, because, subject to political control, he has the duty of care over the entire competitive performance of his security community. Deliberately, for the sake of clarity I state the matter in extreme terms. In contrast, the general with his generalship moves his military pieces, the whole puzzle-worth of assets available to him, for advantage in regard to a particular geographical battlespace. In the event that a war comprises but a single battle in a single campaign in a single geographical theatre, then truly, albeit rarely, strategy and operational-level command would be fused. But in any historical case where particular episodes of operational artistry do not constitute the whole of the warfare in a war, there will be need for a centralizing military strategist to provide higher level direction to the campaigning general.

Generals (and admirals) exercising their generalship perform at the operational level, a level that typically is close to comprising a politics-free, certainly a politics-light, zone. Generalship overwhelmingly is a military function. However, not infrequently generals perform better in their generalship if they achieve a sound understanding of the character of the war within which they are waging warfare. For a clear example, one of the major reasons why Ulysses S. Grant succeeded as the senior military commander for the Union in the American Civil War was because he comprehended the kind of war to which he was committed. He came to appreciate the necessity not only to succeed in pitched battles, but also to bring Southern society to full-frontal recognition of the hopelessness of its prospects.[32]

The mission of the military strategist is to decide how the enemy is to be defeated. It is his task to invent a theory of military victory. That theory has to be expressed and revealed in plans, which are contingent predictions of an extended kind, and it must be commanded by the generals to whom the strategist delegates some restricted command authority. Whether or not the strategist wishes or is able to function as a general also, must vary with historical circumstance. Command style and the command philosophy that it expresses can range from the personally heroic, and therefore extremely personally dangerous, to the emphatically unheroic, even bureaucratic. While the military strategist can function as general, witness Adolf Hitler's exciting brief career as sole strategist and supreme operational military commander, so also he can perform as grand strategist. Indeed, the supreme military command of a polity either at war, or in a period of rivalry short of war, cannot possibly function responsibly and competently if its decisions are taken in isolation from extra-military considerations. Armies do not fight, rather do societies and their polities fight with their armies, inter alia.

The military strategist per se cannot perform as grand strategist save in the context of the complementary expertise provided by those well informed about the health of the polity's non-military assets and situation. Of course, the military dimension to a society's competitive behaviour typically assumes pre-eminent importance in time of war, and the higher the level of command the narrower becomes the gap between policy and strategy. For example, by late 1944 allied division, corps, and even army, commanders in France and the Low Countries had little seriously to concern them beyond plainly military challenges (which is not to deny the humanitarian task that they could not ignore entirely). By way of the sharpest of contrasts, the generals and admirals who constituted the Combined Chiefs of Staff Committee had little to concern them of an exclusively military character. Close to all of their dilemmas and arguments were political concerns, explicit or implicit, or both. Everything that subordinate military commanders succeeded or failed to achieve with their exercise of command in north-west Europe in the campaign of 1944–5 had strategic effect and then political effect. But how far up the chain of command must one climb in order to reach the altitude of the strategist, even the merely military strategist, let alone the grand strategist. Did General Dwight D. Eisenhower make decisions critical to the overall course of the warfare he was designated to command in a supposedly 'supreme' military capacity? The answer is largely in the negative. He was subordinate to the Combined Chiefs of Staff and he was obliged by the scale of the theatre of military endeavour to delegate operational command to his squabbling army, later army group, commanders. This is not to deny the truly important exception of Eisenhower's command decision to postpone the invasion of France from 5 June to 6 June 1944. His responsibility in that instance was of a character that could have paralysed the will of lesser men.[33]

The lion's, but by no means only, share of the British imperial effort to defeat Germany and its allies in the First World War was committed to the Western Front in France and Belgium. General, then Field Marshal, Sir Douglas Haig had a theatre command of paramount continental significance in his role as Commander in Chief of the British Expeditionary Force (BEF). However, his was only an operational level of command, albeit one of historically exceptionally heavy relative weight. Haig did not make, or strive to make, general war policy. He did not exercise command over British or Imperial troops other than those on the Western Front. He had no authority over the literally vital maritime dimension to his country's war effort. Also, notwithstanding the significance of his command responsibility as the primary military consumer of his country's resources, he had no say of much note on the relevant civil policies of his government. To reinforce this narrowly military picture, it is interesting to note the facts that Haig did not play an important role in the political decision to offer Germany an armistice, he did not contribute at all to British political planning for a post-war world, and he did not even attend the great, epoch marking and making Versailles Conference in 1919.[34] The contrast with the role of the Duke of Wellington in Vienna in 1814 and 1815 could hardly be more stark. Haig did not make British national military strategy, though his performance in command, his generalship, for good or ill was key to the quality of British and overall allied strategic performance.

Million-man-plus armies cannot be led heroically by their directing strategist and supreme commander exercising personal generalship in the style of a warrior leading by personal example on the battlefield. Wellington could exercise personal direct generalship. Indeed, time after time he needed to do so, not least at Waterloo. With an army of ca. 70,000 men deployed for combat in a battlespace extending no more than a few miles at most in breadth and depth, a general can exercise personal command. Needless to add, perhaps, he stands a non-trivial chance of death or injury in so doing. But, from the mid-nineteenth century to the present day, the character of warfare has evolved in ways that typically have served to separate military chiefs physically from their troops. The scale of armies and the expansion of the battlespace have denied scope for the exercise of first-hand generalship (and admiralship), while the evolution of communications technologies has enabled commanders to exercise their command and control functions at some distance from the violent action. In point of fact, quite aside from the issue of personal hazard, typically the only position from which overall military command could be exercised was, and remains, fairly well behind the lines, when there were lines, whence communications with all elements commanded ought to be feasible. As historians have observed, it was the great misfortune for the generation of 1914–18 that, uniquely among the greater wars in world military history, the dominant technical characteristics of contemporary warfare denied generals both the means to command in battle in real-time, as well as the ability to exploit battlefield success rapidly.[35] These two technical conditions mightily constrained the scope for the exercise of generalship in the Great War. When trans-battlefield communication and tactical mobility is as limited, and often near non-existent, as it was from 1914 to 1918, it is difficult to achieve decisive success in battle, even if one has the talent.

There is, and can be, no rule for the exact arrangements most likely to provide superior command performance. Every item in the listings in Table 6.1 points to a function and role that needs to be performed somehow by someone or ones through some process of governance. Tradition and culture, personalities, and historical circumstance determine how the strategic function is performed, as well as who performs it and how they perform it. Strategy must be guided by policy, else it cannot know what it must attempt. While, also, it must be made with the selection of military means, military ways, and military goals, all nested in the choices among and conduct of grand strategy's non-military elements. Once made, strategy has to be conducted as command performance at every level from the most inclusive down to the lowest tactical. And that mandates the selection and guidance of competent subordinate military commanders. Also it requires that the army be trained in the lore of best or, at least, good enough, current practice for its job, which is to fight effectively. Such training mandates the development and practice of sound military doctrine.

Strategy and command are distinguishable phenomena, as are the roles of strategist and general. In practice, though not quite so often in principle, a polity's chief military strategist should be entrusted with overall military command responsibility, subject only to civilian political authority. Whatever the variety of relationships nominally possible between the functions of strategy and high command, in practice each demands influence, even control over the other. Strategists need to be responsible for the implementation of their guiding strategic concept(s) as plans in action, while high military command must be able to influence the shaping of the plans they are ordered to execute. The relationship between strategy and command should be umbilical. It is well to recall the ironic maxim that 'nothing appears impossible to the man who does not have to do it'. The metaphor of the strategy bridge can be helpful in aiding recognition of the historical reality that the politician-policymaker connects with the tactical military instrument through military strategists, who typically remain based physically close to the central political authority. Civilian policymakers conduct ongoing, possibly daily, dialogue with senior military strategists, while the dynamic outcome of that dialogue provides guidance to combatant commanders in all geographical locations.

The theory of strategy does not insist that the strategist must be competent as theorist-planner, manager-bureaucrat, leader, politician-diplomat, and educator-persuader. Fortunately for strategic performance, omnicompetence is no more essential to strategic success than is a high score on the scale of genius. All that the general theory claims is that every role just cited needs to be performed somehow, by some person or persons, through some processes of governance. Strategic success is not strictly dependent upon satisfactory, let alone superior, performance of each of the roles specified. Strategy may be uninspired, strategy-making in the planning process can be muddled and dysfunctional because of bureaucratic mismanagement, while military command may be held by generals who fail to provide inspiring leadership. Happily for the strategist, the very complexity of the elements that contribute to strategic performance allows a wide scope for improvised, even serendipitous and plain accidental, compensation. An army can fight well enough even if it is poorly led, though this is not a judgement from which one should derive much comfort.[36]

Enablers

What enables a strategist to be successful? The answer, full-blown, could be extracted from interpretation of the somewhat forbidding architecture of the general theory of strategy presented in Chapters 1 and 2. However, from the abundance of factors and complex interdependencies which the theory has extracted, abstracted, and reduced from all of strategic history, a select shortlist of great, perhaps greater, enablers of strategy merits special notice. These most favoured compound factors are four in number: they comprise strategic education, leadership, fighting power, and opportunity. We are inclined to emphasize the personal, certainly the human over the intellectual, the organizational, the technological, the contingent, and the contextual. Each has enablers or triggers of its own, should one be willing to explore the matter more deeply than is strictly necessary for our purpose.[37] It is somewhat true that generals can find themselves in technological, military, strategic, and political contexts wherein they have scant scope to demonstrate their skill in generalship. It is less true to claim that a successful strategist is dependent upon the good fortune of finding himself present at one of history's conveniently 'strategic moments', as the phrase will have it. The strategist is charged with effecting a satisfactory purposeful match between his polity's political needs and the directed efforts of its many assets. Whether or not net strategic advantage is achievable in some year, for example consider 1917 for Britain and Germany, the good strategist will do what can be done, be it ever so modest. In 1917, the Great War could not be won by either coalition, nor could it be declared a draw and settled on mutually tolerable terms. German and Allied strategies, grand and military, could not deliver victory to their polities in that year. If there was fault in 1917, which there certainly was at the level of both overall military strategy and operational art, it lay primarily though certainly not only, in the political realm. Both Germany and the Western Allies demanded more of their military assets than they could deliver. Charles Nivelle for France and Douglas Haig for Britain performed poorly as generals in that they persisted with poorly conceived offensives which should have been terminated more expeditiously than they were. Nonetheless, while granting the unmistakeable failure of generalship in 1917, the root problem lay on the political bank of the strategy bridge. When charged with achievement of the militarily impossible, armies fail to win.[38] One can argue that the competent strategist must educate his political masters as to the bounds of military feasibility, but this particular strategic dialogue is both unequal and can be beset with a host of practical harassments. Political leaders have a way of being unreceptive to military advice that they do not wish to hear.

Clausewitz was acutely aware of the challenge to sound strategy posed by the need for civilians to work purposefully in concert with soldiers. In some justly famous words he advised both that 'a certain grasp of military affairs is vital for those in charge of general policy', and that 'what is needed in the post [of 'minister of war', typically a civilian function, though not in Imperial Germany: CSG] is distinguished intellect and strength of character. He can always get the necessary military information somehow or other.'[39] What Clausewitz is saying is that provided a politician brings a powerful enough brain, a balanced judgement, and strength of will, to the conduct of war, he can rely upon others to feed him with the military information he needs. Unfortunately, 'distinguished intellect and strength of character' not infrequently are hard to find. This well-attested fact should help incline us to look with particular favour upon the first of the great enablers already identified, education in strategy.

Strategic education is of course essential for the designated strategist, the keeper of the strategic flame on his strategy bridge. However, such education also is important, albeit strictly less essential, for the people with whom the authoritative strategist must interact continuously in the chain of consultation and command. Specifically, strategy is likely to be much enabled if not only the strategist himself is well educated in his art, but also if his political masters are not entirely ignorant of strategic matters. Also, it is necessary for the strategist's principal military subordinates to be able to conduct their military operations with some grasp of their strategic context. In the pertinent phrase of historian Robert Lyman, generals should perform better with their generalship if they are able to direct their fights in the light of understanding of their geographically wider and temporally larger strategic implications. In Lyman's words:

> But it is not enough simply to be a good leader under fire, and to be a model of valour. As Socrates identified, generals must also be able to plan, and they must be able to understand and contribute to the strategic as well as the battlefield aspects of warfare. Effective command requires *strategic sense*. Higher commanders need to understand the broader picture and context in which their own military operations take place, and thus to structure, plan and mount operations that meet the requirements of this wider strategy. They may not themselves be involved in the construction of grand strategy, but it is paramount that they understand why these decisions are made so that they can make battlefield decisions intelligently.[40]

Strategic education can be acquired in several ways, most obviously by purposeful study, as well as by incidental learning through serendipitous and incidental exposure, and by first-hand experience. Explicit formal mastery of the twenty dictums presented in Chapters 1 and 2 is by no means the entirety of strategic education, though such could only be of benefit to the student. Rather is some education in strategy, which is to say in the fundamental ideas and many of their interconnections, more often acquired piece by piece: in the classroom for most people to some degree; possibly as partially registered half-truths from history courses at school; from the History Channel, inter alia, for many; from movies, history books, and novels; and from the general experience of life which exposes us all to the ebb and flow of news events and episodes which have some strategic features, and which obliges everyone to attempt to function strategically in their efforts to adjust ends, ways, and means. The general theory of strategy may be more than a little arcane and challenging when approached as a coherent, highly distilled body of professional knowledge. It is much less forbidding when its many concepts and interdependencies appear in historically specific situations and typically in some material form. Individuals and people in groups, including organizations, are able to learn how to attempt to perform strategically, though not reliably, not at a predictable rate, and not necessarily wisely.[41] Nonetheless, the body of understanding required as the basis for an education in strategy, which is to say its general theory, is available and accessible to all. The appointed strategist cannot function competently unless he is strategically well educated— by study, experience, or, one must admit, by a gift of biology that bequeaths instinctual genius. Instinctive good strategic judgement certainly is a historical reality, but intellectual understanding and insight from can only be of assistance, improving its batting average. As for a general with the duty to exercise operational-level command, although he will not make strategy or execute strategic decisions, unless he has some of the strategic sense to which Lyman refers, he is unlikely to grasp well enough his strategic commander's intent, and this can matter.[42]

If some education in strategy logically must be our first great enabler, then leadership has to be the second. It may be worthwhile reminding ourselves, particularly if we are civilians, that strategy is about, and really is all about, command performance. Polities and would-be polities are not rewarded in the course of history for the quality of their strategies, or the apparent brilliance of their strategists, but rather for the effectiveness of their strategic behaviour in the political realm. Ideas are vital, but not as ideas. Strategic ideas truly are vital only as fuel for action and purposeful inaction. These ideas are applied to specific situations as candidate solutions to actual historical problems in the form of plans in a process of military planning at several levels of inclusiveness. And these plans will need to be adapted, often entirely rewritten, in the light of events. Our theory of victory meets the enemy's theory of victory, and both of us are likely to be surprised by the course of events propelled by our interwoven efforts. One of us is near certain to be unpleasantly jolted by the strategic and political outcome to the conflict. In Chapter 4, we explained that between them, the enemy and war's inherent complexity provide both a monumental heap of problems and, paradoxically, the principal means to overcome or evade the challenges. The enemy may be thwarted by the surprises that we might succeed in springing upon him, while the sheer complexity of the strategist's world ensures at least the possibility that compensation for particular weakness can be found and applied. These are significant points, but in a sense they can be subsumed under the umbrella of command by strategically effective leadership.

Commentators, theorists, and even historians are apt to refer to people as strategists, commanders, leaders, and generals, without overmuch care as to the precise meaning of each title. With only rare historical exceptions leadership is not explicit in a military rank or title, rather is it a necessary, but formally unstated, function of effective command at all levels. The Third Reich's Waffen-SS and Britain's Royal Air Force (RAF), to cite two of those exceptions, did include 'leader' in its rank structure (e.g. *Hauptsturmbahnführer*, squadron leader). It should be needless to add that in making a quasi-religion of the leadership principle (*Führerprinzip*), Nazi Germany may have had the effect of rendering guilty by association a necessary function, task, and quality. Hitler's Germany has a lot for which to answer. For example, not only did it sully the concept of leadership, also it cast a pall over the idea and subject of geopolitics that required nearly half a century to dissipate.[43] The German contribution to strategic history since the beginning of the nineteenth century has been so potent that there can be no escaping its reach. Recall that this book agreed with a declared determination to rewrite, certainly to write, the general theory of strategy, while striving to survive suffocation by the excellence of Clausewitz's *On War*. To this task, we must add the necessity to employ geopolitical analysis, despite its mainly unjust, but unavoidable, Nazi taint. And now we have to accord leadership its due as probably the greatest among the shortlist of strategy's great enablers.

Lest the point be lost amidst the jumble of concepts and terms that jostle for priority attention—command, leadership, generalship, orders, duty, follower, loyalty, trust, charisma, among many others in a conceptually crowded field—it is helpful to recall the competency and context of a military force. When all is said and done, polities raise and sustain armies because they either need, or suspect strongly that they might need, a body of soldiers some of whom need to be true warriors, effective in combat to protect them from ill-wishers abroad or malcontents at home. The defining core of the competencies of an army is fighting. When one thinks about the possibility of war of any character, one could do worse than draw upon, who else, Clausewitz with his superb terse summary of war's 'climate': 'danger, exertion, uncertainty, and chance'.[44] All military strategists, and most grand strategists, cannot perform their duties unless their schemes, great and small, are done, 'in the field', by soldiers willing to be led in that physically and psychologically horrendous circumstance of the most acute personal peril. Troops can be commanded by soldiers empowered by legal authority to issue orders, but whether or not they lead their soldiers depends upon whether or not those soldiers consent to be led. In other words, since leaders cannot lead without enough willing, not necessarily enthusiastic, followers, the exercise of effective military command needs in addition to be an exercise in leadership. Also, soldiers may well follow as their duty minimally demands, but they might not follow with determination, let alone enthusiasm. Such a personally prudent attitude translates readily into a potentially fatal moral disadvantage, should the enemy score much higher on the willingness-to-fight scale.

The fighting power, or combat effectiveness, of a military force is by no means solely determined by the quality of its leaders. Nonetheless, there are good reasons to believe that superior leadership is the single most significant contributor to what nearly all people agree is by far the most important ingredient in fighting power, morale. This somewhat vaporous elusive quality, morale, is key to the willingness of men to fight. More to the point, perhaps, it is key to the degree of determination to fight on in the face of awesome ample reasons for discouragement. For illustration of this point, we can identify the humble German *Landser*, Private Heinrich Sewelow of the 352nd infantry division, who almost certainly personally killed more Allied soldiers than did anyone else on D-Day (except, unfairly backtracked, the Allied military command, i.e. General Dwight D. Eisenhower serving at the pleasure of the Allied Combined Chiefs of Staff). This ordinary soldier did so with his MG-42 from a position on top of the bluffs overlooking Omaha beach, for a personal total tally certainly in the hundreds. He fired his machine gun and then his carbine quite literally until he ran out of ammunition (respectively, he shot off 12,000 and then 50 rounds). He did his duty in part, he explained, simply because he was a good German, and it was his duty to resist the enemy. But rather more important was his open ended, unlimited, determination to fight on while he could out of loyalty to, one could possibly say love for, his lieutenant. That young officer, who died early on in the day, was a leader, and the machine gunner was an obedient, but entirely willing, follower.[45] Of course, obedience to orders issued by proper authority is expected, indeed is required, sometimes on pain even of death, in all armies. But, for soldiers willingly to risk their lives in ways that exceed minimal or perhaps only token compliance, there is always need for a dose of the ingredients that make for high enough morale. The ingredients can be chemical (vodka, rum, indeed anything alcoholic), spiritual (trust, inspiration, self-confidence), or a lack of alternatives (desperation). The military, sporting, and business literatures abound with theories and anecdotal histories purporting to reveal the mysteries of morale in its several guises. Those guises all translate as the will to win, at least the will not to allow the enemy to win cheaply. This will, or determination, may be optimistic, fatalistic, and more or less well founded in materially and spiritually objective realities (e.g. how strong is the enemy soldier's will to win?). No matter. What does matter is recognition that morale is a spectrum between the extremes, on the one hand, of a determination unto death not to accept defeat until the last round has been fired, and, on the other hand, a willingness to surrender when the near future looks acutely dangerous. The strategist, grand, military, or both ultimately is enabled by human beings deciding where on this spectrum of the will to resist they choose to place themselves at this hour on this day. For soldiers to decide that they will fight truly hard, they need to be led by people whom they trust. Moreover, to emphasize the point and connect the dots, at every level of command, from the highest down to the single soldier and very small group, the most essential basis for voluntary, sometimes personally outrageously risky, combat effort, is trust.

In his memoir of the siege of Dien Bien Phu in 1954, Dr Paul Grauwin, the head surgeon of the garrison, attests to the potency of trust when he notes that '[e]ach time a battalion was dropped [parachuted in: CSG] enthusiasm and confidence mounted throughout the camp. "France and the higher command are not going to let us fall; they are sending us the best blokes of the lot [élite paratroop units]".[46] Grauwin, himself a hero of the desperate struggle, tells us that

> Towards the middle of April, a special order of the day, signed by General de Castries [then a colonel, garrison commander: CSG], informed us that in response to a request from the commander-in-chief, thousands of men in all branches of the service had volunteered to drop on Dien-Bien-Phu, without making any preliminary drop or having any previous training.
>
> It was unbelievable, unprecedented; we could hardly believe our eyes as we read. Our hearts were filled with relief; around me I could hear the soldiers, visitors and wounded, expressing their joy and enthusiasm. Now they were convinced that everything would be done for Dien-Bien-Phu, that the higher command had decided to hold on to the end—until victory.[47]

Dien Bien Phu was one of those many episodes in strategic history when the politicians, pursuing a policy of hasty scuttle, were unworthy of their soldiers and, most especially, their local allied dependents, military and civilian. Martin Windrow records the fact that in spring 1954 'France's moral obligation to the peoples of North Vietnam would be discarded with humiliating speed'.[48] Trust may well be persistently undeserved in strategic affairs, but there can be no doubting its efficacy as fuel for effort by gullible, perhaps simply desperate, people. It was with good reason that Clausewitz laid emphasis upon the 'moral elements' that 'constitute the spirit that permeates war as a whole'.[49] He proceeds to liken the physical and the moral factors in war, respectively, to 'the wooden hilt, while the moral factors are the precious metal, the real weapon, the finely-honed blade'.[50] Clausewitz is surely correct, but he does risk misleading the reader. His emphasis on the moral, on the power of will, can incline the incautious to be unduly disdainful of material considerations. The spirit is a potent source of compensation for missing resources, but it has its limits, as an historian of Robert E. Lee's Army of Northern Virginia notes

> Confederates went to war with inferior weapons, if any at all, and they fought with ammunition that failed to measure up to Union standards. To compensate, Lee's Army had to rely on superior leadership and combat effectiveness. But as the army drained manpower in battle after battle, and its pool of talented officers and enlisted men diminished, these advantages became harder to sustain. The Union could rely on better equipment and greater resources and manpower to compensate for battlefield losses. The Confederacy had no such luxury.[51]

Each level of military performance that contributes finally to overall strategic effect is energized and guided by the level immediately above. This applies to frightened infantry in waterlogged ditches, as well as to planning staffs suffering sleepless nights far behind the battlespace. For satisfactory performance, it may well suffice simply to be ordered to do one's duty. Most armies in most circumstances of actual or imminent combat enforce discipline more or less brutally, both formally and informally. But there can be a world of difference in the fighting power generated between a unit that merely obeys orders, that complies, and one that literally does all of which it is physically and emotionally able, even possibly for a tactical goal that transcends the commander's plain intent.[52] One obvious reason why morale is so important is because warfare is so unpredictable in its course that the chaos of the battlespace obliges units, down to individuals, to behave at their own discretion. Modern technology enables command and attempted control in any level of detail that doctrine and the personalities of commanders prefer. However, perceived personal or group necessity, not excluding an instinctual panic, will always be liable to override command by remote control, should those locally in danger, humans at the tip of the strategist's spear, not trust the personal integrity of those above them in their chain of command.

For a commander to be a leader with willing followers, he must pass the test of trust. This trust can be expressed as relating to the soldier's, perhaps better simply the subordinate's, belief that those in authority over him accept a 'duty of care', for the contemporary phrase, for his well-being. The soldier, at every level that contributes to the quality of the strategist's command performance, should be able to trust his superior(s): to care enough about him so as not to waste his life or health; to be so competent in the conduct of his duties that the soldier's life and effort will be ordered into harm's way only in the doing of what needs to be done; and, possibly for a sentiment too far, not to be indifferent to the soldier's fate save for a functional concern for the loss of, or damage to, a military 'asset'. For morale to be high, every level of the military hierarchy needs to be able to trust the personal integrity and the professional competence of the levels above it. Proceeding downwards, the military strategist-commander and his subordinates in command have to be confident that they do not require more of their men than those men can be trusted to deliver. It is necessary to insist that high morale requires reciprocal trust not only up and down the chain of command, but also horizontally among tactical units. In the Second World War, the *Wehrmacht* routinely demanded of its soldiers in all grades a total personal commitment to the fight, an insistence that most ranks met to a degree that is extraordinary in historical terms.[53] For example, it is incredible but true that no fewer than 500 of Nazi Germany's 1,400 generals and admirals lost their lives or were missing in action in the war.[54] That was possibly an unprecedented number of fatalities for general officers in war. 'Château generalship' was well and truly dead and buried for Nazi Germany.[55]

Because this is a work of general strategic theory, we are not obliged to probe deeply the sources of morale. However, we are required to register the preeminence of leadership, and its paired phenomenon, willing followership, as the most significant among morale's contributors. Leadership is most obvious in, say, the battlefield heroism of then Major General Erwin Rommel fighting personally at the head of the engineers and infantry of his Seventh Panzer Division as it struggled to cross the River Meuse at Sedan on 13 May 1940. This was leadership in its most ancient guise. Rommel led by personal example in a rubber boat under fire with his men.[56] He was in constant touch with his men; his life was in as much danger as was theirs. They saw the leader of their war-band leading. Every army requires some heroic leaders who are warriors by inspiring, even shaming, personal example. However, the overall grand or military strategist cannot sensibly lead as a warrior in combat, save by reputation from an early danger-filled career, at least he cannot survive for very long doing so. What the strategist must do is provide guidance, including orders, that will be obeyed in spirit as to broad intent, as well as in good measure in some detail. He must communicate what he wants to achieve and how he intends to achieve it. His subordinates, as staff officers, field commanders, and those providing essential logistical and other support, must function competently or better in the great chain of command. Moreover, the whole chain, and what it commands at every level, will perform better the closer the command relationship is to one characterized by leadership and followership. Orders, duty, residual loyalty, and local peril may suffice for the sharper points of the spear to do what needs to be done. It is vital for the strategist as effective commander to be able to communicate clearly with his army. In varying amounts of detail, and by a wide variety of means, the strategist-commander-leader needs to explain to his troops, all his troops, what he intends to do, why he intends to do it, and how it will be done— at least he will do so within the limits of security and in ways tailored to his particular audiences. The good leader will emphasize the common elements in the risky military enterprise. He will talk about 'our' purposes, and he will sound firm and confident in claiming what 'we' will do. There must be no Freudian slips of the tongue which appear to suggest that 'your' effort and sacrifice will assist 'my' promotion. Nonetheless, should the enemy prove cunning, unexpectedly skilled, and should he be lucky, ordinary, meaning minimally acceptable, military performance at many levels of the human military machine will be unlikely to suffice for victory; indeed, even good may not be good enough.

The third of the great enablers of command performance by the strategist is fighting power. We have suggested already that morale, eternally and universally, has been and remains the principal ingredient in this power. Admittedly the concept of fighting power is extraordinarily analytically challenging, because it is so compounded. In this respect, it has much in common with Clausewitz's employment of the literally mechanical metaphor of 'friction' as a figure of speech that aids understanding of 'the factors that distinguish real war from war on paper'.[57] Fortunately, the general theorist of strategy is not required to specify exactly the ingredients that produce fighting power. That can and needs to be done, though it is necessary to appreciate that fighting power is always situational. What the concept of fighting power brings to this feast is explicit recognition that the strategist needs a combat arm. Elegant concepts, ingenious plans, and some inspiring leaders, much effective equipment, and even well-trained and tolerably willing soldiers, inter alia, are all more or less necessary for adequate overall strategic performance. However, just how potent as a fighting force is the strategist's military instrument of decision? When he turns the command key from on high at his political masters' behest, how good in the field will his army prove to be? More to the point, how good will it prove to be against the army of a specific enemy at a particular time? Warfare is not like golf, rather is it akin to tennis or indeed any sport wherein the performance of an active rival must decide both how good one needs to be, as well as how good one can be. War is a duel, to recite holy writ yet again. The strategist is enabled not by a potent army, but rather by what his potent army can do against a particular enemy. For the understatement of the book, this requires a quality of judgement far beyond the ordinary. Anticipating the net performance of his army in the duel that is warfare, the strategist must ask of his army's apparent fighting power, 'so what?'. He has to answer the question, 'given what policy instructs me to achieve by military means, is my fighting power in all its possible combinations adequate to do the job at a cost my society will judge bearable?'. As we have had occasion to observe several times already, the function of strategy cannot safely be entrusted to the strategically ill-educated, the faint-hearted, or the physically frail. The inescapable consequence is that strategy needs to be entrusted primarily to a person who is likely to be borderline arrogant, overconfident, impatient of those with lesser talent, and difficult to fit into a team, even as team leader. George C. Patton and Bernard Law Montgomery spring to mind. Donald Jagoe expresses the irony nicely when he writes that '[t]he concept of *development process* [of new doctrine] is both problematic and complex. When one finds the aforementioned brilliant and exceptional leaders [he cites Nelson, Rodney, and Spruance, to which one could add, for today, Petraeus: CSG] one may also find particularly resolute egos.'[58] As Douglas Waller has written of the flamboyant air power theorist-theologian, General William 'Billy' Mitchell:

> Great leaders, particularly those in wartime, have outsized egos. Institutional mavericks, whistle-blowers, critics who press for reform in bureaucracies all tend to be abrasive, outspoken, hard to get along with. Prophets by nature are opinionated and overconfident. Agents of change break china, make people angry, and uncomfortable, leave enemies in their wake.[59]

It seems to be close to a rule for command performance, that extraordinary natural talent comes somewhat offset by scarcely less extraordinary negatives of personality. Few among history's great strategist-commanders have been both saintly as human beings and effective as practitioners of strategy.

The fighting power of an army must be enhanced by its development and adoption of suitable military doctrine. It is well to recognize, though, that superior doctrine, even when married to excellent weapons and logistical adequacy, are all irrelevant should the troops not be inclined to fight hard. They may believe that they have 'done their bit', and more, already—the condition of several British regiments following their tough service in North Africa from 1940 or 1941 to early 1943—or they may lack confidence in the generalship of their operational-level commander.[60] For good doctrine to reward its authors, it has to meet with the approval of those who must implement it. Should they disagree with its precepts, they will either ignore it, or comply only reluctantly and more than a little subversively. The higher the level of military performance addressed, the less prescriptive is doctrine. General instruction for operational-level command assuredly is feasible, and indeed is provided in most countries' colleges of higher military education. That granted, the most vital specific choices that have to be made by an operational-level commander, always assuming he is delegated the necessary discretion, cannot possibly be taught by general precept. His level of generalship requires the making of historically discrete choices in a unique context. Formal education in strategy's theory, instinct—perhaps instinctual knowledge—and experience should suffice to equip the operational commander to plan competently for his challenge, but no doctrine can provide a reliable template for success.[61] However, this is not to argue that operational-level doctrine, and certainly tactical doctrine, lacks value.

At the level of the strategist himself, it is all too obvious that while he can be educated in strategy, should he prove educable, he cannot be taught how to win. To repeat the familiar mantra, his function as a strategist is to translate his political masters' voice (which may well be produced by a forked tongue or be audible as voices) into strategic effect through the agency of a theory of victory, a strategy, performed well enough by his exercise of command achieved by sufficiently willing followers through his leadership. Reading Sun Tzu and Thucydides, for the leading examples, should help prepare the strategist for his practical duties, but even they cannot instruct him as to probable 'best practice', to borrow a vital concept from the realm of doctrine, for, by way of illustration, the defeat of Imperial Japan in the Second World War. There is no such animal as the general 'best practice' for this, or indeed any, necessarily historically unique mission. Doctrine can be important, but can only be as useful as it finds its way into practice. Since the strategist must be enabled, or disabled, by the fighting power, whence cometh the net military effectiveness, of his army, he cannot be disinterested in the quality of that army's tactical and operational doctrine.[62] As for best practice by the strategist, he can turn to the great educators among the classic authors of general theory for intellectual assistance to his personal assets, and to help offset his limitations should that be possible, which often it is not.

In his essential role as trainer, perhaps more accurately as educator and trainer of the trainers, of his troops, the strategist-commander must educate and instruct in what he believes to be the best practices of which his army is capable against the enemy of the day in the circumstances in which it finds itself. As we have argued already, military doctrine is both a potentially vital enabler of success, as well as being a possible source of grave peril. When developed objectively and applied adaptably with discretion, not dogmatically, and if it is correct enough, then it should greatly enhance fighting power. But doctrine, even if basically sound, can mislead in specific instances when actual people have to decide on their behaviour. And, to repeat a point that bears repetition, no matter how robust the tactical doctrine, prudent the operational doctrine, and wise the so-called strategic doctrine, if the troops lack the will to fight, the quality of the authoritative doctrines will count for nothing. In other words, military doctrine should be a potent enabler of command performance, *ceteris paribus*.

The last of my four enablers for emphasis is the admittedly analytically suspect factor of historical opportunity. Rephrased, I wish to suggest that a strategist often is enabled to be successful, if that is not too strong a suggestion, by being the right enough person at the time and in the place wherein opportunity beckons the bold, the competent, or possibly just the healthy, the lucky, and the politically or socially acceptable. This argument is analytically challengeable because it seems to be notably tautological. I may appear to be claiming that the strategist is able to be successful when he is able to be successful. One wants to argue that the good strategist shows his strategic mettle in any context, no matter how adverse. For example, Roman grand and military strategy in the Second Punic War rose magnificently to the challenge of repeated battlefield disasters. Eventually, and one must emphasize the relatively *longue durée*, Hannibal was defeated tactically in a decisive battle with conclusive strategic and political effect at Zama in 202 BCE. But the ultimate military demise of Carthage was the result of Roman grand strategy which defeated what passed for strategy in Hannibal's calculations.[63] Battle is truly decisive beyond the narrowest of military confines only when it is the enabling agent for strategic decision, and the potential worth of that decision frequently is squandered by political incompetence in the tough area that is peacemaking.

The strategist knows that victory in battle can only be a means to his strategic ends. In addition, though, he knows that defeat in battle can rarely, if ever, have a positive influence upon the course of his grand designs. Battlefield defeat need not prove strategically fatal, but it saps the morale of his troops, shakes confidence in the strategist-commander's competence on the part of his subordinate commanders, and reduces his self-confidence. Also, of fatal moment for his contribution and reputation, defeat in the field inclines politicians to look for people, or a person, upon whom shame and blame plausibly can be heaped. This latter phenomenon, eternal and universal in its reflection of human nature, is aptly characterized by the plea, 'anyone but me [is responsible]'.

Paradoxically and ironically, the successful strategist can be one who succeeds not only in averting disaster, but even one who copes as well as fair judgement decides could be done in circumstances so disadvantageous that the limitation of damage had to be the practicable summit of strategic ambition. For example, most historians believe that although the balance of inherent advantage was loaded severely against the Confederate States of America, they are not agreed that Union victory was a foregone conclusion to the Civil War, as if historical necessity allowed no discretion to human effort. It is possible to argue with some measure of plausibility either that the Confederacy did not have to lose, or that it could have waged a more effective war than it did, had it only enjoyed the services of a superior strategist and strategy. I am unpersuaded by such speculation. What the South lacked, apart from non-trivial deficits in people and material assets, was a sufficiency of good enough generals. It prospered in the Civil War's early years partly because Union military leadership ranged only between appalling and poor. But from the summer of 1863 until the close of hostilities in April 1865, it was a very different story.[64]

There is something to be said for the proposition that the strategy bridge is tested most severely when the military going is relatively easy, as opposed to severely contested. For two recent examples, in 2001 and 2003 US military, even grand, strategy handily won two interstate wars. It so happened, though, that both were won in ways and by means that had consequences fatal for the prospects for a satisfactory political settlement following the brief episodes of regular warfare. US military and political strategies to take down the Taliban, then the Baathist, regimes succeeded in genuinely exemplary fashion. Had those short episodes of warfare, and those particular, discrete, wars been all that US strategy needed to conduct, then undoubtedly it would have been appropriate to declare, as did President George W. Bush, famously, 'mission accomplished', and distribute the congratulations and medals. But in both cases the promptness of the military success functioned as tempting opportunities for the demonstration of strategic incompetence. Strategic history rarely disappoints when it is offered such juicy occasions to punish hubris.[65]

As Luttwak argues persuasively, strategy is paradoxical and ironic.[66] There is little safety in success because such a happy condition is the breeding ground for future failure. The competent strategist is one who can deal well enough both with some operational-level misfortune—say Britain in 1940—and, for probably the greater challenge, with apparently unstoppable, though incomplete, operational success. The latter, termed the malady of 'victory disease', impaired the mental condition of Germany's *Führer* and military commanders in 1940–41.[67] If one has been persuaded by victories in the field that one is blessed by divine grace, or whatever, as a brilliant strategist, it can be difficult to assess the enemies still at large at all accurately, or to take proper account of future history's possible negative contingencies. Often it is difficult to know quite how to account for success. When in doubt, let alone when not in doubt, it is all too human simply to invite and accept the praise for victory, whether or not it is deserved. Ironically, history is apt to punish the successful by inviting in the victor of today an unwarranted self-confidence. Truly delusional self-belief is far from uncommon. With reference to an admittedly extreme example, it is worth noting Antulio Echevarria's wry comment on Osama bin Laden's strategic performance, post 9/11: 'It is difficult to analyze one's strategy and tactics critically if they are considered divinely inspired.'[68]

For the purpose of locating strategists contextually, historical opportunity is specified here as a great enabler. Strategists are much enabled by their education, by the leadership they can provide and encourage, and by the combat potency they should realize from their military instrument. In addition, however, strategists must function in historical, geographical, and political contexts, inter alia, very much not of their personal choice or construction. Whether or not they can shape and reshape the stage(s) on which they must act out their several roles is a measure of their skill/their luck, and the skill, luck and assets of their enemies. Circumstance, both of huge adversity as well as of great advantage, must test severely the ability of the strategist to produce a satisfactory, let alone an outstandingly successful, command performance.

Payoff: The Good Enough Strategist

Perhaps as an 'afterword' more than a conclusion, there is need to reemphasize the value of education through exposure to the general theory of strategy for the strategist who has to try to connect purposefully and effectively all of the dots in his command performance. The meta-narrative of strategy may be the political story that provides the key motivation, but by far the most influential factor in strategy, as it is in war, warfare, and indeed in peace and crisis, is the complex human one. Strategy is conducted for and by people. Command performance, the critical output of the strategist, is performance by people, enabled by other people, and conducted to shape and even control the will of the adversarial. Other, the enemy.

If strategy is enabled, still it needs to be done well enough by the person or persons thus duly enabled. Such a person or persons cannot, save by blind luck, command a winning performance if he stumbles at the first and highest fence on the conflict course. This fence is the one that obliges

> the statesman and commander to establish by that test [of fit with policy] the kind of war on which they are embarking: neither mistaking it for, nor trying to turn it into, something that is alien to its nature. This is the first of all strategic questions and the most comprehensive.[69]

Clausewitz is right, of course, but nonetheless potentially misleading. The words just quoted imply strongly that a particular war must have a distinctive character, one which reflects its political purposes. What is misleading about these words is the suggestion that the statesman and commander should take the politics, and hence the military strategic and operational, character (not 'nature' as Clausewitz says) of the conflict as all but objective realities that have to be understood and whose special features need to be accommodated. In point of historical fact, the exact political character of war, most obviously the political stakes, will not be fixed and open to reliable and verifiable stable identification. Furthermore, the character of the warfare that matches the political stakes quite typically will not be readily identifiable from a firm grasp of policy. Among the considerations that Clausewitz does not proffer for our education is the disturbing thought that the 'test' of policy can yield different correct answers, depending upon which polity is conducting the examination. For example, Clausewitz's political test for American effort in warfare for Vietnam in the mid- to late 1960s would, indeed did, oblige Washington to wage a distinctly limited war.[70] Unfortunately for American strategy, the North Vietnamese policy test for their military effort, inter alia, mandated total societal commitment. Had American strategists and would-be strategists grasped the fact of this all but existential asymmetrical political reality, what should they have recommended? Was it reasonable to assume that the United States and its local and regional allies could win through the conduct of a significantly limited style in warfare against an enemy who could not afford to be so constrained? Arguably, Clausewitz's famous logic, as quoted, can be more of a hindrance than a help to strategic education. As I have ventured before, in the words of the great fictional detective, Sherlock Holmes, 'these are very deep waters', to which one would add, 'and dangerous'.

Strategy must be both made, and then made to exercise such guidance to, and hopefully achieve some control over, events as to deliver strategic, then political, advantage, success, and possibly decisive victory.[71] Decisive victory in war has to be achieved in such a manner, especially military, so as not to mortgage fatally the political purpose of it all, which is of course the establishment and maintenance of a tolerably stable peace. For such a peace to be stable by reasonable definition, all relevant parties need genuinely to be either major stakeholders in the new architecture and terms for order, global, regional, or local domestic (should the war have been civil, as the inapposite adjective designates), or close to definitively strategically disenfranchized. So much should be thoroughly obvious. Indeed, if it is not obvious at this very late juncture in the text, my mission with this work must be judged a failure. Alas, history in all periods, not excluding the current, provides a rich harvest of examples, occasions as well as protracted episodes, wherein many if not most of the vital connections from strategist up to politician, and down through the chain of command to the combat edge, plainly were broken.

By his command performance, it is the strategist above all others who must 'join up the dots' from political intention, back to political achievement, via the centralized direction of varied effort in conflict. This is the function of the strategist, and it is why his bridge needs to be kept in good enough repair for the two-way strategic traffic to flow. It can be fortunate that war by definition is a duel, because this means that the strategist does not have to exhibit undeniable genius; he need only perform well enough to win against the competitive command performances of enemies who also are likely to be copiously flawed strategically.

It is fitting to close this chapter with a telling quote from a contemporary American strategist, General David Petraeus. With a terseness that is eloquent, these few words convey most of the content of this chapter, indeed of this book:

> There are three enormous tasks that strategic leaders have to get right . . . The first is to get the big ideas right. The second is to communicate the big ideas throughout the organization. The third is to ensure proper execution of the big ideas.[72]

NOTES

1. Carl von Clausewitz, *On War*, tr. Michael Howard and Peter Paret (1832–4; Princeton, NJ: Princeton University Press, 1976), 75.
2. T. E. Lawrence, *Seven Pillars of Wisdom: A Triumph* (New York: Anchor Books, 1991), 192.
3. Luttwak has yet to attract intellectual biographical attention, but Schelling is the subject of the following efforts: Phil Williams, 'Thomas Schelling', in John Baylis and John

Garnett, eds., *Makers of Nuclear Strategy,* (New York: St. Martin's Press, 1991), 120–36; and especially Robert Ayson, *Thomas Schelling and the Nuclear Age: Strategy as Social Science* (London: Frank Cass, 2004).

4. The strategic thought of Bernard Brodie can be seen at its best in the following: 'Strategy as a Science', and 'The Absolute Weapon', in Thomas A. Mahnken and Joseph A. Maiolo, eds., *Strategic Studies: A Reader* (Abingdon: Routledge, 2008), respectively 8–21 (original 1949), and 183–223 (original 1946); *Strategy in the Missile Age* (Princeton, NJ: Princeton University Press, 1959); and *War and Politics* (New York: Macmillan, 1973). It needs to be said that Brodie's work merits much greater attention than it has received to date. That claim registered, the following are helpful: Fred Kaplan, *The Wizards of Armageddon* (New York: Touchstone, 1983); Ken Booth, 'Bernard Brodie', in Baylis and Garnett, eds., *Makers of Modern Strategy*, 19–56; Barry H. Steiner, *Bernard Brodie and the Foundations of America's Nuclear Strategy* (Lawrence, KS: University Press of Kansas, 1991); Bruce Kuklick, *Blind Oracles: Intellectuals and War from Kennan to Kissinger* (Princeton, NJ: Princeton University Press, 2006), 55–60; and Alex Abella, *Soldiers of Reason: The RAND Corporation and the Rise of the American Empire* (Orlando, FL: Harcourt, 2008).

5. Basil H. Liddell Hart (1895–1970) was severely wounded on the Somme in 1916 while holding a temporary commission in the King's Own Yorkshire Light Infantry (KOYLI), the regiment in which he served from 1914 until 1924. By temperament, he was not well suited to a peacetime career as a regular soldier. It is worth noting that Liddell Hart persisted in employing his modest rank of captain throughout his civilian life. Among a plethora of studies of his theories see the two leading intellectual biographies: Brian Bond, *Liddell Hart: A Study of His Military Thought* (New Brunswick, NJ: Rutgers University Press, 1977); and, for an unusually literate as well as lively read, Alex Danchev, *Alchemist of War: The Life of Basil Liddell Hart* (London: Weidenfeld and Nicolson, 1998). For tough analytical assessments of Liddell Hart's theories, see: John J. Mearsheimer, *Liddell Hart and the Weight of History* (Ithaca, NY: Cornell University Press, 1988), which is strongly negative; and Azar Gat, *Fascist and Liberal Visions of War: Fuller, Liddell Hart, Douhet, and Other Modernists* (Oxford: Clarendon Press, 1998), pt. II, which is more positive.

6. In quantity and typically in quality also, J. F. C. Fuller's output was prodigious. He made his theoretical mark most especially with regard to the employment of tanks. Large and eventually influential though that mark was, in truth Fuller ranged over the whole field of modern warfare, an exercise that more and more came to be overtaken by his military historical studies, some of which have come to be recognized as minor classics. His studies of historical cases of outstanding generalship in particular have stood the test of some time and much additional scholarship very well indeed (e.g. Fuller's studies of Alexander the Great and of Ulysses S. Grant continue to be widely respected). Studies of Fuller are not exactly abundant, but there are four works, at least, that are worthy of their brilliant, if irascible, subject: Brian Holden Reid, *J. F. C. Fuller: Military Thinker* (New York: St. Martin's Press, 1987); id., *Studies in British Military Thought: Debates with Fuller and Liddell Hart* (Lincoln, NE: University of Nebraska Press, 1998), see esp. the bibliography of Fuller and Liddell Hart's principal writings, 269–73; Gat, *Fascist and Liberal Visions of War*, esp. ch. 2; and useful though of somewhat lesser weight, Anthony J. Trythall, *'Boney' Fuller: The Intellectual General, 1878–1966* (London: Cassell, 1977). In the small library that comprises the Fuller oeuvre, his energetic argument for the domination by technology in warfare remains an all too relevant fallacious thesis: see his

Armament and History: A Study of the Influence of Armament on History from the Dawn of Classical Warfare to the Second World War (London: Eyre and Spottiswoode, 1946).

7. The original is not to be missed. See Giulio Douhet, *The Command of the Air* (1921, 1927; New York: Arno Press, 1972). Italian General Douhet has yet to receive intellectual biographical treatment in English worthy of his historical significance, though Gat, *Fascist and Liberal Visions of War*, ch. 3, is more than merely helpful, as also is Phillip S. Meilinger, 'Giulio Douhet and the Origins of Airpower Theory', in Meilinger, ed., *The Paths of Heaven: The Evolution of Airpower Theory* (Maxwell AFB, AL: Air University Press, 1997), 1–40. Julian S. Corbett published much excellent British naval history, but most students of strategy today mainly are familiar with his book, *Some Principles of Maritime Strategy* (1911; Annapolis, MD: Naval Institute Press, 1988). It is perhaps ironic that Corbett's maritime theorizing appears much less dated now than it did through the whole of Britain's short twentieth century, with its repeated great (European) continental strategic fixation (1914–18, 1939–91). Educated by Clausewitz to take a holistic view of war and warfare, Corbett's fairly wide-angle maritime, rather than narrow naval, lens, yielded a view that has persisting merit. His principal focus was upon 'the function of the fleet in war', not its function in battle at sea: see Corbett, *England in the Seven Years' War: A Study in Combined Strategy*, vol. 1 (1907; London: Longmans, Green, 1918), ch. 1, 'Introductory—The Function of the Fleet in War'. Needless to say, perhaps, Corbett's breadth of strategic vision did not please all of the senior sailors of his day; men reared in the strategically unhelpful anachronistic tradition of mindless veneration of a misunderstood Horatio Nelson as the god of naval victory through decisive battle. See Eric Grove's first-rate biographical essay in *Some Principles of Maritime Strategy*, xi–xiv; while Donald M. Schurman, *Julian S. Corbett, 1854–1922: Historian of British Maritime Policy from Drake to Jellicoe* (London: Royal Historical Society, 1981), is essential. In addition, Azar Gat, *The Development of Military Thought: The Nineteenth Century* (Oxford: Clarendon Press, 1992), 204–25, is characteristically acute. If Corbett is judged, rightly I believe, to be the finest maritime theorist of all time in terms of intellectual merit, his American contemporary Alfred Thayer Mahan, with his focus on the battle fleet, enjoyed the greater measure of contemporary fame and influence. However, Mahan's stock did sink precipitately, much as had that of his mentor in theory, Antoine Henri de Jomini, and for much the same reason. A radically changing strategic context appeared to render Mahan's views irrelevant to the challenges of the day. Nevertheless, having suffered an eclipse for many decades, he found a worthy champion in the hugely scholarly person of Jon Tetsuro Sumida in the 1990s. See his boldly innovative study, *Inventing Grand Strategy and Teaching Command: The Classic Works of Alfred Thayer Mahan Reconsidered* (Baltimore: Johns Hopkins University Press, 1997). Also see Gat, *Development of Military Thought*, 174–204. Gat's assessments of Corbett and Mahan need to be read in tandem, as they are placed in his book. As for Mahan's own writings, they are voluminous, and to the best of my knowledge Sumida is the only historian who claims to have read them all, including the Correspondence. See Sumida's listing of the Mahanian *oeuvre*, *Inventing Grand Strategy*, 119–21. As an entrée to the Mahanian canon, the prime selection is unavoidable: *The Influence of Sea Power upon History, 1660–1783* (1890; London, Methuen, 1965).

8. Martin van Creveld attracts the adjectives brilliant and controversial in equal measure: the two descriptors are probably stapled together unavoidably. Over the course of thirty years, he has written a succession of highly original military historical studies, each of which has made a lasting mark on scholarly debate and understanding. See his books:

Supplying War: Logistics from Wallenstein to Patton (Cambridge: Cambridge University Press, 1977); *Command in War* (Cambridge, MA: Harvard University Press, 1985); and *Technology and War: From 2000 B. C. to the Present* (New York: Free Press, 1989). These are frontier works, and even beyond. For example, it is no mean achievement to write an exciting controversial book of historical case studies on logistics. However, van Creveld's claim to fame as a strategic, almost an anti-strategic, theorist rests principally upon two books in which he challenges head-on the assumption that is most fundamental to the Clausewitzian paradigm of war and warfare. He dares to argue against the thesis that war is an instrument of policy, a means to an end. This is both apostasy and heresy from a distinguished military historian and sometimes insightful interpreter of Clausewitz. See his more radical studies: *The Transformation of War* (New York: Free Press, 1991), and *The Culture of War* (New York: Ballantine Books, 2008).

9. 'Classic Ground', *The Times* (London), editorial, 17 October 2009, 2.
10. There is much to recommend the view expressed by Ken Booth and Eric Herring in their speedy history of modern strategic studies, when they write: 'For many years strategic studies in the nuclear age was something that was done rather than written about.' *Keyguide to Information Sources in Strategic Studies* (London: Mansell Publishing, 1994), 16.
11. See Colin S. Gray, *Strategic Studies and Public Policy: The American Experience* (Lexington, KY: University Press of Kentucky, 1982); Brodie, *War and Politics*, chs. 9–10; and Lawrence Freedman, *The Evolution of Nuclear Strategy*, 3rd edn. (Basingstoke, UK: Palgrave Macmillan, 2003).
12. Martin van Creveld raises the interesting question of 'whether military experience is or is not essential in writing about war and its history'. *Culture of War*, 180.
13. Brodie, *War and Politics*, esp. 475.
14. In his tour de force, *The Face of Battle* (London: Jonathan Cape, 1976), John Keegan somewhat startled the military history profession by reminding it that individual soldiers 'did' their history, but, alas, he had little impact upon the mainstream of strategic studies. From time to time Keegan has betrayed an uncertain grasp of the meaning and functions of strategy and strategic theory. This is not to deny that his anti-strategic bias, though apt to encourage him unwisely to discard the strategy baby with the bathwater of depersonalized 'strategese' or perhaps 'strategism'—to coin neologisms for unsound writing on strategy—can serve a useful intellectual purpose in jolting unduly settled minds and approaches. In his book, *The Mask of Command* (New York: Viking Penguin, 1987), Keegan writes, tantalizingly, that 'I am increasingly tempted towards the belief that there is no such thing as "strategy" at all, and that international relations and military affairs would prove more manageable callings if it could be banished from their vocabularies', 7.
15. Keegan, *Mask of Command*, 3.
16. Ibid. 2.
17. For John Keegan's distinctly unsound assault upon Clausewitz, see *A History of Warfare* (London: Hutchinson, 1993), 16–28; and *War and Our World: The Reith Lectures, 1998* (London: Hutchinson, 1998). In the latter work, Keegan disdained intellectual restraint when he claimed that '[t]he success with which it [the First French Republic: CSG] waged ideological war prompted the Prussian soldier, Carl von Clausewitz, to promulgate the most pernicious philosophy of war making yet conceived', 42. Keegan translates Clausewitz's thesis that war is a continuation of policy by other means as the claim that 'war, in short, is a value-free activity, outside the moral sphere; but the implication is that politics is too . . .' He proceeds to explain that

'I call Clausewitz pernicious because his political philosophy underlies that of the totalitarian state'. Keegan's evidence for this potent claim is that 'the state's use of force works in a continuum that begins with the punishment of its own citizens who defy its interests. Therefore, nothing can or should restrain the state's right to act violently except the threat of superior violence in return', 47. By way of icing on the poisoned cake, Keegan reminds us, accurately enough, that his '[Clausewitz's: CSG] is the only name mentioned in Hitler's political testament', Ibid. Readers of *War and Our World* also will be told that Clausewitz 'was polluting civilised thought [in the 1810s and 1820s: CSG]', 43. Suitable commentary is provided in Christopher Bassford, 'John Keegan and the Grand Tradition of Trashing Clausewitz', *War in History*, 1 (November 1994), 319–36. See also Bassford's valuable comprehensive study, *Clausewitz in English: The Reception of Clausewitz in Britain and America* (New York: Oxford University Press, 1994).

18. Gary Mead, *The Good Soldier: The Biography of Douglas Haig* (London: Atlantic Books, 2008), 394–5. A far less generous view of Haig's role and competence is taken in J. P. Harris, *Douglas Haig and the First World War* (Cambridge: Cambridge University Press, 2008). Harris notes dismissively that '[t]he fact that for most of the period 18–22 October Haig was absent [at home and in London: CSG] from GHQ while campaigning was in full swing is indicative of the extent to which his GHQ staff and the armies could now run the war without him', 509.

19. Mead, *Good Soldier*, 343.

20. Ibid.

21. On the seductions and alleged consequences of Haig's somewhat enforced style of château generalship, see Keegan, *Mask of Command*, 333–5.

22. This elementary point, which is easy enough to explain logically and to illustrate by historical example, possibly is so simple that it escapes general notice. As a careful strategic theorist, J. C. Wylie does provide the necessary caveat, though I believe he could have made the warning stronger. Having defined strategy well enough, indeed better, as '[a] plan of action designed in order to achieve some end . . .' he moves on prudently to acknowledge that '[o]ne can concede readily that it is possible to prepare a plan for doing something with only a vague notion of what the result will be—too many men have done that too often for any of us to believe otherwise—but I do contend that it would be a very difficult job indeed adequately to assess the validity of any strategy without a rather clear appreciation of its purpose.' *Military Strategy: A General Theory of Power Control* (1967; Annapolis, MD: Naval Institute Press, 1989), 14, 15.

23. The leading works of theory on counter-insurgency (COIN) have been authored by soldiers, regular or—rarely—wartime temporary. See David Galula, *Counterinsurgency Warfare: Theory and Practice* (1964; Westport, CT: Praeger Security International, 2006); John A. Nagl, *Learning to Eat Soup with a Knife: Counterinsurgency Lessons from Malaya and Vietnam* (Chicago: University of Chicago Press, 2005); and David Kilcullen, *The Accidental Guerrilla: Fighting Small Wars in the Midst of a Big One* (London: C. Hurst, 2009). Galula was a lieutenant colonel in the French Army, Nagl was a lieutenant colonel in the American, and Kilcullen was a lieutenant colonel in the Australian. The understandable, if not entirely fortunate, military dominion over COIN theory may be gauged from US Army and US Marine Corps, *Counterinsurgency Field Manual: U. S. Army Field Manual No. 3–24, and Marine Corps Warfighting Publication No. 3–33.5* (Chicago, IL: University of Chicago Press, 2007), esp. 391–5

(annotated bibliography); Ian F. W. Beckett, *Modern Insurgencies and Counter-Insurgencies: Guerrillas and Their Opponents Since 1750* (London: Routledge, 2001), which succeeds admirably in being both historically broad as well as deep in analysis and understanding; and Daniel Marston and Carter Malkesian, eds., *Counterinsurgency in Modern Warfare* (Oxford: Osprey Publishing, 2008), which also is first rate, though it sacrifices some desirable depth in the interest of historical breadth. COIN is a security challenge that attracts many fallacies, two among which merit special notice. First, while there is a canon of sound precepts that apply to all COIN cases, it is a serious mistake to believe that the practices that yielded success in one COIN episode can serve reliably as a template for others. Second, although it is true to claim that COIN must not be planned and executed as a military campaign alone, it is a grave, indeed it is a lethal, error to underestimate the significance of COIN's necessary military dimension. Military success, in isolation, cannot win a COIN endeavour, but persisting military failure assuredly will lose it. The local populace cannot afford to back a military loser.

24. When professional military persons introduce a strategist as a 'defence intellectual', or an 'academic strategist', the intention usually is to express disdain, not to flatter. The adjective employed might as well have been 'armchair', for the full ironic treatment.

25. Clausewitz, 607.

26. Ibid. 610.

27. Eliot A. Cohen quoted in Thomas E. Ricks, *The Gamble: General Petraeus and the Untold Story of the American Surge in Iraq, 2006–8* (London: Allen Lane, 2009), 99. Also see Cohen, *Supreme Command: Soldiers, Statesmen, and Leadership in War* (New York: Free Press, 2002).

28. Ricks, *Gamble*, 92.

29. Gérard Chaliand, ed., *The Art of War in World History: From Antiquity to the Nuclear Age* (Berkeley, CA: University of California Press, 1994), 125.

30. Theatre strategy is a concept approved in Luttwak, *Strategy*, chs. 8–10, a fact which, admittedly, stands in its favour. The idea of strategy fit for purpose in a particular geographical domain does make sense, of course.

31. See, for example, Bob Breen and Greg McCauley, *The World Looking over Their Shoulders: Australian Strategic Corporals on Operations in Somalia and East Timor*, Study Paper 314 (Canberra: Land Warfare Studies Centre, August 208). The concept of the 'strategic corporal' was first popularized by US Marine Corps Commandant, General Charles C. Krulak in 'The Strategic Corporal: Leadership in the Three Block War', *Marine Corps Gazette*, 83 (1999), 18–22.

32. See J. F. C. Fuller, *The Generalship of Ulysses S. Grant* (London: John Murray, 1929); and Keegan, *Mask of Command*, ch. 3.

33. Carlo D'Este, *Eisenhower: A Soldier's Life* (New York: Henry Holt, 2002), ch. 6–8, is outstanding. D'Este's military biographical oeuvre, comprising his triptych on Patton, Eisenhower, and Churchill, elevate him to the enviable status of leading military biographer of our time.

34. Mead, *Good Soldier*, esp. 350–1.

35. An exceptionally fine explanation of the grim context for the exercise of generalship in 1914–18 is John Terraine, 'The Substance of the War', in Hugh Cecil and Peter H. Liddle, eds., *Facing Armageddon: The First World War Experienced* (London: Leo Cooper, 1996), ch. 1.

36. The combat performance of the US Army in Europe in 1944–5 improved into a zone of more than adequacy, but as a broad judgement it was poorly or averagely

commanded and much of it was not well led. Before I am accused of patriotic bias, I must hasten to add that a similar assessment applies to the British Army in those campaigns (Italy and France, the Low Countries, and Germany). One cannot doubt that the armies of the Western Allies were commanded and fought well enough to satisfy the needs of high policy, but it is difficult to be more positive than that. While the American and British armies of the Second World War cannot be confused with the greatest fighting forces of all time, it is well to remember that the *Wehrmacht* was indeed the enemy from hell. For a sporting analogy that British readers will appreciate, to fight the Germans is, more accurately was, akin to playing cricket against Australians. To beat Germany in war, one needed both to be competent and to enjoy large advantages for which the Germans lacked adequate compensation. The same judgement applies to playing cricket against Australia. And in both cases some luck is required also. It is sobering to note what hard work the Western Allies made of their land campaigns in Europe in 1945, when the bulk of the enemy's forces were deployed on the Eastern Front. Time after time I have needed to lay emphasis upon the fact that war is a duel. An important reason why Western Allied land power (and its joint air power) in Europe did not glitter with military distinction in 1944–5, was because of the potency of the enemy's combat performance. The Germans were still militarily formidable in 1944–5, despite the massive attrition they had already suffered, and despite the dysfunctionality of their High Command under the *Führer's* less than well inspired leadership. It is a general truth that the enemy determines how competent you need to be, but also—alas—how good you are able to be. Unsurprisingly, a rather more favourable assay of American military performance is offered in the excellent American authored study by Williamson Murray and Allan R. Millett, *A War to Be Won: Fighting the Second World War* (Cambridge, MA: Harvard University Press, 2000). Also unsurprising is the critical, but strategically not unempathetic, assessment in Max Hastings, *Armageddon: The Battle for Germany, 1944–45* (London: Macmillan, 2004), with which this Anglo-American strategist generally is in accord. In addition, the following provide some useful historical breadth and depth: Michael D. Doubler, *Closing with the Enemy: How GIs Fought the War in Europe, 1944–1945* (Lawrence, KS: University Press of Kansas, 1994); David French, *Raising Churchill's Army: The British Army and the War against Germany, 1919–1945* (Oxford: Oxford University Press, 2000); and Timothy Harrison Place, *Military Training in the British Army, 1940–1944: From Dunkirk to D-Day* (London: Frank Cass, 2000).

37. The abominable wording, if not concept, of the 'strategic moment' periodically reappears to blight scholarship, commentary, and policymaking. This is simply yet another abuse of the strategic adjective, in this case meaning unusually important. Presumably if we can find ourselves embarrassed, or perhaps blessed, by the extraordinary dilemmas and high opportunities gifted by one of history's 'strategic moments', logically there ought to be a host of merely 'tactical' and up the scale, 'operational moments' also. Whether or not the concept is a nonsense, and the matter can be argued either way, assuredly it is a crime against conceptual discipline so to deploy the adjective 'strategic'.

38. This is somewhat contestable scholarly terrain, though the ever renewed lively debate among historians largely has been confined to the issue of how well, and poorly, the generals and their unfortunate armies performed, given the fact that in 1917 they were seeking to support and realize a policy goal of total victory that was well beyond military reach that year. The literature is vast, but see: Robert B. Asprey, *The German High Command at War: Hindenburg and Ludendorff and the First World War* (Boston:

Little, Brown, 1993); Holger H. Herwig, *The First World War: Germany and Austria-Hungary, 1914–1918* (London: Arnold, 1997), chs. 8 and 9; Peter H. Liddle, ed., *Passchendaele in Perspective: The Third Battle of Ypres* (London: Leo Cooper, 1997); Mead, *Good Soldier*, ch. 11; and Harris, *Douglas Haig and the First World War*, chs. 11–15.

39. Clausewitz, 608.

40. Robert Lyman, *The Generals: From Defeat to Victory, Leadership in Asia, 1941–45* (London: Constable, 2008), 341 (emphasis in the original).

41. See Nagl, *Learning to Eat Soup with a Knife*, for a comparative study of the British and American armies as 'learning' institutions.

42. The vital concept of commander's intent is explained briefly and effectively in Paul K. Van Riper, *Planning for and Applying Military Force: An Examination of Terms* (Carlisle, PA: Strategic Studies Institute, US Army War College, March 2006), 10–13.

43. Holger H. Herwig, '*Geopolitik:* Haushofer, Hitler and Lebensraum', in Colin S. Gray and Geoffrey Sloan, eds., *Geopolitics, Geography and Strategy* (London: Frank Cass, 1999), 218–41. See Hans W. Weigert, *Generals and Geographers* (New York: Oxford University Press, 1942).

44. Clausewitz, 104.

45. Transcript of 'Slaughter at Omaha Beach', Sky tv Military History Channel, 11 December 2008, 8–9. Sewelow's exemplary conduct should be regarded in the historical context of a German anti-invasion garrison army, especially those infantry divisions deployed expendably right on the coast, whose morale was not officially assessed as high. The semi-official German history of the Second World War offers this judgement on the general condition of the army: 'For a whole series of reasons, the combativeness of the individual units [in early 1944: CSG] was also much lower than in the early years of the war'; and 'most divisions stationed there [in the West] had been formed from disparate remnants of other units. As a result, their troops had widely varying combat experience, and—if only because of their heterogeneous age structure—it was hard for them to recapture the fighting spirit of earlier years.' Horst Boog, Gerhard Krebs, and Detlef Vogel, *Germany and the Second World War: vol. vii, The Strategic Air War in Europe and the War in the West and East Asia, 1943–1944/5* (Oxford: Clarendon Press, 2006), 546. See also Antony Beevor, *D-Day: The Battle for Normandy* (London: Viking, 2009), ch. 7, esp. 112–13. One cannot help but observe that if the German defence of Normandy in the summer of 1944 was the product of a somewhat demoralized, far from elite—except for the Panzer and paratroop divisions—army, far advanced in its decline, the Allies would have stood little chance of success against the enemy at an earlier date.

46. Major (Paul) Grauwin, *Doctor at Dien-Bien-Phu* (London: Hutchinson, 1955), 204.

47. Ibid. 205. For some detail on Grauwin, a reserve major who was flown into the fortress, the '*base aero-terrestre*', on 21 December 1953 as head of the Twenty-Ninth Mobile Surgical Team, see Martin Windrow, *The Last Valley: Dien Bien Phu and the French Defeat in Vietnam* (London: Weidenfeld and Nicolson, 2004), 340–1, 674–5 n72.

48. Windrow, *Last Valley*, 630. Twenty-one years later, history would repeat itself, with only the identity of the betraying polity changed.

49. Clausewitz, 184.

50. Ibid. 185.

51. Joseph T. Glatthaar, *General Lee's Army: From Victory to Collapse* (New York: Free Press, 2008), 266–7.

52. On the important concept of fighting power, see Martin van Creveld, *Fighting Power: German and U. S. Army Performance, 1939–1945* (Westport, CT: Greenwood Press, 1982). Some readers may prefer the somewhat competing concept of military effectiveness to fighting power. For the latter, see Williamson Murray, *German Military Effectiveness* (Baltimore: The Nautical and Aviation Publishing Company of America, 1992), esp. ch. 1. Murray also was key to the organization of a seminal three volume study of the subject. See Allan R. Millett and Murray, eds., *Military Effectiveness, 3 vols: The First World War, The Interwar Period,* and *The Second World War* (Boston: Allen and Unwin, 1988). For some rigorous, albeit highly contestable, analysis of the baseline concept of military power itself, see Stephen Biddle, *Military Power: Explaining Victory and Defeat in Modern Battle* (Princeton, NJ: Princeton University Press, 2004). Conceptual and analytical battle over Biddle's theory was joined productively in the less than dazzled cluster of essays, 'Military Power: A Roundtable Review', *Journal of Strategic Studies*, 28 (June 2005), 413. Poor Professor Biddle did not escape unwounded from debate with an élite team of scholars: Eliot A. Cohen, Lawrence Freedman, Michael Horowitz and Stephen Rosen, and Martin van Creveld.

53. See the fine discussion in Kevin W. Farrell, 'Culture of Confidence: The Tactical Excellence of the German Army of the Second World War', in Christopher Kolenda, ed., *Leadership: The Warrior's Art* (Carlisle, PA: Army War College Foundation Press, 2001), ch. 10.

54. This figure is reported in Keegan, *Mask of Command*, 300.

55. Ibid. 333–6, is outstanding on 'château generalship'.

56. Dennis Showalter says of Rommel's crossing of the Meuse, '[f]or the next couple [of] hours, the verifiable record reads like something out of a comic book'. *Patton and Rommel: Men of War in the Twentieth Century* (New York: Berkeley Caliber, 2005), 179. Whether by calculation or educated instinct—the classic *coup d'oeil*—Rommel, a supreme tactician and tactical leader, provided what Keegan so aptly calls 'the imperative of example'. He advises persuasively that '[t]he first and greatest imperative of command is to be present in person. Those who impose risk must be seen to share it, and expect that their orders will be obeyed only as long as command's lesser imperatives require that they shall'. *Mask of Command*, 329. Alexander the Great, Julius Caesar, and Erwin Rommel all understood the necessity for (highly dangerous) personal example.

57. Clausewitz, 119.

58. Donald Jagoe, 'United States Naval Doctrine and Professional Military Education', in Michael Duffy, Theo Farrell, and Geoffrey Sloan, eds., *Doctrine and Military Effectiveness*, Strategic Policy Studies 1 (Exeter: Strategic Policy Studies Group of the Britannia Royal Naval College and Exeter University, 1997), 30 (emphasis in the original).

59. Douglas Waller, *A Question of Loyalty* (New York: Harper Perennial, 2004), 363–4.

60. French, *Raising Churchill's Army*, ch. 8.

61. Instinctual knowledge should not be confused with a raw uneducated instinct. Even outstanding natural gifts can be augmented by lifelong learning. It is worth reflecting on these apposite words by Carlo D'Este: 'Patton was an authentic and flamboyant military genius whose entire life was spent in preparation for a fleeting opportunity to become one of the great captains of history. No soldier in the annals of the U. S. Army ever worked more diligently to prepare himself for high command than did Patton. However, it was not only his astonishing breadth of professional reading and writing that separated Patton from his peers, but that intangible, instinctive sense of what must be done in the heat and chaos of battle: in short, that special genius for war that

has been granted to only a select few, such as Robert E. Lee and German Field Marshal Erwin Rommel. Who but Patton would have tramped the back roads of Normandy in 1913 with a Michelin map to study the terrain because he believed he would someday fight a map battle there?' *A Genius for War: A Life of George S. Patton*, vol. 1 (London: Harper Collins Publishers, 1995), 3–4. Even genius can benefit from careful preparation. It so happens that Field Marshal Sir Henry Wilson, when Director of Military Operations before the Great War, had bicycled up and down the Franco-Belgian frontier, for precisely the reason that Patton was busy doing likewise in 1913.

62. Since Great Captains require the assistance of some approximation to Great Armies, it is advisable for scholars of strategy not to neglect the 'sword' that the strategist has available to wield. Just as Field Marshal Herbert Lord Kitchener was right in his assertion that '[w]e cannot make war as we ought, we can only make it as we can', so we could assert as a complementary maxim that 'sometimes we must fight with the army that we have, and not with the army we would like to command'. Kitchener is quoted in Terraine, 'Substance of the War', 14. The following writings are exceptionally helpful in understanding the roles and importance of military doctrine; Yehoshafat Harkabi, *Theory and Doctrine in Classical and Modern Strategy*, Working Papers 35 (Washington, DC: Wilson Center, Smithsonian Institution, 30 October 1981); Barry R. Posen, *The Sources of Military Doctrine: France, Britain, and Germany between the World Wars* (Ithaca, NY: Cornell University Press, 1984); Duffy, Farrell, and Sloan, eds., *Doctrine and Military Effectiveness*; John Gooch, ed., *The Origins of Contemporary Doctrine*, The Occasional 30 (Camberley: Strategic and Combat Studies Institute, September 1997); and Harold R. Winton, 'An Imperfect Jewel: Military Theory and the Military Profession', paper presented to the Society for Military History Annual Conference, Bethesda, MD, 22 May 2004; Holley, *Technology and Military Doctrine*; US Army and Marine Corps, *Counterinsurgency Field Manual*, is an example of functional doctrine.

63. Superior treatments of Roman strategy include Alvin Bernstein, 'The strategy of a warrior-state: Rome and the wars against Carthage, 264–201 B.C.', in Williamson Murray, MacGregor Knox, and Bernstein, eds., *The Making of Strategy: Rulers, States, and War* (Cambridge: Cambridge University Press, 1994), 56–84; and Adrian Goldsworthy, *The Roman Army at War, 100BC–AD200* (Oxford: Oxford University Press, 1996). Goldsworthy issues a useful warning against anachronistic interpretation of Roman strategy, 76–8.

64. Gary Gallagher, *The Confederate War* (Cambridge, MA: Harvard University Press, 1997), concludes fairly persuasively that '[t]he final failure [of the Confederacy: CSG] lay not so much with Confederate strategy as with the men available to Davis to carry it out', 153. Because of the large asymmetry in resources between the belligerents, the South was unequally vulnerable to the damage wrought by poor generalship. Unfortunately for the Confederate States of America (CSA), once one allows for the typical, though not invariable, excellence of Robert E. Lee and Thomas 'Stonewall' Jackson, Lee was lethally short of excellence in command among his principal lieutenants. Also, as 'Stonewall's' sad case illustrates all too poignantly, battlefield leadership, even for generals, was a dangerous occupation in America from 1861–5. The excellence of Lee and, for a while, of 'Stonewall', eventually was matched well enough by Lincoln's elevation of Ulysses S. Grant and his protégé, William Tecumseh Sherman. Indeed, the South on balance was overmatched, given Stonewall's death by 'friendly fire' at the Battle of Chancellorsville on 2 May (d. 10 May) 1863.

65. It is too early at this time of writing to identify reliable analyses of, let alone judgements on, the US-led strategic adventures in Afghanistan and Iraq in the 2000s. However, the following three books on the Iraq imbroglio appear to have exceptional merit: Stephen Metz, *Iraq and the Evolution of American Strategy* (Washington, DC: Potomac Books, 2008), which is as scholarly as one can ask of a current history; and two outstanding works by journalist Thomas E. Ricks, *Fiasco: The American Military Adventure in Iraq* (New York: Penguin Press, 2006), and *Gamble.*

66. Luttwak, *Strategy.* To the best of my knowledge, only Antulio J. Echevarria, *Clausewitz and Contemporary War* (Oxford: Oxford University Press, 2007), 197 n5, among contemporary strategic theorists has ventured even to suggest scepticism over strategy's allegedly paradoxical nature.

67. See Karl-Heinz Frieser, *The Blitzkrieg Legend: The 1940 Campaign in the West* (Annapolis, MD: Naval Institute Press, 2005), 349–53.

68. Echevarria, *Clausewitz and Contemporary War,* 118.

69. Clausewitz, 88–9.

70. See Stephen Peter Rosen, 'Vietnam and the American Theory of Limited War', *International Security,* 7 (fall 1982), 83–113.

71. I have fished in the conceptually murky waters of advantage, success, and victory, in my *National Security Dilemmas: Challenges and Opportunities* (Washington, DC: Potomac Books, 2009), ch. 2.

72. David Petraeus quoted in Ricks, *Gamble,* 129.

Part III

Context and Purpose

7

Conclusion: Bandit Country and the Strategist's Quest for Control

THE STRATEGIST AS HERO

With undergoverned space as its context, the purpose of strategy is to secure control of that turbulent zone. More often than history books recognize, the political and military battlespace for the strategist is, or certainly approaches, a condition of chaos. The master theme of this book, sometimes explicit, more often just implicit, is the struggle by the strategist to devise, sustain, and satisfactorily conclude purposeful behaviour. I dare not risk the hubris shown by T. E. Lawrence with his subtitle, 'A Triumph', to *Seven Pillars of Wisdom*.[1] But, throughout the text, and most especially in these concluding pages, I do intend to signal some satisfaction with strategists' achievements, performances frequently conducted in the face of heavy odds against success. The subtitle which opens this conclusion, 'the strategist as hero' comes close to saying it all. Whether or not strategists are heroes, there are grounds for doubt. However, there is little room for scepticism over the proposition that the strategist's profession is a heroic one, so many and potentially damaging are the impediments even to adequate, let alone superior, strategic accomplishment.

One can photograph an army, but not the strategy that seeks to direct it. One can have paintings of Carl von Clausewitz, but not of his theory. Strategy is ethereal. It can be explained and understood, but in common with love, happiness, pain, fear, or security, for example, it cannot be represented directly. Its presence or absence, as well as its quality, can be inferred from behaviour as registered in the course of events, but then only if there is a plausible connection between known intention and that record. It is notable that the media, print and especially electronic, do not often try to address strategy. Rare indeed are the books on 'great, or poor, strategists', while the television channels that provide vicarious military excitement for armchair warriors, almost go out of their way to avoid discussing strategy. When, rarely, strategy is the subject, more often than not one finds that the programme limits its ambition to coverage of operational level effort. One must sympathize. The medium, be it printed text, film, or PowerPoint, has a way of commanding its subject more than it ought. And, of course, one should not forget the client. Publishers can sell books about famous generals or admirals, but not about little known strategists (e.g. Nelson but not John Jervis, Montgomery but not Alanbrooke, or Patton but not Marshall). Strategy is a familiar word, and is widely believed to be important, but it is barely comprehended. Indeed, even today it is little understood that the concept commonly is wrongly identified and the word, especially the adjective, is misapplied. There is all too little that can be done to raise strategy's profile, to render it better understood, or even to help enable would-be strategists perform the strategic function better. However, what little might be done at least should be attempted; hence this book.

For reasons that we have sought to make clear, strategy is as important as unquestionably it is awesomely difficult to do well enough. The substantive title of this conclusion is not a casual choice. Only rarely are medals for outstanding performance in strategy won easily. The subject truly is challenging and the strategist's role, properly understood, should be recognized as heroic. To be performed well, its multiple demands require extraordinary natural gifts, advantages that need nurturing by education and experience. That granted, successful strategic conduct should not be so difficult as to evade plausible explanation. The body of the text must speak for itself, but it is necessary to extract from the analysis some major positive claims that comprise the core of the argument, as well as to strike some cautionary notes. Together, arguments and cautions may help explain how theory and practice in actuality are a unity, even though in principle they are clearly distinguishable. Not only is strategic practice directed and misdirected by the application of strategic theory; in addition it is accurate to claim that nearly always there is theory lurking in disguise and as practice. The only exception is the category of purposeless violence known as expressive. In order to attempt this mission, six broad, more than a little compounded and generally positive claims are assessed. These are succeeded by five cautions, or caveats, significant for both the theory and practice of strategy.

THE ARGUMENT

The Purpose of Strategy

De quoi s'agit-il?—'what is it (all) about?'—'what is the problem?' to borrow both from Marshal Ferdinand Foch and from Bernard Brodie who was not as empathic as he might have been to the thought and conduct of the French soldier-strategist.[2] If the strategist's most potent question is 'so what?', Foch's question must be directed at strategy itself. Strategy functions as the only purpose built bridge connecting political ends with the methods and means for their attempted achievement, most especially the military tools given the focus of this study. While the basic function of this metaphorical bridge necessarily is to connect, say, policy and army, the purpose for which this key task is performed is in order to achieve some degree of control over the polity's security context. Those holding the strategy bridge are charged, in effect, with the planning and higher orchestration of the policy instruments that in threat and action should impress themselves upon the bodies and minds of those who ought to be concerned by such behaviour. The strategist needs to be able to influence enemies, allies, and neutrals, which means minds and actions, foreign and domestic. To bend an enemy's will to resist, and if required to reduce his military means in their capacity to do harm, the strategist needs to seek control over the course of events. For this heroic task to be feasible, the strategist first must ensure that he controls his own capacity to reach out to do the harm he intends. This is the practice of command. Not for nothing is command twinned with control in the standard military formula. Indeed, so complementary are the two concepts that in effect 'command and control' are fused as a meta-concept, and might one day be melded into a single word. The purpose of command is to control friendly armed forces so that they can prevail in combat with an enemy whose strategists also are exercising command in search of control, in their case over us, so as to shape and even dictate the course of strategic history. This is what strategy is all about. This is the answer to Foch's fundamental question. But as we explain, the strategist as would-be controller of history is ever locked into a struggle against severe odds. The political-bureaucratic policymaking, the military execution, and the political consequences, of the strategy process in those distinctive but more than marginally temporally overlapping phases, always threaten to dissolve process into chaos. Preparation for war, as well as war itself and its warfare, inherently are hostile environments for what one might ironically term good order in strategy. Unfortunately for good predictive order, a disorder verging upon chaos is close to constituting the natural condition of war writ large and of its warfare, as well as being a constant menace to the invention, development, and execution of rational and reasonable strategy. The strategist must operate in 'bandit country', and that country has both domestic and foreign provinces. The enemy is apt to be the single largest factor among the problems that can frustrate the strategist with his preferred strategy. But a more than marginally dysfunctional policymaking process at home and among allies, and a much less than suitably tailored, razor-sharp military sword, will come close equal second.

Strategy and Strategies: Theory and Practice

It would be unwise, though not wholly implausible, to risk an unwelcome historical echo by declaiming for strategy what might read as a severely parsimonious declaration of faith: 'One theory, One theorist, One historical challenge!' Translated, this Trinitarian credo would claim that there is only one general theory of strategy; there is only one strategic theorist fully worthy of the job title; and there is only one set of strategic problems, eternally and universally. This extreme example of reductionism happens to be useful, because it does highlight two all but axiomatic truths, while it exaggerates a justifiable, though arguable claim. First, there has been, is, and can only be a single general theory of strategy. We are not at liberty to rearrange the law of strategy as though it were merely strategic lore. Different theorists will present this theory in ways that reflect the conditions unique to their historical context as well as their personalities, but nonetheless they must all paint pictures of the same essentially unchanging landscape. This thesis is a vital assumption; I contend that it is founded inductively, not only deductively.

Second, it is not wholly unreasonable to argue that the one general theory of strategy is located and explained well enough, albeit not ideally, by Carl von Clausewitz in *On War*. I do not—perhaps it would be more honest for me to admit that I no longer—endorse this judgement. However, it is entirely appropriate to record a massive, though not preclusive, note of confidence in Clausewitz's theorizing. Certainly there is scope for argument, but I am prepared to defend the claim that our general theory of strategy is to be found in ten books at most, and that these more or less canonical ten break fairly clearly into four categories of objective merit. Table 7.1 (and Appendix B) provides the details. Each of the nine authors additional to Clausewitz augments, enriches, and corrects the Prussian sufficiently to warrant the stamp of approval for membership in the classical elite. This is not to deny the widely varying merit among all these books, a fact that explains the hierarchy of categories.

Table 7.1 The Classics of General Strategic Theory[3]

1. **First Division**
   upper class
   Carl von Clausewitz, *On War* (1832–4)
   lower class
   Sun-Tzu, *The Art of War* (ca.490 BCE)
   Thucydides, *The Peloponnesian War* (ca. 400 BCE)

2. **Second Division**
   Niccolo Machiavelli, *The Art of War* (1521)
   The Prince (1522)
   Discourses on Livy (1531)
   Antoine Henri de Jomini, *The Art of War* (1838)
   Basil Liddell Hart, *Strategy: The Indirect Approach* (1941)
   J. C. Wylie, *Military Strategy: A General Theory of Power Control* (1967)
   Edward N. Luttwak, *Strategy: The Logic of War and Peace* (2001)

3. **Third Division**
   Bernard Brodie, (ed.), *The Absolute Weapon: Atomic Power and World Order* (1946)
   Strategy in the Missile Age (1959)
   War and Politics (1973)

4. **Fourth Division**
   Thomas C. Schelling, *The Strategy of Conflict* (1960)
   Arms and Influence (1966)

Other Contenders

Julius Caesar, *Commentaries* (d. 44 BCE)
Alfred Thayer Mahan, *The Influence of Sea Power upon History, 1660–1783* (1890)
Julian S. Corbett, *England in the Seven Years' War* (1907)
                    Some Principles of Maritime Strategy (1911)
J. F. C. Fuller, *Armament and History* (1946)
John R. Boyd, *A Discourse on Winning and Losing* (1987)
Martin van Creveld, *The Transformation of War* (1991)
                    The Culture of War (2008)

Note: Membership in the First Division is beyond sensible argument. The Second and Third Division entries are robust, though not entirely beyond contention. It should be well understood that the books cited in the Second and Third Divisions, as well as those by Other Contenders, with the exceptions of Julius Caesar (two books of Commentary) and J. C. Wylie, comprise but a small fraction of their authors' complete oeuvres. No doubt many readers will differ over my selection of some of the entries.

See Appendix B, for strategic theorists claimed here to have authored the classical canon of general strategic theory.

Third, it is reasonable, indeed strictly it is unavoidable, to argue that one general theory, and potentially even one general theorist, has eternal and universal validity because the fundamentals of strategic challenge do not alter. Each of the authors here identified speaks to the problems that every practising strategist has to solve, regardless of his circumstances and historical location. This is less true of Brodie's writings, but some of his strategic analyses, despite their period-piece Cold-War foci and flavour, nonetheless reflect an exceptional awareness of the general theory of strategy. For just one example, he contributed an excellent essay to the now standard English language version of Clausewitz's *On War*.[4]

It is vital to recognize the persisting authority of a single general theory of strategy, no matter that it is presented in various forms and styles. Such singularity has a fundamental authority over a vastly variable historical domain. This imperium, for that is its nature, the whole course of strategic history, witnesses the creation and execution of specific strategies keyed to command and control in unique strategic contexts. Thus, the realm of general strategic theory is unchanging, while that of the practicing executive strategist is always liable to alter by evolution and even revolution.

An important qualification to the argument advanced needs registration. There is an inescapable sense in which the apparently clear conceptual distinction between theory and practice may mislead. Although making and executing strategy as a plan for action lies, of course, within the realm of practice, every such plan inherently is a theory, paradoxical though this may seem at first glance. A strategy expressed in the form of a plan, formal or informal, must be a theory of victory, however defined for its historical context. This strategic plan or strategy, more or less detailed, more or less optimistic, predicts a desirable course of events. In effect, the plan, which is to say the strategy, explains how military, inter alia, success will be made to happen. It will specify, in whatever detail is appropriate for its level (overall military, operational, tactical), and in more or less discretionary terms, who will do what, with what, where it will be done, and when it will be done. The strategy may or may not explain why tasks are to be performed. Anchored in time, place, and hence strategic context, the pragmatic and responsible executive strategist is obliged to practice theory. To plan is to theorize. Theories appear in many guises, but nonetheless the practicable looking military solution to a pressing real-world problem is, in a vital sense, a theory. The practicing strategist must engage in 'if . . . then' logic and prediction. Strategy in action is all about the consequences of behaviour, and those consequences cannot be predicted with exactitude. The logic cannot be evaded; the executive strategist practises theory. How else can he reason? If military behaviour truly was bereft of strategic theoretical intention, then it could only be mere expressive violence. When committed by the military agents of polities great, small, or still aspirant, expressive violence at worst is a crime, at best is a strategic irrelevance.

Whereas all strategies are plans, not all plans are strategies. Military action may be guided by a plan, but the plan might simply direct forces to be used in a tactically effective manner, with no careful attempt to relate such intended use to the achievement of goals that have much operational, strategic, or political value. Many of strategic history's so-called war plans have been nothing of the kind. They can fail the strategy test in several ways. For example, they may be designed with no discernible ambition in mind more elevated than the intention to bring on a 'decisive' battle. In the best Napoleonic tradition one would manoeuvre in order to fight at an advantage. But this could be in the worst Napoleonic tradition of not having a clear idea how victory would conclude a war satisfactorily; just what would the purportedly decisive battle decide? For another class of example, armed forces can be committed to the fight in the absence of any reasonable expectation that the fight, no matter how well or poorly conducted, will achieve any positive result. An all too plain example of this second category of mainly expressive violence would be a large-scale bilateral nuclear war. Nuclear war plans, so-called, are a practical necessity, but in execution above a very modest level of well-calibrated fire power delivered for intended coercive effect, they must require destructive behaviour indulged for its own sake. In actuality, the use of nuclear weapons on a large scale would mean only that their owner could think of nothing else to do, even though such action could serve no strategic or political purposes. Of course, one might try to argue that an utterly astrategic revenge might be purpose enough, sought under the banner of a grim retributive justice.[5]

The literature on war planning is voluminous, but typically is so concerned to turn over every bureaucratic stone that as a result the plot at several levels often is lost.[6] The context for, and consequences of, specific cases of war planning have a way of evading the attention they merit. Furthermore, of particular moment for this text, the kind of professional expertise that deep knowledge of war planning experience both needs and attracts is not an expertise often inclined to spark creative theorizing by its owner. On the one hand, historical war planning experience is reasonably well understood by historians, but they tend to be professionally allergic to bold theorizing, including that with a strategic focus. On the other hand, our contemporary war planners, competent and even occasionally creative as they may be, are inhibited from contributing to the theory of strategy with respect to the role of planning both by the need for official secrecy, and by their own lack of professional proficiency in such theorizing. The predictable result of the situation just described is a strategic studies literature that is weak in its general understanding of the roles and significance of what, generically, has been known as war planning, though today often is called defence planning. Plans, formal and informal, explicit and implicit, are of crucial significance for the translation of politically guided, strategically educated, intention into military achievement. Boomerang-like via effects, in their several forms, the consequences of plans, which is to say actions, reverberate back to the political level. It is easy to see why the general theory of strategy, if it is to contribute usefully to the world of practice, requires competence in those who must translate the canon lore of general theory into actual historical planning agencies, processes, and instruments.

The Value of Strategic Theory

For many defence professionals, military and civilian, theory is a word and concept more likely to induce hostility, certainly indifference, than respect. Pragmatic strategists, their staffs, other advisors, and their executive agents in the military field can have no small difficulty grasping the connection between, say, most of Clausewitz's philosophizing about the nature of war and solutions to their own contemporary problems. Beatrice Heuser argues effectively that:

> In many respects, Clausewitz is thus providing something that few military practitioners seek. They tend to be in search of teachable and learnable rules of thumb that can be applied to a wide range of different situations, and can help them find short-cuts to decision-making in stressful combat situations. But, apparently alas Clausewitz mainly supplies philosophical reflections on the nature of war that are difficult to translate into simple, memorable prescriptions for action. He is not easily Powerpointable.[7]

Officials usually are not deeply interested in the nature of strategy. Instead, for example they need to know how best to bring down Hitler's Reich, or how best to invade his empire. Strategic philosophy can seem more useful for alleviating insomnia, or supporting a damaged table leg, than as a source of useful advice. The practical strategist, locked into a contextually unique challenge, will look in vain to the classics of strategic theory in his search for usable specific answers to very particular problems. In 1944, Dwight D. Eisenhower and his master commanders on the Combined Chiefs of Staff committee needed to decide how to win the war in the West in the context of the war(s) as a whole, European and Asian–Pacific. They could have found few usable particular answers in the pages of Sun Tzu, Thucydides, or Clausewitz. This is not to deny that the Chinese sage might have inspired their resort to exceptionally cunning plans, especially with regard to the potential value of deception.[8]

The general theory of strategy, however it is presented—mingled in a historical narrative (Thucydides), all but PowerPointed cryptically (Sun Tzu), or more than a little entangled in a somewhat challenging philosophical exposition (Clausewitz)—can only educate, it cannot instruct with specific advice for today. The general theory explains the nature of strategy everywhere, for all times, and for all conditions. What it can do, if its students are receptive, is so to educate practising executive strategists that they are mentally equipped to tackle their historically unique problems as well as they can be so enabled. In short, the practising strategist is taught, if he is reachable, how to think about, how to approach, his real-world challenges. By category, he knows what he needs to worry about and he understands, again by broad category, how he might succeed in evading or defeating many of the causes for his anxiety. Alert to both complexity and to the wholeness of his subject, the strategist also knows that the categories he employs to achieve some mental order all interpenetrate to help produce messily well-compounded strategic effects and consequences. Between high theory and command practice for and in combat lies the enabling agency of doctrine. Only the educated strategist can be trusted to develop the multi-level body of doctrine that must serve to staple together synergistically efforts in performance at every level of warfare.

Clausewitz, who else, provides thoroughly persuasive explanation of why theory has value for practice. In justly honoured language, we are advised that:

> Theory exists so that one need not start afresh each time sorting out the material and plowing through it but will find it ready to hand and in good order.[9]

He advises that 'theory need not be a positive doctrine, a sort of *manual* for action'. Rather, 'it is meant to educate the mind of the future commander, or more accurately, to guide him in his self-education, not to accompany him to the battlefield'.[10] In vigorous prose, Clausewitz makes an unanswerable case for strategic theory:

> Theory should cast a steady light on all phenomena so that we can more easily recognize and eliminate the weeds that spring from ignorance; it should show how one thing is related to another, and keep the important and unimportant separate . . . Theory cannot equip the mind with formulas for solving problems, nor can it mark the narrow path on which the sole solution is supposed to lie by planting a hedge of principles on either side. But it can give the mind insight into the great mass of phenomena and of their relationships, then leave it free to rise into the higher realms of action.[11]

No one has said it better; indeed it is hard to imagine how the merit in theory could be better explained, especially given the handicap to clarity inseparable from translation from the German. The case for general strategic theory is inscribed in the whole practice and malpractice of strategy throughout history. Theory requires clarity of definition, suitability of definition, and the specification of relationships among distinguishable elements in the structure of the subject. Also, not least, theory provides explanation of causation. When policymakers, soldiers, and commentators are ill educated in strategic theory, they misuse concepts and such misuse contributes readily to unsound planning and faulty behaviour. For a leading example, a fundamental lack of intellectual grip upon the distinctive natures of policy, strategy, and tactics licenses appalling self-harming misuse of the adjective strategic. If theory does not educate as to the difference between a policy instrument and that instrument itself, as, for a historical example, in the *Strategic* Air Command, or *strategic* missiles, or the *strategic* deterrent, then the strategy function is unlikely to be well served. If a particular military force is called strategic, an existential meaning of that force is asserted. Such a claim is a logical, and often will be a practical, absurdity. Since the behaviour of all troops has strategic consequences, be they ever so modest, it follows that the adjective is deprived of any sense.

By no means can the general theory of strategy provide all the education that a practising executive strategist requires and should be able to employ usefully. In addition to book-learnt theory, the strategist will be educated by professional enculturation, informal as well as formal, by personal experience, and by wider, extra-strategic learning. Probably the example of examples was the influence of Homer on Thucydides, and indeed on all Greeks of that period.[12] Whatever may be said in praise of the *Iliad* and the *Odyssey*, in the military dimension they are far more tactical than strategic. How much, how well, and what the strategist acquires by way of strategic education will depend considerably upon his biology, psychology, and the accidents of time and place that provided the unique contexts, perhaps the strategic moments, for his instruction. The strategist learns his strategy not only with reference to what the classics, and culture, and events, bring to him. As much, the strategist's education is shaped, even sometimes determined, by what the mind and body of the individual human being brings to the education on offer. It is agreeable to note that Clausewitz advises that:

> [theory] must also take the human factor into account, and find room for courage, boldness, even foolhardiness. The art of war deals with living and with moral forces. Consequently, it cannot attain the absolute, or certainty; it must always leave a margin for uncertainty, in the greatest things as much as in the smallest.[13]

Truly, these words should shake the confidence of theorists who seek to purvey a science of strategy. There continue to be theorists who believe that, for example, war's fog and friction can be dispersed and avoided by thoroughly reliable material means. Such foolish people fail, at least refuse, to recognize that the most significant dimension to the strategic function is the human. Moreover, a noteworthy aspect to this human dimension of difficulty and achievement is the adversary's nature and character.

Stripped to the barest, one can claim that strategic theory is an aid to clear, perhaps just clearer, thinking about all aspects of war and peace, nested in political and other contexts, domestic and foreign. In its general form, this theory provides clarity in definition, in identification of relationships, and in causation, which is to say in the crucial matter of consequences. In truth, strategic theory is not an optional extra. All practical strategists practice the theory of strategy. They differ only in the quality of their practice, a quality that most historical experience tries to tell us can and should owe much to strategic education.[14] All too naturally, there will always be ineducable strategists, just as there will be strategists who, in a vital sense, fail because their assignments are beyond possibility of successful completion. To this last point we need to add the thought, little comfort though it must provide, that the superior strategist for a failing cause may be able to lose more gracefully, less painfully, than would a less-skilled strategist. If one loses, but not very badly, let alone catastrophically, that verdict of the battlespace should be exploitable politically to improve the terms on which the conflict is settled. Moreover, the political outcome to a war, which after all is what the war in question must be about, need not reflect with entire accuracy the imbalance of net strategic advantage and disadvantage recorded in the actual warfare. For a somewhat contentious example, notwithstanding the dominant contemporary German assessment, the Versailles settlement of 1919 was by no means as draconian as the German military defeat might have licensed politically. The settlement was remarkable, though, in that it provided maximum offence to German opinion, thereby providing potent fuel for a rematch, without systematically weakening Germany in noteworthy measure.[15] Germany secured the armistice on 11 November 1918 not because of the strategic skills of its dysfunctional leadership, but rather because its army, demoralized and beaten though it was, could still have exacted a heavy tactical price upon the Allies should they have sought to proceed and conclude hostilities on German soil.

Strategy Is Possible, but Difficult

Strategy is not an illusion, a chimera.[16] However, it is so difficult to do well enough, let alone brilliantly, that a security community needs to provide some redundancy of high competence in the activities most vital to strategic performance in order to have to hand a reserve supply of strategists to replace those who appear to fail. This means that the strategist's role needs to be well supported by prudence in policy, efficiency in organizational system, method in process, and—last but not least—by effectiveness in the combat power available. The less prudent his policy guidance, the more constipated the organizational machinery of strategy-making and execution by the chain of command, and the less impressive the fighting power of his soldiers, the heavier the burdens that must be laid upon strategy and the strategist. More often than not, the contemporary strategist will lack a spark of genius sufficient to compensate, personally, for the multiple dysfunctionalities, the friction, that harass and inhibit his overall command performance.

The bad news for the would-be strategist is truly forbidding in severity, scope, and number. An adequate grasp of the range of difficulties by category for the strategist, cannot afford to note less than eight such. These can be summarized thus: (*a*) existential (misunderstanding of the nature and purpose of strategy); (*b*) the enemy (frequently neglected, almost invariably misassessed); (*c*) currency conversion (command performance as military events in the five geographies of battlespace need to be converted into strategic and then political consequences); (*d*) strategy-making (poor, even dysfunctional, organization and process for strategy-making); (*e*) human performance (reflecting the influences, not always positive, of culture, biology, psychology, and historical situation); (*f*) complexity (there are too many things that can go wrong for them all to be evaded); (*g*) friction (the mainly unknowable and unpredictable unknowns that can impair performance); and (*h*) civil–military relations (dysfunctional asymmetries among soldiers, politicians, and civil servants).

Each of the eight categories of problems for the strategist has the potential to harm his ability to perform the bridging function between policy and army. Some of the eight are well known and appreciated, but others merit more explicit recognition. For example, there continues to be an existential problem of understanding that hinders strategic performance. Rephrased, although strategic effect must be generated simply by the consequences of all tactical behaviour and misbehaviour, with or without much operational direction, a deficit in the grip needed for purposeful strategic command is apt to prove fatal in the waging of war as a whole. Tactically one may win, at least not lose, most of the warfare, yet because there was a strategy deficit the war must be lost. Examples abound. Napoleonic France; Imperial and Nazi Germany; France in Algeria; the United States in Vietnam; the United States and Britain in Iraq (2003–7); and the United States, Britain, and NATO in Afghanistan from 2001 to the present day. And these are just a handful of the cases of strategy deficiency syndrome (SDS) that all but beg for notice. It is hard to treat a malady of which one is unaware. An overconfident Napoleon was not aware of his failure to perform strategically. Similarly, America's Johnson administration behaved as if it was unaware of the need for a strategy bridge. It had policy goals in and connected to Southeast Asia, in fact it had too many such goals, and it waged warfare in abundance. But between politics-policy and tactics-operations there lurked an unrecognized black hole wherein strategy should have resided, provided by people holding the eponymous metaphorical bridge.

Since military behaviour always must have some strategic effect on the course of history, the absence of a strategy, a theory of victory in war worthy of the name, does not mean that that behaviour must lack strategic consequences. Far from it. For illustration of my claim one need look no further than to America's record of warfare waged tactically with adequate competence in Southeast Asia between 1965 and 1973, and the apparently paradoxically abysmal strategic and political result.[17] Parallel illustration is on offer with the French demonstration of its SDS in Algeria from 1954 to 1962.[18] Since history abhors a vacuum, the gap that the strategy bridge should span is filled by encroachment on the part of the political, operational, and tactical functions. Such mission creep may be characterized as the politicization and tacticization of strategy, though it might be more perceptive to recognize that enhanced roles for politics and tactics substitute for, rather than capture, strategy.[19] The strategy bridge cannot be seized by politics or by tactics (or operations). If the bridge is not manned by strategists it does not function, period.

It is important to be clear as to the inherent difficulty of purposeful strategic performance. It is no small task so to plan military operations that one should be able to control events militarily in such a way and to such a degree that the political future is shaped favourably. This strategic function necessarily entails prediction in the face of typically formidable problems. Moreover, ironically, if one succeeds militarily far beyond one's expectations—the Germans in May–June 1940, for example—the challenge is extreme in deciding how far, indeed how, to exploit such success. Again more than a little ironically, if one is dealt too weak a military hand to succeed tactically and operationally, strategic excellence may, or may not, be demonstrated in the way in which one copes with defeat.

Several senior American military professionals, whose names must be withheld in order to protect the guilty, have confided to this theorist an astrategic, bordering on an anti-strategic, proposition. They have suggested that when a country is so potent in the quantity and tactical effectiveness of its armed forces that it should always win the warfare, it has scant need for strategy. Rephrased, perform well enough tactically, and perhaps operationally, and strategy, as the necessary strategic effect, will take care of itself. This is a vintage misreading of Field Marshal Helmuth Graf von Moltke's expression of apparent disdain for strategy in favour of tactics.[20]

Of all the problems that beset the strategist, problems that usually cluster, compound, and fuel yet further difficulties, the super category of sheer complexity and consequent potential for multiple disharmonies warrant special mention. No matter how clearly the human actors leading a belligerent polity in war and warfare understand the essential unity of all their behaviours, the reality of performance on the different levels of conflict unavoidably promote what can be a lethal cumulative mega-disharmony. In theory, each of war's levels should complement each other. War is so much a gestalt that the relations among policy, grand strategy, military strategy, operations, and tactics need to be understood to be horizontal in their interdependencies, as well as vertical in their chain of command authority.[21] But each of these standard levels of behaviour has its own nature, reflected in unique dynamics, needs and concerns, inter alia. For example, tactical performance does not naturally serve operational design optimally. And operational success need not contribute to strategic achievement in a way at all proportionate to its costs. For a capstone negative, we have to note that even a conflict strategically well, certainly eventually well enough, conducted, might not be succeeded by a stable political order. When military and strategic performances retire from centre stage, largely to be replaced by active diplomacy (and relevant domestic politics), there will be no guarantee that the blood and treasure expended will be cashed competently by the politicians. Tolerable harmony among the levels of a polity or coalition's effort in conflict has to be made to happen, but such harmonization will never be a natural process that can safely be left to some hidden hand of history that functions on autopilot.

Incredibly, purposeful centralized strategy does function in practice, though rarely as well as in theory; not always and rarely elegantly, but frequently well enough. How can this be, given the problems that can and do threaten to render it irrelevant or worse? Several answers are necessary. One could emphasize the human dimension; the ever repeated fact of human ability to rise to meet extraordinary challenges adequately. This crucial point, and its limitations, is discussed below. For now it can suffice to cite and lay emphasis upon just two broad reasons why strategy is not an illusion. Fortunately, they can be stated simply, though they do appear historically in all but infinite specific variety.

First, every category of difficulty that in principle must threaten to defeat a belligerent strategically, also must menace its enemy, likewise in principle. One can hardly repeat too often the grossly reductionist Clausewitzian mantra that 'war is nothing but a duel on a larger scale'.[22] There is no need to excel strategically in order to win a war or succeed in competition. Rather is there need only to perform to better net strategic effect than does the enemy. Second, war's very complexity contains within its diversity the possibilities of compensation for particular failures and weaknesses. Provided a competitive weakness is not unduly imperial in domain and severity, a catastrophic collapse in the morale of the polity's main army—for example the Italian army at and following the disastrous battle of Caporetto (24 October–12 November 1917)—fungibility may be commanded to ride to the rescue.[23] For a while the US Navy loses its battle-line in the Pacific because of the tactical loss at Pearl Harbor, so the fleet aircraft carriers must step up to take the strain. Of course, there will be occasions when no compensation fit for purpose can be located and applied. However, not for nothing is the strategist's second master question 'what are the alternatives?' The first question, we should recall, is 'so what?' The US Navy in 1941–2 did not answer the second of the strategist's questions by refraining from offensive action pending the restoration to health of its battleship inventory in the Pacific.

Strategists, Command, and Strategic Effect

With what may seem to be tedious regularity, this text has striven never to lose the central plot, the master narrative, of strategy. So, yet again we claim that: for political reasons strategy provides the bridge between policy goals and policy instruments, and it is held by strategists who seek by their command performance to secure the strategic effect necessary for victory, success, advantage, or the limitation of damage (select the preferred language). The strategy bridge, like Florence's Ponte Vecchio, can carry many buildings (as well as, incredibly, a secret tunnel), but it is the human strategist, singular or plural, who must make the bridge work. Strategist is a familiar informal job descriptor, but it is both rare for it to be explicit as a job title, or, rarer still, for all of its necessary roles, and the essential connections among them, to be recognized adequately. There is, and can be, no template for strategist, because political, social-cultural, and technological, inter alia, contexts drive the historically specific detail. Nonetheless, we can identify with confidence a completely standard set of distinguishable roles that always need to be performed if purposeful centralized strategy is to be a reality. Table 6.1 laid out the full story tersely. For a polity to have and attempt to execute a strategy, it must provide for performance of the following roles: policymaker, theorist-planner, and commander who has to manage and lead. In principle, the three functions indicated almost with unduly graphic clarity by the bridge metaphor are purpose, strategy, and tools (ends, ways, and means). To add some useful detail to the bare structure of the metaphor, the bridge need not only simply be anchored on its political and military banks; rather it can extend some distance overland from the water. Since the nature of the broad strategic function is to staple military and other behaviour to political interests, motives, and goals, it is obvious that, save in theory, there cannot be barriers at each end of the bridge. The executive strategist, as contrasted, say, with a scholar writing strategic theory, has some need to think and talk politically in order to under-stand and try to influence the content of his policy guidance for a better fit with his practicable ways and available means. Also, often he will be better served should he be able to improve the strategic and military education of both his political masters and his military and civilian subordinates. In the latter regard, the development and promulgation of up-to-date, permissive not restrictive, military doctrine is essential. The military machine at the strategist's command should, in its entirety, sing from the same hymnal of faith as to best current practice. Needless to add, some doctrinal variety may provide a measure of protection against the ill consequences of the military choir singing the wrong tactical tune harmoniously. Doctrine can be wrong. However, this powerful caveat is not a sound reason for hostility to doctrine per se.

The strategic function, and hence the domain of the strategist, cannot be confined to the realm of ideas, even when those are expressed in plans and doctrine manuals. After all, 'strategic theory is a theory for action'.[24] The strate-gist is not an amusing and possibly erudite adornment to the world of practice, at least he should not only be such. His strategy exists strictly as a contingent theory for victory, a plan devised to solve, or at the general level to help solve via education, actual or anticipated problems. It follows that the role of the strategist is meaningless absent provision for strategy execution. Whether or not the principal conceptualizer of a strategy is designated to command its implementa-tion in the field, there can be no doubt that the function of command must feature prominently on the strategy landscape. Both as general theory and as historically unique plans, the purpose of strategy is to improve a polity's compet-itive performance. And the quality of that performance should be influenced to advantage by a choice of strategy executed by armed forces commanded by people who endeavour to achieve a purposeful control of events. This apparently com-plex, yet essentially simple, process is most likely to happen net advantageously when all the many behaviours commanded are controlled for complementary and synergistic impacts and consequences. Such command and control, no doubt devolved as it must be to and among many layers in the military hierarchy, are integral to the strategic function. To repeat the logic, a master strategic idea, a dominant narrative, should drive the design of actual plans, and those plans must be executed by forces that are commanded and controlled so that their efforts serve a common centrally intended purpose. The existence, promulgation, understanding, and use of a single coherent body of authoritative sound military doctrine should contribute notably to the achievement of such purpose. In different historical eras, and even in the same era among distinctive characters of competition and warfare, the strategic function writ as large as suggested here has been performed by fewer, or by more, people. There is no external and universal formula doctrine that can yield a current general answer with much merit to the particular question of precisely how the strategic function should be performed, and how its several aspects ought to be delegated.

What does strategy produce? The answer is as challengingly opaque as it is unavoidable—strategic effect. Apparent tautology or not, this concept has to be the keystone in the arch of the strategy bridge. Performance of the strategic function can only be to generate desired effect upon the future course of events. Our subject is as simple as this, even though all matters of strategy design, decision, and execution in an adversarial environment are inherently complex and typically are uncertain far into the zone of unpredictability. Strategic effect is one among those mysterious qualities that cannot be observed and measured directly—security, love, happiness, and grief are examples of others. But, even if we are unable to record strategic effect exactly, we can and must try hard to recognize evidence of its current condition. Its future impact typically will be a topic fit only for guesswork, but we can find material evidence of its recent and current presence. For example, the hasty retreat towards the frontier of the Reich in August 1944 by the ragged remainder of the German army from Normandy yielded unmistakable evidence of massive positive strategic effect achieved by Allied command performance. But what did this German retreat-come-rout mean? Would the war be over in 1944? How much fight was there left in the *Wehrmacht*? How would the negative effect of retreat and defeat trade against the will to defend German soil for the first time, in a context of improved logistics as the distance for resupply shortened dramatically? The answer could not be computed.

Strategists cannot escape the laws of physics even though their job requires them to seek to control some aspects of the future. Although competent strategists and more than adequate commander-managers often do succeed in shaping events to a broadly advantageous outcome, it is never possible for them to remove entirely the potentially sovereign role of chance in war. Yet again, Clausewitz is thoroughly persuasive. He specified chance and its dependent associate, uncertainty, as an organic component of the 'climate of war'.[25] No matter how cunningly theorists strive, they cannot eliminate the uncertainty from war. In truth, knowledge of nearly everything about the future, in almost any detail below the generic—for example, the prediction that human affairs will continue to be governed in good part by the malign influences of 'fear, honour, and interest'—is precisely unknowable.[26] And yet, the strategist's core duty is to develop, and see commanded in physical performance, plans that are predictions and intentions, in other words theories. The strategist's plans purport to explain how desired end states will be achieved.

Strategic effect, the dynamic and more than a little unpredictable result of the strategist's labours, is the product of every element specified as acting and interacting in the many dicta that comprise the complete general theory of strategy. In principle, nothing in this general theory is irrelevant to any particular historical context, but the many subjects of the dicta must play roles of variable significance from case to case. The strategist's plan must seek to anticipate how tactical action, commanded for operational level consequences, will shape the course of future events; assessed overall, this is strategic effect. For more reasons than it would be sensible to attempt to itemize comprehensively, it is difficult to perform even competently as a strategist, let alone as a strategist of true historical distinction. Happily for most of history's would-be strategists, which is to say for those with average biological endowment, education, experience, and luck, there is need only to be good enough. Readers may recall the point repeated in these pages that the enemy's high command too, one hopes, is not blessed with undoubtable genius in strategy.

It may be helpful to conclude this discussion by placing emphasis upon two features of this vital concept, and physical and psychological reality, of strategic effect. First, the effect is felt and has consequences in stages, across levels of conflict, and the transitions from one level to another are not reliably predictable. By stages, strategic effect happens, is felt, in first-order, second-order, probably third-order and beyond, consequences, untraceable in confirmable detail. There may be some apparent order in, even design to, the strategic universe, but chaos theory does offer a few insights of value.[27] Tactical first-order effects should have second-order tactical and operational effects, and those effects should have meaning in strategic effect. Alas, strategy is apt to be curved in its trajectory of consequences. Tactical behaviour may well be the trackable product of a grand strategic design, but in its turn it could blow back to reshape the strategy itself. Perhaps we need to consider the simile of comparing strategic performance with the trajectory of a well-thrown boomerang.

Second, theorists of a metric persuasion who strive against the heavy odds to convert the art of strategy into applied quantifiable science are always going to be outmanoeuvred fatally by the authority of the contextuality of events. Strategic effect and its achievement via command performance strategically, operationally, and tactically must be a product whose weight is determined by somewhat dynamic and unique circumstances. Defeat in battle may, or may not, so demoralize an army or a nation that its morale sags beyond recovery.[28] The strategic meaning of tactical and operational success and failure can be anticipated, guessed intelligently, but by no means can it be predicted with rock-like reliability. This second point of emphasis translates easily as a restatement of one of the fundamental terms of engagement for the practicing strategist. He is obliged by duty to try to achieve a sufficient control over the course of strategic history for the political purposes he is given, and that is a heroically challenging mission indeed.

CAUTIONS

Accepting the risk of seeming unduly downbeat, I am persuaded that this book should not short-change the case for caution. Given the stakes in strategy and the inherent uncertainty of all strategic projects, the message, *caveat emptor*, seems to me obligatory. Five cautions should suffice to alert those who place a suitably high value on prudence.

First, here and elsewhere history has been lauded as a, if not the, principal source for strategic education, and hopefully for strategic wisdom. Without denying such praise to history, it is necessary to be careful lest we heap undue praise upon historians. Although there is a real historical record, the past, to reveal, explain, and understand, what we read as history are the opinions of historians. These paladins for truth are apt to have contemporary agendas, whether recognized by themselves or not. Historians cannot help but be people encultured by their own life and times. The insightfully bold and scholarly historian Jeremy Black, writes about *The Curse of History*, a malediction he identifies as an anti-historical contextual tendency among his fellow historians who permit their own moral judgements to drive their professional assessments.[29] While granting the validity of Black's indictment, there is a yet deeper 'curse of history' against which there can be no effective protection. Specifically, the historian is cursed by the knowledge of what happened, in greater or lesser detail. This knowledge, if not quite understanding, all but commands the historical scholar to reason backwards, employing his inalienable temporal rear-view mirror. He can hardly help locating what appear to have been the necessary causes for events, when all that may be identifiable are sufficient ones. When one holds major facts of undeniable truth and significance, for example, the outbreak of the Second World War in early September 1939, it is literally impossible to recover fully how and why people reasoned about issues of war and peace in the 1920s and the very different 1930s. Why? Because we know that a very great war occurred, we know when it occurred, and we know that it was the greatest, possibly the most awful war, in all of history. A politician or general in the 1930s could know none of this. For a rather different point, on the one hand historical perspective is essential if we are to grasp, via the tool of the *longue durée*, the meaning of events and episodes. On the other hand, however, lengthy historical perspective ensures that the historian of today, whenever that is, could not have been anywhere close to the scene of the crime. The consequence, as this author can attest personally from years of teaching strategic studies, is that while students of history may secure a plausible grasp of the meaning of past happenings, the perspective that donates such candidate wisdom also serves to minimize empathy for historical players. Today we can review, appalled, the conduct of the nuclear arms competition in the great East–West Cold War (1947–89). But understanding of the reasons for the decisions taken in those years about the competition is becoming ever more tenuous.[30] Historical perspective is both a blessing and a curse. For example, today it is hard to find a historian of Republican or Imperial Rome who has even visited that grand polity as a tourist, let alone as a scholar. This unavoidable absence of first-hand knowledge has it advantages, but it comes at a price. Strategic studies must make the best use it is able of what seems to be reasonable historical judgement on the past. But this judgement is to a degree cursed, as noted here somewhat reluctantly and certainly regretfully.

Second, the human element is by far the greatest source of contingency in strategic affairs. This is a less than startling revelation, but it is too important to merit other than high emphasis.[31] This book has sought to give the human dimension to strategy its massive due, but still I am troubled lest inadvertently I have understated its significance. While the general theory of strategy can and must acknowledge the human contribution only generically, the application of the theory in historical practice is thoroughly, pervasively, in human hands at every level of concern to strategy. Machines matter, but they are always employed by people, and not just people as a military-strategic, even cultural, abstraction, but rather as individual persons or groups. And people differ in their 'cultural thoughtways' and behaviour.[32] Moreover, their behaviour will vary with context. There is a place for historical grand narrative, but it must never be permitted to hide the often key role of individuals. There are historical contexts wherein individual, even quite large groups, choice is either strictly limited or even unimportant, so compelling is the power of the energy derivative from the structural forces that comprise circumstances. That granted, it still is generally valid to argue that contingency, especially a quintessentially human contingency, typically makes some difference. Recall that as the phenomenon of morale the human mind and the emotions it recognizes and episodically promotes, is judged by military professionals to be the most important contributor to fighting power. We do not wish to risk overstating this caution, but we must convey the warning that human beings, including individuals, matter in strategy. They are not just 'bit players' in the grand narrative of history, let alone entirely hapless victims of chance. In the 'Afterword' to his terrifyingly convincing history of the Cuban Missile Crisis, Michael Dobbs offers conclusive judgement on the significance of the individual human factor for the course of history. He writes, 'The Cuban Missile crisis demonstrates the sometimes pivotal role of personality in politics. Character counts.'[33] Dobbs shows plausibly why and how it was that the personality of John F. Kennedy and Nikita Khrushchev prevented our known world from being terminated with extreme prejudice on 27–8 October 1962. Both at the time and in some retrospect, it seems that the human race had a very close call with catastrophe. And the personalities of the two key individuals mattered decisively. That said, it is a little alarming to be obliged to recognize that in addition to the most obviously key human players in the drama of high politics about war or peace, such persons as Kennedy and Khrushchev, a single humble Soviet naval officer may well have been scarcely less key.[34] Furthermore there is need to recognize the distinctly human dimension in the 'mind-sets' that shaped and drove judgements about intelligence information.[35]

Third, it may seem ironic, but in a book devoted to explanation, in some measure even to the promotion, of strategy as a virtuous function, it is necessary to issue a warning against the subject. Hastily, I must explain that the villain in question is not so much strategy, rather is it what can be called 'strategism'. This malady often takes the form of reification. Strategy per se is praised and advocated as the all purpose solution to security challenges. To promote strategy, empty of content, is useful if it educates for recognition of a broad need. But such promotion often is undertaken with no particular content in mind. For a hypothetical example, it is probably true to assert that, say, 'America (Russia, India . . .) must have a strategy'. Good advice, one might suppose. However, what should be asserted is that 'America (Russia, India . . .) needs the right, or a right enough, strategy'. Strategy per se is necessary, but can never be sufficient. In fact, as history does for once try to report in a loud voice, the wrong strategy is likely to prove lethal. It is one thing to understand the importance of the function of the strategy bridge, it is quite another to offer sound advice on a particular strategy to meet a historically unique strategic challenge. Strategy as strategism is mere wise-sounding verbiage. It offers the appearance of wisdom, while leaving untouched the far more difficult problems of strategic theory for practice. For an important variant of this caution about the virus of strategism, it is well to remember that even if a plausible strategy to answer a pressing problem is specific, somebody, and some bodies, will need to make it happen by their command performance. Strategy is not self-executing by virtue of the genius in its cunning even should it be so blessed. Also, strategy usually cannot substitute for poor or absent policy.

Fourth, the study and practice of strategy has ever been blighted by the presentist fallacy, and by its close associate, indeed its dependant, the fashionable fad of the moment. Because people must live only in the present—those inconvenient laws of nature again—their understanding of the past and the future necessarily is limited. Since the future is terrain upon which we can never walk, it always moves out ahead of us. And because our acquaintance with the past, especially the distant past, is in more or less measure tenuous, our natural inclination is to privilege the present. We tell ourselves that today is a time of exceptional significance, which it is, to us, now, and is of unusual historical importance viewed from a long-term perspective, which is possible, but unlikely. More to the point, our understanding of today, accurate or not (and who knows, objectively?), is held to provide reliable pointers to the character of tomorrow. This is the presentist fallacy. For all its contestability, the historical record does demonstrate the capacity of the course of events to reveal and effect rapid, and hard to anticipate, change in only a brief time span. For example, somehow a 1920s that witnessed a road to peace, became a 1930s that, rather more firmly, recorded a march towards war; or so a great deal of scholarship seeks to inform us. The present of the late 1920s could not plausibly predict the actual present of 1937–45. This is but one among any number of candidate examples of the limitations of the present as a sound basis from which to anticipate or predict the future.

The necessary caution is not to the effect that because the future is unforeseeable in character, strategists ought not to try to anticipate it. Strategists as defence planners have no choice other than to strive to anticipate the future, notwithstanding their inescapable ignorance. The caution holds that the strategist does not necessarily see the future in what he sees today and saw yesterday. The strategist's future comprises the unpredictable secondary, tertiary, and beyond effects of the forces at play both now and in the time between now and then. A possibly classic example of the presentist fallacy is the fashionable contemporary conviction that the future of warfare must be largely irregular in character.[36] How do our present day strategic seers know this? Because the insurgent, the guerrilla, and the terrorist constitute the dominant present belligerent reality.

Fifth and finally, it is necessary to provide the reminder that all strategic practice, all command performance, is pervasively contextual. The general theory of strategy is not, indeed cannot be, contextual. It is what the nature of the strategic function, not the circumstances of needful practice, demands that it must be. And that nature cannot change. However, would-be strategic templates usually do not work well when lifted from one setting to another anachronistically. We have suggested that the strategist must ply his trade with reference to the particulars of seven contexts: political, social-cultural, economic, technological, military, geographical, and historical. Such contextual awareness should alert the military strategist to his situation nested in grand strategy. This awareness is akin to, albeit even stronger than, the need for the operational level military commander to enjoy a strategic sense. Context provides meaning to events. Would-be strategists who lack contextual sensitivity cannot succeed. Strategy has no autarchic meaning or value. An instrument, and strategy is nothing if not such, is valuable only for its utility in service of some purpose outside itself. It is possible to overemphasize contextuality. If one stresses the significance of context, and is somewhat loose in one's definition of what is and what is not contextual, the behaviour duly contextualized can be in danger of sliding out of focus, if not out of sight. An example is the genre of 'war and society' scholarship that addresses just about everything to do with war save only for its defining centrepiece, the politically motivated organized violence at its core that is warfare.

THE GOOD (ENOUGH) STRATEGIST

To strike a moderately upbeat note, strategy is possible, the strategist often can succeed because true excellence in his calling is rarely necessary. The victorious strategist need not even be the particularly good strategist. Because the strategist has to perform as a duellist, he need only be a good enough strategist to achieve by his command performance a necessary measure of control over the enemy's decisions. The quality and quantity of that enemy (and enmity) decides just how good the strategist has to be, always assuming obedience to the rule of prudence in the provision of his political guidance. For some comfort, it is more than a little encouraging to reflect upon these words by the journalist-novelist Robert Harris: 'In the absence of genius there is always craftsmanship'.[37] The strategist strictly does not require the right stuff, only enough of the right enough stuff to meet the challenge of the day. For him to do that he can only benefit from some education by a general theory designed and refined to assist practice.

Happily, perhaps, although the general theory of strategy can be rewritten endlessly, with each drafting reflecting the time, place, circumstance, and personality of the theorist, it does not necessarily register progress in comprehension. The general theory can be identified and explained at any time and in any place and circumstance in history. This theory for the strategic function must be expressed in the manner characteristic of the period of its several major literary eruptions, but it does not have a linear intellectual narrative. Clausewitz is superior in important respects to Thucydides and Sun Tzu, but that is not because he wrote 2,200 and more years later than did they. The strategic function is universal and eternal, and is not the product of culturally circumscribed conceptualization. It follows, therefore, that great works of general strategic theory in principle can have equal value for today and tomorrow, can be written at any location and at any of history's many moments, those both allegedly 'strategic' and those that plainly are not. I honour the good sense with which Thucydides and Clausewitz commended the finest products of their intellectual labours to posterity. The Greek general-historian aspired as follows:

> I have written my work, not as an essay which is to win the applause of the moment, but as a possession for all time.[38]

While, with a little more apparent modesty, the mighty Prussian confessed, that

> It was my ambition to . . . write a book that would not be forgotten after two or three years, and that possibly might be picked up more than once by those who are interested in the subject.[39]

Everything there is to know about strategy as the basis for general theory was as knowable in ancient Greece as it was in early nineteenth-century Prussia, and as it is today. Strategy, not strategies, endures.

NOTES

1. T. E. Lawrence, *Seven Pillars of Wisdom: A Triumph* (New York: Anchor Books, 1991).
2. Marshal (Ferdinand) Foch, *The Principles of War*, tr. Hilaire Belloc (London: Chapman and Hall, 1921), 14. See Bernard Brodie, *Strategy in the Missile Age* (Princeton, NJ: Princeton University Press, 1959), ch. 2; id., *War and Politics* (New York: Macmillan, 1973), ch. 1.
3. Carl von Clausewitz *On War*, tr. Michael Howard and Peter Paret (1832–4; Princeton, NJ: Princeton University Press, 1976); Sun Tzu, *The Art of War*, tr. Ralph D. Sawyer (ca. 490 BCE; Boulder, CO: Westview Press, 1994); Thucydides, *The Landmark Thucydides: A Comprehensive Guide to 'The Peloponnesian War'*, ed. Robert B. Strassler, rev. tr.

Richard Crawley (ca. 400 BCE; New York: Free Press, 1996); Basil Liddell Hart, *Strategy: The Indirect Approach* (1941; London: Faber and Faber, 1967); id., *The Revolution in Warfare* (London: Faber and Faber, 1946); J. C. Wylie, *Military Strategy: A General Theory of Power Control* (1967; Annapolis, MD: Naval Institute Press, 1989); Edward N. Luttwak, *Strategy: The Logic of War and Peace*, rev. edn. (Cambridge, MA: Harvard University Press, 2001); Niccolo Machiavelli, *The Art of War*, tr. Ellis Farneworth (1521; Indianapolis, IN: Bobbs-Merrill, 1965); id., *Discourses on Livy*, tr. Julia Conaway Bondarella and Peter Bondarella (1531; Oxford: Oxford University Press, 2003); id., *The Prince*, tr. Peter Bondarella and Mark Musa (1532; Oxford: Oxford University Press, 1998); Antoine Henri de Jomini, *The Art of War* (1838; London: Greenhill Books, 1992); Bernard Brodie, ed., *The Absolute Weapon: Atomic Power and World Order* (New York: Harcourt Brace, 1946); id., *Strategy in the Missile Age*; id., *War and Politics*. See Appendix B for a brief justification for these selections. The following works are selected for honourable mention in a porous and debateable 'Other Contenders' division: Julius Caesar, *Caesar's Commentaries: 'On The Gallic War' and 'On The Civil War'*, tr. W. A. MacDevitt (50s and 40s BCE; El Paso, TX: El Paso Norte Press, 2005); Alfred Thayer Mahan, *The Influence of Sea Power upon History, 1660–1783* (1890; London: Methuen, 1965); id., *The Problem of Asia and Its Effect upon International Policies* (Boston: Little Brown, 1905); Julian S. Corbett, *Some Principles of Maritime Strategy* (1911; Annapolis, MD: Naval Institute Press, 1988); id., *England in the Seven Years' War: A Study in Combined Strategy*, 2 vols. (1907; London: Longman, Green, 1918); J. F. C. Fuller, *Armament and History: A Study of the Influence of Armament on History from the Dawn of Classical Warfare to the Second World War* (London: Eyre and Spottiswoode, 1946); John R. Boyd, *A Discourse on Winning and Losing*, unpub. briefing (August 1987); Martin van Creveld, *The Transformation of War* (New York: Free Press, 1991); id., *The Culture of War* (New York: Ballantine Books, 2008).

4. Bernard Brodie, 'The Continuing Relevance of *On War*', in Clausewitz, 45–58.
5. A period piece that alas has residual significance is Desmond Ball and Jeffrey Richelson, eds., *Strategic Nuclear Targeting* (Ithaca, NY: Cornell University Press, 1986). Also see Lawrence Freedman, *The Evolution of Nuclear Strategy*, 3rd. edn. (Basingstoke: Palgrave Macmillan, 2003); and Keith B. Payne, *The Great American Gamble: Deterrence Theory and Practice from the Cold War to the 21st Century* (Fairfax, VA: National Institute Press, 2008).
6. General wisdom on war planning is in short supply; as so often, one should begin with Clausewitz, Book Eight, 'War Plans'. After *On War* one is, admittedly, struggling to find much enlightenment. Some help can be derived from Steven T. Ross, *American War Plans, 1941–1945* (London: Frank Cass, 1997), xiii–xx, and Talbot C. Imlay and Monica Duffy Toft, eds., *The Fog of Peace and War Planning: Military and Strategic Planning under Uncertainty* (Abingdon: Routledge, 2006). Good examples of historians' literature include Paul Kennedy, ed., *The War Plans of the Great Powers, 1880–1914* (London: Allen and Unwin, 1979); Mark Jacobsen, Robert Levine, and William Schwabe, *Contingency Plans for War in Western Europe, 1920–1940*, R-3281-NA (Santa Monica, CA: RAND, June 1985); Michael Stephen Partridge, *Military Planning for the Defense of the United Kingdom, 1814–1870* (Westport, CT: Greenwood Press, 1989); Graydon A. Tunstall, Jr., *Planning for War Against Russia and Serbia: Austro-Hungarian and German Military Strategies, 1871–1914* (New York: Columbia University Press, 1993); Steven T. Ross, *American War Plans, 1945–1950* (London: Frank Cass, 1996); and Terence Zuber, *Inventing the Schlieffen Plan: German War Planning, 1871–1914* (Oxford: Oxford

University Press, 2002), a highly controversial study that, at least in the mind of this theorist, implicitly raises the interesting question, 'when is a war plan a war plan, as opposed to being something else?' The something else in the 1905 case at issue being allegedly only a *Denkschrift* (study), not the grand design to win a war swiftly (forty-two days or so) in a single decisive campaign.

7. I am grateful to Beatrice Heuser, *Reading Clausewitz* (London: Pimlico, 2002), 12, for this important thought.
8. 'Warfare is the way (Tao) of deception.' Sun Tzu, 168.
9. Clausewitz, 141.
10. Ibid. (emphasis in the original).
11. Ibid. 578.
12. See M. I. Finley's 'Introduction' to *Thucydides: History of the Peloponnesian War*, tr. Rex Warner (ca. 400; London: Penguin Books, 1972), 9–32.
13. Ibid. 86.
14. One should distinguish among the great, here called classical, general theorists of strategy; the great executive strategists-planners and commanders; and the great writers who influenced the strategic theorists and practitioners, whether or not their work had much, or indeed any, explicitly strategic content.
15. The literature on Versailles and its alleged consequences is enormous and necessarily inconclusive. Was Germany a fairly normal European great power waiting to re-emerge in the post-war world, whose re-emergence was aborted by the domestic political impact of the Great Depression? We can never know, but for informed reassessments of Versailles 1919, see Manfred F. Boemke, Gerald D. Feldman, and Elisabeth Glaser, eds., *The Treaty of Versailles: A Reassessment After 75 Years* (Cambridge: Cambridge University Press, 1998); Michael Dockrill and John Fisher, eds., *The Paris Peace Conference, 1919: Peace without Victory?* (Basingstoke: Palgrave, 2001); and Zara Steiner, *The Lights that Failed: European International History, 1919–1933* (Oxford: Oxford University Press, 2005), pt. 1.
16. See Richard K. Betts, 'Is Strategy an Illusion?' *International Security*, 25 (fall 2000), 5–50.
17. For a range of perspectives, see: Andrew F. Krepinevich, Jr., *The Army and Vietnam* (Baltimore: Johns Hopkins University Press, 1986); Jeffrey Record, *The Wrong War: Why We Lost in Vietnam* (Annapolis, MD: Naval Institute Press, 1998); Mark W. Woodruff, *Unheralded Victory: Who Won the Vietnam War?* (London: Harper Collins Publishers, 1999); and C. Dale Walton, *The Myth of Inevitable U. S. Defeat in Vietnam* (London: Frank Cass, 2002).
18. See the classic English language narrative, Alistair Horne's magnificent *A Savage War of Peace: Algeria, 1954–1962* (London: Penguin Books, 1979). Martin S. Alexander and J. F. V. Keiger, eds., *France and the Algerian War, 1954–62: Strategy, Operations and Diplomacy* (London: Frank Cass, 2002), is a first-rate collection of essays on a conflict that is much under-studied in the Anglophone world.
19. Although by definition warfare is waged for political ends, this necessary fact does not mean that politics and warfare are fused. Acts of organized violence committed for political purposes may be regarded as a form of political behaviour—war is armed politics, and suchlike formulae—but warfare has a lore and dynamic all its own, no matter what the political intentions might be. Clausewitz is admirably explicit on this point. 'Its [war's] grammar, indeed, may be its own, but not its logic', 605. On the malady of the tacticization of strategy, see Michael I. Handel, *Masters of War: Classical Strategic Thought*, 3rd edn. (London: Frank Cass, 2001), 355–60.

20. Helmuth von Moltke, *Moltke on the Art of War: Selected Writings*, tr. Daniel J. Hughes, and Gunther E. Rothenberg (Novato, CA: Presidio Press, 1993), 47.

21. See Handel, *Masters of War*, 353–60.

22. Clausewitz, 75.

23. German General Otto von Below assaulted forty-one Italian divisions with thirty-five (seven German, twenty-eight Austro–Hungarian) divisions and routed them in a classic panic. The Italians lost 40,000 casualties, and 275,000 were taken prisoner. The loss of materiel was formidable, also (e.g. 2,500 guns were captured by von Below's storming troopers). But his victorious forces lacked the logistical means to convert a tactical victory into either operational or strategic decision. The complexity of war and warfare has a way of frustrating those who are only tactically outstanding.

24. Bernard Brodie, *War and Politics* (New York: Macmillan, 1973), 452.

25. Clausewitz, 104.

26. Thucydides, *Landmark Thucydides*, 43.

27. See Glenn E. James, *Chaos Theory: The Essentials for Military Applications*, Newport Papers 10 (Newport, RI: Naval War College, October 1996); David S. Alberts and Thomas J. Czerwinski, eds., *Complexity, Global Politics, and National Security* (Washington, DC: National Defense University Press, 1997); Tom Czerwinski, *Coping with the Bounds: Speculations on Nonlinearity in Military Affairs* (Washington, DC: National Defense University Press, 1998); and Robert Jervis, *System Effects: Complexity in Political and Social Life* (Princeton, NJ: Princeton University Press, 1999). But some readers may find the argument in Colin S. Gray, *Strategy for Chaos: Revolutions in Military Affairs and the Evidence of History* (London: Frank Cass, 2002), esp. ch. 4, agreeably less challenging to follow.

28. For example, in the estimation of the victor, Hannibal Barca, the catastrophic defeat of the army of the Roman Republic at Cannae in 216 BCE should have led to Rome suing for the best peace terms with Carthage that it could negotiate. In the instructive words of Adrian Goldsworthy, '[b]y his own understanding of war Hannibal won the Second Punic War at Cannae, but the Romans were following a different set of rules and when they did not admit defeat there was little more that he could do to force them', *Roman Warfare* (London: Cassell, 2002), 85. Britain's defeat in Flanders in May 1940 was far less bloody than was Rome's at Cannae, but it appeared to place her in scarcely more hopeful a strategic situation.

29. Jeremy Black, *The Curse of History* (London: Social Affairs Unit, 2008).

30. I attempt to explain this difficulty in achieving empathy in my *Modern Strategy* (Oxford: Oxford University Press, 1999), chs. 11 and 12.

31. The human dimension to warfare is well presented in Hugh McManners, *The Scars of War* (London: Harper Collins Publishers, 1993); and Michael Evans and Alan Ryan, *The Human Face of Warfare: Killing, Fear and Chaos in Battle* (St. Leonards, Australia: Allen and Unwin, 2000).

32. Ken Booth, *Strategy and Ethnocentrism* (London: Croom Helm, 1979), 14.

33. Michael Dobbs, *One Minute to Midnight* (London: Arrow Books, 2009), 351.

34. See Peter Ashdown, *Fate, Chance and Desperate Men: Six Studies of the Role of Chance in Twentieth Century History* (Brighton: Book Guild Publishing, 2009), 106–15.

35. Kenneth Michael Absher, *Mind-Sets and Missiles: A First Hand Account of the Cuban Missile Crisis* (Carlisle, PA: Strategic Studies Institute, August 2009), is an insightful study by a participant-observer. Most aspects of intelligence are profoundly human.

36. Probably the firmest disciple of a largely irregular character form to twenty-first century warfare, one cannot say most authoritative because there are no authorities

on the future, is Rupert Smith, *The Utility of Force: The Art of War in the Modern World* (London: Allen Lane, 2005). Colin S. Gray, *Another Bloody Century: The Future of Warfare* (London: Phoenix, 2006), offers a somewhat contrasting view, amidst the expression of many reservations about prediction, strategic and other.

37. Robert Harris, *The Ghost* (London: Hutchinson, 2007), 141.
38. Thucydides, 16.
39. Clausewitz, 58.

Appendix A

The Dicta of Strategy

NATURE AND CHARACTER OF STRATEGY

1. Grand strategy is the direction and use made of any or all of the assets of a security community, including its military instrument, for the purposes of policy as decided by politics.
2. Military strategy is the direction and use made of force and the threat of force for the purposes of policy as decided by politics.
3. Strategy is the only bridge built and held to connect policy purposefully with the military and other instruments of power and influence.
4. Strategy serves politics instrumentally by generating net strategic effect.
5. Strategy is adversarial; it functions in both peace and war, and it always seeks a measure of control over enemies (and often over allies and neutrals also).
6. Strategy usually requires deception, is paradoxical, and frequently is ironic.
7. Strategy is human.
8. The meaning and character of strategies are driven, though not dictated and wholly determined, by their contexts, all of which are constantly in play and can realistically be understood to constitute just one compounded super context.
9. Strategy has a permanent nature, while strategies (usually plans, formal or informal, expressing contingent operational intentions) have a variable character driven, but not mandated, by their unique and changing contexts, the needs of which are expressed in the decisions of unique individuals.

MAKING STRATEGY

10. Strategy typically is made by a process of dialogue and negotiation.
11. Strategy is a value-charged zone of ideas and behaviour.
12. Historically specific strategies often are driven, and always are shaped, by culture and personality, while strategy in general theory is not.

EXECUTING STRATEGY

13. The strategy bridge must be held by competent strategists.
14. Strategy is more difficult to devise and execute than are policy, operations, and tactics: friction of all kinds comprise phenomena inseparable from the making and conduct of strategies.
15. Strategy can be expressed in strategies that are direct or indirect, sequential or cumulative, attritional or manoeuverist-annihilating, persisting or raiding (more or less expeditionary), coercive or brute force, offensive or defensive, symmetrical or asymmetrical, or a complex combination of these nominal but often false alternatives.

16. All strategies are shaped by their particular geographical contexts, but strategy itself is not.
17. Strategy is an unchanging, indeed unchangeable, human activity in thought and behaviour, set in a variably dynamic technological context.
18. Unlike strategy, all strategies are temporal.
19. Strategy is logistical.
20. Strategic theory is the most fundamental source of military doctrine, while doctrine is a notable enabler of, and guide for, strategies.

CONSEQUENCES OF STRATEGY

21. All military behaviour is tactical in execution, but must have operational and strategic effect, intended and otherwise.

Appendix B
General Strategic Theory, the Classical Canon

> A classic is a book (hence a race, building, human activity) about whose value it is assumed that there can be no argument.
>
> *The Times (London)*, 17 October 2009

The general theory of strategy has universal and eternal validity and arguably is located, to date, in the works of no more than ten authors who have written over the course of 2,500 years. The general theory relates to the particular plans and strategies of history by means of educating strategists in their profession. General theory translates into actual behaviour via actionable plans implemented by commanders. It is useful to identify four divisions in the ranks of classic general strategic theorists.

The first division has these three entries:

1. Carl von Clausewitz, *On War* (1832–4). This is the most profound book on the theory of war and strategy ever written. It is long, philosophical, and challenging to the reader who needs to engage closely with the text. It was written between 1816 and 1831 and its argument reflects major shifts in the author's understanding, changes which sometimes are transcribed imperfectly into the text. Nonetheless, *On War* is the richest mine of strategic wisdom available.

2. Sun Tzu, *The Art of War* (ca. 490 BCE). As cryptic, indeed axiomatic, in style as Clausewitz frequently is prolix and philosophical, Sun Tzu's is a brilliant terse treatise. It is barely a simple edit away from readiness to serve as an ancient Chinese PowerPoint briefing. Unlike Clausewitz, Sun Tzu offers direct advice to help his reader be victorious in war. But, also unlike Clausewitz, Sun Tzu writes not just narrowly about war, but rather about war and strategy in the context of statecraft.

3. Thucydides, *The Peloponnesian War*, is best studied in the version, Thucydides, *The Landmark Thucydides: A Comprehensive Guide to 'The Peloponnesian War'*, (ca. 400 BCE). Thucydides did not set out to write a general theory of strategy. However, *The Peloponnesian War* contains some of the finest literary examples of grand strategic reasoning ever committed to paper, as well as a host of richly detailed cases of military strategy in their political setting. The reader receives a general strategic education from the superb description and analysis in historical context.

The second division of classical authors of strategic theory has five members (listed historically).

4. Niccolo Machiavelli's three books, *The Prince* (1532), *Discourses upon Livy* (1531), and *The Art of War* (1521), demand inclusion, admittedly controversially, in the classical canon (notwithstanding the definition of a classic suggested in the epigraph to this appendix, one must always allow for exceptions to claimed rules). He rested his specific analyses and recommendations for the situation of his time firmly and consistently on

the general theory of politics, statecraft, and war that he developed. The weakest work of the three here cited is *The Art of War*, a book vulnerable to criticism for its massive flights of military anachronism and its particular errors in judgement, most famously the author's refusal to be impressed by the promise in gunpowder weapons. Nonetheless, Machiavelli wrote with insight about the intimate connections between an army and the society it should serve. Indeed, his wisdom on the higher conduct of war in the context of domestic and foreign politics, stands in clear contrast to his shortage of tactical brilliance. Readers should be relaxed about much of Machiavelli's unduly backward looking admiration for the Roman army of the republican era, and be content to learn from the political-military education scattered throughout these works, though mainly in *The Prince* and the *Discourses*.

5. Baron Antoine Henri de Jomini, *The Art of War* (1838). Unquestionably not in the same class as the trio in the first division, but still a work of high merit. In fact, Jomini is undervalued today, so far has his mantle of authority slipped from his paramount position in the middle of the nineteenth century. He was probably the most perceptive interpreter of Napoleon's way of warfare. Although his *Art of War* is severely flawed, certainly dated, in much of its detailed advice, it is, nonetheless, well populated with significant insights into war as a whole, warfare, strategy, operational art, tactics, technology, logistics, and much else besides. It deserves to be read, albeit with care, naturally, by strategists today.

6. Basil H. Liddell Hart, *Strategy: The Indirect Approach* (1941), is a work of great breadth and depth, marred principally by the author's determination to sell the 'indirect approach' as the magical elixir that delivers success reliably. But, despite its ability to resist disciplined definition, the indirect approach is a valid and important idea. However, since it can have no meaning other than being whatever the enemy does not expect (the direct approach), it cannot serve as the all-context key to victory that its prophet claims; its logic is fatally circular.

7. J. C. Wylie, *Military Strategy: A General Theory of Power Control* (1967), is probably the most competent, and notwithstanding its brevity, the deepest work on the general theory of strategy written in the twentieth century. Following Clausewitz, Wylie wisely insists that the purpose of war is some measure of control over the enemy.

8. Edward N. Luttwak, *Strategy: The Logic of War and Peace*, rev. edn. (2001), though very recent, plainly has undeniable classic features. The author treats the several levels of war systematically, emphasizing brilliantly the pervasiveness of paradox and irony as inherent features of strategy. Furthermore, his insight that there is no natural harmony among policy, strategy, operations, and tactics, though hardly original, nonetheless is both profound and of huge practical significance. Friction reigns but need not rule.

The third division has a single member.

9. Bernard Brodie, as revealed in three of his books, (ed.) *The Absolute Weapon: Atomic Power and World Order* (1946), *Strategy in the Missile Age* (1959), and *War and Politics* (1973), deserves inclusion at least as an outlying member of the highly exclusive category of great theorists of strategy. Although most of the oeuvre was focused on American defence problems in the emerging nuclear and missile ages, his strategic theoretical range was extensive and his judgements were profound. I predict that he will merit reading a century from now, a judgement that should confer at least brevet-classic status.

The fourth division also has only a single entry.

10. Thomas C. Schelling, in his two books, *The Strategy of Conflict* (1960), and *Arms and Influence* (1966), made lasting contributions to our understanding of the structure of interdependent rational strategic choice, and provided theory literally vital to the comprehension of the management of risks. The first book rationalized the political utility of suicidal threats, inter alia; the second is a user's guide to coercion.

Below the four divisions, with just ten theorists identified above, there are many 'Other Contenders' for serious notice, some of which are identified in Table 7.1, 'The Classics of General Strategic Theory'.

Appendix C

Conceptual '*Hueys*' at Thermopylae? The Challenge of Strategic Anachronism

Neither Sparta nor Persia could deploy Bell UH-1 '*Huey*' helicopters at Thermopylae in 480 BCE. Material anachronism in fiction or on film usually is starkly self-evident, but the like conceptual error is less readily detected, though it may be strongly suspected. As a structural plot device for fiction, including fiction intended to bear a serious message, anachronism can be powerful indeed. Prominent among the more accomplished examples of the genre, with time travel as the postulated key structural enabler, is novelist Harry Turtledove's impressive story, *The Guns of the South*.[1] In this tale, Robert E. Lee and his enemy discover how useful the AK-47 assault rifle can be, especially when the enemy is confined to the weapon technologies of the 1860s. A little hindsight–foresight about the foe also proves helpful. The reason for this appendix is because whereas novelists and other entertainers employ anachronisms of all kinds knowingly and purposefully, albeit not always effectively, contemporary scholars of strategy have been known to employ them innocently. Whether or not this matters, and if it matters how much does it matter, are issues that I am obliged to address. This unexpected necessity derives from the fact that in the course of writing *Strategy Bridge*, one or two respected friends and colleagues from the tribe known as historians have challenged me to justify my fundamental claim that strategy is eternal and universal.[2] I undertake this mission here in an appendix, because the subject is both too important to be treated adequately in a footnote, yet is unduly scholastic for the main text of the book.

The beginning of wisdom has to repose with clear enough definition of vital terms. By anachronism, I understand 'the attribution of a custom, event, etc., to a period to which it does not belong; anything out of harmony with its period'.[3] Anachronism thus has a significantly pejorative connotation. The charge of anachronism has been levelled by professional historians at the defence professionals who have practised modern strategic studies since 1945. In sum, we contemporary strategists are accused of so far lacking in cultural empathy for the people who did defence in past centuries and millennia, that we are apt inappropriately, which is to say anachronistically to apply the concepts, the intellectual tool-kit, of today, to the mental worlds of people in times long past. Given that times past comprise a more or less foreign, even alien Other, country, such strategic anachronism has to be fraught with peril. Or is it?

It is the position of this defence professional and strategic theorist that the historians' somewhat parochial tribal accusation is an important one that merits a much more considered answer than it has received to date, hence this small essay. But it is also the opinion of this author that the charge ought to have only trivial merit. One must offer the aspirational qualifier, because obviously strategic anachronism can be employed, perhaps committed, both ignorantly and egregiously and in a manner that undermines the authority of the point that is made. Let me summarize what seems to be valid among historians' complaints:

1. Modern students of strategy are wont to plunder the history books in search of illustrative support for their contemporary arguments. So rich is the past (what actually happened), and so much richer is history (what competing historians claim happened), that the modern strategist will always find what he seeks by way of views he can use.

2. The modern strategist/defence professional may well strive honestly and competently to find right enough, which is to say truthful, best-guess answers to the questions of today, but he is not likely to be quite so scrupulous about the candidate evidence he deploys from history books. His presumable objectivity quotient by and large is expended upon meeting the challenges of now, not in weighing the arguments of competing historical narratives. Generally speaking, he will not be competent to do this anyway. For example, since professional historians do not agree on why, or even really whether, the Western Roman Empire truly declined and then 'fell' in 476 CE, it is unsurprising if we modern strategists are able in quite good conscience to pick the villain(s) we prefer for our historical illustrations. It was barbarian pressure, variably explained, or internal decadence and decline, or more likely both together, and so forth.[4]

3. When modern strategists parade a strategic historical anecdote or two in order to enliven an otherwise lacklustre PowerPoint briefing, usually they can do so confident that their audience is even less familiar with the historical story thus exploited than are they themselves. When historically inexpert strategists tell short, but pointed, historical tales to historically innocent audiences, the absence of any real quality control over the illustrative evidence is likely to prove lethal to the merit in the anecdotes. Except, of course, that the strategic historical decoration is probably intended more for amusement, for light relief, than to convey meaning in itself.

4. Modern strategists inadvertently are careless, because ignorant, with language. To cut to the chase, strategists uncritically deploy modern concepts to explain the behaviour of historical figures who we think we know did not employ the key words at issue here. Most specifically, strategy in its modern meaning, or some close approximation to it, was not in philological circulation in any language prior to the 1770s.[5] Historians have been known to challenge modern scholars of strategy with the following bluntly unnuanced logic: since there was no word for what today we mean by strategy prior to the late eighteenth century, literally it was not possible for people to conceptualize, to think, strategically; and if they could not think strategically, which we know to have been the case because they lacked the vital concept word, plainly they could not intend to behave strategically. This is not exactly a potent chain of logic, one must hasten to add, but it does refer both to an elementary truth and to more than a grain of a deeper and possibly troubling source of confusion.

Lest my plot line be less than well lit, I need to register the claim that my pre-eminent concern here is with the authority of strategy's general theory. In the main text, I claim that the theory has such authority as the whole history of man's unpleasantness to man is able to convey as relevant evidence. I assert that my twenty-one dicta are valid for all times and all places. This hugely imperial claim must be undermined or worse, should the nominally complementary, but sometimes rival (to strategists), historians' tribe be able to demonstrate that modern strategy is exactly, and strictly only, that—modern. Paradoxically, perhaps, even if historians were able to provide conclusive evidence that my understanding of strategy and purposefully strategic behaviour is utterly inapplicable to the global historical record prior to 1771, such a victory for historical empathy and consequent authenticity would not itself damage the authority of my take on strategy's general theory for today. However, it would certainly be a wound, even if a survivable one. It might seem to follow that if strategy, with behaviour at least shaped by the prevailing conceptualization, can be dated only from the 1770s, then it may prove to be merely a periodic truth and not an eternal verity. Could there be a strategic era (a long strategic moment), much like the prospectively 200-year-long era of the world's oil-based economy (ca. 1900–2100)?

Sorting sense from nonsense in the competing arguments about strategy in history has not been much helped by the gross indiscipline with which supposedly careful professionals, scholars and officials, military and civilian, use and abuse the nouns strategy and strategist, and the adjective strategic. Truly, one could specify a confusion of strategists as the most appropriate collective noun.

As the main body of *Strategy Bridge* seeks to make plain, taut definitions, employed consistently, are essential to clear thinking and occasionally even to rationally sound and reasonable practice. Words and their meaning do matter. I am entirely at one with the historians on this basic point. There is no current dispute over the relevant linguistic history. The word for strategy in French, German, and English does not appear in military and political literature until the 1770s (French and German), and the 1810s (English). But so what? What is of interest? We are looking for some approximation to what we understand as the strategy/tactics, the higher/lower, distinction. It may be useful to remind ourselves that all that is called strategic may not be so, at least not in our contemporary conceptual universe. Adoption of a word carries no guarantee of the adoption of a meaning preferred by us today. Also one needs to repeat the lament that although language changes over time, so also the meaning even of words that endure can change, while in addition the words strategy and strategic are used today in several senses. Language and meanings alter, but such change need not signify progress in understanding. For the most pertinent illustration of this point, it would be absurd to seek to argue that strategy was discovered in the late eighteenth century. By analogy, if Alfred Thayer Mahan discovered sea power, just what was it that England possessed, and did at and by sea, from the mid-sixteenth century until 1890?

The challenge here is not so much to argue plausibly that strategy was practised prior to the 1770s, but rather to take serious account, as one should, of the historians' valid point that the Ancients, as well as those who came much later, did not conceive of their world as do we of ours. Not only is the past a foreign country, it is foreign in ways that we cannot recover with thorough reliability. Even time travel would provide only limited assistance to understanding, because time travellers would be tourists so conceptually encultured by their period of origin that they could not think 'in period'. It is tempting to try to settle the scholars' dispute by asserting the maxim that by their recorded deeds and material artefacts shall we know them. But, neither deeds nor words from times past, let alone very long past, can be taken fully on trust as to their full meaning.

On reflection, and after no little argument, this modern strategist has come to the following conclusions:

1. Strategy, employed in contrast to tactics, was not a word used in English prior to the 1800s. Dr Samuel Johnson's great *Dictionary* of 1755 certainly had no entry for strategy.[6] Furthermore, no other language with which this theorist has some familiarity employed a single word that meant strategy as, for the case in point, it is defined in this book, and which was contrasted with activities deemed tactical. (My definition of military strategy is 'the direction and use made of force and the threat of force for the ends of policy as decided by politics'.)

2. It is not only persuasive, it is obvious to the point of banality, to argue that very Other people in very Other times had *mentalités*, world views, distinctive from our own. Given

the cultural differences among people alive today, it is not at all difficult to grasp this point, at least in principle. However, I detect some readiness among scholars to be overimpressed by cultural distance.[7] The main text of *Strategy Bridge* insists that 'so what' is the first question in the strategist's intellectual armoury. He needs to pose the question to those who erroneously would parade tactical or even operational-level prowess as being self-referentially significant. But, also, he should direct the question at those who deem somewhat alien appearances in words and ways to have self-evident implications for behaviour that must differ greatly from ours, even if largely in motivation. The good (enough) strategist should be both open minded and scepti-cal—hence the 'so what' question—with respect to undeniable human differences. Whether those differences are contextually cultural but contemporary, or whether they are contextually both cultural and historically more or less distant, the strategist should not prejudge the apparent evidence. If King Archidamus of Sparta talks in 432 BCE about his polity's challenges in terms that read to us today as grand strategy, then it should be safe, as they say in law about a verdict, to assume that it was indeed grand strategy that Thucydides records him as having examined.[8]

3. *Ab extensio*, also it is persuasive to claim that today we are unable to recover with high confidence the pertinent conceptualization by Greek, Roman, ancient Chinese, inter alia, statesmen, 'strategists', and tacticians. Did the Romans conceive of grand strategy? If they did not, could they nonetheless design and implement one in practice? Not according to historian Benjamin Isaac in his full-frontal assault on Edward N. Luttwak's bold study of *The Grand Strategy of the Roman Empire*.[9]

4. But, if we think of strategy as a function, much of the potential merit in the historians' challenge vanishes. After long cogitation and no small number of inter-tribal scholarly arguments, this modern strategist concludes that: when it is regarded as a function, which in this case translates as a need to find ways to match the use of available means to the achievement of desired ends, strategy indeed should be deemed eternal and universal. This claim can accommodate fully historians' plausible arguments over change in *mentalités*, and their accurate (to the best of my knowledge) assertion that strategy as it is, or should be, understood today is not to be discovered in a single word in times past in any language.

As should be crystal clear from the definitions provided early in Chapter 1, the twinned core ideas, the two suns, of strategy for this strategic theorist are 'direction and use made of means of various kinds'. Whether the subject is strategy as a broad function with content unspecified, whether it is grand strategy, or whether it is military strategy, the formula of 'direction and use made of means' captures what must be located, snared, and bounded. My take on strategy is, of course, more inclusive than was that favoured by Clausewitz.[10] However, my preference is a direct extrapolation from the master's central distinction. This distinction, the one so frequently obscured in our contemporary usage, is between the activity, which is tactics, and the guidance, employment, and consequences of the activity, which is strategy. In other words, action and its purpose have to be distinguishable and distinguished, notwithstanding their practical interdependence.

As Beatrice Heuser among other notable scholars has recognized, the common meaning of strategy has indeed migrated upwards since Clausewitz's day.[11] Unfortunately, it has migrated not only with benefit towards and into the vital category of grand strategy, but, alas, also so far up the chain of command that it overlaps, and is readily confused with, policy. Whereas Clausewitz's definition of strategy plausibly approximates what the twenty-first century typically understands by operations, though that is not wholly true in my opinion, at least he drew an unmistakeable line between tactics and strategy. As my main text suggests, the modern conceptual and doctrinal insertion of an operational level of war between strategy and tactics is not entirely the blessing that most theorists and practitioners today assume to be the case. Whatever the merits of the idea of an operational level, and they are substantial, it does have the potential, and indeed the actual, ability to confuse players in the categories both below and above it in the hierarchy of functions. Skilled strategists can neglect tactics, because they may believe it is a lesser but included activity that can safely be left to the attention of operational-level commanders. Similarly, many people worried about the use made of tactical effort, can be seduced by the organizational and doctrinal existence of the operational level of war into assuming that strategic consequences comprise a subject well enough handled by that intermediate level. As Edward N. Luttwak has observed tellingly, there is no natural harmony among what we can identify as distinguishable levels of war or, indeed, for an expansion upon his thought, among those levels in relevant peacetime activities either.[12] It is helpful to remember that as a general, though not absolute, rule the fewer the moving parts comprising articulated, but supposedly cooperating, bodies, the fewer must be the sources for friction. When a chain of command grows additional links, there will be costs as well as benefits. It is only sensible to conceive of, plan for, and when politically so commanded, practice, operations, occasionally even grand operations of war (warfare). But to exercise one's operational artistry as a general need not mean that one is performing at some reified operational level. What one would be doing would be orchestrating so as to link engagements, tactics, as strategic guidance demands, *ceteris paribus*. Historical experience and commonsense both tell us that conceptual and military institutional affirmation of the idea of an operational level of warfare tends to have consequences harmful to strategic performance. It increases the probability that tactical behaviour will be directed and commanded not so much for strategic ends, but rather for operational purposes that may or may not stand careful strategic audit. The more robust a military's doctrinal and institutional commitment to a postulated operational level of warfare, the more likely is it that the distinctive perspective of that level will be permitted to usurp the practical authority of strategy.

Both such of the historical record, the past, as we are able to recover, albeit only as history, as well as the admittedly unreliable guide that is our deeply encultured and therefore biased commonsense, try to tell us that the strategic function is inalienable from an eternal human condition. Regardless of the size, political organization, temporal historical placement, and circumstances, of a human community, it has had no prudent option other than purposefully to try to direct and employ its means by chosen ways in order to achieve its desired goals. I admit to the occurrence of exceptional cases of purely expressive, irrational, though scarcely wholly random, violence, to which strategy must be judged a stranger. However, to grant that much is not to concede anything of real substance that could undermine the argument here. Overwhelmingly, security communities have acted with intent when they have decided upon a course of action; hence they behaved *strategically*. The intention may be unwise, the decisions ill considered, and the action might be poorly performed. But the strategic function itself would be operating. To armour the argument even more, I claim that even though communities have been known to neglect explicit attention to the strategic function, it has always been the case, regardless of their time and place, that they ought not to have been thus negligent. The need for strategy on any reasonable definition is eternal and universal.

Professional historians are right to chide modern strategists for their frequent ana-chronisms when they venture as casual tourists into the foreign country of the past for purportedly valuable illustration of arguments framed for the security challenges of today.

We strategists can be guilty of accidental anachronism, and it might matter that our concepts are indeed out of harmony with the lands and times into which we thrust them carelessly. Many an important debate on a defence topic has been amply, though not accurately, decorated with purportedly telling illustrative historical analogies. It is probably true to claim that historical analogy is not merely a feature of contemporary defence debate, rather is it a heavy staple item. Since all that we can claim to know with some confidence has to refer to that which has, or is believed to have, happened in the near or distant past, really there is no escaping the benefits and seductions of argument and counterargument by claimed analogy.

All that I can offer by way of justification for occasional anachronism by myself and my colleagues among modern strategists is that although we do our best to avoid historically unharmonious usage, the hazards are not comprehensively preventable, save at unacceptable cost. Understanding anachronism in the standard pejorative definition deployed at the beginning of this essay, the only way for a strategist to avoid it with high confidence would be by a total eschewal of historical evidence-by-illustration in his arguments. Bernard Brodie famously complained that many of his distinguished colleagues at RAND were, to rephrase him, at best history-lite.[13] I doubt if it is even possible for a modern strategist, no matter how technical or future focused he may be, to exclude some historical material from his argument. The inevitability of this is readily appreciated when one poses the question, 'when does history end and something else begin?' Is the American war in Vietnam history? Or Gulf War I (1991), or even II (2003)? Where does one draw the line in the sands of time?

The unsatisfactory existential truth appears to be that we modern strategists are damned if we do and damned if we do not, with respect to the use of history that is certain to have at least some anachronistic flavouring that will jar the tribal susceptibilities of a few professional historians. On the one hand, if contemporary strategists stay firmly dug in only on their small temporal island of the present, rightly they are accused of ignoring past experience and of eschewing gratuitously the education they ought to gain from access to it. But, on the other hand, when strategists take advice and seek a measure of familiarity with the past, they cannot help but bring to that feast the fruits of their contemporary professional and other enculturation. Dare I say it? Even anachronism-sensitive professional historians cannot help but be cursed by their rear-view mirrors which grant hindsight that must colour judgement. Also unavoidably, they are condemned to hold contemporary attitudes and ideas unhelpful for historical empathy. Although it is necessary for historians to alert their non-historian strategist peers to the perils of anachronism, they do need to be aware of the costs of undue tribalism. While a modern strategist, and possibly even an historian, cannot reliably recover the conceptual kit that, say, ancient practitioners of statecraft and the art of war brought to their tasks, he can attempt carefully to guess at the ancient's intentions. Often the evidence of several kinds is not entirely missing, rather is it more or less frustratingly incomplete and hard to interpret. Furthermore, for a dangerous postulate, I invite my historian colleagues at least to consider the possibility that our contemporary strategic ideas and methods, albeit in notable ways apparently anachronistic for the past, sometimes can make good enough sense for today of historical episodes.

It may well be a suggestion too far for professional historians, but I am moved, not entirely mischievously, to venture the thought that it does not really matter whether an explanation is direly, even egregiously, anachronistic, provided it does its intended job plausibly and has substantive contemporary resonance for us. I recognize that I may be suggesting that bad history occasionally can serve a useful purpose. Some years ago I hazarded the truly perilous thought that what matters in our reading of Clausewitz is what we are able and choose to make of him, given our unavoidably historically specific enculturation.[14] That distinctly fragile postulate can be contrasted with the historians' view, which requires, correctly and virtuously, that one must strive to comprehend the messages(s) of *On War* as they were intended by its author—as best we are able to recover his intentions. In order to achieve such empathy, one needs to command understanding of the theorist's life and times in all his contexts (including the historical). I am deeply respectful of the historians' perspective, as I am of the demand that Clausewitz, inter alia, should be read in the situation of his place and time in so far as that is possible. Nonetheless, the rebellious social scientist in me at least half believes that it is right and proper, as well as inescapable, that today we bring to the classics of strategic theory, as we do to all of history, our own perspective and our pressing concerns. We should not apologize for that which we cannot avoid. Moreover, for the twenty-first century, we may recover part of a narrative from *On War*, say, that is not the one its author sought to privilege. We should take what we can from the past, and we should do so only critically, including self-critically. But the general theory of strategy exists primarily for the benefit of practice today. Antiquarianism has its justifications, but they are not relevant to modern strategy. It is far more important that we find the best value for our times that we can in Clausewitz's theorizing, as opposed to our striving to recover with full confidence exactly what the Prussian most probably meant, across the barriers of time and language. This is not to condone mistranslation, grossly anachronistic linguistic usage, and casual context-free extraction of partial points from *On War*. But it is to claim that it is our duty to read Clausewitz for our education, not to be faithful to the master after the fashion of a medieval copyist seeking to preserve a sacred text for unquestioning veneration entirely in its original form.

Inadvertently, this appendix may give the appearance of libelling historians with an undue inclusivity. It is a matter of well-published record that very many historians generally are comfortable with the use of modern strategic concepts to help explain behaviour in times past.[15] The theme of this essay has not been a dispute between two disciplined tribes of historians and (today typically social scientific) strategists. Some strategists do seek depth in historical understanding, and some historians, often with mild explicit caveats, are not averse to borrowing concepts from modern strategy. The final judgement in this discussion is provided by a most distinguished scholar-practitioner, Louis J. Halle.

> Thucydides, as he himself anticipated, wrote the history not only of the Peloponnesian War. He also wrote the history of the Napoleonic wars, World War I, World War II, and the Cold War.[16]

It would seem to be the case that when one thinks of strategy as a function, much of the sting goes away from the charge of strategic anachronism across time and culture.

NOTES

1. In Harry Turtledove, *The Guns of the South* (New York: Ballantine Books, 1992), late apartheid era South Africa employs time travel in order to effect a decisive intervention in the American Civil War in favour of the Confederate States of America.

2. I am especially grateful to Hew Strachan for his endeavours to save me from the potentially mortal sin of anachronism. His article, 'The Lost Meaning of Strategy', *Survival*, 47 (autumn 2005), 33–54, is proving seminal for contemporary debate.

3. Judy Pearsall and Bill Trumble, eds., *The Oxford English Reference Dictionary (OERD)*, 2nd edn. (Oxford: Oxford University Press, 1996), 46.

4. The cottage industry of speculation about the end of the Roman Empire in the West is in a healthy condition. For good recent products, see Peter Heather, *The Fall of the Roman Empire* (London: Macmillan, 2005); and Adrian Goldsworthy, *How Rome Fell: Death of a Superpower* (New Haven, CT: Yale University Press, 2009). Lest I be accused of professional parochialism at the expense of historians, I must record the fact that for our part we modern strategists and other theorists of the contemporary world enjoy debating why it was that the greatly unlovable USSR declined and fell. One recent offering for this debate asserts with some plausibility that the collapse of the oil price to a mere $10 a barrel in 1985–6 succeeded rapidly (May 1986) by the nuclear meltdown at Chernobyl, both in the context of an emerging military defeat in Afghanistan, proved fatal. '[T]he sudden collapse of oil prices turned out to be cataclysmic, in fact the beginning of the end.' Michael Stuermer, *Putin and the Rise of Russia* (London: Phoenix, 2009), 91. It is, and will long remain, open season on why the USSR departed. There will never be a definitive simple explanation.

5. In 1771, Lt. Colonel Paul Gideon Joly de Maizeroy, a leading French military theorist of the age, translated the *Taktika* (ca. 905) of Byzantine Emperor Leo VI ('the Wise', 886–912), wherein the author's original *strategike* (Greek) was somewhat freely translated as the art of the general. The translator recognized explicitly in his commentary the high significance of Leo's strategy/tactics distinction, but was not quite ready to commit to the term strategy, notwithstanding his appreciation of the ca. 905 wisdom of the Emperor. I am exceedingly grateful to my colleague, Beatrice Heuser, for sharing this product of her successful detective work with me. Maizeroy overcame his reluctance to employ the word strategy when he published his *Théorie de la guerre, Où l'on expose la constitution et formation dé l'Infanterie et de la Cavalerie, leurs manoeuvres élémentaires, avec l'application des principes à la grande Tactique, Suivie de démonstration Sur la Stratégique* (Lausanne: 1777). The year 1777 would seem to have been truly a 'tipping point' as some theorist might say, for explicit modern recognition of a clear difference between tactics and strategy. I am grateful to my colleague, Beatrice Heuser, again, for the significant information that 1777 also saw the publication of volume one of Johann W. von Bouscheid's translation of Emperor Leo VI's *Taktika* with the German title, *Kaiser Leo der Philosopher Strategie und Taktik*, 5 vols. (Vienna: Trattner, 1777–81). See Alexander P. Kazhdan, edn., *The Oxford Dictionary of Byzantium*, vol. 3 (New York: Oxford University Press, 1991), 2008, 'Taktika of Leo VI'.

6. Samuel Johnson, *A Dictionary of the English Language: In Which the Words Are Deduced from Their Originals, and Illustrated in Their Difference Significations by Examples from the Best Writers: To Which Are Prefixed, a History of the Language, and an English Grammar*, vol. II (1755; London: W. Strachan and others, 1773), 743, can offer an entry only on 'stratagem', which is close to strategy, but, alas, not close enough. *The Oxford English Dictionary Online [OEDO]*, 2nd edn. (1989) cites C. James, *Military Dictionary*, 3rd edn. (1810), as the first modern use of strategy. OEDO's definition is tolerable, though it is not as clear as it should be in the distinction it needs to register vis-à-vis operations. OEDO informs us that strategy is '[T]he art of a commander-in-chief [so far so good: CSG]; the art of projecting and directing the larger military movements and operations of a campaign [this muddies the water: CSG]. Usually

distinguished from *tactics*, which is the art of handling forces in battle or in the immediate presence of the enemy [this is sound on tactics, but it risks serious confusion both by neglecting to locate operations between tactics and strategy, and also by implying that strategy involves the handling of forces other than when the enemy is present: CSG], <http://dictionary.oed.com/cgi/entry/50238986?query_type=word&-queryword=strategy> accessed 21 June 2009. Pearsall and Trumble, eds., OERD, do slightly better with their effort. For them, strategy is '(1) the art of war. (2a) the management of an army or armies in a campaign. (b) the planning and direction of the larger military movements and overall operations of a campaign. (c) an instance of this or a plan formed according to it. (3) a plan of action or policy in business or politics etc.' 1428.

7. Patrick Porter, *Military Orientalism: Eastern War Through Western Eyes* (London: C. Hurst, 2009), is a potent vaccine against the virus of the temptation to make too much of obvious cultural differences.

8. Thucydides, *The Landmark Thucydides: A Comprehensive Guide to The Peloponnesian War*, ed. Robert B. Strassler, rev. tr. Richard Crawley (ca. 400 BCE; New York: Free Press, 1996), 45–7.

9. Benjamin Isaac, *The Limits of Empire: The Roman Army in the East* (Oxford: Clarendon Press, 1990). Isaac insists that the Romans did not conceive of strategy, grand or military, in terms dominant among the ranks of strategic analysts today. He argues that '[t]hese questions [the motives which led to decisions to go to war: CSG] are often discussed [today by modern strategists: CSG] in terms of strategy, and it is assumed without further ado that the Romans were capable of realizing in practice what they could not define verbally. The assumption is that we can distil theoretical concepts from a reality that can be grasped through the interpretation of literary sources and archaeological remains. There is, however, the danger of imposing an inadequate evidence on interpretation that seems attractive only because we know so little', 374–5. Isaac insists that 'there was no Grand Strategy underlying Roman frontier policy', 416. '[T]he constituent elements of Roman frontier policy were not of a kind to produce a Grand—or even merely consistent—strategy... Rome expanded where it could, not where it should.' 416. Isaac is in no doubt that '[i]n the case of imperial Rome... anachronistic judgements are often imposed... The moral qualities attributed by the Romans to good leaders were quite different from those demanded today... The concepts of state, territory, and borders were different. The limitations of ancient geography and cartography resulted in views of the interrelationship between political power and military action unlike those held in our times. Modern logic cannot adequately explain the choice of ancient frontier lines', 419. Isaac is scholarly and cogent, but is he right? Almost as much to the point, even if he is right enough, so what? Can we find lessons for us in Roman behaviour, even if our best efforts to recover Roman motivation are academically unsafe? A principal target for Isaac's mighty blast was Edward N. Luttwak's bold work, *The Grand Strategy of the Roman Empire: From the First Century A.D. to the Third* (Baltimore, MD: Johns Hopkins University Press, 1976). Also highly relevant to this debate is Luttwak's more recent venture into distant strategies, and especially the Appendix, 'Was Strategy Feasible in Byzantine Times?' in *The Grand Strategy of the Byzantine Empire* (Cambridge, MA: Harvard University Press, 2009), 421–2. Luttwak is magisterially dismissive of his critics, whose view of strategy he regards as too narrow and too modern. The latter is a nicely ironic judgement with which to bomb some professional historians. He insists that the question of whether or not strategy was feasible for the Romans and Byzantines 'rests on how strategy is defined'.

Luttwak raises his standard thus: 'I hold that strategy is not about moving armies, as in board games, but rather comprehends the entire struggle of adversarial forces, which need not have a spatial dimension at all [he wonders if his critics confuse strategy with 'the discredited "pseudo-science of Hausoferian-sic-geopolitics"': CSG], as with the eternal competition between weapons and countermeasures.' 421. Although Isaac argues well and does score some plausible points, the core of Luttwak's position is by far the more persuasive of the two. It cannot be conclusive, but certainly it is indicative that the distinguished Byzantinist, Walter Emil Kaegi, Jr., can write: 'Byzantine strategists tend to discuss strategy, operations, and tactics together with stratagems even though Byzantine writers are aware of distinctions between, at a minimum, tactics and strategy.' *Some Thoughts on Byzantine Military Strategy* (Brookline, MA: Hellenic College Press, 1983), 3. The Byzantines were, of course, the direct heirs of Ancient (Greek and Roman primarily, albeit with Persian and other influences) culture on matters of statecraft, including military subjects. See Victor Davis Hanson, ed., *Makers of Ancient Strategy: From the Persian Wars to the Fall of Rome* (Princeton, NJ: Princeton University Press, 2010).

10. Carl von Clausewitz, *On War*, tr. Michael Howard and Peter Paret (1832–4; Princeton, NJ: Princeton University Press, 1976), 128 ('strategy, *the use of engagements for the object of the war*,' emphasis in the original), and 177 ('[s]trategy is the use of the engagement for the purpose of the war').

11. See Beatrice Heuser, *The Evolution of Strategy: Thinking War from Antiquity to the Present* (Cambridge: Cambridge University Press, 2010), ch. 1, 'Introduction: What is Strategy?'. I am grateful to Professor Heuser for letting me read her manuscript prior to its publication.

12. Edward N. Luttwak, *Strategy: The Logic of War and Peace*, rev. edn. (Cambridge, MA: Harvard University Press, 2001), xii.

13. Bernard Brodie offered the following pertinent thoughts: 'Thus, where the great strategic writers and teachers of the past, with the sole and understandable exception of Douhet [Giulio Douhet, who wrote on air power: CSG], based the development of their art almost entirely on a broad and perceptive reading of history—in the case of Clausewitz and Jomini mostly recent history but exceptionally rich for their needs—the present generation of "civilian strategists" are with markedly few exceptions singularly devoid of history.' *War and Politics* (New York: Macmillan, 1973), 475. Brodie proceeded to examine critically the excuse or explanation that the nuclear revolution severed contemporary strategy from the past. He pointed out convincingly that the dominant role of politics in strategy—the source of strategy's 'ends'—has endured, regardless of technical change.

14. Colin S. Gray, *Modern Strategy* (Oxford: Oxford University Press, 1999). In this book, I insisted that 'we do not use *On War* to mislead'. Also I expressed disdain for the raiding of Clausewitz for 'decorative quotation'. However, I insisted then, as I continue to emphasize, that 'one should not be afraid to treat *On War* much as innovative actor-directors handle Shakespeare when they present the bard in modern dress', 82. I apologize for the sin of quoting myself.

15. For example, see the essays in Williamson Murray, MacGregor Knox, and Alvin Bernstein, eds., *The Making of Strategy: Rulers, States, and War* (Cambridge: Cambridge University Press, 1994); Murray and Richard Hart Sinnreich, eds., *The Past as Prologue: The Importance of History to the Military Profession* (Cambridge: Cambridge University Press, 2006); and Murray and Jim Lacey, eds., *The Making of Peace: Rulers, States, and the Aftermath of War* (Cambridge: Cambridge University Press, 2009).

A fourth book in this long-running series from a distinctly professional historians' stable (with the exception of myself) is forthcoming on the subject of leadership in grand strategy, again with cases ranging from imperial Rome nearly to the present: Williamson Murray, Richard Hart Sinnreich, and Jim Lacey, eds., *Grand Strategy: Nations and Militaries* (New York: Cambridge University Press, forthcoming 2010). Geoffrey Parker, *The Grand Strategy of Philip II* (New Haven, CT: Yale University Press, 1998), is a study in great depth which bears strongly on the subject of this appendix.

16. Louis J. Halle, *The Elements of International Strategy: A Primer for the Nuclear Age, vol. x* (Lanham, MD: University Press of America, 1984), 15.

Appendix D
Potent Trinities: Fourteen Skeleton Keys of Theory for the Strategist

Strategy inherently is a complicated subject, while its theorists are easily seduced into rendering it even more complicated than it needs to be by accidental and ironic consequence of ill-directed efforts to identify and unravel its mysteries. Unfortunately, strategy in its many relevant, associate, and adjunct parts is much simpler to dissect and analyse piece by piece, than it is as a more than marginally indigestible whole. In striving to explain the nature and working of strategy, the earnest theorist is always in danger of some surrendering of overall understanding as a price paid for capture of the individual parts. Strategic thought should offer helpful guidance to the individual trees in the strategy forest, but as a consequence of so doing it may be unable to discern the nature, shape, and extent of the forest itself. Erudition and energy in research and analysis have been known to strand the scholar ever more hopelessly in a morass of unmanageable detail.

The theorist and the practitioner of strategy need conceptual survival aids to help bring intellectual order to the confusing mass of disparate detail with which they must cope. One category of such aids is Trinitarian conceptualization.[1] This theorist is not claiming that trinities necessarily are superior to pairs or quartets, among others. All that is claimed is that the authors of strategic and strategy related thought for 2,500 years have been attracted to Trinitarian theorizing. This preference is manifested in a body of Trinitarian theories, perhaps pre-theories that are useful for strategists today. Struck by the modest proliferation of more or less helpful trinities, I decided to gather and offer the more potent among them in an appendix.

The way to approach the fourteen trinities itemized below is as if they are a bunch of skeleton keys with much overlapping competence. A strategist who carries these conceptual skeleton keys cannot fail to find them either helpful or essential, depending upon the challenges he must address. These are keys to be used individually and in combination with discretion for the purpose of the hour. Readers might like to regard this appendix as an aid to the book's main text, but not, I hope, as a substitute for it. I insist only that these trinities can be important in opening doors to understanding, not that individually or collectively they indicate, and perhaps contain, everything important to the strategist. This should be true, but I do not offer the claim with a money back guarantee as to its accuracy. Indeed, almost as always is the case, recognition of the trinities is much easier than is their pragmatically effective, and appropriate rather than harmfully anachronistic, application to particular historical situations.

(STRATEGIC METHOD): ENDS, WAYS, AND MEANS

This is the strategic function; it is what strategy does. As is true of most of the trinities identified here, the logically correct character of the connections among the three items will by no means necessarily be the actual ones in a dynamic historical narrative. The self-evidently sequential cascade from purposes, by chosen methods, with tools, often is reversed in practice.

(HOW TO STUDY): WIDTH, DEPTH, AND CONTEXT

Michael Howard argues that military history—though it could be any kind of history, I believe—needs to be studied over a long period, the subject in particular focus should be probed deeply, and that that subject has to be fully situated in its surrounding and affecting circumstances.[2] This advice is broadly relevant to most matters of concern to the strategist.

(HOW TO WRITE GOOD THEORY): DEEP THOUGHT, GREAT THEORY, SHORT BOOK[3]

Classic books are not always short, but they would likely be even better were they less prolix. Clausewitz and Thucydides certainly were not brief, which is a contrast with Sun Tzu who was unduly economical with his ideographs. Just as a little theory typically is more useful to practice than is a lot of theory, so a smaller architecture of theory is likely to be more refined and profound than is a theoretical structure of monumental complexity. It is hard to find a large book on strategic ideas that would not benefit from a conceptual and linguistic cull (most probably not excluding this one!). Short books can be too short, admittedly, but when the author truly is master of his subject there is everything to be said in praise of economy of expression.

(POWER): INTELLECTUAL, PHYSICAL, AND PSYCHOLOGICAL

Kautilya tells us that this trio are the three kinds of power. 'Intellectual strength provides the power of [good] counsel; a prosperous treasury and a strong army provide physical power and valour is the basis for [morale and] energetic action.'[4]

(ETHICS AND STRATEGY): FORCE, ORDER, AND JUSTICE[5]

To be normative as well as descriptive, a condition of order is likely to be stable when the force that polices it is committed to behave justly and, above all else, when the society thus ordered believes that the order extant is tolerably just. Judgement as to what is and is not just is of course profoundly cultural as well as situational.

(STRATEGIC BEHAVIOUR): POWER, EFFECT, CONTROL

This trinity offers another (to that offered as in '(Strategic method): ends, ways, and means' above) perspective on the strategic function. Strategists develop and employ conceptually ever contestable power, in order to achieve the strategic effect that should be rewarded with some control, at least leverage, over the adversary.[6]

(POLICY): CAPABILITIES, DECLARATIONS, AND ACTIONS

What is policy? When is policy not really policy? The concept of policy is clear enough; it is a course or principle of action agreed upon by authority, hence with authority. However, in practice for the strategist who must endeavour to support it, reality is apt to be more opaque than the dictionary definition just provided suggests should be so. The trinity specified here brackets policy words (declarations) between vital categories of evidence, capabilities, and action. Whether policy can be policy when a polity behaves contrary to its proclaimed aspirations, or when it cannot behave at all because it lacks the means to do so, is a matter for individual scholarly taste. This trinity is useful in helping alert us to the reality that all is not always as it seems in the realm of claims for policy. And when a policy is not obviously doing much purposeful driving from its driving seat, the strategist cannot do strategy as he should. When policy ends are weak and wobbling at best, the strategist virtually is obliged by default to allow operational and tactical opportunism to serve as his pragmatic guide. Strategy worthy of the name cannot be done in the absence of political direction.

(MOTIVES FOR THE COLLECTIVE BEHAVIOUR OF SECURITY COMMUNITIES): FEAR, HONOUR, AND INTEREST

Thucydides' justly famous triptych has never been bettered as a terse formula able both to accommodate every significant impulsion behind political behaviour, yet to accomplish that heroic task without banality.[7] It is all but incredible that three concepts linked in ever dynamic interrelations can help critically to organize explanation and understanding of so complex and messy an actuality as the course of strategic history. If we modernize honour to mean culture, inclusively defined, the authority of the triptych is augmented—though, admittedly, it is hard to improve on near perfection.

(NATURE OF WAR, I): 'HOSTILITY, PURPOSE, AND CHANCE' (OR VIOLENCE, CHANCE, AND REASON)

This is the core of Clausewitz's primary trinity, which expresses the nature of war. This ordering and rendition of the trio of elements is the one most favoured by Antulio J. Echevarria, with whose choices I concur.[8] Alternatively, so flexibly adaptable is it, this trinity can be rendered as violence, chance, and reason, the words and ordering I employ in Chapter 3. The relative weight of each element varies with time and circumstance, notwithstanding the formal strategic logic of the descending relative weight of ends, ways, and means.

(NATURE OF WAR, II): PEOPLE, GOVERNMENT, ARMY

This is Clausewitz's secondary trinity presented to correspond with the order of presentation in '(Nature of war, I): "hostility, purpose, and chance" (or violence, chance, and reason)' above.[9] The great Prussian was careful to specify that the elements in what we can best regard as his primary trinity (hostility, purpose, chance) 'mainly concern' (his words), not wholly respectively concern, the agencies he identified as the people, government, and the army. Between them, Clausewitz's two not-quite-synonymous trinities can tolerate any degree of variation in historical detail (e.g. tribal society, ancient city state, feudal kingdom, modern state, even contemporary terrorist organization).

(LEVELS OF WAR): POLICY, STRATEGY, TACTICS

This is the logic of Clausewitz. It collapses politics and policy into the single compound of policy (with politics assumed, not unreasonably), and by implication it collapses operations into tactics. This trinity is austere by today's standards, but it is all the more useful by virtue of the economy in that discipline. However, the virtuous parsimony of this stark trinity may blind rather than illuminate. Given the complexity of the subject, less thoughtful Anglophone users of this trinity could fail to appreciate the continuous relevance of politics for policy, and the depth of the challenge posed by the need to harness tactical behaviour to strategic purpose. It is useful to rework this familiar trinity into functional terms and understand it to refer to political skill, the creative management of (largely military) assets, and fighting power.

(LEVELS OF WAR): STRATEGY, OPERATIONS, TACTICS

This trinity is authoritative in doctrine in many countries today, including the United States and Britain. It postulates an operational level of war intervening between strategy (purpose) and tactics (behaviour). The rationale for these three postulated levels is unexceptionable, since the concept of operations refers reasonably enough, indeed intelligently, to the need for generalship in orchestration of distinct though hopefully connected military engagements. Of course, it can and has been objected that such operational artistry rather should be regarded as a task for strategy.[10] The major problem with this trinity is that it totally excludes the purposeful world of politics and policy. Such exclusion is defensible only if one can justify omitting to accommodate recognition of the variable strength and content of the political grip upon strategy, and the cascade of consequences from that reach. I believe that such an economical exclusion is unwise or worse.

(COMBAT): FIRE, MANOEUVRE, SHOCK

These are the three basic, variably interdependent, behaviours that produce military combat performance. Military forces pursue their tasks by means of ever changeable combinations of these three options.

(THE FIRST TEAM OF GENERAL THEORY): CLAUSEWITZ, *ON WAR* (1832–4); SUN TZU, *THE ART OF WAR* (CA. 490 BCE); THUCYDIDES, *THE HISTORY OF THE PELOPONNESIAN WAR* (CA. 400 BCE)

The general theory of strategy begins and arguably might be claimed not implausibly to end with just these three theorists. They are the first division of strategic theory (see Appendix B).

The fourteen trinities are specified and recommended as conceptual tools, by functional analogy as skeleton keys. They can be helpful on a 'pick and mix' basis to strategists who need help to penetrate the fog, and seek some order out of the confusion, that always menaces their performance.

NOTES

1. See the useful discussion of Clausewitz's liking for trinities in Hew Strachan, *Clausewitz's On War: A Biography* (New York: Atlantic Monthly Press, 2007), 85–7. One suspects that although Trinitarian organization typically is a sensible compromise between the undue reductionism and simplicity of binary analysis and the perilously excessive categorization by quartets, the obvious preference for threesomes was more aesthetic than analytical.
2. Michael Howard, *The Causes of Wars and Other Essays* (London: Counterpoint, 1983), 215–17.
3. This somewhat syncopated, Chinese-style, Trinitarian form has been coined by the author as good advice that he wishes he could follow. A worthy model of a classic text that is both short yet is long enough, and which gains energy from the concentrated thought required by brevity is J. C. Wylie, *Military Strategy: A General Theory of Power Control* (1967; Annapolis, MD: Naval Institute Press, 1989). By way of some contrast, Sun Tzu's *The Art of War*, tr. Ralph D. Sawyer (ca. 490 BCE; Boulder, CO: Westview Press, 1994), is shorter, but could have been improved by being longer.
4. Kautilya, *The Arthashastra*, tr. L. N. Rangarajan (4th century BCE; New Delhi, Penguin Books, 1992), 559.
5. I am indebted to Robert E. Osgood and Robert W. Tucker for my liking for this trinity. See their book, *Force, Order, and Justice* (Baltimore: Johns Hopkins University Press, 1967).
6. This logic is central to the general strategic theory in the main text of this book. I am in good company. See Carl von Clausewitz, *On War*, tr. Michael Howard and Peter Paret (1832–4; Princeton, NJ: Princeton University Press, 1976), 75, and Wylie, *Military Strategy*, 66–7, 124, 152.

7. Thucydides, *The Landmark Thucydides: A Comprehensive Guide to The Peloponnesian War*, ed. Robert B. Strassler, rev. tr. Richard Crawley (ca. 400 BCE; New York: Free Press, 1996), 43.

8. For Clausewitz's trinity see *On War*, tr. Michael Howard and Peter Paret (1832–4; Princeton, NJ: Princeton University Press, 1976), 89. I am obliged to Antulio J. Echevarria II, *Clausewitz and Contemporary War* (Oxford: Oxford University Press), 91.

9. Clausewitz, *On War*, 89.

10. For some contrasting opinions on the concept of an operational level of war, see Edward N. Luttwak, 'The Operational Level of War', *International Security*, 5 (winter 1980/1), 61–79; Echevarria, *Clausewitz and Contemporary War*, 140; Strachan, *Clausewitz's On War*, 109–10; and Justin Kelly and Mike Brennan, *Alien: How Operational Art Devoured Strategy* (Carlisle, PA: Strategic Studies Institute, US Army War College, September 2009).

Bibliography

Abella, Alex, *Soldiers of Reason: The Rand Corporation and the Rise of the American Empire* (Orlando, FL: Harcourt, 2008).

Adams, Michael C. C., *Our Masters the Rebels: A Speculation on Union Military Failure in the East, 1861–1865* (Cambridge, MA: Harvard University Press, 1978).

Alexander, Martin S., and J. F. V. Keiger, eds., *France and the Algerian War, 1954–62: Strategy, Operations and Diplomacy* (London: Frank Cass, 2002).

Alger, John I., *The Quest for Victory: The History of the Principles of War* (Westport, CT: Greenwood Press, 1982).

Allison, Graham, *The Essence of Decision: Explaining the Cuban Missile Crisis* (Boston: Little, Brown, 1971).

Andres, Richard B., 'Deep Attack against Iraq', in Thomas G. Mahnken and Thomas A. Kennedy, eds., *War in Iraq: Planning and Execution* (Abingdon: Routledge, 2007), 69–96.

Andrew, Christopher, *Defence of the Realm: The Authorized History of MI5* (London: Allen Lane, 2009).

Aron, Raymond, *Peace and War: A Theory of International Relations* (Garden City, NY: Doubleday, 1966).

Asprey, Robert B., *The German High Command at War: Hindenburg and Ludendorff and the First World War* (Boston: Little, Brown, 1993).

Auerswald, David, Janet Breslin-Smith, and Paula Thornhill, 'Teaching Strategy Through Theory and Practice', *Defence Studies*, 4 (spring 2004), 1–17.

Bahnsen, John C. (Doc.), 'Charisma', in Christopher Kolenda, ed., *Leadership: The Warrior's Art* (Carlisle, PA: Army War College Foundation, 2001), 259–75.

Ball, Desmond, and Jeffrey Richelson, eds., *Strategic Nuclear Targeting* (Ithaca, NY: Cornell University Press, 1986).

Bassford, Christopher, *Clausewitz in English: The Reception of Clausewitz in Britain and America* (New York: Oxford University Press, 1994).

Baylis, John, and John Garnett, eds., *Makers of Nuclear Strategy* (New York: St. Martin's Press, 1991).

——and others, eds., *Strategy in the Contemporary World: An Introduction to Strategic Studies*, 2nd edn. (Oxford: Oxford University Press, 2007).

——James Wirtz, and Colin S. Gray, eds., *Strategy in the Contemporary World*, 3rd edn. (Oxford: Oxford University Press, 2009).

Baynes, John, *Morale: A Study of Men and Courage* (Garden City Park, NY: Avery Publishing Group, 1988).

Beckett, Ian F. W., *Modern Insurgencies and Counter-Insurgencies: Guerrillas and Their Opponents Since 1750* (London: Routledge, 2001).

Beevor, Antony, *D-Day: The Battle for Normandy* (London: Viking, 2009).

Bellamy, Chris, *The Future of Land Warfare* (New York: St. Martin's Press, 1987).

——*Absolute War: Soviet Russia in the Second World War* (London: Macmillan, 2007).

Benbow, Tim, *The Magic Bullet? Understanding the Revolution in Military Affairs* (London: Brassey's, 2004).

Beringer, Richard E., *Why the South Lost the Civil War* (Athens, GA: University of Georgia Press, 1986).

Berlin, Isaiah, *The Hedgehog and the Fox: An Essay on Tolstoy's View of History* (New York: Mentor Books, 1957).

Bernstein, Alvin, 'The Strategy of a Warrior-State: Rome and the Wars against Carthage, 264–201 B. C.', in Williamson Murray, MacGregor Knox, and Bernstein, eds., *The Making of Strategy: Rulers, States, and War* (Cambridge: Cambridge University Press, 1994), 56–84.

Betts, Richard K., 'Is Strategy an Illusion?', *International Security*, 25 (fall 2000), 5–50.

Beyerchen, Alan, 'Clausewitz, Nonlinearity, and the Unpredictability of War', *International Security*, 17 (winter 1992–3), 59–90.

——'Clausewitz and the Non-Linear Nature of Warfare: Systems of Organized Complexity', in Hew Strachan and Andreas Herberg-Rothe, eds., *Clausewitz in the Twenty-First Century* (Oxford: Oxford University Press, 2007), 45–56.

Biddle, Stephen, *Military Power: Explaining Victory and Defeat in Modern Battle* (Princeton, NJ: Princeton University Press, 2004).

——and Jeffrey A. Friedman, *The 2006 Lebanon Campaign and the Future of Warfare: Implications for Army and Defense Policy* (Carlisle, PA: Strategic Studies Institute, U.S. Army War College, September 2008).

Biddle, Tami Davis, *Rhetoric and Reality in Air Warfare: The Evolution of British and American Ideas about Strategic Bombing, 1914–1945* (Princeton, NJ: Princeton University Press, 2002).

Black, Jeremy, *Rethinking Military History* (Abingdon: Routledge, 2004).

Blainey, Geoffrey, *The Causes of War* (London: Macmillan, 1973).

Boemke, Manfred F., Gerald D. Feldman, and Elisabeth Glaser, eds., *The Treaty of Versailles: A Reassessment After 75 Years* (Cambridge: Cambridge University Press, 1998).

Bond, Brian, *Liddell Hart: A Study of His Military Thought* (New Brunswick, NJ: Rutgers University Press, 1977).

Boog, Horst, ed., *The Conduct of the Air War in the Second World War: An International Comparison* (New York: Berg, 1992).

——et al., *Germany and the Second World War: Vol. VI, The Global War* (Oxford: Clarendon Press, 2001).

——Gerhard Krebs, and Detlef Vogel, *Germany and the Second World War: Vol. VII, The Strategic Air War in Europe and the War in the West and East Asia, 1943–1944/5* (Oxford: Clarendon Press, 2006).

Boorman, Scott A., 'Fundamentals of Strategy: The Legacy of Henry Eccles', *Naval War College Review*, 62 (spring 2009), 91–115.

Booth, Ken, *Strategy and Ethnocentrism* (London: Croon, Helm, 1979).

——'Bernard Brodie', in John Baylis and John Garnett, eds., *Makers of Nuclear Strategy* (New York: St. Martin's Press, 1991), 19–56.

——and Eric Herring, *Keyguide to Information Sources in Strategic Studies* (London: Mansell Publishing, 1994).

Bourke, Joanna, *An Intimate History of Killing: Face-to-Face Killing in Twentieth-Century Warfare* (London: Granta Books, 1999).

Boyd, John R., 'A Discourse on Winning and Losing', unpub. briefing (August 1987).

Bratton, Patrick C., 'A Coherent Theory of Coercion? The Writings of Robert Pape', *Comparative Strategy*, 22 (October–November 2003), 355–72.

Breen, Bob, and Greg McCauley, eds., *The World Looking over Their Shoulders: Australian Strategic Corporals in Operations in Somalia and East Timor*, Study Paper 314 (Canberra: Land Warfare Study Centre, August 2008).

Brodie, Bernard, 'The Continuing Relevance of *On War*', in Clausewitz, 45–58.

Brodie, Bernard, *The Absolute Weapon: Atomic Power and World Order* (New York: Harcourt, Brace, 1946).

——*Strategy in the Missile Age* (Princeton, NJ: Princeton University Press, 1959).

——*War and Politics* (New York: Macmillan, 1973).

——'Strategy as a Science', in Thomas G. Mahnken and Joseph A. Maiolo, eds., *Strategic Studies: A Reader* (Abingdon: Routledge, 2008), 8–21.

Brown, Ian Malcolm, *British Logistics on the Western Front* (Westport, CT: Praeger Publishers, 1998).

Builder, Carl H., *The Masks of War: American Military Styles in Strategy and Analyses* (Baltimore, MD: Johns Hopkins University Press, 1989).

——'Keeping the Strategic Flame', *Joint Force Quarterly*, 14 (winter 1996–7), 76–84.

——and James A. Dewar, 'A Time for Planning? if Not Now, When?', *Parameters*, 24 (summer 1994), 4–15.

Bull, Hedley, 'Strategic Studies and Its Critics', *World Politics*, 20 (July 1968), 593–605.

Bungay, Stephen, *The Most Dangerous Enemy: A History of the Battle of Britain* (London: Aurum Press, 2000).

Caesar, Julius, *Caesar's Commentaries: 'On the Gallic War' and 'On The Civil War'*, tr. W. A. MacDevitt (50s and 40s BCE; El Paso, TX: El Paso Norte Press, 2005).

Callwell, Charles E., *Small Wars: A Tactical Textbook for Imperial Soldiers*, 3rd edn. (1906; London: Greenhill Books, 1990).

Carnegie Endowment for International Peace, *Report of the International Commission to Inquire into the Causes and Conduct of the Balkan Wars* (New York: The Endowment, 1914).

Chaliand, Gerard, ed., *The Art of War in World History: From Antiquity to the Nuclear Age* (Berkeley, CA: University of California Press, 1994).

Chambers, John Whiteclay, ed., *The Oxford Companion to American Military History* (Oxford: Oxford University Press, 1999).

Chandler, David G., ed., *Napoleon's Marshals* (London: Weidenfeld and Nicolson, 1987).

——*The Military Maxims of Napoleon*, tr. George C. D'Aguilar (1901; New York: Macmillan, 1987).

Charnay, J.-P., 'Strategy', in Andre Corvisier, ed., *A Dictionary of Military History*, ed. John Childs, tr. Chris Turner (Oxford: Blackwell Reference, 1994), 768–74.

Chiabotti, Stephen D., 'A Deeper Shade of Blue: The School of Advanced Air and Space Studies', *Joint Force Quarterly*, 49 (2nd qtr. 2008), 73.

Cimbala, Stephen J., *The Background and Effects of Nuclear War Complacency* (Westport, CT: Praeger Publishers, 2002).

Citino, Robert M., *Quest for Decisive Victory: From Stalemate to Blitzkrieg in Europe, 1899–1940* (Lawrence, KS: University Press of Kansas, 2002).

——*Blitzkrieg to Desert Storm: The Evolution of Operational Warfare* (Lawrence, KS: University Press of Kansas, 2004).

——*The German Way of War: From the Thirty Years' War to the Third Reich* (Lawrence, KS: University Press of Kansas, 2005).

Clausewitz, Carl von, *On War*, tr. Michael Howard and Peter Paret (1832–4; Princeton, NJ: Princeton University Press, 1976).

Clayton, Anthony, *Paths of Glory: The French Army, 1914–18* (London: Cassell, 2003).

Cleary, Thomas, *The Japanese Art of War: Understanding the Culture of Strategy* (Boston: Shambhala, 1992).

Coates, A. J., *The Ethics of War* (Manchester: Manchester University Press, 1997).

Cohen, Christopher, *Waging War Without Warriors? The Changing Culture of Military Conflict* (Boulder, CO: Lynne Rienner Publishers, 2002).

—— *The Warrior Ethos: Military Culture and the War on Terror* (Abingdon: Routledge, 2007).

Cohen, Eliot A., *Supreme Command: Soldiers, Statesmen, and Leadership in Wartime* (New York: Free Press, 2002).

Copeland, Dale C., *The Origins of Major War* (Ithaca, NY: Cornell University Press, 2000).

Corbett, Julian S., *England in the Seven Years' War: A Study in Combined Strategy*, 2 vols. (1907; London: Longmans, Green, 1918).

—— *Some Principles of Maritime Strategy* (1911; Annapolis, MD: Naval Institute Press, 1988).

Corum, James S., and Wray R. Johnson, *Airpower in Small Wars: Fighting Insurgents and Terrorists* (Lawrence, KS: University Press of Kansas, 2003).

Corvisier, Andre, ed., *A Dictionary of Military History*, ed. John Childs, tr. Chris Turner (Oxford: Blackwell Reference, 1994).

Cox, Sebastian, and Peter W. Gray, eds., *Air Power History: Turning Points from Kitty Hawk to Kosovo* (London: Frank Cass, 2002).

Creveld, Martin van, *Supplying War: Logistics from Wallenstein to Patton* (Cambridge: Cambridge University Press, 1977).

—— *Fighting Power: German and U. S. Army Performance, 1939–1945* (Westport, CT: Greenwood Press, 1982).

—— *Command in War* (Cambridge, MA: Harvard University Press, 1985).

—— *The Transformation of War* (New York: Free Press, 1991).

—— Creveld, Martin van *The Culture of War* (New York: Ballantine Books, 2008).

Crowl, Philip A., 'The Strategist's Short Catechism: Six Questions Without Answers', in Harry R. Borowski, ed., *The Harmon Memorial Lectures in Military History, 1959–1987* (Washington, DC: Office of Air Force History, U. S. Air Force, 1988), 377–88.

Czerwinski, Thomas J., *Coping with the Bounds: Speculations on Nonlinearity in Military Affairs* (Washington, DC: National Defense University Press, 1998).

Danchev, Alex, *Alchemist of War: The Life of Basil Liddell Hart* (London: Weidenfeld and Nicolson, 1998).

Davis, Richard G., *Bombing the European Axis Powers: A Historical Digest of the Combined Bomber Offensive, 1939–1945* (Maxwell AFB, AL: Air University Press, April 2006).

Deptula, David A., *Effects-Based Operations: Change in the Nature of Warfare* (Arlington, VA: Aerospace Education Foundation, 2001).

D'Este, Carlo, *A Genius for War: A Life of George S. Patton*, 2 vols. (London: HarperCollins Publishers, 1995).

—— *Eisenhower: A Soldier's Life* (New York: Henry Holt, 2002).

—— *Warlord: A Life of Churchill at War, 1874–1945* (London: Allen Lane, 2009).

Dixon, Norman F., *On the Psychology of Military Incompetence* (London: Futura Publications, 1976).

Dobbs, Michael, *One Minute to Midnight* (London: Arrow Books, 2009).

Dockrill, Michael, and John Fisher, eds., *The Paris Peace Conference, 1919: Peace without Victory?* (Basingstoke: Palgrave, 2001).

Doubler, Michael D., *Closing with the Enemy: How GIs Fought the War in Europe, 1944–1945* (Lawrence, KS: University Press of Kansas, 1994).

Doughty, Robert A., *Pyrrhic Victory: French Strategy and Operations in the Great War* (Cambridge, MA: Harvard University Press, 2005).

Douhet, Giulio, *The Command of the Air* (1921, 1927; New York: Arno Press, 1972).

Dower, John W., *War Without Mercy: Race and Power in the Pacific War* (New York: Pantheon Books, 1986).

Dueck, Colin, *Reluctant Crusaders: Power, Culture, and Change in American Grand Strategy* (Princeton, NJ: Princeton University Press, 2006).

Duffy, Michael, Theo Farrell, and Geoffrey Sloan, eds., *Doctrine and Military Effectiveness*, Strategic Policy Studies 1 (Exeter: Strategic Studies Group of the Britannia Royal Naval College and Exeter University, 1997).

Dupuy, T. N., *A Genius for War: The German Army and General Staff, 1807–1945* (London: MacDonald and Jane's, 1977).

Eberle, Henrik, and Matthias Uhl, eds., *The Hitler Book: The Secret Dossier Prepared for Stalin*, tr. Giles McDonogh (London: John Murray, 2005).

Eccles, Henry E., *Military Concepts and Philosophy* (New Brunswick, NJ: Rutgers University Press, 1965).

Echevarria II, Antulio J., 'Dynamic Inter-Dimensionality: A Revolution in Military Theory', *Joint Force Quarterly*, 15 (spring 1997), 29–36.

——*After Clausewitz: German Military Thinkers Before the Great War* (Lawrence, KS: University Press of Kansas, 2000).

——*Challenging Transformation's Clichés* (Carlisle, PA: Strategic Studies Institute, U. S. Army War College, December 2006).

——*Clausewitz and Contemporary War* (Oxford: Oxford University Press, 2007).

——*Imagining Future War: The West's Technological Revolution and Visions of Wars to Come, 1880–1914* (Westport, CT: Praeger Security International, 2007).

Edmonds, James E., *History of the Great War, Military Operations, France and Belgium, 1918: 2, March-April: Continuation of the German Offensive* (London: Macmillan, 1937).

Engels, D. W., *Alexander the Great and the Logistics of the Macedonian Army* (Berkeley, CA: University of California Press, 1980).

Enthoven, Alain, and K. Wayne Smith, *How Much Is Enough? Shaping the Defense Program, 1961–1969* (New York: Harper and Row, 1971).

Esdaile, Charles J., 'De-Constructing the French Wars: Napoleon as an Anti-Strategist', *Journal of Strategic Studies*, 31 (August 2008), 515–52.

Evans, Michael, and Alan Ryan, eds., *The Human Face of Warfare: Killing, Fear and Chaos in Battle* (St. Leonards, Australia: Allen and Unwin, 2000).

Farrell, Kevin W., 'Culture of Confidence: The Tactical Excellence of the German Army of the Second World War', in Christopher Kolenda, ed., *Leadership: The Warrior's Art* (Carlisle, PA: Army War College Foundation, 2001), 177–203.

Finley, M. I., 'Introduction', to Thucydides, *History of the Peloponnesian War*, tr. Rex Warner (ca. 400 BCE; London: Penguin Books, 1972).

Fitzsimmons, Michael, 'The Problem of Uncertainty in Strategic Planning', *Survival*, 48 (winter 2006–7), 131–46.

Fleming, Colin M., 'New or Old Wars? Debating a Clausewitzian Future', *Journal of Strategic Studies*, 32 (April 2009), 213–41.

Foch, Marshal (Ferdinand), *The Principles of War*, tr. Hilaire Belloc (London: Chapman and Hall, 1921).

Foley, Robert, *German Strategy and the Path to Verdun: Erich von Falkenhayn and the Development of Attrition, 1870–1916* (Cambridge: Cambridge University Press, 2005).

Fort, Adrian, *Archibald Wavell: The Life and Times of an Imperial Servant* (London: Jonathan Cape, 2009).

Freedman, Lawrence, *The Revolution in Military Affairs*, Adelphi Paper 318 (London: International Institute for Strategic Studies, 1998).

——— *The Evolution of Nuclear Strategy*, 3rd edn. (Basingstoke: Palgrave Macmillan, 2003).

——— *The Transformation of Strategic Affairs*, Adelphi Papers 318 (London: International Institute for Strategic Studies, 2006).

Freir, Nathan, *Known Unknowns: Unconventional Strategic Shocks in Defense Strategy Development* (Carlisle, PA: Strategic Studies Institute, U. S. Army War College, November 2008).

French, David, *The Strategy of the Lloyd George Coalition, 1916–1918* (Oxford: Clarendon Press, 1995).

——— *Raising Churchill's Army: The British Army and the War Against Germany, 1919–1945* (Oxford: Oxford University Press, 2000).

Frieser, Karl-Heinz, *The Blitzkrieg Legend: The 1940 Campaign in the West* (Annapolis, MD: Naval Institute Press, 2005).

Fruhling, Stephan, 'Offense and Defense in Strategy', *Comparative Strategy*, 28 (November–December 2009), 463–77.

Fuller, J. F. C., *The Generalship of Ulysses S. Grant* (London: John Murray, 1929).

——— *Armament and History: A Study of the Influence of Armament on History from the Dawn of Classical Warfare to the Second World War* (London: Eyre and Spottiswoode, 1946).

Gaddis, John Lewis, 'What Is Grand Strategy?', Lecture delivered at the conference 'American Grand Strategy after War', sponsored by the Triangle Institute for Security Studies and the Duke University Program in American Grand Strategy, 26 February 2009.

Gallagher, Gary W., *The Confederate War* (Cambridge, MA: Harvard University Press, 1997).

Galula, David, *Counterinsurgency Warfare: Theory and Practice* (1964; Westport, CT: Praeger Security International, 2006).

Gartner, Scott Sigmund, *Strategic Assessment in War* (New Haven, CT: Yale University Press, 1997).

Gat, Azar, *The Origins of Military Thought: From the Enlightenment to Clausewitz* (Oxford: Clarendon Press, 1989).

——— *The Development of Military Thought: The Nineteenth Century* (Oxford: Clarendon Press, 1992).

——— *Fascist and Liberal Visions of War: Fuller, Liddell Hart, Douhet, and other Modernists* (Oxford: Clarendon Press, 1998).

——— *War in Human Civilization* (Oxford: Oxford University Press, 2006).

Gentile, Gian P., *How Effective Is Strategic Bombing? Lessons Learned from World War II to Kosovo* (New York: New York University Press, 2001).

Glantz, David M., and Jonathan M. House, *The Battle of Kursk* (Lawrence, KS: University Press of Kansas, 1999).

Glatthaar, Joseph T., *General Lee's Army: From Victory to Collapse* (New York: Free Press, 2008).

Glenn, John, Darryl Howlett, and Stuart Poare, eds., *Neorealism Versus Strategic Culture* (Aldershot: Ashgate, 2004).

Goerlitz, Walter, *History of the German General Staff, 1657–1945* (New York: Frederick A. Praeger Publishers, 1953).

Goldsworthy, Adrian, *The Roman Army at War, 100BC–AD200* (Oxford: Oxford University Press, 1996).

——— *Roman Warfare* (London: Cassell, 2002).

——— *How Rome Fell: Death of a Superpower* (New Haven, CT: Yale University Press, 2009).

Gooch, John, ed., *The Origins of Contemporary Doctrine*, The Occasional 30 (Camberley: Strategic and Combat Studies Institute, September 1997).

Gordon, Andrew, 'The Doctrine Debate: Having the Last Word', Michael Duffy, Theo Farrell, and Geoffrey Sloan, eds., *Doctrine and Military Effectiveness*, Strategic Policy Studies 1 (Exeter: Strategic Studies Group of the Britannia Royal Naval College and Exeter University, 1997), 46–50.

Gordon, Michael R., *The Generals War: The Inside Story of the Conflict in the Gulf* (Boston: Little, Brown, 1994).

——and Bernard E. Trainor, *Cobra II: The Inside Story of the Invasion and Occupation of Iraq* (London: Atlantic Books, 2006).

Grauwin, Paul, *Doctor at Dien Bien Phu* (London: Hutchinson, 1955).

Gray, Colin S., *Strategic Studies and Pubic Policy: The American Experience* (Lexington, KY: University Press of Kentucky, 1982).

——*House of Cards: Why Arms Control Must Fail* (Ithaca, NY: Cornell University Press, 1992).

——*Modern Strategy* (Oxford: Oxford University Press, 1999).

——*Strategy for Chaos: Revolutions in Military Affairs and the Evidence of History* (London: Frank Cass, 2002).

——*Another Bloody Century: Future Warfare* (London: Weidenfeld and Nicolson, 2005).

——*Strategy and History: Essays on Theory and Practice* (Abingdon: Routledge, 2006).

——*Fighting Talk: Forty Maxims on War, Peace, and Strategy* (Westport, CT: Praeger Security International, 2007).

——*Schools for Strategy: Teaching Strategy for 21st Century Conflict* (Carlisle, PA: Strategic Studies Institute, U. S. Army War College, November 2009).

——*National Security Dilemmas: Challenges and Opportunities* (Washington, DC: Potomac Books, 2009).

——and Geoffrey Sloan, eds., *Geopolitics, Geography and Strategy* (London: Frank Cass, 1999).

Gray, J. Glenn, *The Warriors: Reflections on Men in Battle* (New York: Harpertorch Books, 1967).

Griffith, Charles, *The Quest: Haywood Hansell and American Strategic Bombing in World War II* (Maxwell AFB, AL: Air University Press, September 1999).

Grossman, Dave, *On Killing: The Psychological Cost of Learning to Kill in War and Society* (Boston: Little, Brown, 1995).

Guangqian, Peng, and Yao Youzhi, eds., *The Science of Military Strategy* (Beijing: Military Science Publishing House, 2005).

Guibert, Jacques-Antoine Hyppolite Comte de, *Défence du systéme de querre moderne* (Paris: 1779).

Hall, David Ian, ed., 'The Relevance and Role of Military History, Battlefield Tours and Staff Rides, for Armed Forces in the 21st Century', *Defence Studies*, 5 Special Issue (March 2005).

Hall, Richard C., *The Balkan Wars, 1912–1913: Prelude to the First World War* (London: Routledge, 2000).

Hall, R. Cargill, ed., *Studies in Strategic Bombardment* (Washington, DC: U. S. Government Printing Office, 1998).

Halle, Louis J., *The Elements of International Strategy: A Primer for the Nuclear Age, vol. X* (Lanham, MD: University Press of America, 1984).

Handel, Michael I., 'Clausewitz in the Age of Technology', in Handel, ed., *Clausewitz and Modern Strategy* (London: Frank Cass, 1986), 51–92.

——ed., *Clausewitz and Modern Strategy* (London: Frank Cass, 1986).

——*Masters of War: Classical Strategic Thought*, 3rd edn. (London: Frank Cass, 2001).

Hansell, Jr., Haywood, *The Air Plan that Defeated Hitler* (New York: Arno Press, 1980).

Hanson, Victor Davis, *The Western Way of War: Infantry Battle in Classical Greece* (London: Hodder and Stoughton, 1989).

——ed., *Makers of Ancient Strategy: From the Persian Wars to the Fall of Rome* (Princeton, NJ: Princeton University Press, 2010).

Harkabi, Yehoshafat, *Theory and Doctrine in Classical and Modern Strategy*, Working Papers 35 (Washington, DC: Wilson Center, Smithsonian Institution, 30 October 1981).

Harris, J. P., *Douglas Haig and the First World War* (Cambridge: Cambridge University Press, 2008).

Hastings, Max, *Armageddon: The Battle for Germany, 1944–45* (London: Macmillan, 2004).

Heather, Peter, *The Fall of the Roman Empire* (London: Macmillan, 2005).

Henrickson, Rune, 'Warriors in Combat—What Makes People Actively Fight in Combat?', *The Journal of Strategic Studies*, 30 (April 2007), 187–223.

Herberg-Rothe, Andreas, *Clausewitz's Puzzle: The Political Theory of War* (Oxford: Oxford University Press, 2007).

Herspring, Dale R., *The Pentagon and the Presidency: Civil-Military Relations from FDR to George W. Bush* (Lawrence, KS: University Press of Kansas, 2005).

Herwig, Holger H., *The First World War: Germany and Austria-Hungary, 1914–1918* (London: Arnold, 1997).

——'*Geopolitik*: Haushofer, Hitler and Lebensraum', in Colin S. Gray and Geoffrey Sloan, eds., *Geopolitics, Geography, and Strategy* (London: Frank Cass, 1999), 218–41.

Heuser, Beatrice, *Reading Clausewitz* (London: Pimlico, 2002).

——*The Evolution of Strategy: Thinking War from Antiquity to the Present* (Cambridge: Cambridge University Press, 2010).

Hoffman, Frank G., *Conflict in the 21st Century: The Rise of Hybrid Wars* (Arlington, VA: Potomac Institute for Policy Studies, December 2007).

——'Hybrid Warfare and Challenges', *Joint Force Quarterly*, 52 (first qtr. 2009), 34–9.

Holley, I. B., *Technology and Doctrine: Essays on a Challenging Relationship* (Maxwell AFB, AL: Air University Press, 2004).

Holmes, Richard, *Firing Line* (London: Penguin Books, 1987).

Honig, Jan Willem, 'Clausewitz's *On War*: Problems of Text and Translation', in Hew Strachan and Andreas Herberg-Rothe eds., *Clausewitz in the Twenty-First Century* (Oxford: Oxford University Press, 2007), 57–73.

Hooker, Richard D., Jr., *Manoeuvre Warfare: An Anthology* (Novato, CA: Presidio Press, 1993).

Horne, Alistair, *A Savage War of Peace: Algeria, 1954–1962* (London: Penguin Books, 1979).

Howard, Michael, *Studies in War and Peace* (London: Temple Smith, 1970).

——'The Forgotten Dimensions of Strategy', *Foreign Affairs*, 57 (summer 1979), 975–86.

——*The Causes of Wars and Other Essays* (London: Counterpoint, 1983).

——'Men Against Fire', in Peter Paret, ed., *Makers of Modern Strategy: From Machiavelli to the Nuclear Age* (Princeton, NJ: Princeton University Press, 1986), 510–26.

——*The Invention of Peace and the Reinvention of War* (London: Profile Books, 2001).

——*Clausewitz: A Very Short Introduction* (Oxford: Oxford University Press, 2002).

——*Captain Professor: The Memoirs of Sir Michael Howard* (London: Continuum UK, 2006).

Howard, Michael, *Liberation or Catastrophe? Reflections on the History of the Twentieth Century* (London: Continuum UK, 2007).

—— *War and the Liberal Conscience* (London: C. Hurst, 2008).

Hughes, Matthew, and Matthew S. Seligman, *Does Peace Lead to War? Peace Settlements and Conflict in the Modern Age* (Stroud: Sutton Publishing, 2002).

Hull, Isabel V., *Absolute Destruction: Military Culture and the Practices of War in Imperial Germany* (Ithaca, NY: Cornell University Press, 2005).

Hundley, Richard O., *Past Revolutions, Future Transformations: What Can the History of Revolutions in Military Affairs Tell Us about Transforming the U.S. Military?* MR-1029-DARPA (Santa Monica, CA: RAND, 1999).

Huntington, Samuel P., *The Soldier and the State: The Theory and Politics of Civil-Military Relations* (New York: Random House, 1964).

Imlay, Talbot C., and Monica Duffy Toft, eds., *The Fog of Peace and War Planning: Military and Strategic Planning under Uncertainty* (Abingdon: Routledge, 2006).

Isaac, Benjamin, *The Limits of Empire: The Roman Army in the East* (Oxford: Oxford University Press, 1990).

Jager, Sheila Miyoshi, *On the Uses of Cultural Knowledge* (Carlisle, PA: Strategic Studies Institute, U. S. Army War College, November 2007).

Jagol, Donald, 'United States Naval Doctrine and Professional Military Education', in Michael Duffy, Theo Farrell, and Geoffrey Sloan, eds., *Doctrine and Military Effectiveness*, Strategic Policy Studies 1 (Exeter: Strategic Policy Studies Group of the Britannia Royal Naval College and Exeter University, 1997), 26–33.

James, Glenn E., *Chaos Theory: The Essentials for Military Applications*, Newport Papers 10 (Newport, RI: Naval War College, August 1996).

Jervis, Robert, *System Effects: Complexity in Political and Social Life* (Princeton, NJ: Princeton University Press, 1999).

Johnson, David E., *Learning Large Lessons: The Evolving Roles of Ground Power and Air Power in the Post-Cold War Era*, MG-405 (Santa Monica, CA: RAND, 2006).

Johnson, Jeannie L., Kerry M. Kartchner, and Jeffrey A. Larsen, eds., *Strategic Culture and Weapons of Mass Destruction: Culturally Based Insights into Comparative National Security Policymaking* (New York: Palgrave Macmillan, 2009).

Johnson, Julia A., *Selected Articles on War—Cause and Cure* (New York: H. W. Wilson, 1926).

Johnson-Freese, Joan, *Space as a Strategic Asset* (New York: Columbia University Press, 2007).

Jomini, Baron Antoine Henri de, *The Art of War* (1838; London: Greenhill Books, 1992).

Jones, Archer, *The Art of War in the Western World* (Urbana, IL: University Press of Illinois, 1987).

Jones, Michael K., *Stalingrad: How the Red Army Survived the German Onslaught* (Philadelphia, PA: Casemate, 2007).

Jordan, David and others, *Understanding Modern Warfare* (Cambridge: Cambridge University Press, 2008).

Kaegi, Jr., Emil, *Some Thoughts on Byzantine Military Strategy* (Brookline, MA: Hellenic College Press, 1983).

Kagan, Frederick W., *Finding the Target: The Transformation of American Military Policy* (New York: Encounter Books, 2006).

Kahn, Herman, *On Thermonuclear War* (Princeton, NJ: Princeton University Press, 1960).

—— *Thinking About the Unthinkable* (New York: Horizon Press, 1962).

Kane, Thomas M., *Military Logistics and Strategic Performance* (London: Frank Cass, 2001).

Kaplan, Fred., *The Wizards of Armageddon* (New York: Simon and Schuster, 1983).

Kautilya, *The Arthashastra*, tr. L. N. Rangarajan (fourth century BCE; New Delhi: Penguin Books, 1992).

Keegan, John, *The Face of Battle* (London: Jonathan Cape, 1976).

—— *The Mask of Command* (New York: Viking Penguin, 1987).

—— *A History of Warfare* (London: Hutchinson, 1993).

—— *War and Our World: The Reith Lectures 1998* (London: Hutchinson, 1998).

Kelly, Justin, and Mike Brennan, *Alien: How Operational Art Devoured Strategy* (Carlisle, PA: Strategic Studies Institute U. S. Army War College, September 2009).

Kennedy, Paul, ed., *The War Plans of the Great Powers, 1880–1914* (London: Allen and Unwin, 1979).

—— *The Rise of Anglo-German Antagonism, 1860–1914* (London: George Allen and Unwin, 1980).

—— ed., *Grand Strategies in War and Peace* (New Haven, CT: Yale University Press, 1991).

Kent, Glenn A., *Thinking About America's Defense: An Analytical Memoir* (Santa Monica, CA: RAND, 2008).

—— Randall J. Devalk, and D. E. Thayer, *A Calculus of First-Strike Stability (A Criterion for Evaluating Strategic Forces)*, N-2526-AF (Santa Monica, CA: RAND, June 1988).

Kilcullen, David, *The Accidental Guerrilla: Fighting Small Wars in the Midst of a Big One* (London: C. Hurst, 2009).

Knox, MacGregor, 'Conclusion: Continuity and Revolution in the Making of Strategy', in Williamson Murray, Knox, and Alvis Bernstein, eds., *The Making of Strategy: Rulers, States and War* (Cambridge: Cambridge University Press, 1994), 614–45.

—— and Williamson Murray, ed., *The Dynamics of Military Revolutions, 1300–2050* (Cambridge: Cambridge University Press, 2001).

Kolenda, Christopher, ed., *Leadership: The Warrior's Art* (Carlisle, PA: Army War College Foundation Press, 2001).

Kramer, Alan, *Dynamics of Destruction: Culture and Mass Killing in the First World War* (Oxford: Oxford University Press, 2007).

Krepinevich, Andrew F., Jr., *The Army and Vietnam* (Baltimore, MD: Johns Hopkins University Press, 1986).

Krulak, Charles C., 'The Strategic Corporal: Leadership in the Three Block War', *Marine Corps Gazette*, 83 (1999), 18–22.

Kublick, Bruce, *Blind Oracles: Intellectuals and War from Kennan to Kissinger* (Princeton, NJ: Princeton University Press, 2006).

Kugler, Richard L., *Policy Analysis in National Security Affairs: New Methods for a New Era* (Washington, DC: National Defense University Press, 2006).

Lambeth, Benjamin S., *The Transformation of American Air Power* (Ithaca, NY: Cornell University Press, 2000).

—— *NATO's Air War for Kosovo: A Strategic and Operational Assessment* (Santa Monica, CA: RAND, 2001).

Lantis, Jeffrey S., and Darryl Howlett, 'Strategic Culture', in John Baylis and others, eds., *Strategy in the Contemporary World: An Introduction to Strategic Studies*, 2nd edn. (Oxford: Oxford University Press, 2007), 82–100.

Lawrence, T. E., *Seven Pillars of Wisdom: A Triumph* (New York: Anchor Books, 1991).

Lee, John, *The Warlords: Hindenburg and Ludendorff* (London: Weidenfeld and Nicolson, 2005).

Lengel, Edward G., *To Conquer Hell: The Battle of Meuse-Argonne, 1918* (London: Aurum Press, 2008).

Liang, Qiao, and Wang Xiangsui, *Unrestricted Warfare: Assumptions on War and Tactics in the Age of Globalization*, tr. FBIS (Beijing: PLA Literature Arts Publishing House, February 1999).

Libicki, Martin C., *Conquest in Cyberspace: National Security and Information Warfare* (Cambridge: Cambridge University Press, 2007).

Liddell Hart, Basil H., *The Revolution in Warfare* (London: Faber and Faber, 1946).

——*Strategy: The Indirect Approach* (1941; London: Faber and Faber, 1967).

Lind, William S., *Maneuver Warfare Handbook* (Boulder, CO: Westview Press, 1985).

Lonsdale, David J., *Alexander: Killer of Men. Alexander the Great and the Macedonian Art of War* (London: Constable, 2004).

——*Alexander the Great: Lessons in Strategy* (Abingdon: Routledge, 2007).

Luttwak, Edward N., *The Grand Strategy of the Roman Empire: From the First Century A.D. to the Third* (Baltimore, MD: Johns Hopkins University Press, 1976).

——*Strategy and Politics: Collected Essays* (New Brunswick, NJ: Transaction Books, 1980).

——'The Operational Level of War', *International Security*, 5 (winter 1980–1), 61–79.

——*On the Meaning of Victory: Essays on Strategy* (New York: Simon and Schuster, 1986).

——'Strategy', in John Whiteclay Chambers, ed., *The Oxford Companion to American Military History* (Oxford: Oxford University Press, 1999), 683–6.

——*Strategy: The Logic of War and Peace*, rev. edn. (Cambridge, MA: Harvard University Press, 2001).

——*The Grand Strategy of the Byzantine Empire* (Cambridge, MA: Harvard University Press, 2009).

——'Errors of Backsight Forethought', *The Times Literary Supplement* (16 October 2009), 22–3.

Lyman, Robert, *The Generals: From Defeat to Victory, Leadership in Asia, 1941–45* (London: Constable, 2008).

Lynn, Gene M., and Louis Morton, *Schools for Strategy: Education and Research in National Security Affairs* (New York: Frederick A. Praeger Publishers, 1965).

Lynn, John A., ed., *Feeding Mars: Logistics in Western Warfare from the Middle Ages to the Present* (Boulder, CO: Westview Press, 1993).

Macaulay, Lord, *Horatius Keeps the Bridge* (1842; London: Phoenix, 1996).

Machiavelli, Niccolo, *Art of War*, tr. Christopher Lynch (1521; Chicago, IL: University of Chicago Press, 2003).

——*Discourses on Livy*, tr. Julia Conaway Bondarella and Peter Bondarella (1531; Oxford University Press, 2003).

——*The Prince*, tr. Peter Bondarella and Mark Musa (1532; Oxford: Oxford University Press, 1998).

Mahan, Alfred Thayer, *The Influence of Sea Power upon History, 1660–1783* (1890; London: Methuen, 1965).

——*The Problem of Asia and Its Effect upon International Policies* (Boston: Little, Brown, 1905).

Mahnken, Thomas G., *Technology and the American Way of War Since 1945* (New York: Columbia University Press, 2005).

——and Thomas A. Keaney, eds., *War in Iraq: Planning and Execution* (Abingdon: Routledge, 2007).

Maizeroy, Paul Gideon Joly De, *Théorie de la guerre, Où l'on expose la constitution et formation de l'Infanterie et de la Cavalerie, leurs manoeuvres élémentaires, avec l'applica-*

tion des principes a la grande Tactique, Suivie de démonstration Sur la Stratégique (Lausanne: 1777).

Marcella, Gabriel, ed., *Teaching Strategy: Challenge and Response* (Carlisle, PA: Strategic Studies Institute, U.S. Army War College, March 2010).

Marshall, A. W., J. J. Martin, and H. S. Rowen, eds., *On Not Confusing Ourselves: Essays on National Security in Honor of Albert and Roberta Wohlstetter* (Boulder, CO: Westview Press, 1991).

Marston, Daniel, and Carter Malkesian, eds., *Counterinsurgency in Modern Warfare* (Oxford: Osprey Publishing, 2008).

Martel, Robert, *The Meaning of Military Victory* (Boulder, CO: Lynne Rienner Publishers, 2006).

Martel, William C., *Victory in War: Foundations of Modern Military Policy* (Cambridge: Cambridge University Press, 2007).

Mattis, James N., 'USJFCOM Commander's Guidance for Effects-Based Operations', *Joint Force Quarterly*, 51 (4th qtr. 2008), 105–8.

Maurice (Emperor), *Maurice's Strategikon: Handbook of Byzantine Military Strategy*, tr. George T. Dennis (ca. 600 AD; Philadelphia, PA: University of Pennsylvania Press, 1984).

Mawdsley, Evan, *Thunder in the East: The Nazi–Soviet War, 1941–1945* (London: Hodder Arnold, 2005).

Mc Ivor, Anthony D., *Rethinking the Principles of War* (Annapolis, MD: Naval Institute Press, 2005).

McManners, Hugh, *The Scars of War* (London: HarperCollins Publishers, 1993).

McMaster, H. R., *Dereliction of Duty: Lyndon Johnson, Robert McNamara, the Joint Chiefs of Staff, and the Lies that Led to Vietnam* (New York: HarperCollins, 1997).

McPherson, James M., *Battle Cry of Freedom: The Civil War Era* (New York: Oxford University Press, 1988).

Mead, Gary, *The Good Soldier: The Biography of Douglas Haig* (London: Atlantic Books, 2008).

Mearsheimer, John J., *Liddell Hart and the Weight of History* (Ithaca, NY: Cornell University Press, 1988).

Megargee, Geoffrey P., *Inside Hitler's High Command* (Lawrence KS: University Press of Kansas, 2000).

Meilinger, Phillip S., ed., *The Paths of Heaven: The Evolution of Airpower Theory* (Maxwell AFB, AL: Air University Press, 1997).

——'Giulio Douhet and the Origins of Airpower Theory', in Meilinger, ed., *The Paths of Heaven: The Evolution of Airpower Theory* (Maxwell AFB, AL: Air University Press, 1997), 1–40.

Metz, Stephen, 'A Wake for Clausewitz: Toward a Philosophy of 21st Century Warfare', *Parameters*, 24 (winter 1994–5), 126–32.

——*Iraq and the Evolution of American Strategy* (Washington, DC: Potomac Books, 2008).

'Military Power: A Roundtable Review', *Journal of Strategic Studies*, 28 (June 2005).

Miller, Donald L., *Eighth Air Force in Britain: The American Bomber Crews in Britain* (London: Aurum Press, 2008).

Millett, Allan R., and Williamson Murray, eds., *Military Effectiveness*, 3 vols.: *The First World War, The Interwar Period, The Second World War* (Boston: Allen and Unwin, 1987).

Moltke, Field Marshal Helmuth Graf von, *Moltke on the Art of War: Selected Writings*, ed. Daniel J. Hughes, tr. Hughes and Gunther E. Rothenberg (Novato, CA: Presidio Press, 1993).

Moltz, James Clay, *The Politics of Space Security: Strategic Restraint and the Pursuit of National Interests* (Stanford, CA: Stanford University Press, 2008).

Mombauer, Annika, *Helmuth von Moltke and the Origins of the First World War* (Cambridge: Cambridge University Press, 2001).

——'Of War Plans and War Guilt: The Debate Surrounding the Schlieffen Plan', *Journal of Strategic Studies*, 28 (October 2005), 857–85.

Murray, Williamson, *German Military Effectiveness* (Baltimore, MD: Nautical and Aviation Publishing Company of America, 1992).

——and Allan R. Millett, *A War To Be Won: Fighting the Second World War* (Cambridge, MA: The Belknap Press of Harvard University Press, 2000).

——and James Lacey, eds., *The Making of Peace: Rulers, States, and the Aftermath of War* (Cambridge: Cambridge University Press, 2009).

——and Mark Grimsley, 'Introduction: On Strategy', in Murray, MacGregor Knox, and Alvin Bernstein, eds., *The Making of Strategy: Rulers, States, and War* (Cambridge: Cambridge University Press, 1994), 24–55.

————'Introduction: On Strategy', in Murray, MacGregor Knox, and Alvin Bernstein, eds., *The Making of Strategy: Rulers, States, and War* (Cambridge: Cambridge University Press, 1994), 1–23.

——and Richard Hart Sinnreich, eds., *The Past as Prologue: The Importance of History to the Military Profession* (Cambridge: Cambridge University Press, 2006).

——MacGregor Knox, and Alvin Bernstein, eds., *The Making of Strategy: Rulers, States, and War* (Cambridge: Cambridge University Press, 1994).

Nagl, John A., *Learning to Eat Soup with a Knife: Counterinsurgency Lessons from Malaya and Vietnam* (Chicago, IL: University of Chicago Press, 2005).

Newland, Samuel J., *Victories Are Not Enough: Limitations of the German Way of War* (Carlisle, PA: Strategic Studies Institute, U. S. Army War College, December 2005).

Oberg, Jim, *Space Power Theory* (Washington, DC: U. S. Government Printing Office, 1999).

Olsen, John Andreas, *John Warden and the Renaissance of American Air Power* (Washington, DC: Potomac Books, 2007).

——ed., *A History of Air Warfare* (Washington, DC: Potomac Books, 2009).

Otter, T. G., and Keith Neilson, eds., *Railways and International Politics: Paths of Empire, 1848–1945* (Abingdon: Routledge, 2006).

Overy, Richard J., *The Air War, 1939–1945* (New York: Stein and Day, 1985).

—— *Why the Allies Won* (London: Jonathan Cape, 1995).

Palmer, R. R., 'Frederick the Great, Guibert, Bülow: From Dynastic to National War', in Peter Paret, ed., *Makers of Modern Strategy: From Machiavelli to the Nuclear Age* (Princeton, NJ: Princeton University Press, 1986), 91–119.

Pape, Robert A., *Bombing to Win: Air Power and Coercion* (Ithaca, NY: Cornell University Press, 1996).

Paret, Peter, *Clausewitz and the State* (New York: Oxford University Press, 1976).

——ed., *Makers of Modern Strategy: From Machiavelli to the Nuclear Age* (Princeton, NJ: Princeton University Press, 1986).

Parker, Geoffrey, *The Grand Strategy of Philip II* (New Haven, CT: Yale University Press, 1998).

Payne, Keith B., *The Great American Gamble: The Theory and Practice of Deterrence from Cold War to the Twenty-First Century* (Fairfax, VA: National Institute Press, 2008).

Peters, Ralph, *Fighting for the Future: Will America Triumph?* (Mechanisburg, PA: Stackpole Books, 1999).

Place, Timothy Harrison, *Military Training in the British Army, 1940–1944: Dunkirk to D-Day* (London: Frank Cass, 2000).

Platias, Athanasios G., and Constantinos Koliopoulos, *Thucydides on Strategy: Athenian and Spartan Grand Strategies in the Peloponnesian War and their Relevance Today* (Athens: Eurasia Publications, 2006).

Pois, Robert, and Philip Langer, *Command Failure in War: Psychology and Leadership* (Bloomington, IN: Indiana University Press, 2004).

Poore, Stuart, 'Strategic Culture', in John Glenn, Darryl Howlett, and Poare, eds., *Neorealism Versus Strategic Culture* (Aldershot: Ashgate, 2004), 45–71.

Porter, Patrick, 'Good Anthropology, Bad History: The Cultural Turn in Studying War', *Parameters*, 37 (summer 2007), 45–58.

——*Military Orientalism: Eastern War Through Western Eyes* (London: C. Hurst, 2009).

Posen, Barry R., *The Sources of Military Doctrine: France, Britain, and Germany between the World Wars* (Ithaca, NY: Cornell University Press, 1984).

Pratt, Edwin A., *The Rise of Rail-Power in War and Conquest, 1833–1914* (Philadelphia, PA: J. B. Lippincott, 1916).

Quade, Edward S., ed., *Analysis for Military Decisions: The RAND Lectures on Systems Analysis* (Chicago, IL: Rand McNally, 1964).

——and W. I. Boucher, eds., *Systems Analysis and Policy Planning: Applications in Defense* (New York: American Elsevier Publishing Company, 1968).

Record, Jeffrey, *The Wrong War: Why We Lost in Vietnam* (Annapolis, MD: Naval Institute Press, 1998).

Reid, Brian Holden, *J. F. C. Fuller: Military Thinker* (New York: St. Martin's Press, 1987).

——*Studies in British Military Thought: Debates with Fuller and Liddell Hart* (Lincoln, NE: University of Nebraska Press, 1998).

Ricks, Thomas E., *Fiasco: The American Military Adventure in Iraq* (New York: Penguin Press, 2006).

——*The Gamble: General Petraeus And The Untold Story Of The American Surge In Iraq, 2006–2008* (London: Allen Lane, 2009).

Rip, Michael Russell, and James M. Hasik, *The Precision Revolution: GPS and the Future of Aerial Warfare* (Annapolis, MD: Naval Institute Press, 2002).

Roberts, Andrew, *Masters and Commanders: How Roosevelt, Churchill, Marshall and Alanbrooke Won the War in the West* (London: Allen Lane, 2008).

Rock, Stephen R., *Why Peace Breaks Out: Great Power Rapprochement in Historical Perspective* (Chapel Hill, NC: University of North Carolina Press, 19890.

Rosen, Stephen Peter, 'Vietnam and the American Theory of Limited War', *International Security*, 7 (fall 1982), 83–113.

——*War and Human Nature* (Princeton, NJ: Princeton University Press, 2005).

Ross, Stephen T., *American War Plans, 1945–1950* (London: Frank Cass, 1996).

——*American War Plans, 1941–1945* (London: Frank Cass, 1997).

Rowland, David, *The Stress of Battle: Quantifying Human Performance in Combat* (London: Stationery Office, 2006).

Sagan, Scott D., *The Limits of Safety: Organizations, Accidents, and Nuclear Weapons* (Princeton, NJ: Princeton University Press, 1993).

Sawyer, Ralph D., *The Seven Military Classics of Ancient China*, tr. Sawyer (Boulder, CO: Westview Press, 1993).

—— *The Tao of Deception: Unorthodox Warfare in Historic and Modern China* (New York: Basic Books, 2007).

Schelling, Thomas C., *The Strategy of Conflict* (Cambridge, MA: Harvard University Press, 1960).

—— *Arms and Influence* (New Haven, CT: Yale University Press, 1966).

—— and Morton H. Halperin, *Strategy and Arms Control* (New York: Twentieth Century Fund, 1961).

Schlieffen, Alfred von, *Alfred von Schlieffen's Military Writings*, tr. and ed. Robert T. Foley (London: Frank Cass, 2003).

Schurman, Donald M., *Julian C. Corbett, 1854–1922: Historian of British Maritime Policy from Drake to Jellicoe* (London: Royal Historical Society, 1981).

Sheffield, Gary D., ed., *Leadership and Command: The Anglo-American Experience Since 1861* (London: Brassey's UK, 1997).

Showalter, Dennis E., *Railroads and Rifles: Soldiers, Technology and the Unification of Germany* (Hamden, CT: Archon Books, 1975).

—— *Patton and Rommel: Men of War in the Twentieth Century* (New York: Berkeley Caliber, 2005).

Simpson, Howard R., *Dien Bien Phu: The Epic Battle America Forgot* (Washington, DC: Brassey's, 1996).

Smith, Hugh, *On Clausewitz: A Study of Military and Political Ideas* (Basingstoke: Palgrave Macmillan, 2005).

Smith, Malcolm, *British Air Strategy between the Wars* (Oxford: Clarendon Press, 1984).

Smith, Rupert, *The Utility of Force: The Art of War in the Modern World* (London: Allen Lane, 2005).

Sobek, David, *The Causes of War* (Cambridge: Cambridge University Press, 2009).

Sondhaus, Lawrence, *Strategic Culture and Ways of War* (Abingdon: Routledge, 2006).

Sorley, Lewis, *Thunderbolt: From the Battle of the Bulge to Vietnam and Beyond: General Creighton Abrams and the Army of His Times* (New York: Simon and Schuster, 1992).

Steiner, Barry H., *Bernard Brodie and the Foundation of American Nuclear Strategy* (Lawrence, KS: University Press of Kansas, 1991).

Steiner, Zara, *The Lights that Failed: European International History, 1919–1933* (Oxford: Oxford University Press, 2005).

Strachan, Hew, 'Making Strategy: Civil–Military Relations After Iraq', *Survival*, 48 (autumn 2006), 59–82.

—— *The Changing Character of War* (Oxford: Europaeum, 2007).

—— *Clausewitz's On War: A Biography* (New York: Atlantic Monthly Press, 2007).

—— and Andreas Herberg-Rothe, eds., *Clausewitz in the Twenty-First Century* (Oxford: Oxford University Press, 2007).

—— 'Strategy and the Limitation of War', *Survival*, 50(February–March 2008), 31–53.

Stuermer, Michael, *Putin and the Rise of Russia* (London: Phoenix, 2009).

Sumida, Jon Tetsuro, *Inventing Grand Strategy and Teaching Command: The Classic Works of Alfred Thayer Mahan Reconsidered* (Baltimore, MD: Johns Hopkins University Press, 1997).

—— *Decoding Clausewitz: A New Approach to On War* (Lawrence KS: University Press of Kansas, 2008).

Sun Tzu, *The Art of War*, tr. Samuel B. Griffith (ca. 490 BCE; Oxford: Clarendon Press, 1963).

——*The Art of War*, tr. Ralph D. Sawyer (ca. 490 BCE; Boulder, CO: Westview Press, 1994).

——*Sun Tzu's Art of War: The Modern Chinese Interpretation*, ed. Tao Hanzhang, tr. Yuan Shibing (ca. 490 BCE; New York: Sterling Innovation, 2007).

Terraine, John, 'The Substance of the War', in Hugh Cecil and Peter H. Liddle, eds., *Facing Armageddon: The First World War Experience* (London: Leo Cooper, 1996), ch. 1.

'Theory and Evidence in Security Studies: Debating Robert A. Pape's *Bombing to Win*', *Security Studies*, 7 (winter 1997–8), 91–214.

Thompson, Julian, *The Lifeblood of War: Logistics of Armed Conflict* (London: Brassey's, 1991).

Thorpe, George C., *Pure Logistics* (Washington, DC: National Defense University Press, 1986).

Thucydides, *The Landmark Thucydides: A Comprehensive Guide to The Peloponnesian War*, ed. Robert B. Strassler, rev. tr. Richard Crawley (ca. 400 BCE; New York: Free Press, 1996).

——*History of the Peloponnesian War*, tr. Rex Warner (ca. 400 BCE; London: Penguin Books, 1972).

Trythall, Anthony J., *'Boney' Fuller: The Intellectual General, 1878–1966* (London: Cassell, 1977).

Turtledove, Harry, *The Guns of the South* (New York: Ballantine Books, 1992).

(UK) Cabinet Office, *The National Security Strategy of the United Kingdom: Security in an Interdependent World*, Cm. 7291 (Norwich: Stationery Office, 2008).

U. S. Army And Marine Corps, *Counterinsurgency Field Manual: U. S. Army Field Manual No. 3–24, and Marine Corps Warfighting Publication No. 3–33.5* (Chicago, IL: University of Chicago Press, 2007).

U. S. Marine Corps, *Warfighting*, MCDP-1 (Washington, DC: U. S. Government Printing Office, 1997).

——*Strategy*, MCDP1–1 (Washington, DC: U. S. Government Printing Office, 1998).

Van Evera, Stephen, *Causes of War: Power and the Roots of Conflict* (Ithaca, NY: Cornell University Press, 1999).

Van Riper, Paul K., *Planning for and Applying Military Force: An Examination of Terms* (Carlisle, PA: Strategic Studies Institute, U. S. Army War College, March 2006).

Vasquez, John A., *The War Puzzle Revisited* (Cambridge: Cambridge University Press, 2009).

Vego, Milan N., 'Effects-Based Operations: A Critique', *Joint Force Quarterly*, 41 (2nd qtr. 2006), 51–7.

Waller, Douglas, *A Question of Loyalty* (New York: Harper Perennial, 2004).

Walsh, George, *'Damage Them All You Can': Robert E. Lee's Army of Northern Virginia* (New York: Tom Doherty Associates, 2002).

Walton, C. Dale, *The Myth of Inevitable U. S. Defeat in Vietnam* (London: Frank Cass, 2002).

Waltz, Kenneth N., *Man, the State, and War: A Theoretical Analysis* (New York: Columbia University Press, 1959).

Walzer, Michael, *Just and Unjust Wars: A Moral Argument with Historical Illustrations*, 3rd edn. (New York: Basic Books, 1997).

Warden III, John, *The Air Campaign: Planning for Combat* (Washington, DC: Pergamon-Brassey's, 1989).

——'Employing Air Power in the Twenty-First Century', in Richard H. Shultz, Jr., and Robert L. Pfaltzgraff, Jr., eds., *The Future of Air Power in the Aftermath of the Gulf War* (Maxwell AFB, AL: Air University Press, July 1992).

Watts, Barry D., *Clausewitzian Friction and Future War*, McNair Paper 68, rev. edn. (Washington, DC: Institute for National Strategic Studies, National Defense University, 2004).

Wavell, Archibald, *Speaking Generally: Broadcasts, Orders and Addresses in Time of War (1939–43)* (London: Macmillan, 1946).

Weigert, Hans W., *Generals and Geographers* (New York: Oxford University Press, 1942).

Weinberg, Gerhard, *A World at Arms: A Global History of World War II* (Cambridge: Cambridge University Press, 1994).

Wendt, Alexander, *Social Theory of International Politics* (Cambridge: Cambridge University Press, 1999).

Wette, Wolfram, *The Wehrmacht: History, Myth, Reality* (Cambridge, MA: Cambridge University Press, 2002).

Wiest, Andrew, ed., *Rolling Thunder in a Gentle Land: The Vietnam War Revisited* (Oxford: Osprey Publishing, 2006).

Windrow, Martin, *The Last Valley: Dien Bien Phu and the French Defeat in Vietnam* (London: Weidenfeld and Nicolson, 2004).

Winters, Harold, *Battling the Elements: Weather and Terrain in the Conduct of War* (Baltimore, MD: Johns Hopkins University Press, 1998).

Winton, Harold W., 'An Imperfect Jewel: Military Theory and the Military Profession', paper presented to the Society for Military History Annual Conference, Bethesda, MD, 22 May 2004.

Woodward, David R., *Lloyd George and the Generals* (London: Frank Cass, 2004).

Wright, Quincy, *A Study of War*, 2 vols. (Chicago, IL: University of Chicago Press, 1942).

Wylie, J. C., *Military Strategy: A General Theory of Power Control* (1967; Annapolis, MD: Naval Institute Press, 1989).

Yarger, Harry R., *Strategic Theory for the 21ˢᵗ Century: The Little Book on Big Strategy* (Carlisle, PA: Strategic Studies Institute, U. S. Army War College, February 2006).

—— *Strategy and the National Security Professional: Strategic Thinking in the 21ˢᵗ Century* (Westport, CT: Praeger Security International, 2009).

Zabecki, David T., *The German 1918 Offensives: A Case Study in the Operational Level of War* (Abingdon: Routledge, 2006).

—— ed., *Chief of Staff: The Principal Officers Behind History's Great Commanders*, 2 vols. (Annapolis, MD: Naval Institute Press, 2008).

Zamoyski, Adam, *1812: Napoleon's Fatal March on Moscow* (London: HarperCollins Publishers, 2004).

Zuber, Terence, *Inventing the Schlieffen Plan: German War Planning, 1871–1914* (Oxford: Oxford University Press, 2002).

—— *The Battle of the Frontiers: Ardennes, 1914* (Stroud: Tempus Publishing, 2007).

Index

Printed and bound by CPI Group (UK) Ltd, Croydon, CR0 4YY